The Social Roots of Authoritarianism

The Social Roots of Authoritarianism

NATALIA FORRAT

OXFORD
UNIVERSITY PRESS

Oxford University Press is a department of the University of Oxford. It furthers
the University's objective of excellence in research, scholarship, and education
by publishing worldwide. Oxford is a registered trade mark of Oxford University
Press in the UK and certain other countries.

Published in the United States of America by Oxford University Press
198 Madison Avenue, New York, NY 10016, United States of America.

© Oxford University Press 2024

All rights reserved. No part of this publication may be reproduced, stored in
a retrieval system, or transmitted, in any form or by any means, without the
prior permission in writing of Oxford University Press, or as expressly permitted
by law, by license, or under terms agreed with the appropriate reproduction
rights organization. Inquiries concerning reproduction outside the scope of the
above should be sent to the Rights Department, Oxford University Press, at the
address above.

You must not circulate this work in any other form
and you must impose this same condition on any acquirer.

CIP data is on file at the Library of Congress

ISBN 978-0-19-779035-9

DOI: 10.1093/oso/9780197790359.001.0001

Printed by Marquis Book Printing, Canada

Contents

Acknowledgments	ix
Introduction	1
Unity and Division as the Social Roots of Authoritarianism	3
Statist and Antistatist Societies	5
Autocracy—Democracy—Autocracy	7
Russia as a Research Site	10
Two Empirical Approaches and the Structure of the Book	11
What the Book Does and Does Not	13
Democracy Support	15
1. Authoritarian Power in Statist and Antistatist Societies	17
Statist versus Antistatist Societies	18
Group Authority and the Third Face of Power	19
Group Authority and the State	23
Grassroots Politics in Statist and Antistatist Societies	31
Infrastructural State Power and Civil Society	32
Political Functions of Public Organizations	36
The State as the Driver of Informality	38
Chapter Summary	40
2. A Tale of Four Regions	42
The Puzzle of the 2012 Presidential Election	43
Regional Political Machines	45
Nested Analysis and Case Selection	46
Regional Socioeconomic Profiles	50
The Regional Histories of State Formation	54
Tatarstan	54
The Kemerovo Region	57
The Republic of Altai	59
The Rostov Region	61
Chapter Summary	64
3. Team State versus Outsider State: Public Organizations in Statist and Antistatist Societies	65
The Team State in the Kemerovo Region and Tatarstan	66
The State as Protector	66
"Is It Bad to Help the Poor?"	68
The Developmental State	69
Pride and Loyalty	71

The Outsider State in the Rostov Region and Altai 72
 Social Norms and Safety Net in Nonstate Communities 72
 The Legitimate Authority of Nonstate Community Leaders 75
Centralized Public Organizations in the Kemerovo Region
and Tatarstan 77
 Community Centers and Residential Councils in Kemerovo 78
  Elena's Residential Council 78
  The Infrastructure of Residential Councils and Community
  Centers in Kemerovo City 79
  Activities of Community Centers and Residential Councils 82
 Youth Organizations in Tatarstan 86
  The Origins of Tatarstan's Youth Organizations 86
  The Infrastructure and Activities of Youth Organizations 88
  State Leadership beyond the Formal State 92
Decentralized Public Organizations in the Rostov Region and Altai 94
 Organizational Autonomy from the State 94
 State Strategy of Minimal Interference 97
The State, Civil Society, and "Collective Institutions" 101
Chapter Summary 103

4. The Political and the Civic: Political Machines in Antistatist and
Statist Societies 104
Buying Loyalty: Political Machines in Antistatist Societies 105
 Pluralist Political Environment 105
 Utility Maximization as the Driver of Clientelist Political Machines 107
 The Challenge of Stable Electoral Performance 110
 Reproduction of the Boundary between the Civic and the Political 110
Building Unity: Political Machines in Statist Societies 112
 The Blurred Boundary between the Civic and the Political 113
 The Distorted Idea of Representation 115
Political Functions of Public Organizations 117
 Mobilization and Co-optation 117
 Management of Existing and Potential Discontent 119
 Control of Public Space and Discourse 121
 Stability of Electoral Performance 124
How the State Hijacked a Social Movement: The Story of the
Kemerovo Veterans' Councils 125
 A Short History of Veterans' Councils in the Soviet Union and
 Post-Soviet Russia 126
 Aman Tuleyev's Takeover of the Veterans' Councils in the
 Kemerovo Region 128
 The Expansion of the Veterans' Councils in the Kemerovo Region
 after 2003 130
 How Social Statism Makes Social Movements Vulnerable 134

The Achilles' Heel of State-Led Unity	134
Chapter Summary	135
5. The Riddle of Russian Authoritarianism	137
Russian Statism: The Case of Vladimir Putin's Regime	138
Personalism	139
Nationalism	140
Performance Legitimacy and the Social Contract	142
The Search for a Just State and the Russian Political Culture	143
The Foundations of State Authority in Russia	147
Resistance and Compliance in Tsarist Russia	150
The Search for a Just State in the Soviet Union	152
Compliant Activism	154
Active Resistance	156
Passive Resistance	157
The Search for a Just State in Post-Soviet Russia	159
Evidence of Social Statism in Public Opinion Polls	160
Yeltsin versus Putin	161
Compliant Activism and the Social Roots of Putin's Support	164
Passive Resistance	167
Active Resistance	168
Repression, Resistance, and Compliance Shortly before and after the 2022 Invasion of Ukraine	172
Chapter Summary	177
Conclusion	179
Statist and Antistatist Societies around the World	179
Explaining Politics, Society, and Democratization through the Statist/Antistatist Lens	181
Appendix 1. Quantitative Analysis	185
Appendix 2. Fieldwork Data Collection and Analysis	199
Appendix 3. Data on Social Policy in the Kemerovo Region	205
Appendix 4. Newspaper Publications Related to Residential Committees and Community Centers in Kemerovo and to Their Role in Politics	209
Appendix 5. Newspaper Publications Related to Veterans' (Pensioners') Organizations and Their Role in Politics	215
Appendix 6. List of Interviews	223
References	227
Index	253

Acknowledgments

This book has been in the making for a decade. Over this time, I accumulated numerous debts to people and institutions without whose support the book would have never crossed the finish line. The project started as my dissertation, and I am very grateful to Northwestern University for supporting my doctoral studies. My dissertation advisors, Ann Orloff, Bruce Carruthers, and James Mahoney, would probably not recognize this work, as it has changed so much since they saw it last, but it was their patience, support, and encouragement that set this project on the right track. Linda Cook from Brown University served as my external dissertation committee member and became my mentor and supporter for many years. She shared ideas, advice, and networks that helped me tremendously. I am also grateful to the members of the Comparative-Historical Social Science workshop at Northwestern for the feedback on the earliest iterations of this project.

Several other institutions provided funding and the intellectual environment that shaped this book. The year I spent at Stanford's Center for Democracy, Development, and the Rule of Law (CDDRL) was incredibly stimulating and resulted in a breakthrough in my thinking about the data I collected for this project. I thank Francis Fukuyama and Kathryn Stoner for their mentorship during my time at Stanford and afterward. My fellow postdocs at CDDRL, Lauren Young, Shelby Grossman, Dan Mattingly, and Dinsha Mistree, were a big part of my social and intellectual environment at Stanford. Separately, I thank the Stanford library for providing me with several incredible primary sources that were not easily accessible even in Russia.

The Kellogg Institute for International Studies at the University of Notre Dame was a great place to focus on writing and workshop ideas. I thank all my colleagues there for both their feedback and companionship. In particular, I am grateful to Michael Coppedge for a perspective on how my theory might work for Latin American countries.

Finally, the bulk of this manuscript's writing took place at the University of Michigan. Dan Slater and the members of our postdoc group at the Weiser Center for Emerging Democracies (Fiona Shen-Bayh, Jean Lachapelle, Katlyn Carter, Jundai Liu, Adam Casey, Matthew Cebul, Marilia Correa, Iza Ding, and Hanisah Sani, among others) read many drafts, challenged my ideas, and helped me refine the concepts and arguments in the pages that follow. I am very grateful to the participants of my book workshop, Dan Slater, Graeme Robertson, Martin

Dimitrov, Pauline Jones, and Sam Greene, for a thorough read and a deep engagement with the argument.

Different parts of this book were presented at numerous conferences, workshops, and talks. I thank all the colleagues who provided me with the opportunity to present my findings and receive feedback at the conferences of the Association for Slavic, Eastern European, and Eurasian Studies; American Political Science Association; Midwest and Southern Political Science Associations; and Social Science History Association as well as at various workshops and talks at the University of Wisconsin–Madison, University of Iowa, Indiana University, Western Michigan University, Northwestern University, and the University of Oxford. As the manuscript was taking its final shape, it also benefited from the feedback from Linda Cook, Paul Goode, Daniel Tavana, and two anonymous reviewers. I am grateful to David McBride at Oxford University Press for his patience and encouragement throughout the journey of this manuscript to publication. Needless to say, I bear all the responsibility for mistakes, omissions, and less-than-perfect implementation of all the useful advice I received.

No amount of support from mentors and colleagues would enable me to write this book if dozens of people in Russia did not help me to collect and understand the data. This includes my colleagues from different regions who shared their insight and knowledge, helped with travel logistics, and introduced me to important contacts. A lot of credit goes to my interviewees, who allowed me to look inside their worlds and shared their thoughts, hopes, achievements, and frustrations. Many of them were true professionals who sincerely cared about the work they did, struggled with difficult questions, and provided me with insights that informed my own thinking. I owe a special debt of gratitude to librarians in local history departments of regional libraries who introduced me to their collections and who continue doing the important work enabling research like mine every day. I wish I could name all these people here, but in this day and age, I must protect their identities. Nevertheless, I want them to know that I remember and greatly appreciate their contributions.

Working on a book project for a decade requires stamina and mental health few people can maintain without friends and family. I thank Margarita Rayzberg for being the best friend one may wish for in any emergency situation and for always being fun to have a chat and a laugh. My husband, Greg Stille, has been my rock as I navigated through the storms of academia and the grief and sorrows in my part of the world. Finally, my parents, Liubov and Vladimir Forrat, ensured I always had a home to return to and, to my surprise, continued to care about this book even though they would not be able to read a word in it.

Introduction

Authoritarianism has struck back in the 21st century after a period of democratization in the second half of the 20th century.[1] Autocracies came in different forms and shapes. They emerged on the left and the right of the political spectrum as well as in weird hybrid forms. They learned to use many tools of democratic politics to serve their interests. And even though autocrats have been sharing a lot of their toolkit, the contrasts between some autocracies are striking and puzzling.

Take such an exemplary autocracy as Russia. On February 24, 2022, Russia invaded Ukraine and brought 20th-century warfare back to Europe after decades of peace. The war killed many thousands and displaced millions of Ukrainians, revealed the strength of the Ukrainian civic identity, and revived the West as a political alliance based on democratic values. Inside Russia, the invasion came as a shock for many. Before the war, the state-controlled media claimed Russia had zero intent to invade. Even among very high-ranking state officials, few knew about Putin's plan. Despite the shock, though, Russian public opinion and discourse adapted quickly. The antiwar resistance was swiftly forced underground; hundreds of thousands of Russians who did not support the invasion left the country. Already in March 2022, public opinion polls showed public support of the war at the level of 70%–80%.[2] At least in the public space, unity was quickly restored.

A few years before that, on the other side of the world, Venezuela, another authoritarian country, saw a governmental crisis that highlighted the longstanding cleavages in society. The centrist-conservative opposition to the sitting leftist president, Nicolás Maduro, secured parliamentary majority and entered a prolonged conflict with him. The conflict involved the collection of millions of signatures to recall Maduro, a state of emergency declared by Maduro and rejected by the parliament, the dissolution the legislature by the supreme court and a series of new, very competitive elections. During the conflict, both the supporters of Maduro and the opposition engaged in massive street protests

---

[1] "Freedom in the World 2023."
[2] Scholars debate whether this number should be trusted, how many of these 80% actually supported the war, and how many were simply disengaged from politics (see, e.g., Rosenfeld, "Survey Research in Russia"; Zavadskaya, "On the Harmfulness of Russian Polls.").

The Social Roots of Authoritarianism. Natalia Forrat, Oxford University Press. © Oxford University Press 2024.
DOI: 10.1093/oso/9780197790359.003.0001

and violent clashes involving police forces, which left at least dozens killed and hundreds injured. After several years of the conflict, the Venezuelan economy was in shambles. Severe shortages of basic goods left people starving and dying from lack of medicine. Millions left the country. Yet, the conflict between the two political camps continues, and the international efforts to facilitate peaceful negotiations have had limited success.

In both Russia and Venezuela, the political patterns of unity and division have had a long history. For the most part of its history, Russia has been characterized by the domination of one political institution—the monarchy, the party-state, or the presidency—that enforced political unity in the public space and, to a large degree, in the minds of Russian citizens. Venezuelan society, on the other hand, has been divided, which made politics very competitive and often provided the military—the institution that promised to restore order—with an upper hand. Ideological and socioeconomic cleavages ensured that even during the periods of dictatorship the supporters of different camps continued to accuse each other of corruption and prepare for the next opportunity to take power.

Both Russia and Venezuela are considered autocracies. The "Freedom in the World" report classifies both countries as "Not free." Russia's 2022 score of global freedom stands at 16; Venezuela's 2021 score is very similar—15.[3] The difference in competitiveness, which is often at the core of distinction between political regimes, is paradoxically obscured as we try to fit the countries into broader regime classifications.

Russia and Venezuela are not the only authoritarian regimes with vastly different levels of political competitiveness. Many other authoritarian countries can also be divided into those with a high degree of social and political unity and those with a high degree of internal division. The regimes in China, North Korea, Vietnam, Cuba, and, to a large degree, Iran, capitalize on and cultivate unity. They have one political institution—a party, a religious institution, or a presidency—dominating politics, and any official competition is only allowed on the condition of loyalty of all parties to this institution. Societies these regimes rule, even if not completely united, don't have cleavages deep enough to fuel political competition not sanctioned by the dominant institution.

Other authoritarian regimes thrive on existing social divisions. Syria, Turkey, Libya, Yemen, Afghanistan, Sudan, Burundi, Chad, Cameroon, Kyrgyzstan, and Myanmar, to name a few, are the countries where authoritarian regimes exacerbate long-standing ethnic, religious, and regional cleavages. Even though there is no lack of attempts to establish political monopoly in these countries, they often break under the pressure from rival groups. Elections in these countries are usually competitive, even though they do not follow democratic norms.

---

[3] "Freedom in the World 2023."

And in the absence of developed democratic institutions that would provide common ground and peaceful means for different groups to share power, opposing parties often resort to violence, which sometimes leads to civil wars and prolonged periods of insecurity.

How is it possible that both unity and division can be used by autocrats to build and strengthen their rule? And what does it mean for our understanding of democracy and autocracy if both political unity and political competition can result in authoritarianism? This book answers these questions by unpacking the *grassroots mechanism* of how authoritarian institutions connect to their two social roots—unity and division—and discusses how this idea impacts our understanding of autocracy and democracy.

Unity and Division as the Social Roots of Authoritarianism

There are many tools an autocrat can use to build an authoritarian regime. Easily available financial resources, such as oil, often help.[4] Autocrats also use political institutions, such as parliaments and parties, to create a veneer of democracy and help manage bargains with the elite.[5] A developed coercive apparatus is a must. Autocrats must be able to repress in case they are challenged by the elites or the masses, and they also want to prevent such challenges using secret services and surveillance if they can.[6]

No authoritarian regime, however, survives on coercion alone. Even the most repressive regimes have at least some legitimacy with at least some population groups. And many invest in the creation of an image and a narrative portraying the autocrat or the regime as the true leader of the people. These narratives appeal to the national history and character; they can talk about the great power glory, or dedication to holy scriptures, or the centuries-long history, or the past battles with enemies, or all of the above.[7] The regime in these narratives is presented as the embodiment of the nation's true self, and it is this connection with identity that provides the autocrat with the followship and charisma often ascribed to them. To the degree that autocrats use propaganda and various components of identity as their tool, they amplify these identities and deepen the divide between groups.

---

[4] Ross, "What Have We Learned about the Resource Curse?"
[5] Gandhi, *Political Institutions under Dictatorship*.
[6] Albertus and Menaldo, "Coercive Capacity and the Prospects for Democratization."
[7] See, for example, von Soest and Grauvogel, "Identity, Procedures and Performance"; Rock, *Authoritarian Argentina*; Cannady and Kubicek, "Nationalism and Legitimation for Authoritarianism"; Paget, "Again, Making Tanzania Great."

The core of this book's argument is the idea that autocrats' use of group identity can take the route of unity or division depending on the structure of society they rule. Although in most societies there are multiple groups and identities, they often have unequal influence on country politics. Historically, a country may form a clear dominating identity or have multiple competing ones. In both types of countries, autocrats deepen divide between groups; the difference is whether those divides lie within society or between that society and the outside world. Russia is an example of a country where authoritarianism thrives on cultivating a common identity while subjugating and suppressing any group identities alternative to the dominant one. At the same time, it deepens the divide between Russia and the allegedly hostile world. Contrary to this, Venezuela is an example of a country where autocracy capitalizes on long-standing internal class divisions, and out-of-the-country political players matter only inasmuch they support or oppose one of the competing camps.[8]

Rulers do not choose the structure of societies they rule. Politically salient groups and identities as well as social cleavages form historically, often over the course of centuries. Even in the cases of radical transformation of social structures, such as the creation and dissolution of the Soviet Union, legacies of the past continue to influence politics in the present.[9] The only choice rulers have is whether they use the group structure to build an authoritarian system and secure their power or bring the country in a more democratic direction.

Authoritarian regimes built on unity and division possess several opposite qualities. First, division-based regimes are usually more competitive than unity-based ones. In Turkey, for example, opposition politicians won mayor posts in major cities and close to 50% support at the 2023 presidential election with barely any access to the major media—a situation hardly conceivable in countries such as Russia, China, or Vietnam. Venezuela, mentioned earlier, is divided approximately in half between the regime and the opposition, and this rivalry was behind the last prolonged conflict between the president and the parliament. In many other authoritarian regimes, opposition parties not only legally exist but also have a stable social base even though the conditions under which they compete at the ballot box are hardly democratic.

Second, unity-based regimes rely on propaganda a lot more than division-based ones, which use violence more often. In division-based regimes, propaganda is less effective outside of the core group of regime supporters as it fights against preexisting group identities. Mexican PRI, for example, tried to cultivate a common identity through educational institutions, and was met with significant

---

[8] For a differently structured argument about overpoliticization and depoliticization as autocrats' tools, see Gerschewski, *The Two Logics of Autocratic Rule*.
[9] Lankina, *The Estate Origins of Democracy in Russia*; Pop-Eleches and Tucker, *Communism's Shadow*.

resistance from below.[10] In such situations, autocrats are forced to either buy population's loyalty if they have economic resources or repress the groups that would not concede. When violence is the only tool of political competition left, it may result in a prolonged fight with guerrilla groups and civil wars.

Third, the grassroots-level political structures—something this book analyzes in-depth—also differ between unity- and division-based authoritarian regimes. Unity-based regimes capitalize on the common identity and the willingness of the population to cooperate with the state that stems from this common identity. They build centralized top-down structures driven by the teamwork ethos and volunteer effort. Division-based regimes, in their turn, rely on bottom-up clientelistic networks driven by material interests and personalized mutual obligations.

In general, politics in unity- and division-based authoritarian regimes are driven by opposite logics. Unity-based authoritarian regimes rely on *teamwork logic*: the members of the group either win together or lose together. It uses social pressure to penalize individuals who deviate from the group and cultivates the common identity to strengthen this power mechanism. Party-states (the Soviet Union, China, Cuba, Vietnam) are all great examples of autocracies that used unifying social pressure to suppress resistance. In contrast, division-based authoritarianism relies on *utility-maximization logic*, which is the centerpiece of rational choice models. The PRI regime in Mexico is a great illustration: it created a system of material redistribution ensuring that cooperation with the regime provided the best individual returns.[11]

Statist and Antistatist Societies

There is a very important caveat to the thesis about the role of unity and division in authoritarianism. Not all countries with a unifying identity are equally prone to authoritarianism. In many countries, the growth of a common civic identity and overcoming earlier social divisions is associated with the growth of robust democratic institutions, some examples of such countries being the United States in the early 20th and Ukraine in the early 21st century.[12] In European countries, support for the welfare state, which reduces social inequalities, has also been related to the existence of a common identity.[13]

---

[10] Vaughan, *Cultural Politics in Revolution*.
[11] Magaloni, *Voting for Autocracy*.
[12] Clemens, *Civic Gifts*; Kulyk, "National Identity in Ukraine."
[13] Eger and Breznau, "Immigration and the Welfare State"; Burgoon and Rooduijn, "'Immigrationization' of Welfare Politics?"

For authoritarianism to thrive in a society with a unifying identity, that identity must be connected to the state—not only to the nation as the collective of the people but also to the state as the institution that embodies these people. Joel Migdal's famous work has shown how the state and other institutions compete for the right to set social norms governing everyday life and how the state's inability to win this right over from other groups leads to weak state capacity, which is often an obstacle to democratization.[14] The situation of identity connected to the state, which I refer to, is the opposite: the state may be so successful in suppressing other groups' influence on people's lives that it becomes the main institution people identify with. The state rather than the nation dominates the country mythology and people's understanding of who "we" are.

Whether the state dominates national identity and everyday life or not impacts *how* people view the state and to what degree they are willing to cooperate with it. When the state competes for societal influence with other powerful social institutions, such as clans or religion, people are more likely to view the state *as an outsider* and even a potential predator. Family, local community, or religious institutions are sources of support, the social safety net, while the state is an external institution that looks to take away their money as taxes and sons as army recruits as well as punish them for noncompliance with laws. People cooperate with families and local communities, while avoiding and resisting the state as much as they can. If, however, the state succeeds in creating an identity around itself and taking over the role of the safety net while suppressing nonstate institutions as alternative authorities, people come to view the state *as their collective leader* rather than a predator. They expect guidance from it and are more willing to cooperate with it for the benefit of the common good. While the state may or may not live up to them, these expectations are in place.

In this book, I will call these kinds of societies *statist* and *antistatist*. The difference in the vision of the state and population's willingness to cooperate with it in these societies determines the tools available to the autocrat at the grassroots level to build and maintain the regime. Statist social norms create favorable conditions for a unity-based authoritarian regime, while antistatist social norms are conducive to a division-based one (Figure I.1). Further in the book, I will look in detail at the grassroots organizational structures in statist and antistatist societies and the different logics they follow.

The distinction between statist and antistatist societies is important as an analytical tool highlighting the opposite internal logics of these political environments and authoritarian regimes existing in them. These ideal types do not and cannot capture the historical richness of each case. Empirically, it

---

[14] Migdal, *Strong Societies and Weak States*.

Statist social norms ⟶ Unity-based authoritarianism

Antistatist social norms ⟶ Division-based authoritarianism

Figure I.1 Statism and types of authoritarianism.

is useful to think about statist and antistatist societies as a continuum rather than two rigid categories. Some societies may clearly fall close to one of the poles. For example, China would be close to the statist pole, given the extensive role the Chinese state plays in people's everyday life, while Ethiopia would be close to the antistatist pole given the long-standing ethnic divisions in the country. Other societies will see a mixture of these logics depending on how the competition between the state and nonstate institutions played out historically. For example, in Iran, the state and religion have historically been rivals—until 1979, when religion subjugated the state. The Islamic Revolution created a polity, in which a unifying revolutionary identity mixed with somewhat meaningful political competition. Any larger country, such as Russia, studied in this book, is likely to have regional variation of political environments. To understand the opposite grassroots mechanisms of authoritarian power that create this variation, though, it is important to distinguish statist and antistatist societies.

Autocracy—Democracy—Autocracy

The distinction between statist and antistatist societies is important also because it sheds new light on the relationship between democracy and authoritarianism. One of the key implications of this distinction is that unity-based and division-based authoritarianisms *lack different elements of democracy*.

In divided countries like Syria, Sudan, or Ethiopia, divisions along ethnic, class, or religious lines result in competition for power and unequal access to state resources. When one group gains power, they often use the state to favor their own group members and deprive others of resources. For example, in Syria, the al-Assad family has been channeling resources to Alawite minority communities and used their fear of the Sunni majority population to secure political support. In Ethiopia until 2018, the ruling EPRDF party has been informally dominated by the Tigray people, while the Oromos were deprived of economic and education opportunities. After the rise to power of Abiy Ahmed, the first Oromo leader of Ethiopia in 2018, the government used the military to suppress Tigray's resistance, while depriving the Tigray region from basic resources. Regimes in divided political environments thrive on differential treatment of citizens and poor enforcement of common rules and procedures. Autocrats there use group identities to maintain *internal divisions* and retain their rule.

In contrast, unity-based regimes like those in Russia, China, or Cuba, have an abundance of equalizing and universalizing policies, which are relatively well enforced by state institutions. While these societies are not free from everyday xenophobia, loyalty to the regime, rather than religion, ethnicity, or class, is the main condition of access to state resources and careers. The Soviet Union, for example, had institutionalized diversity policies geared toward recruiting ethnic minorities and economically disadvantaged groups to party and state apparatuses. The only people such regimes mistreat are those who express loyalty to competing centers of power. This is why the Soviet Union suppressed resistance of ethnic minorities to the Soviet rule while having official and enforced diversity policies for those minority individuals who agreed to recognize Soviet authorities as legitimate. Lack of competing centers of power leaves the state unconstrained and makes state officials the privileged group, who abuse their access to state resources, while being relatively inclusive at the lower levels of the state apparatus. In this environment, *internal unifying identity* and successful repression of competing centers of power help maintain authoritarian rule.

Unity- and division-based authoritarian regimes require opposite solutions to democratize. Division-based authoritarianism needs a stronger state authority that would transcend the interests of specific groups and enforce universal laws. It needs to develop independence of the state apparatus from the influences of different societal groups competing for state power. State officials must enforce the law in the same way regardless of which group currently leads the nation. To grow popular support for such neutral authority of the state, divided societies also need a stronger, common, civic identity. When such unifying identities grow, equalizing democratic institutions and norms take root in society. In the examples mentioned above, the United States in the early 20th century, the growth of civic identity made it possible to counteract clientelism and corruption and strengthen the democratic basis of political institutions.

Unity-based authoritarianism, in contrast, needs to constrain the authority of the state and state officials by strengthening resistance to the state. Supporting alternative centers of power would help grow institutions systematically constraining state officials and making sure they do not extend their privileges beyond what is necessary for proper functioning of the state apparatus. These alternative power centers may be rooted in ethnic or religious communities as well as in regional divisions most countries have. For example, the political system in West Germany after World War II was designed to give significant power to

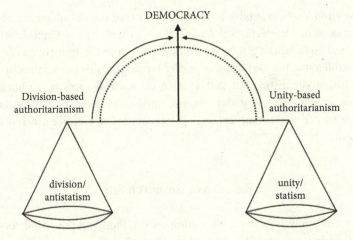

Figure I.2 Democracy as the balance point.

regional authorities, at least partially to ensure they could constrain the central state and prevent another dictator from rising to power.[15]

Democracy, therefore, is the balance of forces enabling and restricting the state. This is not a new idea. From Tocqueville to Fukuyama to Acemoglu and Robinson, democracy theorists have emphasized the importance of such balance.[16] This book contributes to this picture by spelling out the different logics of authoritarian regimes that result from a political system lacking this balance and tilting one or the other way. By developing the concepts of unity- and division-based authoritarianisms, I construct *a different continuum of democracy and autocracy*. Instead of treating democracy and autocracy as the poles, I position division- and unity-based authoritarianisms on the opposite ends of this continuum, while placing democracy in the middle, at the point of balance between the forces enabling and restricting the state (Figure I.2).

This new vision of a democracy–autocracy continuum expands the existing literature on the variety of authoritarianisms. Scholars have developed a range of typologies, many of which focus on either political elites or electoral institutions. Geddes, Write, and Frantz, for example, look at groups that seize power and distinguish between military regimes, single-party regimes, and monarchies.[17]

---

[15] Renzsch, "German Federalism in Historical Perspective."

[16] Tocqueville, *Democracy in America*; Fukuyama, *The Origins of Political Order*; Fukuyama, *Political Order and Political Decay*. Acemoglu and Robinson describe three equilibria between the state and society, which is similar to the ideas presented here. However, they view the state as the elites and society as nonelites who compete with each other, while I argue that both the state and societal groups should be viewed as authority centers that can organize collective action (Acemoglu and Robinson, "Weak, Despotic, or Inclusive?").

[17] Geddes, Wright, and Frantz, *How Dictatorships Work*.

Levitsky and Way distinguish hybrid regimes based on a combination of characteristics related to elections.[18] And Guriev and Treisman distinguish between "fear" and "spin" dictators, based on how rulers use the information space.[19] Without denying the usefulness of earlier typologies, this book introduces another important distinction that focuses on societal roots of authoritarian regimes. It uncovers the grassroots mechanisms of authoritarian power and explains why certain authoritarian tools are more or less useful in different social environments.

Russia as a Research Site

Almost any study is better with a comparison. Studying the social roots, or microfoundations, of authoritarianism through cross-country comparison, though, is challenging. As numerous scholars have demonstrated, authoritarian regimes vary along many institutional and elite-related dimensions. Controlling for these macro-level factors in a cross-country study would be difficult while trying to analyze micro-level processes. Another approach, taken in this book, is to use the regional variation of social and political environments within a bigger country, in which all regions exist within the same macro-level institutional framework.[20]

Russia, studied in this book, is possibly one of the best research sites for such regional comparisons. Not only is it large territorially but also its regions have very different histories and relations with the central state. Some regions already had distinct regional identities and institutions before they were subjugated by the Russian empire or joined it voluntarily. Others formed and developed their identities and institutions as parts of Russia with varied attitudes to Moscow. Such variation provides rich material to study contrasting social environments, their connection to historically formed identities and the grassroots mechanisms of authoritarian power.

Russia is also a very important research site for studying the microfoundations of authoritarianism. For centuries, it experienced authoritarianism returning after short democratic periods, and scholars have tried to find an explanation for this pattern. Some pointed to authoritarian political culture and the inclination to follow authority as the mechanism behind reproducing authoritarianism. Others argued that structural economic and political factors explain the Russian

---

[18] Levitsky and Way, *Competitive Authoritarianism*.
[19] Guriev and Treisman, *Spin Dictators*.
[20] For a recent example of such approach, see Gerschewski, *The Two Logics of Autocratic Rule*. On the methodological principles of using subnational comparisons, see Snyder, "Scaling Down."

historical trajectory perfectly well, and its political culture is not significantly different from other countries.[21]

The theory of unity and division as the two social roots of authoritarianism reconciles these two approaches. In addition to analyzing its regional variation, the book argues that Russian political history as a whole fits well the model of unity-based authoritarianism. This authoritarianism manifests in distinct political culture placing the state in the center of collective identity as well as in political contention driven by people's search for a just state. This culture is often caricatured by political commentators as the desire to have a benevolent tsar, which precludes an unbiased analysis of this phenomenon. By treating both unity and division as possible social roots of authoritarianism, though, this book recognizes the existence of this culture, while also explaining how it fits with the universal analytic categories that present Russia as no different from other countries.

Resolving this puzzle about Russia also allows for better understanding of other countries with similar political histories. One obvious parallel is China, which has an even more consistent history of authoritarianism and state-centered political culture. While Russia and China are different in many respects, understanding how societal unity helps reproduce authoritarianism at the micro-level opens the possibilities for many analytically interesting comparisons of these countries.

Two Empirical Approaches and the Structure of the Book

To investigate unity and division as the social roots of authoritarianism, this book uses two empirical approaches. The first and the main one consists of the comparison of four regions that focuses on grassroots political processes and organizations. This approach allows me to develop a theory of how autocrats build their regimes in social environments with contrasting views of the state. The second approach analyzes Russia as a whole, looking at its political dynamics in historical perspective (see Table I.1). This approach demonstrates how the theory of unity- and division-based authoritarianism can explain a country's political trajectory and the patterns of state–society relations.

This project started as an attempt to explain the difference in performance of political machines in Russian regions: Why was it that in some regions, political machines had a more stable performance than in others? The puzzle came from my earlier study revealing that Russian schoolteachers were part of electoral machines delivering the vote at the 2012 presidential election

---

[21] For a more detailed discussion of these issues, see Chapter 5 of this book.

Table I.1 *The Empirical Strategy of the Book*

	Empirical Study Designs	
	Subnational Comparison (chapters 2–4)	**Russia as a Case (chapter 5)**
Theoretical argument	Authoritarianism is built and reproduced through • *unity* or in-group mechanisms (e.g., conformity with the state) in *statist* social environments; • *division* or intergroup mechanisms (e.g., clientelistic exchanges) in *antistatist* social environments.	
Empirical arguments	Putin's electoral performance in 2012 was *more resilient in the regions with statist societies* than in those with antistatist societies.	Russian historical trajectory and state–society relations fits the model of *unity-based authoritarianism in a statist society*. The main tension driving domestic politics is the *mismatch between the ideal of a just state and the reality of an oppressive state*.
Unit of analysis	a Russian region	Russia as a country case
Research methods	- A static, side-by-side comparison of four Russian regions; - quantitative analysis of regional-level statistics; - analysis of primary documents and interviews for each of the four regions.	- A dynamic, historical view of Russia as a case; - analysis of secondary academic sources; - analysis of primary sources related to the recent events in Russian domestic politics at the national level.

(see Appendix 1). They worked in precinct-level electoral commissions and altered electoral results to favor Vladimir Putin by either engaging in canvassing or through direct falsification of vote count. The effect of teachers was statistically significant and robust, but across the country, it only explained 13% of regional variation in voting for Putin. The differences between regions were large, and their causes were unclear.

This quantitative analysis, however, allowed me to choose strategically the regions for qualitative research. I nested my case studies in the scatterplot of predicted outcome values based on regression results by choosing two regions where political machines' performance was unusually stable and two more where it was unusually unstable. During the fieldwork, I focused on organizations connecting the state and society that could reveal why these political machines performed so differently.

This qualitative comparison of grassroots politics in different regions revealed opposite patterns of state–society relations. Those regions where political machines delivered the vote more consistently had statist societies, that is, people viewed the state as their collective leader and cooperated easily with state representatives for the sake of the common good. In contrast, the regions where the performance of political machines was less stable had antistatist societies. This means that people viewed the state as an outsider and, in their interactions with state officials, tried to maximize their own utility rather than the common good.

In Chapters 2–4 of this book, I explain in detail how the different views of the state translated into different structures of grassroots organizations that performed differently during elections. Before that, in Chapter 1, I develop the theory of statist and antistatist societies by connecting it to earlier research traditions and explaining how the unity of statist societies and division in antistatist ones help reproduce authoritarian power at the grassroots level.

The second empirical approach of this book treats Russia as a single-country case. Unlike the regional comparison, this approach adopts a historical look at Russia and applies the theory of unity-based authoritarianism to explain its political dynamics. In Chapter 5, I apply the concept of unity-based authoritarianism to explain popular support for Vladimir Putin. Then, I look at the history of state–society relations in Russia to argue that the main tension that has been driving Russian domestic politics is the mismatch between the ideal of a just state and the reality of an oppressive state.

What the Book Does and Does Not

The overall purpose of this book is to develop an empirically grounded and internally coherent theory of authoritarian power in different types of societies. As is explained in more detail in Chapter 1, this theory builds on earlier research related to the role of group identity, emotions, and leadership as well as scholarship on the state and authoritarianism. As I connect the different elements of these research traditions, I also challenge some existing ideas and concepts. The reader may find it unusual and counterintuitive, but such challenge is important for continued development of scholarship.

The most important conceptual challenge in this book relates to the role of unity and division in democracies and autocracies. This conceptual challenge is not entirely new. Even the language we use captures the ambivalence of these phenomena: division is usually seen as negative and pluralism as positive; unity is positive, while monopoly or lack of diversity is negative. I purposefully use the term "unity" in the book—not in the formal institutionalist meaning of a unitary state but in the sense of societal unity—to talk about one of the social roots of authoritarianism. The term is widely associated with solidarity, overcoming of social divisions, building a consensus, and finding a common ground, which are all seemingly conducive to democracy. The implication of my theory is that all these things may also be conducive to authoritarianism—if a society lacks institutions constraining the power of the state. Such institutions may develop in different ways but are often maintained by social divisions, that is, by groups who have different political interests and enough power to act on them. Unity would be indeed conducive to democracy in a society that is "pluralist by default," or, in my terminology, antistatist. But in a statist society, more unity often means moving away from democracy.

The issue of unity-based authoritarianism in statist societies also raises the question about the role of coercion. Why do people in some societies view the state as a leader even when the state mistreats them? Why would they not rise? A very common answer to this question is that people must have been coerced into submission, thus authoritarian power is based on coercion. Coercion is seen as the opposite of legitimate power, to which an individual submits voluntarily, and it is this opposition of coercion and legitimacy that my theory challenges. Authoritarian power in statist societies, that is, in societies where people view the state as their collective leader, marries legitimacy and coercion: it is possible to be coerced by an authoritarian state you see as legitimate. Coercion by a trusted party central to one's identity is very different from coercion by an outsider. I discuss this issue in two places in the book: in Chapter 1, when I analyze the concept of legitimacy, and in Chapter 5, when I describe the typical reactions of Russians to state coercion.

Another concept that I challenge in the book is the concept of political machines and, through that, our understanding of the role of formal and informal institutions in democratic and authoritarian politics. Existing scholarship on political machines usually defines them as informal institutions based on clientelist practices, which, by definition, serve private interests at the expense of common ones. Two out of four regions I study match this description perfectly. The other two, however, go the opposite direction. There, political machines work through formal institutions (municipalities, other institutions of local governance, schools, NGOs, etc.) and use the teamwork logic of contribution to the common good to deliver the vote. I chose to call them political machines as well for two reasons. First, they serve the same purpose as political machines in the other two regions—delivering the vote—even though their internal principles are different. Second, "political machines" is a very good metaphor. These are machines at their core: they are impersonal structures that do their job regardless of whether the goal is enforcing trash-collection rules or delivering the vote for the ruling party.

Using this term for both types of political machines demonstrates that formality and informality do not have a unidirectional relationship to democracy. The common understanding is that informality undermines democratic procedures while formality maintains them. However, if the state is unconstrained and uses its position as the collective leader to undermine pluralism, it is the formal institutions that help the state to achieve its goal, while often maintaining the veneer of democratic procedures and the rule of law.

Democracy Support

Understanding of the opposite principles of how authoritarian power works in statist and antistatist societies is very important not only for advancing knowledge but also for improving the practice of democracy support. If unity- and division-based authoritarianisms lack different elements of democracy, democracy support in these environments should focus on developing these lacking elements. Supporting the same kind of social institutions will move one kind of society closer to democracy, while in another kind of society it may unintentionally strengthen authoritarianism.

The theory developed in this book suggests that the institutions most needed in antistatist societies are those that help develop social consensus, support for common rules of the game, and the independent authority of the state that would enforce these rules. Antistatist societies that have been historically divided usually have little problem with inherent political competitiveness as every competing group has a solid social support base. Lack of equal treatment of different groups, though, may lead to monopolization of power by one of them. To counteract that, the independence of state authority from all parties and its ability to enforce the law uniformly should be supported.

In contrast, statist societies have little problem with social consensus, but they lack inherent competitiveness and the institutions that would limit state power. Strengthening independent state authority will not help here, because the state is already viewed by the people as an impartial leader and the source of the common good. To protect society from state officials overreaching their mandates, though, independent institutions that could hold state officials accountable must be supported. Cultivating alternative centers of power that the population also associates with the common good would help to break the state monopoly on leadership and increase political competitiveness backed up by grassroots support.

Tailoring democracy support programs for every country, of course, is not as easy as choosing between these two options. Manifestations of statism and antistatism are mixed in most countries; they may vary by territory or by level of governance. A careful diagnostic of political environments and social norms is essential for designing effective programs, and the theoretical framework developed in this book can serve as a guide for asking questions and developing new answers.

1
Authoritarian Power in Statist and Antistatist Societies

Dictatorships differ from each other more than democracies do.[1] There are many ways to think about this variety of authoritarian regimes: one can use, for example, the characteristics of groups seizing power,[2] electoral competitiveness,[3] the configuration of legislative institutions and party scenes,[4] and the strength of the coercive apparatus[5] to capture the variety of ways in which authoritarian regimes form and endure. Each of these theories expands our understanding of authoritarianism and provides more tools for researchers to explain how specific regimes succeed or fail.

This book expands the study of the variety of authoritarianisms by turning our attention from the ruling elites and organizations to societal characteristics. I argue that the power of a state ruler, as well as his strategies of consolidating and holding on to this power, are largely shaped by *the kind of group identities dominant in society* and by *how people in society view the state*. In countries, such as Russia or China, where the population views the state as its legitimate collective leader and holds it as the centerpiece of its identity, autocrats use the ideas of social unity and civic duty to build and consolidate institutions maintaining their power. In contrast, in countries such as Venezuela or Sudan, where class, religious, or ethnic identities play the dominant role and divide societies into competing groups, autocrats capitalize on these divisions and particularistic group interests to consolidate their regimes. These *unity- and division-based authoritarianisms* use different playbooks based on the opposite principles, which have not been articulated in the literature before.

This chapter accomplishes two tasks. First, it introduces *the statist versus antistatist* scale, along which societies vary and which highlights the contrasting logics of unity- and division-based authoritarianisms. Second, it introduces the concept of *group authority*, whose connection to the state or lack thereof defines

---

[1] Geddes, Wright, and Frantz, *How Dictatorships Work*, 2–3.
[2] Geddes, Wright, and Frantz.
[3] Diamond, "Thinking about Hybrid Regimes"; Levitsky and Way, *Competitive Authoritarianism*.
[4] Brownlee, *Authoritarianism in an Age of Democratization*; Gandhi, *Political Institutions under Dictatorship*.
[5] Bellin, "The Robustness of Authoritarianism in the Middle East."

statist–antistatist variation. A complete blending of group authority and the state defines the statist end of the scale, while their complete separation defines the antistatist one. Second, it lays out the empirical manifestations of statism and antistatism as well as their implications for autocrats' strategies, infrastructural state power, and civil society.

Statist versus Antistatist Societies

Social scientists have convincingly demonstrated that cultural understandings and social norms related to the state play a major role in the state's ability to govern, shape specific policies, and enforce social order.[6] Comparative institutionalist research showed that people in some societies imagine state leadership as the solution to policy challenges while others lean toward minimizing state interventions. In the first world, the classic studies of this difference focus on the comparison of the United States and Britain to continental Europe.[7] Research on developing countries has primarily focused on the practices of state avoidance.[8]

To bring this insight about social norms related to the state to the study of authoritarianism, I will use the concept of *statist* versus *antistatist* societies. I understand *statism* as a social norm that envisions the state as the centerpiece of collective identity, the default leader who organizes individual efforts into collective action, and the main enforcer of social order. In statist societies, people expect the state to lead and play an active role in organizing their everyday life. Cooperating with the state is considered a civic duty and a contribution to the common good. In contrast, *antistatism* is a social norm that expects the state to keep a limited reach and envisions nonstate institutions (business, civil society, religious institutions, ethnic communities, etc.) as taking responsibility for regulating a big share of everyday interactions.

Statism does not necessarily mean default popular support of any state actions. Rather, it is an expectation of strong, active leadership from the state, which a particular government may or may not satisfy.[9] The best indicator of statism is not the level of support for the government but default solution to collective problems that people have in mind. In statist societies, the default solution to the failure of state leadership is to change the people in power to those who can satisfy the expectation of leadership, that is, to strengthen the state. In antistatist

[6] Morgan and Orloff, *The Many Hands of the State*.
[7] Dobbin, *Forging Industrial Policy*; Fourcade, *Economists and Societies*.
[8] Scott, *The Art of Not Being Governed*; Migdal, *Strong Societies and Weak States*.
[9] On active leadership of the state in popular politics, see Ekiert, Perry, and Yan, *Ruling by Other Means*.

societies, the default solution to the failure of state leadership is to roll back the state and let nonstate institutions take the lead in resolving the problem, that is, to weaken the state. A good example of this is the difference between the attitudes to the welfare state in continental Europe and in the United States: while in continental Europe there are mass protests against rolling the welfare state back, for example, against increasing the pension age, in the United States the public opinion is much less in support of state-run social security programs.[10]

The existence of such social norms impacts the kinds of institutions that form in statist and antistatist societies. It is much easier to build centralized, top-down structures in a society that expects state leadership and views cooperation with the state as a civic duty, while in a society that leans toward limiting the state reach, state officials must negotiate with the leaders of nonstate institutions and communities. This link between social norms and institutional structures is crucial for this book's argument, as it demonstrates how unity and division become the tools of an autocrat.

Statism and antistatism are ideal types that form a continuum rather than binary categories, and these social norms are characteristic of any society, not only authoritarian ones. To understand how exactly these social norms relate to power in general and authoritarian power in particular, we must step back and look at the nature of authority and its connection to group identity and legitimacy.

Group Authority and the Third Face of Power

The state is not the only institution that can play the role of a collective leader. People have always lived in groups—tribes, villages, towns, ethnic or religious communities—and had an idea of who the "we" were. Living in groups has not only provided humans with increased chances of physical survival but also developed a psychological need to connect to others. Being part of a family, tribe, religion, or country associates individual life with a larger group that existed before the person was born and will exist after her demise, thus making her life meaningful.[11] Psychological research shows that losing a sense of meaning and purpose, usually as a result of weakened social connections, devalues the physical existence of a person and may lead to suicide. This need to connect and

---

[10] Breeden, "Why So Many People in France Are Protesting over Pensions"; Brooks and Manza, *Why Welfare States Persist*.
[11] McGregor, "Zeal, Identity, and Meaning"; Castano, Yzerbyt, and Paladino, "Transcending Oneself through Social Identification"; Pearlman, "Moral Identity and Protest Cascades in Syria." See also the evidence of connection between group cohesion and existential threats in the World Values Survey in Inglehart, "From Authoritarian Personality to Authoritarian Reflex."

belong is the main reason why such mechanisms of social cohesion as shame and ostracism work even in most individualistic societies.[12]

"Group authority"—the term I will use in the book—is the power of a group over an individual, which is based on the human need to belong. It is the power to set social norms and enforce compliance. When group authority is possessed by a person or an organization, they have the right to speak on behalf of the group, which is recognized and accepted by its members. Such authority induces voluntary compliance even in the situations when individuals are ordered to sacrifice their own, independent interests for the sake of the collective one. The concept of group authority is close to Weberian legitimate domination as it only applies to voluntary compliance rather than overt coercion.[13]

Examples of group authority can be found wherever social norms are involved. It may be a conservative religious community that denies the right for education to women on the basis that it is not part of a God-given social order. It may be a parliament speaking on behalf of the nation and demanding that citizens give up part of their individual resources in the form of taxes. It may be a leader of a workers' movement speaking on behalf of all workers and calling for her supporters to engage in political action. Or it may be the head of a radical religious organization speaking on behalf of his doctrine and motivating his followers to sacrifice their lives by becoming suicide bombers.[14] In all these cases, a legitimate authority is the one that speaks on behalf of a group and demands that individuals sacrifice their own interests and resources to advance collective goals.[15]

The idea that individuals and organizations can speak on behalf of the group and use group authority to secure compliance has implications for the long-standing debate about power and coercion in the social sciences. The question about the nature of voluntary compliance with the authority is central to this debate: "how do the powerful secure the compliance of those they dominate" if no direct coercion is involved?[16] The two answers to this question provided by social scientists so far resolve the contradiction by disputing either the reality of compliance or its voluntary character. James Scott, for example, argues

---

[12] A large body of works in existential and group psychology addresses these issues. See, for example, Baumeister and Leary, "The Need to Belong"; Solomon, Greenberg, and Pyszczynski, "The Cultural Animal"; Juhl and Routledge, "Putting the Terror in Terror Management Theory"; Castano, Yzerbyt, and Paladino, "Transcending Oneself through Social Identification"; Castano et al., "Ideology, Fear of Death, and Death Anxiety"; Vigilant and Williamson, "Symbolic Immortality and Social Theory"; Case and Williams, "Ostracism"; Williams, "Ostracism."
[13] Weber, *Economy and Society*, 212.
[14] Routledge and Arndt, "Self-Sacrifice as Self-Defence."
[15] For psychological research addressing this phenomenon, see, for example, Stellmacher and Petzel, "Authoritarianism as a Group Phenomenon"; Ent and Baumeister, "Obedience, Self-Control, and the Voice of Culture."
[16] Lukes, *Power*, 110.

that the dominated—the peasants or the working class—are resisting the power of the nobility or the capitalists rather than complying with it, but their resistance is hidden from the public eye.[17] Neo-Marxists, such as Gramsci, as well as Steven Lukes, make the opposite argument, saying that the dominated cannot resist because the powerful take away their agency via hegemony and creation of false consciousness.[18] False consciousness alters how the dominated see their own interests in a way that benefits the powerful. For example, Lukes talked about women accepting and defending their traditional roles even though it reproduces their subordinate position in the patriarchal society.[19]

The same contradiction between agency and compliance makes it difficult to define legitimate authority and authoritarian legitimacy. The concept of legitimate authority is paradoxical: it assumes both individual consent, as legitimacy is the recognition of the right to give orders, and suppression of individual interest, as authority means that people obey even those orders with which they disagree.[20] It is unclear how a person can accept as legitimate an authority that makes this person think and act against her interests. How can a woman, for example, regard religious authorities as legitimate if they deny her right for education, owning property, and having a say in family matters? In a similar vein, how can people living under an authoritarian regime accept its legitimacy if this regime acts in the interests of the powerful few rather than in the interests of all?[21] In light of the debate about power described above, one possible answer is that there is no such thing as authoritarian legitimacy. The only way to obtain legitimate authority is through the process of democratic representation, which gives people a voice in shaping the authority that may one day act against their interests.[22] In the absence of free and fair elections, autocrats cannot achieve true legitimacy and compliance, and as a result, always deal with preference falsification and hidden discontent.[23] Another possible answer is that the power of autocrats to manipulate public discourse and control information flows helps them obscure people's true interests, thus achieving sincere compliance by stripping the population of its political agency.[24]

The concept of group authority provides a different way to understand voluntary compliance and authoritarian legitimacy, which reconciles these two answers and does not deny either the sincerity of compliance or the agency of the

---

[17] Scott, *Domination and the Arts of Resistance*; Scott, *The Art of Not Being Governed*.
[18] Gramsci, *Selections from the Prison Notebooks of Antonio Gramsci*; Lukes, *Power*.
[19] Lukes, 137–44.
[20] Weber, *Economy and Society*, 212; Gilley, *The Right to Rule*, 8; Sadurski, Sevel, and Walton, *Legitimacy*.
[21] Gerschewski, "Legitimacy in Autocracies."
[22] Fukuyama, *State-Building*, 26; Levi, *Consent, Dissent, and Patriotism*.
[23] Kuran, "Now Out of Never"; Kuran, *Private Truths, Public Lies*; Dimitrov, "Understanding Communist Collapse and Resilience."
[24] Treisman, *The New Autocracy*.

dominated. The theories of power discussed above assume that individuals have one set of interests, which includes a mixture of material and cultural as well as individual and social needs. The more of those needs a political leader satisfies, the more legitimate she is. At the same time, the more she can restrict individual interests, the more authoritative she is. In this setup, it is difficult to combine legitimacy and authority.

Unlike these theories of power, group authority assumes that people have two sets of interests—independent needs and the need to belong to a group. Often, these two sets of interests work together and reinforce each other. A Black person or a conservative white man in the United States likely see their individual interests as largely resonating with the interests of their social groups: a Black person believes they are better off when all Black people are better off, and a conservative white man believes his interests are served when conservatives in general have more power. Belonging to a group in these cases resonates with and helps shape the perception of individual interests.

There are many situations, however, when independent needs and the need to belong to a group work at cross-purposes.[25] The independent needs are driven by the universal psychological need for autonomy as, even in most collectivist societies, people value the opportunity to make their own choices and follow social norms voluntarily rather than being forced into it.[26] For example, a religious woman may sincerely want to be a part of her faith community while having a no less sincere desire to make choices about her life. Groups, however, are often intolerant of individual choices and tend to restrict individual freedom. And since they are the center of social connections that the person values and possess group authority over the individual, it is easy to implement such restrictions using shame and ostracism.[27]

The internal conflict between the two human needs—to belong and to be free—is what makes group authority so effective and different from overt coercion. By recognizing the legitimacy of an authority—a religious, ethnic, or state leader—a person claims her membership in a group and satisfies her need to belong. At the same time, this legitimate authority may restrict the individual's ability to make her own choices, thus playing a dual role in her life: it is both an anchor that makes her life meaningful and an institution that restricts her individual freedom. Rather than being deceived and unable to understand their own interests, individuals whose life choices, gender identities, or political

---

[25] For similar ideas in different forms, see Feldman, "Enforcing Social Conformity"; Greenberg, Koole, and Pyszczynski, "Experimental Existential Psychology"; Stosny, *Soar Above*.
[26] Kasser and Sheldon, "Autonomy Is No Illusion."
[27] Altemeyer, *Enemies of Freedom*; Feldman, "Enforcing Social Conformity"; Williams, "Ostracism"; Kuran, *Private Truths, Public Lies*; Ent and Baumeister, "Obedience, Self-Control, and the Voice of Culture"; Haidt, *The Righteous Mind*.

preferences do not conform with the norms of their community face a difficult choice. They can either sacrifice their social belonging and risk losing a sense of larger purpose in life or they can comply with the norms of their community and risk losing their own agency and independent self.

This tough choice explains why it is so difficult to resist group authority and why those who possess it can secure wide compliance with their orders. Resisting such authority means going against not only the group leader but also the group itself and risking ostracism. It often requires not only material resources needed to resist physical or economic coercion but also an alternative community, which would provide a sense that you are not alone. In the absence of such an alternative, many individuals will comply with group authority even when they understand that it works against them.

Group Authority and the State

As group authority induces wide voluntary compliance, politics in all societies is greatly influenced by which institutions—tribes, religions, classes, racial or ethnic groups, or the state—possess such authority and for which parts of the population. All political leaders, whether democratic or authoritarian, must take into account the way social norms divide or unite their societies, as it determines the kind of power they have over the population.[28]

Historically, the state has competed for power with other social institutions.[29] In western Europe and in other parts of the world, landed aristocracy competed with the early states for the right to tax the population.[30] In the Middle East, Islamic authorities represented an alternative power center, which could help shield property from state authorities.[31] In many colonial and postcolonial societies, the state competed with indigenous authorities, and the way it managed these relations impacted the authority the state was able to develop.[32] In

---

[28] One example of analysis that focuses on the intersections of group trust and authority is Charles Tilly's "Trust and Rule." Some other examples: on the importance of group authority in African politics, see Pitcher, Moran, and Johnston, "Rethinking Patrimonialism and Neopatrimonialism in Africa"; on the importance of group identity and its connection to protest behavior, see Pearlman, "Moral Identity and Protest Cascades in Syria."

[29] Migdal, *Strong Societies and Weak States*; Barkey and Parikh, "Comparative Perspectives on the State."

[30] On European cases, see, for example, Tilly, *Coercion, Capital, and European States, AD 990–1992*; Spruyt, *The Sovereign State and Its Competitors*. On lack of competition with landowners as a cause of state-driven industrialization in Asia, see Amsden, "The State and Taiwan's Economic Development."

[31] Blaydes, "State Building in the Middle East."

[32] Callaghy, *The State–Society Struggle*; Azarya and Chazan, "Disengagement from the State in Africa"; Steinmetz, *The Devil's Handwriting*; Slater and Soifer, "The Indigenous Inheritance." See also the literature on communalism, for example, Cammett, *Compassionate Communalism*; Smith-Morris, *Indigenous Communalism*.

Latin America, class divisions and regionalism both facilitated and undermined the central state formation: In some countries, the state was able to use societal cleavages to establish itself as the third party, while in other countries, the state failed to obtain autonomy and served primarily capitalist interest groups.[33]

Autonomy is one of the aspects of state power that is especially important for understanding how the state develops in competition with other social institutions. This concept was reintroduced to the academic discourse in the late 1970s and early 1980s by Theda Skocpol and other scholars, who argued with the Marxist vision of the state as being merely an instrument of the capitalist class.[34] Skocpol showed that the state apparatus may have its own interests, which are independent from class ones, and that state policies may work against societal elites. Along the same line of argument, other scholars emphasized the difference between state autonomy and state capacity.[35] Although both are related to the ability of the state to implement its policies, state capacity is associated with the resources—material and organizational—that the state possesses, while state autonomy determines whether those resources serve the state or a societal interest group. The state may have a large police force and developed organizational infrastructure, but these resources may largely serve the interests of an economic class, an ethnic group, or a religious denomination.

This book builds on the tradition of researching state autonomy and takes it one step further by refocusing the attention from the rulers to the ruled. I argue that politics is influenced not only by whether the state apparatus has interests autonomous from society but also by *whether society views the state as the institution that has the right to speak on behalf of society as a whole, that is, as a legitimate source of power*. Wherever people view the state this way, the state and group authority blend, and I will call such a society *statist*. In a statist society, ethnicities, religious communities, or local clans may exist, but none of them possesses enough authority to induce the same level of society-wide compliance as the state. If, however, people do not endow the state with such authority, nonstate groups are likely to be the main political players who can mobilize the population for collective action. I will call such society *antistatist*.

Statism versus antistatism is a continuum rather than a binary. All state leaders presumably would prefer to deal with a statist society, which is easier to control, rather than with an antistatist one with a high level of resistance, and they often aim to strengthen group authority of the state through providing

---

[33] O'Donnell, "Reflections on the Patterns of Change in the Bureaucratic-Authoritarian State"; Stepan, "State Power and the Strength of Civil Society in the Southern Cone of Latin America"; Soifer, *State Building in Latin America*. See also Slater and Soifer, "The Indigenous Inheritance," on the influence of inherited social cleavage on state-building.
[34] Skocpol, *States and Social Revolutions*; Evans, Rueschemeyer, and Skocpol, *Bringing the State Back In*; Mann, "The Autonomous Power of the State."
[35] Barkey and Parikh, "Comparative Perspectives on the State," 525–26.

public goods or using ideology and education.[36] However, because of their rivalry with other institutions, it may be difficult for states to obtain group authority: societies may resist the imposition of state power for centuries.[37] The various institutional configurations, which we observe in societies throughout history, are the result of interaction between different institutions as well as of historical contingencies. For example, in medieval western Europe, the church possessed significant group authority along with the state, which prevented the state from consolidating absolute power.[38] In Iran since 1979, religious authorities succeeded in taking over the state and worked to expand their group authority by blending in the state functions.[39] Ethnic nationalism may help strengthen the state or weaken it, nurturing separatist movements instead.[40] In some cases, however, the state itself succeeds in obtaining group authority and subordinating the rival institutions to its power.

Research on state formation shows that there are several factors that likely influenced whether the state obtained group authority. In agrarian societies, whose economy required collective effort in constructing complex irrigation systems, the state had more chances to establish its authority.[41] Societies, which experienced persistent external threats, might also be more likely to develop authoritative states.[42] Countries where the state consolidated before the introduction of wide suffrage tended to have states with strong norm-setting power as well.[43]

One factor, however, seems to be especially important: the level of political competitiveness at the time when state rulers consolidated their control over society for the first time, possibly under external threats. If during that historical period, society lacked elites who could rival state rulers, bargain with them, and organize formal bodies to limit their power, the state was in a good position to become the supreme leader of the people.[44] Two examples of such scenario of state formation are the Chinese and the Russian states, which share

---

[36] Vaughan, *Cultural Politics in Revolution*; Harris, *A Social Revolution*; Albertus, Fenner, and Slater, *Coercive Distribution*.

[37] See, for example, Scott, *Domination and the Arts of Resistance*; Scott, *The Art of Not Being Governed*; Belge, "State Building and the Limits of Legibility."

[38] Fukuyama, *The Origins of Political Order*; Grzymala-Busse, *Nations under God*.

[39] Harris, *A Social Revolution*.

[40] See the distinction between state-led and state-seeking nationalism in Tilly, "States and Nationalism in Europe 1492–1992." See also a historical account of how religion or nationalism may legitimize or delegitimize the state in Slater, "Revolutions, Crackdowns, and Quiescence."

[41] Scott, *The Art of Not Being Governed*.

[42] For the debate about the role of war, see Tilly, *Coercion, Capital, and European States, AD 990–1992*; Downing, *The Military Revolution and Political Change*; Hui, *War and State Formation in Ancient China and Early Modern Europe*; Ertman, *Birth of the Leviathan*; Dincecco and Wang, "Violent Conflict and Political Development over the Long Run."

[43] Skowronek, *Building a New American State*; Shefter, *Political Parties and the State*.

[44] Vu, "Studying the State through State Formation," 159–64.

structural similarities despite many differences in historical context. In medieval China (the 7th–9th centuries) and Russia (the 13th–14th centuries), both emperors and princes recruited bureaucrats exclusively from hereditary aristocracy, which had significant political independence. In Russia, these aristocrats owned inherited lands and had the right to change their suzerain, which provided them with bargaining power against their prince. In China, the aristocratic elites formed a coalition bound by marriage ties, which also put them in a strong position against the emperor. Both countries, however, subsequently experienced significant weakening of this hereditary aristocracy, which left the political arena to the state and many weaker, lower-status players who were neither strong nor united enough to compete with the state. In China, many members of the aristocracy were killed during the Huang Chao Rebellion in the 9th century, which forced the Tang dynasty to start recruiting bureaucrats from lower-status groups based on a written exam rather than pedigree. The next, Song dynasty made the system of imperial examination the primary way of recruiting state servants, which further undermined the positions of the aristocracy. In Russia, the massacre of the aristocracy was executed by Ivan the Terrible in the 16th century, after the Moscow princes gradually limited the ownership rights and the right to change one's suzerain in the 15th century. In the 17th century, Russian tsars officially began recruiting bureaucrats without regard to their aristocratic pedigree, and in the 18th century, Peter the Great took the last bits of aristocratic independence away when he abolished their formal titles and made state service the only clear way to the social elite.[45] These examples of China and Russia show one of the ways the state may become the strongest center of political authority.[46]

As the state gradually monopolizes group authority, it shapes both the material and symbolic sides of state–society relations around the logic of *teamwork* rather than the logic of resistance and contention (see Figure 1.1 for a brief characteristic of political environment in statist and antistatist societies). The team state becomes the focus of collective identity, of people's understanding of who the "we" are.

State rulers use *team logic* to develop social contracts, which directly connect them to the population without the brokerage of independent elites. Historically, examples of such contracts can be found in China, Prussia, the Soviet Union, Japan, or Korea.[47] Researchers have analyzed these contracts and noted that they

---

[45] Crummey, *Aristocrats and Servitors*; Tackett, *The Destruction of the Medieval Chinese Aristocracy*; Wang, "China's State Development in Comparative Historical Perspective."

[46] On the Russian case, see, for example, White, *Political Culture and Soviet Politics*, 24–30. On the importance of aristocracy as the force that prevents the state from becoming too powerful, see the classic writing of Moore, *Social Origins of Dictatorship and Democracy*.

[47] Rimlinger, *Welfare Policy and Industrialization in Europe, America, and Russia*; Barkey and Parikh, "Comparative Perspectives on the State," 535; Breslauer, "On the Adaptability of Soviet Welfare-State Authoritarianism"; Beck, *The Origins of the Authoritarian Welfare State in Prussia*; Cook, *The Soviet Social Contract and Why It Failed*; Leung and Nann, *Authority and Benevolence*;

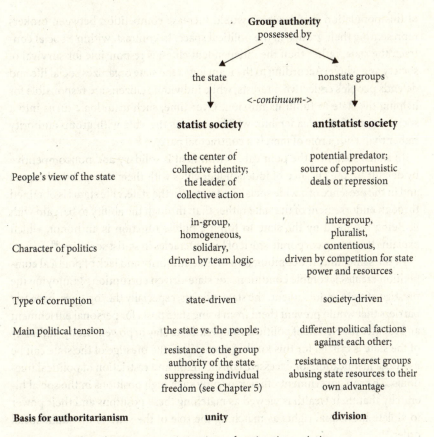

Figure 1.1 Political environment in statist and antistatist societies.

have successfully kept the population quiescent using distribution of material goods to wide population groups. In addition to that, they further neutralized independent elites who might gain popular support and political weight if they became the brokers between the ruler and a population group. These brokers would be viewed as providers and would gain the authority to speak on behalf

Hui, *War and State Formation in Ancient China and Early Modern Europe*, 171–77; Mares and Carnes, "Social Policy in Developing Countries"; Cook and Dimitrov, "The Social Contract Revisited." Scholars have also used the term "social pact" in relation to some countries in the Middle East nowadays, where the state provides a social safety net, jobs, and other public goods, while the citizens comply with the state's political monopoly: see Heydemann, "Social Pacts and the Persistence of Authoritarianism in the Middle East." However, the social pacts in these countries seem to be based less on the authority of the state and more on the authority of religious or ethnic groups that took over the state, and they may easily turn from universal to exclusionary: see Heydemann, "Rethinking Social Contracts in the MENA Region." The popular vision of the state as the leader of collective action also translates into an extended role of the state in economic policies (see Dobbin, *Forging Industrial Policy*; Evans, *Embedded Autonomy*).

of this population group, which would increase competition between brokers representing their groups in the political space. In contrast, within a social contract, the state, rather than the independent elites, is responsible for survival of society as a whole. According to the team logic, the state organizes social life and defends people's collective interests, while individual citizens are responsible for helping the state to fulfill its mission. Over time, such team logic turns into a social norm of state leadership, which provides the state with group authority rather than with a role of merely a contractual party.

In statist societies, the political environment is solidary and noncompetitive by default. In the absence of independent elites with their own political capital and in the presence of a wide social contract with the state, elite status is obtained through endorsement of the state rather than through the ability to bargain with it. Being recruited by the state to fulfill a public function is an honor, which explains the strong corporate spirit of bureaucracies in statist societies.[48]

At the same time, the combination of state authority and lack of political competition creates favorable conditions for state-driven corruption.[49] Enjoying the prestige of state endorsement, the state officials, especially the top ones, have few barriers that would prevent them from using state posts for personal enrichment and further restriction of political competition to stay in power. Group authority of the state is crucial for this kind of corruption: the prestige of the state can be used as a justification for excessive consumption and restriction of political freedoms. The top government officials occupy such high positions in the social hierarchy that their wealth is viewed as matching these positions and their power to violate individual rights as matching the role of the state to maintain social order.[50]

Even though statist societies are characterized by unity rather than division, they have a different kind of political tension—the tension between the unitary state that uses its group authority to restrict individual freedoms and the people who resist it. The dissident movement in the Soviet Union is an example of such resistance, which struggled to break the social conformism in the rest of society and defended individual rights and freedoms. Resistance to the state in a statist society runs into the general difficulty of resisting group authority: Questioning the state ruler means questioning the social order, and the dissenters must be

---

[48] Evans, *Embedded Autonomy*.

[49] For a detailed analysis of the two models of corruption, see Kupatadze, "Political Corruption in Eurasia."

[50] On the connection between social status and corruption, including the case when state officials are perceived as being of higher status than the rest of society, see Granovetter, "The Social Construction of Corruption," 159–60. On how in-group loyalties moderate tolerance for corruption, see Solaz, De Vries, and de Geus, "In-Group Loyalty and the Punishment of Corruption." On the centralized character of corruption in Russia, see Rochlitz, Kazun, and Yakovlev, "Property Rights in Russia after 2009."

willing to risk not only their material well-being but also their social connections and the comfort of group belonging.[51] The state that possesses group authority widely uses the strategy of discreditation and ostracism in combination with selective overt violence against dissenters.[52] The difficulty of resisting group authority of the state does not diminish people's desire for freedom, as some may argue. Rather, it inhibits the active, organized forms of resistance as most people do not trust activists not affiliated with the state to lead collective action.[53] Instead of organized resistance, excessive state pressure breeds hypocrisy, sabotage of state policies, and learned helplessness, which was widespread in late communist regimes.[54]

In contrast to statist societies, in antistatist ones, the state possesses little to no group authority, which means that the most powerful political players are nonstate groups—classes, ethnicities, races, religious groups, or any combination of them. Each of these groups has authority among its own members but not among the members of other groups. With the rare exception of some nation-states, where group authority belongs to an ethnically homogeneous nation whose territorial boundaries exactly match the boundaries of the state, different nonstate groups coexist in one polity and compete for state power. Unlike in statist societies, the competing groups in antistatist ones can use the power of social norms and social conformism to maintain solidarity and compliance only in their own group but not in society as a whole. The tools that the group in power can use to secure compliance of other groups come down to economic concessions or overt repression, which require more material resources to achieve superficial and unstable compliance.[55] Political and economic histories of countries such as Mexico or Turkey are good examples of state attempts to impose its authority onto a highly resistant society.[56]

People's view of the state in antistatist societies matches this pluralist and competitive political environment. The state is the source of perks or punishment

---

[51] See Kharkhordin, *The Collective and the Individual in Russia*, for a historical and cultural account of the collective and peer surveillance in Russia and the Soviet Union. Also, see Owen, "A Genealogy of Kontrol' in Russia."

[52] Gel'man, "The Politics of Fear."

[53] On how repression breeds antiregime attitudes but decreases citizens' contentious behavior, see, for example, Wang, "The Political Legacy of Violence during China's Cultural Revolution."

[54] See, for example, the debate about *Homo soveticus* in Левада, *Простой советский человек: опыт социального портрета на рубеже 90-х*; Гудков, "Человек в неморальном пространстве: к социологии морали в посттоталитарном обществе"; Sharafutdinova, "Was There a 'Simple Soviet' Person?"

[55] Wintrobe, *The Political Economy of Dictatorship*. In some circumstances, the need to seek support outside of one's group and the pragmatic attitude of the outside group members may help combat group loyalties and lead to better governance: Gao, "Tribal Mobilization, Fragmented Groups, and Public Goods Provision in Jordan."

[56] Hamilton, *The Limits of State Autonomy*; Barkey, *The State and the Industrialization Crisis in Turkey*; Magaloni, *Voting for Autocracy*.

rather than the leader of collective action. State posts, rather than being the prestigious positions associated with group authority, are viewed as potential sources of benefits and power that can be used for the good of the individual's own ethnic, religious, or racial group as well as for cultivating clientelistic relations with other groups.[57] The leaders of the competing groups obtain prestige and support if they successfully bargain with state officials or politicians running for state posts in the interests of their group.[58] They maintain their high social status whether they themselves currently occupy a state post or not; however, they would lose this status if the members of their group start doubting their commitment to the group's collective interest.

Lack of group authority possessed by the state creates a favorable environment for society-driven corruption. Unlike the state-driven corruption, it is not the result of excessive state authority and its abuse. Rather, it is driven by strong nonstate group loyalties and the view of the state as a source of short-term benefits. Society-driven corruption often maps onto existing social divisions, for example, lucrative state jobs are distributed to the members of one's own ethnic or religious group. The state here is a means to benefit one of the competing social groups. In contrast, state-driven corruption is focused on serving the interests of the state apparatus itself, which becomes a corporation with its own, autonomous interest rather than a means to satisfy someone else's interests.

As already mentioned above, statism versus antistatism is a continuum, possibly even a spectrum, which can be used to examine the development of every society and the competition of the state with other institutions for group authority. Almost never would a society fall strictly into statist or antistatist category. To determine its position, we need to consider who the main political players are as well as the patterns of power contestation and resistance characteristic of that society. For example, bureaucratic authoritarian states have high autonomy of their bureaucratic apparatus from societal interests, but they exist in societies riven by social cleavages.[59] In fact, it is exactly because of these cleavages that the state was able to play the role of the stabilizing force, and the deeper the cleavage, the more autonomy the state obtained.[60] While the autonomy of bureaucratic authoritarian states may be high, their group authority is still low. The intensity of contentious politics and overt repression in these states shows that the bureaucratic authoritarian state does not induce a high level of voluntary compliance in the population. In the future, these states may achieve group authority if they

[57] Granovetter, "The Social Construction of Corruption," 162–63; Prasad, Martins da Silva, and Nickow, "Approaches to Corruption."
[58] Gottlieb and Kosec, "The Countervailing Effects of Competition on Public Goods Provision."
[59] O'Donnell, "Reflections on the Patterns of Change in the Bureaucratic-Authoritarian State"; O'Donnell, *Bureaucratic Authoritarianism*.
[60] Stepan, *The State and Society*; Stepan, "State Power and the Strength of Civil Society in the Southern Cone of Latin America."

manage to weaken the competing institutions and maintain this position for a long time, which seems unlikely in the modern world. In this historical moment, though, these societies are still antistatist, even though their state apparatus has significant autonomy from societal interests. This example highlights the difference between state autonomy and group authority of the state: While all states that possess group authority are autonomous, not all states that are autonomous possess group authority.

Another important feature of social statism and antistatism is that, unlike state capacity, it does not change fast. State capacity may fluctuate drastically decade to decade and sometimes even faster than that. Economic crises, wars, pandemics, or natural disasters may undermine state resources and the ability of the state apparatus to be a strong political player. Societal preferences, however, take a long time to form and change.[61] State formation literature shows that the states with strong group authority, such as China, Korea, or Japan, took centuries to develop their norm-setting power. There is good reason to believe that the states that did not do it before universal enfranchisement will never be able to weaken societal groups enough to monopolize the leadership role.[62] Societal statism or antistatism is, thus, a product of the *longue durée* of history rather than the legacy of the last decades or the result of actions of current state rulers.

Finally, a very important question about statism and antistatism is related to their relationship to political regimes. This book argues that authoritarianism is possible in both statist and antistatist societies, but the strategies that autocrats must use to consolidate their power in these societies are different. To understand how unity and division become the basis of the authoritarian toolbox, we need to connect social statism and antistatism to the grassroots level organizational infrastructure that rulers must use for governance and political control.

Grassroots Politics in Statist and Antistatist Societies

The different traits of political environments in statist and antistatist societies shape the challenges that autocrats face and the strategies they use to consolidate power. The main challenge of an autocrat in an antistatist society is competition with the leaders of other societal groups for state power.[63] Reducing this competition and consolidating power usually requires either economic concessions that would buy the loyalty of these other groups or repression of those groups

---

[61] For a study that traces the stickiness of statist social norms despite the dramatic swings of state capacity, see Libman and Kozlov, "The Legacy of Compliant Activism in Autocracies."
[62] Skowronek, *Building a New American State*; Shefter, *Political Parties and the State*.
[63] Way, *Pluralism by Default*.

and their leaders.[64] In statist societies, however, political competition happens within the same group that shares an identity and a collective interest. It is competition not just for economic resources but also for the right to speak on behalf of the whole society, that is, to be its legitimate leader and to control society through group authority. To reduce the chance that someone challenges the autocrat, she must develop the means to maintain her legitimacy and control grassroots politics, through which potential challengers may arise.

Later in this chapter, I will focus on these two authoritarian strategies: (1) a combination of economic concessions with repression in antistatist societies and (2) maintenance of ruler's legitimacy and control of grassroots politics in statist ones.

To implement any political strategy, a ruler needs organizational infrastructure. In the next section, I will show how statist and antistatist societies grow different infrastructures of public organizations—both state and nonstate ones—that help autocrats implement their strategies for staying in power. The state organizations in question include state bureaucracies and the public sector, that is, the organizations that researchers see as contributing to infrastructural state power; the nonstate organizations are the ones usually labeled civil society. Although researchers study them separately, I will show below that in statist societies they are best considered together as parts of a larger system of public organizations controlled by the state.

The autocrats' strategies and the organizational models of the public sphere described in this section are theoretical ideal types. The value of distinguishing them lies in spelling out the internal logic of the two different mechanisms of how autocrats can consolidate and hold onto power. In empirical data, however, these models will never be observed in their pure form. No existing state has an absolute monopoly on group authority, and no existing state has no group authority at all. All empirical cases will be a mixture of these logics, although in different proportion in every case. The theoretical separation, however, is necessary, as it makes it possible to trace the two different mechanisms and disentangle them in the empirical data.

Infrastructural State Power and Civil Society

The concept of infrastructural power refers to the organizational development of modern states.[65] Unlike those relying on despotic power, states with

---

[64] Wintrobe, *The Political Economy of Dictatorship*.
[65] Mann, "The Autonomous Power of the State"; Mann, "Infrastructural Power Revisited"; Soifer and vom Hau, "Unpacking the Strength of the State."

infrastructural power have permanent bureaucratic apparatuses that cover the territory of the state and allow it to control various spheres of people's lives. Initially developed for the purposes of taxation, the state apparatus gradually took on the functions of regulation and law enforcement as well as provision of education, healthcare, welfare, and other public goods.

The territorial spread of bureaucracy not only provided the state with tighter control of society but also increased the state's dependence on it. The work of the state apparatus has always been greatly influenced by how cooperative or resistant the population was, which, in its turn, depended on how much group authority the state accumulated over the course of its history on a given territory. I argue here that cooperation or resistance of the population leads to the differences not only in bureaucratic efficiency but also in the structure of the ecosystem of state and nonstate public organizations. These different structures of public organizations provide autocrats with the tools they need to consolidate and hold on to power (see Figure 1.2).

In statist societies, where the state speaks on behalf of the group and is associated with social order, people easily cooperate with the state. Being recruited and trusted by the state is an honor; association with the state elevates one's social status. A good example of that is the prestige of state service in such statist societies as the Chinese or Russian ones, where it has been the way to social elite status for centuries. The Chinese civil service examination ensures that civil servants are selected and promoted based on merit, which reaffirms the role of the state as maintaining social order, harmony, and solidarity.

In contrast to that, in antistatist societies, the state is associated not with social order but rather with an intrusion into it. Nonstate institutions and elites—ethnic, religious, business, or even mafia—bear the primary responsibility for organizing social life, and people cooperate with them unconditionally. The interactions with the state, on the other hand, are viewed with default suspicion and are conditional on the prospect of material gain or avoidance of punishment. As a result, the state seeking cooperation with the population must negotiate with the nonstate elites who effectively control society.[66] The history of empires and colonialism provides numerous relevant examples of how states had to negotiate with local elites to ensure compliance of the population.

This difference in how people view the state and interact with it results in the different structures of state and nonstate public organizations. In statist societies, state officials easily recruit local activists who represent the state on the ground and build ramified top-down organizational structures that penetrate society and greatly increase infrastructural state power. The state bureaucracy is part of this centralized system, and so are the public sector and a big part of civil

---

[66] See, for example, Baldwin, *The Paradox of Traditional Chiefs in Democratic Africa.*

34 THE SOCIAL ROOTS OF AUTHORITARIANISM

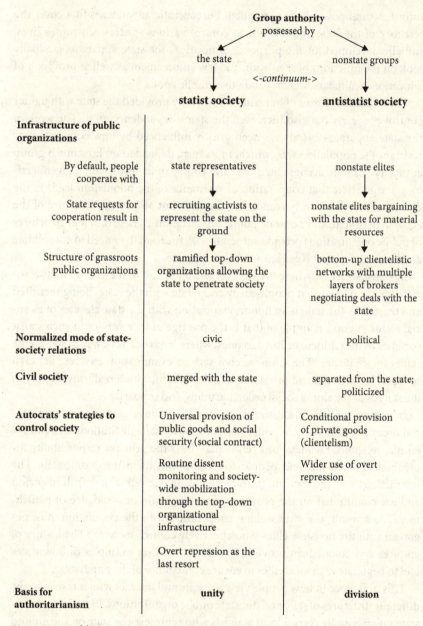

Figure 1.2 Public organizations, civil society, and autocrats' strategies in statist and antistatist societies.

society. As I will show in subsequent chapters, bureaucracies in statist societies work together with the public sector—educational, healthcare, and social security organizations—and with nonstate grassroots organizations that the state supports. The nonstate organizations may vary from youth clubs to neighborhood councils to organizations helping people with disabilities. These organizational connections significantly increase the presence of the state in people's lives, placing state agents near almost every person in the community.

Such highly integrated structure of public organizations blurs the boundary between the state and civil society. Many civil society organizations in statist societies are created by the state and included in the organizational network controlled by it. Researchers often call them GONGOs—government-organized nongovernmental organizations—for lack of a better term.[67] The Soviet Union, for example, was filled with such organizations that united people by profession, hobbies, local activities, sports, and so forth.[68] GONGOs are often considered "quasi-civil society," since they are not independent from the state. However, empirical evidence also suggests that these organizations were not operated by top-down orders. They were often run by local volunteers motivated by the desire to serve the public and provided a significant amount of public goods. They may not have been independent from the state, but they were fueled by the grassroots energy of civic-minded individuals.[69]

This difficulty of understanding GONGOs highlights an important characteristic of state–society relations in statist societies: People view their interactions with the state through the lens of teamwork and civic duty rather than through the lens of political competition. The state for them is a necessary part of the civic,[70] while the opposition to the state is associated with selfishness and greed. The fact that the bureaucracy, the public sector, civil society, and the population easily cooperate with each other reflects this civic unity and social norms rather than direct coercion by the state.[71]

In contrast, in antistatist societies, the state is unable to build a well-integrated system of public organizations because the population refuses to cooperate with the state directly. Instead, state officials must turn to nonstate leaders, who start bargaining with the state on behalf of their groups. As a result, the state's attempts to obtain the population's cooperation results in growth of bottom-up clientelistic networks with multiple layers of brokers, who compete for state resources and power. If these nonstate leaders obtain official posts in the bureaucratic

---

[67] See, for example, Hsu and Hasmath, *The Chinese Corporatist State*; Hasmath and Hsu, *NGO Governance and Management in China*.
[68] Friedgut, *Political Participation in the USSR*; Leitch, "Society in Motion."
[69] Friedgut, *Political Participation in the USSR*; Bahry and Silver, "Soviet Citizen Participation on the Eve of Democratization"; Frolic, "State-Led Civil Society."
[70] Hale, "Civil Society from Above?"
[71] Frolic, "State-Led Civil Society."

hierarchy, it gives them even more access to state resources and the opportunities to increase their own political capital.

In this political environment, the mode of state–society relations habituated and normalized in people's minds is political competition for state resources and power, not teamwork to achieve collective goals. Because of this mindset, the bureaucracy, the public sector, and civil society organizations tend to pursue their narrow goals and closely watch their boundaries. Civil society in such antistatist environment is independent from the state, but at the same time it is often politicized through its involvement in electoral campaigns and other forms of political competition.[72]

Political Functions of Public Organizations

History shows that authoritarianism can thrive in both the unified statist environment and the pluralist antistatist environment. The most vivid examples of statist authoritarian regimes are the USSR and contemporary China, and a good example of a nonstatist authoritarian regime is Mexico in 1929–2000. All of them were formally single-party dictatorships, but the social basis of their power was different. If in the USSR and China the power of the party was based on social consensus and the legitimacy of state leadership, in Mexico the party served as the institutional mechanism of bargains with the different parts of a highly fragmented society.[73]

The characteristics of public organizations I described above help understand the mechanisms through which authoritarian regimes maintain their political monopolies in statist and antistatist societies. They do it by exploiting the opposite qualities of these political environments: in statist societies, they mask their political interests under the veil of civic unity, while in antistatist societies, they exploit the existing social divisions to their own political advantage.

In statist societies, the unified infrastructure of public organizations helps autocrats to hold on to their power because it serves two functions simultaneously. First, it provides a large amount of public goods in many spheres of everyday life: from education and healthcare to public safety to community-building and hobby clubs.[74] People's living environments are shaped by these public organizations, and the vast majority of these activities have clear benefits

---

[72] See, for example, Marchetti and Tocci, *Civil Society, Conflicts and the Politicization of Human Rights*; Sarkissian and Özler, "Democratization and the Politicization of Religious Civil Society in Turkey."

[73] Magaloni, *Voting for Autocracy*.

[74] For an account of a unified infrastructure of public organizations in statist societies, see also Heberer, "Relegitimation through New Patterns of Social Security"; Read, *Roots of the State*.

for communities and are politically benign. The same organizations and communication channels, though, are used by the authoritarian regime for political purposes. For example, residential councils initially created to manage the neighborhood infrastructure and organize community events for children may be used for electoral agitation and mobilization, or educational institutions may serve as a platform for recruiting young activists to the ruling party. Political and civic activities mix within the same organizations and are performed by the same people, which makes it easy to misrepresent political as civic, especially to the population that strongly favors teamwork, views the state as its collective leader, and dislikes competition for power.[75]

In the subsequent chapters, I will show how the infrastructure of public organizations in statist societies is used for at least three political purposes. First, these organizations help mobilize the population and co-opt civic-minded activists. This mobilization and co-optation machine is used for both nonpolitical causes, such as a campaign for road safety, and strictly political ones, such as elections. Second, state-controlled public organizations help monitor and manage population's discontent. Being closely involved with individual citizens and their lives, they serve as the ears of the state and the first point of contact for the citizens who seek help from the state and their community. This information helps the autocrat to alleviate causes of discontent with policy changes before they become the basis for the antiregime mobilization and prevent the growth of the opposition through the early identification of its potential leaders. Third, state-controlled public organizations help the authoritarian regime to control the public space—both physical and informational. They occupy the rooms and buildings, which would be suitable for opposition gatherings, control the neighborhood territory, where electoral agitation might take place, and produce benign, civic-minded contents that fills the informational space and helps stigmatize opposition leaders and political competition as unnecessarily conflictual and selfish.

In antistatist environments, the political functions of the public sector and civil society organizations are driven by the opposite logic. Since the population views the interactions with the state through the prism of rewards and punishments rather than teamwork, the various public organizations serve as an organizational platform for negotiating rewards, punishments, and political coalitions. Be it a school, a teachers' labor union, a village council, a church, or a youth NGO, they may all participate in negotiating political deals with the regime. These negotiations may take the form of pork-barrel politics, individual vote-buying, or other forms of clientelistic exchange of material rewards for

---

[75] For a similar argument about civic participation in Russia and China, see Owen, "Participatory Authoritarianism."

political support. Although these practices are not exclusive to the regime classified as authoritarian in the literature, they play a crucial role in maintaining authoritarian power in antistatist societies.[76]

Overt repression will not be examined in detail in this book, but the logic of the two political environments can be extended to think about the role of overt repression in statist and antistatist societies. Overt repression in statist societies is usually used as a means of last resort, since maintaining legitimacy and controlling grassroots politics remains the optimal strategy for an autocrat. Before using overt repression, the autocrat would try to either discredit the opposition publicly, emphasizing their greed and lack of civic commitment, for example, by accusing them of collaborating with foreign governments, or co-opt them into the existing state apparatus. In rare cases, though, an autocrat in a statist society may use repression indiscriminately and randomly. He may cultivate the feeling of collective threat and use repression of alleged internal traitors to strengthen his image of the guarantor of collective security. In statist societies, the feeling of collective threat makes people seek protection from the state. It increases both people's desire to help identify internal traitors and the stakes of confronting the group for those individuals who might want to resist such repression.[77] This may result in a society-wide witchhunt powered by the state repressive machine with virtually no organized resistance, such as, for examples, Stalin's Great Purge in the Soviet Union in the 1930s or repression in Russia after the 2022 invasion of Ukraine.

In a pluralist antistatist society, repression is the only tool an autocrat has left if economic concessions fail to buy the loyalty of their political opponents. Repression of the disloyal out-groups helps increase the consolidation of the autocrat's own social base. Such repression can be carried out not only by the coercive state apparatus but also by the members of autocrat's own group, which in extreme cases may turn into genocide, as it did in Rwanda in 1994. Disloyal members of the autocrat's own group may be repressed too, but the autocrat must portray these people as having betrayed the group's interest.[78]

The State as the Driver of Informality

The discussion of political functions of public organizations raises the question of how they relate to political machines and informality. Scholars have used the

---

[76] Magaloni, *Voting for Autocracy*. Quasi-democratic institutions, such as the parliament, can be used to manage the requests from different groups and negotiate the loyalty contracts (see Gandhi, *Political Institutions under Dictatorship*). For an account of how community leaders contribute to authoritarian regime durability, see, for example, McLellan, "Delivering the Vote."

[77] Hannah Arendt pointed at the terror directed at the whole society rather than a particular group as the key feature of a totalitarian regime (see Arendt, *The Origins of Totalitarianism*).

[78] Shen-Bayh, "Strategies of Repression."

terms "political machines," "clientelism," and "patronage" to describe a very wide range of phenomena from buying votes for cash to building policy consensus via political appointments.[79] Very often, public organizations are the sites through which these interactions happen.

The theory developed here adds to this discussion an important distinction related to the source of informality. Generally, scholars view informality as undermining the rule of law set by the state, while following formal rules creates a level playing field and equal treatment for everyone. Clientelism and patronage, even though often observed in democracies, are, therefore, threats to the democratic ideal of programmatic politics and professional civil service.[80] The big question, though, is how to move closer to this ideal, and here the issue of the source of informality is of ultimate importance.

In many studies of clientelism and political machines, informality is community-based while the state is the institution that falls prey to these pre-existing community ties and moral obligations.[81] State officials or politicians let their connections to various communities influence their decisions as state officials. They channel money to their communities and expect support at the ballot box or elsewhere in return. They give governmental jobs to the members of their support groups circumventing formal procedures and impartiality principles. All these are the manifestations of how nonstate communities and norms have a stronger influence on the behavior of politicians and state officials than state interests and norms.[82]

This description of informality, though, is only true for antistatist environments. In statist ones, the source of informality is the state itself, as nonstate communities are not strong enough. State officials are the privileged group that has the authority in the eyes of the population to set the rules and distribute material resources in the name of the whole society. Self-preservation as a group rather than maintaining their status in nonstate communities is of ultimate importance to them. Later in the book, I will demonstrate that in statist environments, being a state official provides social status—in contrast to antistatist environments, where social status depends on the person's position in their local, ethnic, religious, or another community.

Political machines in statist societies are, thus, driven by this state self-preservation rather than loyalties to nonstate communities that introduce bias.

---

[79] Hilgers, "Clientelism and Conceptual Stretching."
[80] See, for example, Johnston, *Corruption, Contention, and Reform*; Dahlström, Lapuente, and Teorell, "The Merit of Meritocratization."
[81] Granovetter, "The Social Construction of Corruption"; Solaz, De Vries, and de Geus, "In-Group Loyalty and the Punishment of Corruption"; Prasad, Martins da Silva, and Nickow, "Approaches to Corruption."
[82] See, for example, Reno, *Corruption and State Politics in Sierra Leone*; Blake and Morris, *Corruption and Democracy in Latin America*; Burbidge, *The Shadow of Kenyan Democracy*.

When state officials are pressured from above to deliver the vote, they have enough informal authority and not enough forces restricting them from bending the rules. More than that, they may be convinced themselves that they fulfill an important public mission, and this goal justifies the means. When the ruling party electoral campaign headquarters are set up right in the municipal building, staffed by municipal officials, and an official announcement about it is placed in the media, as happened at least once in Russia—it is a perfect illustration of how the state blends formal and informal authority.

Whether the source of informality is the state or a nonstate community matters for how to fix it. If informality is driven by nonstate communities and ethics, then strengthening state authority and commitment to public good would counterbalance it and reduce the abuse of state offices. If, however, the source of informality is the state itself and state officials use the idea of public good to justify the abuse of formal institutions, a further strengthening of state authority will only reinforce authoritarian grip on power. Further in the book, I will elaborate both on how these models of informality work and on how it matters for democratization strategies.

Chapter Summary

Unity- and division-based authoritarianisms thrive in different types of societies that I call statist and antistatist. In statist societies, group authority—the power of the group over the individual—is possessed by the state, which expands its possibilities to induce the population's compliance. Statist political environments are homogeneous and solidary; they are driven by team logic and the idea that the state is the leader of that team. The main political tension in statist societies is the tension between the state that abuses its group authority to control individuals and the people who dislike state oppression but have trouble acting collectively if the state is not leading them. In contrast, in antistatist societies, group authority is possessed by nonstate groups, which creates a more competitive and divided political environment. Antistatist political environments are pluralist and contentious; they are driven by the utility maximization logic and competition of different groups for state power and resources. The main tension there is between those groups who use their access to state power and resources to the advantage of their group members and other groups who resist such abuse of the state and demand power-sharing.

Authoritarianism is possible in both statist and antistatist societies, but the different qualities of these political environments call for different tools to build and maintain authoritarian regimes. The chapter spells out how authoritarian power works in statist and antistatist societies by looking at the work of public organizations, which include bureaucracies, the social public sector, and state-controlled NGOs. In statist societies, public organizations align into centralized top-down structures that rely on the population's propensity to cooperate with the state and allow the state to penetrate society. These organizations blend political functions into the civic ones: They both provide public goods and help mobilize and control society in the regime's interests. In antistatist societies, public organizations form bottom-up clientelistic networks, and autocrats can use multiple levels of brokers to negotiate private deals with different groups to ensure their quiescence.

The next chapters will apply this theory to Russia. Through the story of regional variation in voting and the investigation of local public organizations and social norms, I will demonstrate how the difference in the population's vision of the state produces different organizational structures. These structures, in their turn, serve as autocrat's tools that help strengthen their grip on power using the opposite logics of unity and division.

2
A Tale of Four Regions

Unity- and division-based authoritarianisms often look similar. Autocrats use all means available—money, censorship, repression—to hold on to power. Whether they distribute money through universalistic benefits programs or conditional payments through brokers, it contributes to popular support of the regime. Repression in all shapes and forms also tends to deter resistance. Controlling the Internet and splitting the opposition are useful for an autocrat regardless of whether they rule a statist or an antistatist society. The distinction between unity- and division-based authoritarianism, thus, is not always obvious when researchers focus on these universal autocratic tools.

Nevertheless, the different internal logics of unity- and division-based authoritarianisms do produce different results that are observable empirically. The theory developed in the first chapter emerged from my search for an explanation for one such difference—the stability of electoral machine performance in Russia. Even though Russian authoritarianism has a distinct face, which I will discuss in the last chapter of the book, the territorial spread of the country and the history of its different parts ensure that there is significant variation in political environments between the regions. The differences in elite relationships, infrastructural penetration of the Russian state, and cultural norms translate into the different configurations and performance of political machines.[1] This regional variation provides the necessary analytical leverage to distinguish the two authoritarian logics.

This chapter pursues three goals. First, it presents the puzzle of the 2012 presidential election, which served as the starting point for formulating the theory. Second, it describes the nested analysis research design, which combines quantitative analysis of electoral statistics and four case studies with maximum variation. Third, it introduces the historical and contemporary socioeconomic profiles of the four regions that constitute the comparison. The regional histories show where the social norms and the views of the state in these regions came

---

[1] Research addressing the regional variation of political environments and political machines in Russia includes Starodubtsev, *Federalism and Regional Policy in Contemporary Russia*; Gel'man, "Politics, Governance, and the Zigzags of the Power Vertical"; Reuter, "Regional Patrons and Hegemonic Party Electoral Performance in Russia"; Frye, Reuter, and Szakonyi, "Political Machines at Work."

The Social Roots of Authoritarianism. Natalia Forrat, Oxford University Press. © Oxford University Press 2024.
DOI: 10.1093/oso/9780197790359.003.0003

from—before the next chapters elaborate on how these social norms formed political structures with opposite qualities.

The Puzzle of the 2012 Presidential Election

In March 2012, Vladimir Putin faced an election that might have been the most difficult in his political career. At the time of his two previous presidential elections, in 2004 and 2008, Putin's public approval was high, which made it relatively easy to convert this approval into a high electoral percentage for himself and his alter ego, Dmitry Medvedev. In 2012, though, that popular approval had significantly decreased as the fast economic growth of the 2000s was replaced by economic stagnation that followed the 2008–2009 financial crisis (see Figure 2.1). In addition, many Russians saw the "castling" maneuver of Putin and Medvedev in September 2011—when they publicly announced that they had decided to switch prime minister and presidential spots a long time ago—as complete contempt for the will of the people. The December 2011 parliamentary elections were marred by large-scale falsifications, and afterward, 100,000 Muscovites, as well as people in other Russian cities, took to the streets to protest.

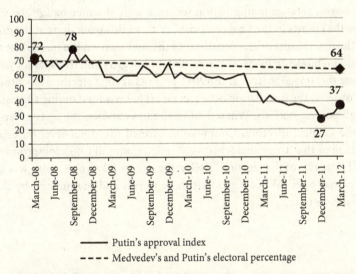

Figure 2.1 Putin's approval index and the regime's presidential candidate electoral percentage, March 2008 to March 2012.

Note: The approval index is the difference between the percentage of those who approve of and those who disapprove of Putin's actions.

Source: Levada-Center, "Indicators."

These protests were the largest Moscow had seen since the fall of the Soviet Union, and they ultimately forced the government to liberalize the electoral legislation. Under these circumstances, a decisive victory at the presidential election in March 2012, only a few months after these large protests, was of utmost importance for the regime. Putin needed it to demonstrate the regime's strength and demoralize the nascent opposition.

On election day, the task was accomplished. Putin received 64% of votes, which was only 6% less than what Dmitry Medvedev had received in 2008, at the height of regime popularity. This official electoral result, combined with the promise of increasing salaries of public-sector employees, limited political concessions, and the efforts to divide the opposition, significantly weakened the protest movement over the next few months, successfully diverting the challenge to the regime survival.[2]

How did Putin manage to obtain an election result that was so out of sync with his popular approval? Seeing an incumbent receive an implausibly high voting percentage is not unusual in electoral authoritarian regimes, where rulers regularly manipulate elections to increase their winning margin.[3] However, despite what some external observers may think, manipulation of electoral results in Russia does not happen by having the chair of the Central Electoral Commission change the final vote count. It happens in thousands of precincts where local authorities work to mobilize the proregime vote, stuff ballot-boxes, arrange manipulation schemes with absentee ballots, or simply change the counts in the final protocols. With all this work done at the ground level, the federal authorities can distance themselves from the fraudulent activities and maintain an image as proponents of integrity and transparency. It was to create this image that, after the 2011 protests against electoral falsifications, Putin ordered the installation of web cameras to broadcast online a live stream from all polling stations. When the live streams exposed the facts of falsification, the Central Electoral Commission blamed the street-level bureaucrats and claimed that these incidents were isolated and did not compromise the overall integrity of the election. Delivering real or fake votes, thus, was a task for regional political machines, which were run and maintained by the regional governors.

---

[2] Right after his inauguration in May 2012, Putin signed his first so-called May Decrees, which directed regional authorities to increase the salaries of schoolteachers and some other public-sector workers to match average salaries in the region by 2018. The salaries of university faculty and researchers were to reach double that level by 2018. These promises never materialized. For more detailed research on presidential decrees in Russia, see Remington, *Presidential Decrees in Russia*.

[3] See Simpser, *Why Governments and Parties Manipulate Elections*, on how winning elections with a large margin helps autocrats.

Regional Political Machines

The regional political machines play a very important role in Russian elections. Unlike in some other countries, the political machines in Russian regions do not rely much on the party structures, which only play a secondary role. Most governors treat the whole regional and local-level bureaucracy, the public sector, and the state-dependent companies as components of their political machines. Every election, the media report that Russian "budgetniki" (the workers whose salaries are paid from the state budget, such as teachers, doctors, social workers, employees of public libraries, museums, etc.) are mobilized by their employers to vote in large numbers.[4]

The 2012 election was not the first one when regional governors and their political machines played a crucial role. Their importance for the electoral process as well as for street politics was behind the twists that federal–regional relations in Russia have gone through during Putin's time in power. In the 1990s, some regional governors were political heavyweights at the federal level and their coalitions counterbalanced the Kremlin in the political arena. To tame the power of regional governors, Putin changed the Russian tax code shortly after he came to power, making regional budgets more dependent on the inflow of federal money. In 2004, he canceled governors' elections replacing them with presidential appointments. These maneuvers realigned governors' political incentives from accumulating their own political capital in the region to serving the Kremlin and thus weakened regional political machines.[5] However, they also backfired, when during the 2011–2012 electoral cycle, it turned out that nonelected governors were unable to control their regions as well as the elected ones used to do. As a result, the governors' elections were brought back in 2012.

---

[4] For examples of media reports, see Мерзликин, ""Голосование—это должностная обязанность." По всей России бюджетников и работников предприятий сгоняют на голосование за поправки в Конституцию—несмотря на коронавирус. Вот как это устроено"; Джанполадова, "Всеобщая мобилизация"; "Губернатор дал поручение мобилизовать бюджетников на выборы." For scholarly analysis of electoral mobilization in the public sector, see Hale, "Explaining Machine Politics in Russia's Regions"; Reuter, "Regional Patrons and Hegemonic Party Electoral Performance in Russia"; Frye, Reuter, and Szakonyi, "Political Machines at Work." For additional evidence that electoral results are clustered by region, see Moser and White, "Does Electoral Fraud Spread?" For the evidence that political machines rely on regional governors and municipal authorities, see Shkel, "Why Political Machines Fail." On the importance of regional-level political machines for the federal-level elections, see Киреев, "Что может искоренить фальсификации на выборах в России." Political machines are also not new to post-Soviet Russia: For the analysis of political machines in the Soviet Union, see Willerton, *Patronage and Politics in the USSR*.

[5] Sharafutdinova, "Gestalt Switch in Russian Federalism"; Sidorkin and Vorobyev, "Extra Votes to Signal Loyalty." For more complete picture of federal–regional relations, though, see Golosov, "The Last Resort of Political Regionalism."

Nested Analysis and Case Selection

During the 2012 election, the performance of regional political machines varied widely. Some of them were able to increase mobilization efforts compared to the 2008 election and compensate for the decreased regime support, while others were unable to do so. For example, in Moscow, where the vote count in March 2012 was relatively honest as authorities feared a new wave of protests, Putin lost 25% compared to Medvedev's 2008 result. At the same time, in Chechnya, he gained 11%. Other regions fell in between.

To understand the causes of this variation, I used a mixed-method research design called nested analysis.[6] The crux of the nested analysis is the strategic choice of case studies to complement and deepen the results of quantitative analysis. If quantitative results are robust and satisfactory, in-depth studies of cases serve the purpose of further model testing. They either provide comprehensive support for the model or reveal theoretical flaws. If, however, the results are not very robust, case studies help model-building by discovering the factors and processes that have not been accounted for by quantitative analysis. For this book, I used a model-building nested analysis design: it nested case studies in the quantitative analysis of electoral results to maximize regional variation, which allowed me to discover the contrast between statist and antistatist political environments.

The quantitative part of the nested analysis research design comes from my previous research, in which I looked at the regional voting disparity and the role of the biggest part of regional political machines—civil servants and public sector workers—in it (see Appendix 1 for the details of this analysis).[7] I considered three possible mechanisms of how the public sector might influence the ability of regional political machines to pass the stress-test of the 2012 presidential election. Looking at whether Putin's support in 2012 rose or fell relative to Medvedev's 2008 support in the same region, I tested whether higher electoral resilience of Putin's regime might be associated with:

1. an increased level of spending on education, healthcare, and social security;
2. an increased number of public sector workers, who vote for proregime candidates in larger numbers; and
3. the higher density of the public sector, which penetrates society and allows the state more control over it, which in the literature is called infrastructural state power.

---

[6] Lieberman, "Nested Analysis as a Mixed-Method Strategy for Comparative Research."
[7] Forrat, "Shock-Resistant Authoritarianism."

The analysis did not find any associations of the regime's electoral resilience with social spending or an increased number of potentially loyal workers. Neither did it show any connection to the dynamic of regional economic indicators, such as personal income, inflation, or unemployment, or the titular (non-Russian) status of the regions, which were used as controls. Both quantitative and qualitative data, however, supported the hypothesis of infrastructural state power, although with a twist.

The part of the state infrastructure that had a pronounced effect on how well a regional political machine was able to deliver high electoral percentage in 2012 was the school network. Schoolteachers, rather than doctors or civil servants, made a difference for the 2012 electoral result, and they did it in two ways. First, they engaged in agitation for Putin, using their position as trusted members of the community and taking advantage of their frequent interactions with the families of their students. Second, they worked as members of precinct-level electoral commissions, most of which were based in schools, where they helped to manipulate the electoral results. Many teachers did it for fear of losing their jobs or benefits. The more teachers a region had, the easier it was for regional authorities to manipulate them by threatening to replace them with competitors. As a result, the regions with largest teacher density were best able to compensate for decreased regime support with falsified results or artificially mobilized votes. And the size of this teacher effect on the electoral result was nontrivial: When this effect was minimized in the quantitative model, it predicted that Putin would have received less than 50%, and the election would have gone to a runoff.

The analysis also showed that this influence of schools varied significantly by region. Political machines in some regions seemed to be a lot stronger than in others with comparable density of the school system. Clearly, some other factors made the political machines in some regions perform better than my quantitative model predicted, while making the political machines in other regions perform worse than the prediction. This variation presented me with the next empirical puzzle, which is central to this book:

Why was it that some regional political machines overperformed under stress, while others underperformed?

To answer this question, I selected two pairs of regions for case studies (see Figure 2.2 and Table 2.1). Two cases were situated above the regression line (the Kemerovo region and the Republic of Tatarstan) and two other cases—below the line (the Rostov region and the Republic of Altai). The regions above the line were a lot more resilient than the density of the school system predicted, while the regions below the line were a lot less resilient than the prediction.

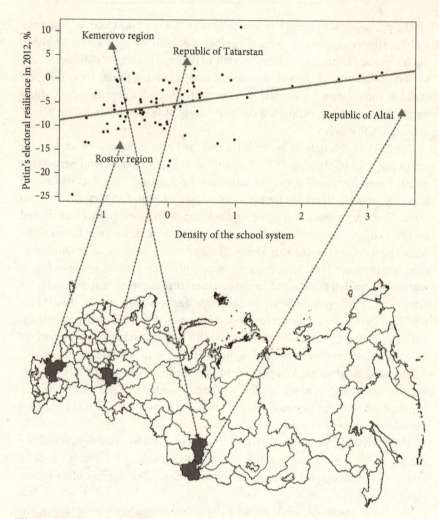

Figure 2.2 Case selection.

Notes:

1. Putin's electoral resilience in 2012 was calculated as the difference between Putin's electoral percentage in 2012 and Medvedev's electoral percentage in 2008 in the same region.

2. Density of the school system was calculated as the number of schoolteachers in the region divided by the regional population and normalized; the scale unit is standard deviation.

3. The regression line is based on a simple OLS regression of Putin's electoral resilience in 2012 on the density of the school system. See Appendix 1 for the full model.

4. Observations on the right have been tested for their influence on the slope of the regression line; the test revealed that these observations do not drive the results but rather follow the trend that exists even without them.

Table 2.1 Case Selection

Electoral Resilience	Density of the School System	
	Low	Medium to High
Lower than expected	Rostov	Altai
Higher than expected	Kemerovo	Tatarstan

In addition to this main selection strategy, I used another criterion. Both among the lower and higher resilience cases, I chose a titular and a nontitular region. Titular regions, that is, the ones that the Soviet government assigned to be the official home of a non-Russian ethnic group, are frequently considered different from nontitular ones by political scientists, who routinely control for this regional status in their regression models.[8] Titular regions have a sizable non-Russian population, stronger ethnic-based social networks, and sometimes even different budgetary relations with the federal center, which formed in the 1990s.[9] These factors impact both the willingness of the governors of these regions to use their influence to boost Putin's electoral percentage and their ability to do so.[10]

It is important to note that these regions have been chosen based on the resilience of Putin's electoral support in 2012 relative to Medvedev's performance in 2008 rather than based on the absolute level of Putin's support. In the last three presidential elections, these regions did not clearly separate into those supporting the proregime candidate more or less (see Figure 2.3). Among the four, Tatarstan and Altai delivered more votes for Putin in 2004; the Rostov region and Tatarstan gave more for Medvedev in 2008, and only in 2012, Tatarstan and the Kemerovo region gave Putin significantly more than the Rostov region and Altai. In addition, none of these four regions performed significantly worse than an average Russian region in any of those elections.

The four chosen regions are, thus, not the ones that necessarily support Putin's regime more or less but whose political machines performed differently under pressure. In other words, they vary not by absolute levels of performance but by reliability in challenging circumstances. In the Kemerovo region and Tatarstan, the governors mobilized their machines in 2012 and delivered a high electoral percentage for Putin despite decreased popular support. In contrast, in the

---

[8] Reuter, "Regional Patrons and Hegemonic Party Electoral Performance in Russia"; Bader and van Ham, "What Explains Regional Variation in Election Fraud?"; Sharafutdinova and Turovsky, "The Politics of Federal Transfers in Putin's Russia."
[9] Shkel, "Bastions of Tradition."
[10] Minaeva and Panov, "Localization of Ethnic Groups in the Regions as a Factor in Cross-Regional Variations in Voting for United Russia."

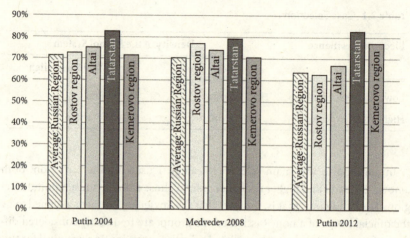

Figure 2.3 Voting percentages of Vladimir Putin and Dmitry Medvedev in presidential elections in 2004, 2008, and 2012.

Rostov region and Altai, the governors were unable to do so, and their machines performed worse in 2012 than they did in 2008. The regression presented in Figure 2.2 demonstrates the performance of regional political machines relative to their potential predicted by the quantitative analysis: The farther away the region is from the regression line, the more its performance deviates from the prediction. One can see that the political machines of the chosen regions performed significantly better or worse than we would expect based on the density of the school system.

Regional Socioeconomic Profiles

The four selected regions vary in many aspects of their geographic and socioeconomic profiles, but none of these differences easily explains why the political machines in the Rostov region and the Republic of Altai would be less reliable than those in the Republic of Tatarstan and the Kemerovo region. The geographic location, economic structures, urbanization level, or ethnic composition of these regions do not systematically vary between the low-resilience regions and the high-resilience ones.

The Rostov region is situated in the south of the European part of Russia, by the Azov Sea and the border with Ukraine. The Republic of Altai occupies

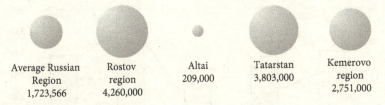

Figure 2.4 Population on January 1, 2012.
Source: Росстат, Регионы России. Социально-экономические показатели: 2013. Статистический сборник.

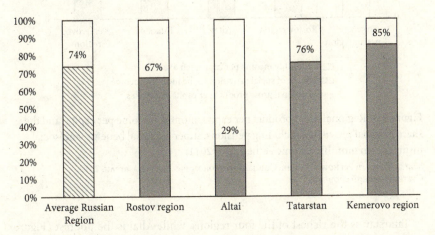

Figure 2.5 Share of urban population on January 1, 2012.
Source: Росстат, Регионы России. Социально-экономические показатели: 2013. Статистический сборник.

a mountainous region in the south of Western Siberia, at the border with Kazakhstan, Mongolia, and China. The Kemerovo region, or Kuzbass,[11] is a highly industrialized area in the south of Western Siberia. And the Republic of Tatarstan is located in the east-central part of European Russia, in the Volga River basin (Figure 2.2).

Altai stands out among the four regions because of its small size and predominantly rural population. The other three regions have populations larger than an average Russian region (Figure 2.4) and comparable urbanization levels (Figure 2.5). The Kemerovo region is the most urbanized of the four, with 85% of its population living in cities. It is the most densely populated and one of the most urbanized areas east of the Ural Mountains.

---

[11] An abbreviation from Kuznetsk (Coal) Basin.

52   THE SOCIAL ROOTS OF AUTHORITARIANISM

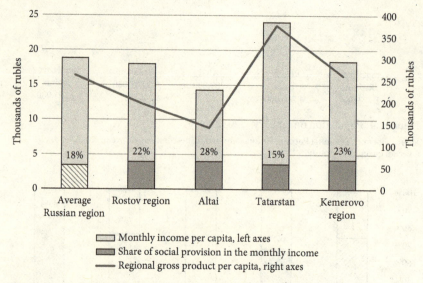

Figure 2.6 Regional gross product per capita, monthly income per capita, and the share of social provision, including pensions, stipends, social benefits, and social insurance, in monthly income at the end of 2011.
Source: Росстат, Регионы России. Социально-экономические показатели: 2013. Статистический сборник.

Tatarstan is the richest of the four regions, while Altai is the poorest (Figure 2.6). Gross regional products of the Kemerovo and Rostov regions are close to the national average. Among the four regions, Altai is highly economically dependent on the federal center: Transfers from Moscow constituted 73% of its budget in 2011, while in the Kemerovo region this number was only 13% (Figure 2.7). Despite all the differences between Altai and Tatarstan, both of them spend a smaller share of their budgets than the national average on social policy, while the Rostov and Kemerovo regions spend more (Figure 2.8).

In terms of the structure of the economy, Altai again stands out: 70% of its small population of 214,000 live in rural areas, where they work mostly in agriculture, especially in raising livestock.[12] In contrast, in the Kemerovo region, only 3.6% of the population (less than half of the national average) work in agriculture, while 10.5% (six and a half times of the national average) work in the mining industry. Mining also produces 27% of gross regional product, which is two and a half times of the average for Russian regions.[13] Tatarstan and the

---

[12] Росстат, *Регионы России. Социально-экономические показатели. 2015,* Table 2.1 and Table 2.3.
[13] The data are for the year 2012 and come from Росстат. *Регионы России, Социально-экономические показатели. 2014,* Table 2.2, Table 2.3, Table 3.4, Table 10.4.

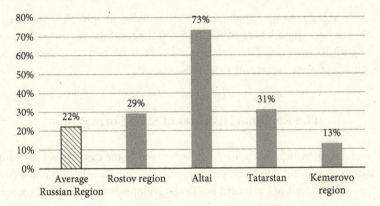

Figure 2.7 Percent of regional budget income that came from federal transfers in 2011.
Source: See sources of data on regional budget variables in Appendix 1.

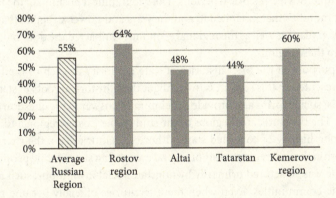

Figure 2.8 Percent of regional budget spent on education, healthcare, and social security in 2011.
Source: See sources of data on regional budget variables in Appendix 1.

Rostov region have more balanced regional economies. Tatarstan is an industrially developed region, whose oil- and gas-refining, chemical, engineering, and light industries as well as food processing make it one of the richest regions in Russia. The economy of the Rostov region is well balanced between heavy industry, such as mining, metallurgy, and machinery; light industry; agriculture and food processing; and energy and transportation.

Finally, the regions also vary in terms of both their ethnic composition and their official ethnic status. Two of the four regions are titular ones, which means that they are an official home of a non-Russian people but does not always mean that the majority of the population there is non-Russian. In Altai, for example, only 34% of the region's population are ethnic Altai people, 57% are Russian, and 6% are Kazakhs, who are concentrated in the southern municipality on the border with Kazakhstan. Tatarstan is split between the two ethnic groups: 53% of its population are Tatars and 40% are Russian.[14]

The Regional Histories of State Formation

The social statism and antistatism that I observed in the case studies raised one more question: Where do these patterns of state–society relations come from? Are they the product of the recent political developments, or are they rooted in long-term regional histories? Based on a brief survey of the literature on regional histories, I would argue that statist and antistatist social norms have been developing over a long period of time rather than being only the product of recent, for example, Soviet, historical periods. The geographical position of the regions, the communities that inhabited it, and the wars and power struggles that might have taken place as well as the regional economies impacted the dominant social norms in these regions.

The purpose of the brief histories of state authority in each of the four regions presented in this section is to highlight these historical roots of statist and antistatist social norms and provide a preliminary answer to the question of their origins. The two antistatist regions in the study—the Rostov region and Altai—had a long history of contested state authority. Centuries ago, their territories were within the realm of interests of several competing states, while people's everyday life was structured primarily by nonstate social institutions, such as clans or ethnic communities. Even when these territories officially became parts of the Russian Empire, the state was unable to uproot the authority of the indigenous institutions. In contrast, the two statist regions—the Kemerovo region and Tatarstan—have never experienced prolonged periods of contestation and, thus, the state was able to establish itself as the primary collective leader in those territories. The description of regional histories I present below, although brief and stylized, pulls together the main historical facts demonstrating the formation of statist and antistatist social norms over time.

Tatarstan

Tatarstan has a long history, in which the state, ethnicity, and religion have closely intertwined, but the state has repeatedly proved itself superior to other

---

[14] *Итоги Всероссийской переписи населения 2010 года.*

social institutions. Tatars as an ethnic group are Turkic people who originated from the Mongols of the Golden Horde. The Mongols settled in the area in the mid-13th century, absorbing the native Bulgar population. In the 15th century, the Golden Horde's power declined, and it split into several states, including the Kazan Khanate that would much later become Tatarstan.[15] This Kazan Khanate, the Tatars' state, was conquered by the Moscow tsar Ivan the Terrible in 1552, making Tatars a "subjugated imperial nation."[16] A large part of the Tatar elite was exterminated during and after the conquest while the rest was incorporated into the Russian state elite.[17]

The subsequent relations of Tatars with the Russian Empire, the Soviet Union, and post-Soviet Russia have been a function of two factors. On the one hand, the ethnic and religious difference between Muslim Tatars and Orthodox Russians led to Russia's attempts to convert and acculturate Tatars, who resisted such attempts through repeated claims for greater autonomy of the Tatar state from the Russian state. On the other hand, Tatars have always sought accommodation within the existing political system rather than proposing its revolutionary change,[18] which I would explain by the strength of their own statist tradition.

During the imperial period of the Russian history, the relations of Russian tsars and tsarinas to Tatars varied, but generally, Tatars integrated into the empire quite successfully. Although some rulers saw them as infidels who must be converted into Christianity, others allowed the practice of Islam and Tatar culture as long as political loyalty to the crown was practiced as well. Catherine the Great, for example, implemented a number of policies that "facilitated a cultural and spiritual rebirth among Volga Tatars simultaneous with the economic development of the Tatar merchant class."[19] Because of Catherine's reforms, by the early 19th century, Tatars had a sizable community of industrialists and merchants who played a role as intermediaries in economic relations between Russia and Central Asia.[20]

During the Soviet period of Tatarstan history, the Tatar state was officially institutionalized and strengthened vis-à-vis the ethnic and religious identities. The Soviet government supported Tatars' distinctiveness under the umbrella of the Soviet "peoples' friendship." Tatarstan officially became a political entity in 1920, when the young Soviet government created the Tatar Autonomous Soviet Socialist Republic. Although in the first Soviet decades, many leading positions in the republic were occupied by Russians, after Stalin's death, ethnic Tatars were

[15] "Tatarstan."
[16] Interview Kaz-11.
[17] Graney, *Of Khans and Kremlins*, 5–6.
[18] Graney, 8.
[19] Graney, 6.
[20] Graney, 4–8.

deliberately recruited to the leadership positions, where they constituted the majority by the late Soviet years.[21] At the same time, Tatars were supposed to join the larger Soviet nation, which worked against important components of their ethnic and religious identities. For example, as the country industrialized and expanded education, the language policies of Russification intensified. The two changes of the alphabet—from Arabic to Roman in 1927 and from Roman to Cyrillic in 1937—isolated the Soviet Tatars from the intellectual tradition of Tatars abroad.[22] The Soviet atheism, meanwhile, undermined Islam as the basis of cultural difference between Russians and Tatars.

As the Soviet state weakened in the 1980s, Tatarstan experienced the rise of an ethnic and religious nationalist movement, whose political interests were aligned with the interests of Tatarstan's state elites at the time.[23] Mintimer Shaimiev, the first leader of the post-Soviet Tatarstan, used the sentiments and arguments of ethnic and religious nationalists to negotiate the future status of Tatarstan in the Russian Federation with Boris Yeltsin.[24] The treaty that they signed in 1994 was controversial and reflected the desire of Tatarstan's elites to push the republic's autonomy within the Russian Federation barely short of complete state sovereignty.[25] Tatarstan obtained the right to have its own constitution, president, and even citizenship, whose ambiguous relationship with Russian citizenship continued to spark disagreements in the years to follow. Among the important economic privileges, Tatarstan obtained the right to control taxes on alcohol, oil, and gas as well as the right to transfer taxes levied on the military-industrial enterprises in the region back from the federal to the regional budget. On top of that, Tatarstan obtained the right to form direct economic relations with foreign countries, bypassing the federal government.[26]

Once the goal of maximum autonomy within Russia was achieved, the interests of Tatarstan's state elites and the leaders of the nationalist movement diverged. Many nationalists regarded the 1994 treaty as a betrayal of their ideal of a sovereign ethnic state. The Tatarstan President Shaimiev, however, split the nationalist movement by co-opting the moderate nationalists into the regional state structures and marginalizing those with extreme nationalist views.[27] Such a split of the movement was easy, as ethnic nationalists have never obtained wide support among the Tatarstan population. Even at the height of the movement, the nationalist political party, which was independent from the regional state

---

[21] Yemelianova, "Islam and Power," 65.
[22] Yemelianova, 81.
[23] For a much more detailed analysis of the relations of Tatar nationalists and the republican state elites, see Kondrashov, *Nationalism and the Drive for Sovereignty in Tatarstan, 1988–92*.
[24] Сагитова and Мухарямов, *Республика Татарстан*, 130–36.
[25] Graney, *Of Khans and Kremlins*, 32–41.
[26] Yemelianova, "Islam and Power," 67; Graney, *Of Khans and Kremlins*, 32–49.
[27] Yemelianova, "Islam and Power," 70–73.

elites, had only 10% support even among the ethnic Tatars.[28] Shaimiev used a similar maneuver with the religious leaders, who were either incorporated into state-controlled organizations or marginalized.[29] Both ethnicity and religion, therefore, served the purpose of regional state-building but could not maintain their influence in opposition to the state.

Because of this position of the state vis-à-vis ethnicity and religion, regional identity in contemporary Tatarstan is, paradoxically, not an ethnic identity. A public opinion poll conducted in 2011–2012 has shown that Russians and Tatars in Tatarstan are remarkably similar in terms of the salience of their ethnic identity as well as attachment to the region and to the country.[30] During the post-Soviet era, Tatarstan's state elites, who are predominantly ethnic Tatars, have successfully moderated the relations and occasional tensions between Russians and Tatars and between the Orthodox and Muslim religious authorities.[31] Some authors even argue that Tatarstan created a civic, not ethnic, nation.[32] I suggest that a better qualification might be to say that the state in Tatarstan has always dominated ethnicity and religion, and therefore, Tatarstan state elites and society have been willing to accommodate multiple ethnicities and religions to strengthen the state.

The Kemerovo Region

The identity of the Kemerovo region is closely intertwined with its economic profile as a heavily industrialized region and its regional identity as the industrial heart of Russia. Mining, especially coal mining, has historically been the major driver of the region's development. The Russian Empire colonized this territory in the early 17th century. About a century later, deposits of coal and iron ore were discovered, which attracted industrialists, who built metallurgical plants. In the late 19th century, the construction of Trans-Siberian railroad facilitated coal mining, and by 1913, 3% of Russian coal was extracted from this area. During the Soviet industrialization in the 1920s–1930s, two dozen new mines and several major industrial plants were built, which made Kuzbass a major coal-mining and metal production area in the country.[33]

---

[28] Yemelianova, 77. See also Kondrashov, *Nationalism and the Drive for Sovereignty in Tatarstan, 1988–92,* 175–76, 189.
[29] Yemelianova, "Islam and Power," 84–86.
[30] Дробижева et al., *Консолидирующие идентичности и модернизационный ресурс в Татарстане,* chap. 2.
[31] Interview Kaz-14; Якупов, *Ислам в Татарстане в 1990-е годы,* 35–39.
[32] Graney, *Of Khans and Kremlins,* chap. 4.
[33] Бобров and Мить, "Кемеровская Область."

The formative period for the region in the 20th century was World War II, when the regional heavy industries directly contributed to the victory of the Soviet Union over Nazi Germany. Over 80 industrial plants from the western part of the country were evacuated to Kuzbass, and many stayed there after the war was over. Kuzbass, which was a part of another region at the time, became the key production site of the Soviet war industry, and in January 1943, the Soviet government granted this area the administrative status of a region. In the postwar decades, the industrial development of the region continued, with mining, metallurgy, and chemical industry playing the major roles in this process.[34]

In the last years of the Soviet Union, Kuzbass became the center of a powerful workers' movement, which demonstrated regional solidarity and potential for collective action.[35] This movement emerged in the situation when Gorbachev's political reforms and the crisis of the command economy had undermined the image of the Soviet state as leader. The workers who used to be the proud contributors to the industrial might of the country now felt betrayed when that country could not provide even basic consumer goods for them. In May 1989, a few months before the fall of the Berlin Wall, Kuzbass miners began a strike that quickly spread nationwide. They demanded economic and political independence from the Soviet government, in large part to be able to use the industrial capacity of the region to improve plummeting living standards. After the fall of the Soviet Union and over the first post-Soviet decade, the miners continued to play an important role in labor strikes, including the "rail war"—blocking the Trans-Siberian railroad in order to make the government listen to their demands. Boris Nemtsov, who negotiated with the striking miners in 1998 as the deputy prime minister of Russia, noted, "Miners do not view [the politicians] as saviors, which is a sign of a high level of maturity. As pilots, they work in harsh conditions and risk their lives every day. And they have a special sense of brotherhood. That's why miners are organized and dangerous for the political regime."[36]

To pacify the region, Boris Yeltsin called on Aman Tuleyev—a politician from the region who skillfully redirected the regional solidarity back into the state-led framework and became the Kuzbass leader for over two decades. Tuleyev not only pacified the miners but also gradually consolidated his own power in the region to such a degree that by the mid-2010s it had acquired a reputation as "a sultanate of Aman Tuleyev."[37] It often had abnormally high official election turnout rates and very high electoral support for Tuleyev as a governor, which

---

[34] Бобров and Мить.

[35] Лопатин, *История рабочего движения Кузбасса (1989–1991 гг.)*; Cook, *The Soviet Social Contract and Why It Failed*; Crowley, *Hot Coal, Cold Steel*.

[36] "У нас пока нет сладких пилюль, чтобы давать вместе с горькими."

[37] Орешкин, "Зазеркалье избирательной кампании."

combined his relatively high popularity in the region with a high estimated level of electoral falsification.[38]

The Republic of Altai

The political history of this region has been shaped by the interactions of the multiple Altai tribes who lived in the area with several large and powerful states that surrounded it. None of these states was able or willing to impose its full authority on this territory for a long time, limiting their relations to taxation in exchange for protection. In the 17th century, many Altai tribes were double-taxed by the Russian Empire and the Mongol state of Dzungaria, which officially agreed on the shared taxation authority. After Dzungaria weakened because of internal conflicts and fell to China in the mid-18th century, many Altai zaisans, that is, tribal heads, sought protection from Russia, which had been strengthening its positions in the region.[39]

The transition of Altai tribes under the rule of the Russian tsar took almost a century. Russia was reluctant at first to provide protection for Altai tribes and risk starting a conflict with China. It suggested relocating these tribes to Kalmyk Khanate, an area north of the Caspian Sea. Some tribes agreed, but in the process of relocation, they lost about a third of their members to cold, hunger, and diseases. Other tribes accepted Russian citizenship but resisted relocation and hid in the mountains, where they were still sometimes attacked by the Chinese and the Kazakhs. For several decades, the Altai territory and the right to tax the Altai tribes were contested by Russia and China, but by the early 19th century, Russia strengthened its positions enough to resist the Chinese pressure. In 1822, the Russian government officially declared the Altai land its territory, which started the process of ethnic Russians relocating to the Altai land. In 1864, Russia signed a treaty with China about the official border between the two states.[40]

Before joining Russia, Altai tribes viewed each other as different peoples, and these tribal divisions significantly contributed to the regional political pluralism. As they interacted more closely with Russians during their time in the Russian Empire, they began to see multiple Altai tribes as one ethnic group consisting of different tribes. Ethnographers usually divide the Altai tribes into northern ones (kumandintsy, tubalary, chelkantsy) and southern ones (altai-kizhi,

---

[38] Шпилькин, "История кемеровской аномалии и немного конспирологии." Different methods of estimating electoral fraud generally agree on which Russian regions have the largest scale of falsifications, although they disagree on the estimates of its absolute scale—see more in Kalinin, "Validation of the Finite Mixture Model Using Quasi-Experimental Data and Geography."
[39] Самаев, *Горный Алтай в XVII–середине XIX в.*; Мукаева, "История административно-территориального устройства Горного Алтая в прошлом и настоящем."
[40] Самаев, *Горный Алтай в XVII–середине XIX в.*

telengity, telesy), which populated the Altai territory by the early 18th century. This multitude of groups was joined by the Russian Old Believers, who began to settle in the region in the second half of the 18th century, and other Russian settlers along with some Kazakhs in the south in the 19th century. While the Russian government provided the Altai tribes with a rather wide autonomy—for example, they were allowed to keep their own internal governance system and practice their own religion and were freed from conscription—the Russian settlers and the Russian Orthodox Church had more strained relations with them.[41] The settlers cultivated the land that the Altai tribes used as pastures for their cattle, while the Orthodox missionaries worked to convert the tribes to Christianity.[42] Most conversions were voluntary but merely ceremonial, as the tribe members continued to practice polytheism.[43] In the early 20th century, the resistance to economic and cultural expansion of the Russians led to the emergence of Burkhanism—a new millenarian religious movement, which united the different clans of the altai-kizhi tribe. It had the potential of uniting other Altai tribes into one nation, but it was suppressed by the Russian and then the Soviet governments.[44]

During the Soviet period, the search for a common identity of the Altai tribes was aided by the Soviet government in a different way. The government's goal was to create a unified Altai ethnicity with a designated place among the other peoples of the Soviet Union. This homogenizing impulse together with collectivization and ideological influence temporarily led to diminishing the role of tribes and clans in the life of indigenous Altai population in the mid-20th century—only to bring them back to the forefront of public discussions once the Soviet Union fell apart.[45]

In the post-Soviet Russia, the indigenous Altai tribes have been simultaneously searching for a common identity for all of them and distinct identities for each one separately, reproducing the pluralist political tradition of the region. They created multiple ethnic organizations, including the Kurultai of the Altai people, elected zaisans for all major tribes, and revived Burkhanism in the form of two new religious movements.[46] These processes have also been impacted

[41] Николаев, *Этнодемографическое развитие коренного населения предгорий Горного Алтая*, 27–28; Мукаева, "История административно-территориального устройства Горного Алтая в прошлом и настоящем."

[42] Русанов, *Национальный суверенитет и процессы суверенизации Горного Алтая (в первой половине XX века)*, 83–84.

[43] Николаев, *Этнодемографическое развитие коренного населения предгорий Горного Алтая*, 23–27.

[44] Данилин, *Бурханизм*; Шерстова, *Бурханизм*; Тадина, "Два взгляда на бурханизм у алтай-кижи."

[45] Николаев, *Этнодемографическое развитие коренного населения предгорий Горного Алтая*, 90–95.

[46] Гончарова, *Горный Алтай*; Чемчиева, *Алтайские субэтносы в поисках идентичности*, 65–67; Шерстова, "Бурханизм и проблема новых идентичностей народов Горного Алтая."

by the Russian state, which formally granted some Altai tribes the status of "indigenous endangered peoples." This status guaranteed the tribe more state resources but, at the same time, alienated them from the rest of the Altai people.[47] Another source of financial support for the cultural heritage of Altai people was the Russian state-owned gas company Gazprom. It was interested in building a gas pipeline through the region and sponsored creation of a spectacular museum of Altai culture in Gorno-Altaisk in an effort to win the hearts and minds of the people.[48] Nowadays, the indigenous Altai population has a multilayered identity, from patrimonial family to Altai nationality, which takes into account tribes and clans as well as their geographic location within Altai.[49]

The search for identity among the indigenous Altai people activated a similar process among the Russians, making the public sphere in the region a vibrant space of production and reproduction of group identities and contesting their relations to each other. Several Russian nationalist organizations emerged in the early 1990s, but they did not have a wide popular appeal despite the large share of regional population being ethnically Russian. Their activities were limited and faced the resistance of both the regional authorities and the stronger Altai nationalist organizations. The leaders of the Russian nationalists in the region had to moderate their views and political agendas in order to participate in regional politics and form coalitions with other political forces, thus, contributing to the political pluralism in the region.[50]

The Rostov Region

The ethnic composition of the regional population in the Rostov region, at the first sight, creates an impression of a high level of homogeneity: about 90% of people in the region identify as Russian.[51] Behind this statistic, however, there is significant diversity in the historical background and identity of the different parts of this large group. Part of those who identify as Russians, are the so-called Cossacks, whose story I will tell below. Another part is the descendants of the several waves of migrant peasants from Central Russia, who relocated to the region in the 18th–19th centuries. Yet another part are the descendants of the

---

[47] Шерстова, "Бурханизм и проблема новых идентичностей народов Горного Алтая," 246; Чемчиева, *Алтайские субэтносы в поисках идентичности*; Тюхтенева, "Личность и общество у алтайцев: От родовой принадлежности до общеалтайской идентичности."
[48] Plets, "Exceptions to Authoritarianism?"
[49] Чемчиева, *Алтайские субэтносы в поисках идентичности*; Николаев, *Этнодемографическое развитие коренного населения предгорий Горного Алтая*; Тюхтенева, "Личность и общество у алтайцев: От родовой принадлежности до общеалтайской идентичности."
[50] Гончарова, *Горный Алтай*, 163–72.
[51] *Итоги Всероссийской переписи населения 2010 года*.

qualified workers and other specialists mobilized and sent to the region by the Soviet government. Finally, the last group are the ethnic Russians who migrated to the region from the Caucasus, especially Chechnya, and Central Asia during the post-Soviet time.[52]

The 10% of the non-Russian population in the Rostov region may seem like a small number, but these people live in consolidated and geographically concentrated communities and play an important role in regional politics.[53] For example, the Armenian diaspora in the region dates back to the 18th century and is concentrated in one of the districts in the regional capital Rostov-on-Don and several villages in a rural municipality. Other ethnic groups, especially in the east and south of the region include Meskhetian Turks, Azeris, Chechens, Georgians, Darghins, and Avars. The Meskhetian Turks relocated to the region from Uzbekistan during the ethnic clashes of 1989, and many Chechens moved in during the two Chechen wars in the mid-1990s and the early 2000s.[54]

The Cossacks in the Rostov region are a Russian subethnic group, whose identity over the centuries has been both fluid and distinct and whose relations with the Russian state have been a mixture of loyalty and rebellion. This group derives from the nomadic communes of Turkic, Slavic, and other peoples who lived in the steppes north of the Black and Caspian Seas in the 14th–15th centuries. This area was the buffer zone between the Ottoman Empire, the future Russian Empire, and the future Polish-Lithuanian Commonwealth. The communes of Cossacks—"the freemen"—have absorbed marginalized people from these states, such as runaway serfs. In the 15th–17th centuries, the Don Cossacks grew to be dominated by Orthodox Slavs and gradually joined Russia, while maintaining significant autonomy from Moscow. They both served the Russian tsar by protecting the borders of the state and periodically spearheaded peasant uprisings against the expansion of Moscow power.[55]

In the 18th–early 20th centuries, the Cossacks' autonomy in the Russian Empire significantly diminished, and they became a military estate that still kept the features of a subethnos. During this time, the tsarist government used the Cossacks to put down peasant and worker riots in different cities across Russia, where the local police might have been reluctant to crush unarmed civilians. Cossacks' loyalty to the Russian state, however, was never guaranteed, as they continued to see themselves as an independent community governed by direct democracy tradition. During the civil war, the Cossacks split between the White

---

[52] Markedonov, "Ethnopolitical Processes in the Rostov Region, the Krasnodar and Stavropol Territories."
[53] Interviews Ros-11, Ros-13.
[54] Markedonov, "Ethnopolitical Processes in the Rostov Region, the Krasnodar and Stavropol Territories."
[55] Ure, *The Cossacks*; Волков, *Казачество как этносоциальный феномен современной России*; Buchanan, "Cossacks."

and the Red Armies, but those who supported the Bolsheviks were later dispersed and starved in the 1930s by Stalin, who saw them as separatists. During World War II, the Cossacks divided again, with some of them joining the Soviet Army and others collaborating with the Nazis while dreaming about the Cossack independence from Soviet domination. After the war, the Cossacks almost ceased to exist as a separate group, only to resurrect once the Soviet Union fell apart.[56]

During the post-Soviet time, the Cossacks continued to search for their identity and the place of the state inside it. The Russian government returned them to a special status but has always been wary of engaging with them too closely, fearing it would be unable to control them at the critical moment. The Russian state now keeps an official host registry for Cossacks, but their identity, governance practices, and folk culture spread well beyond this official relationship with the state. Cossack revival has been driven by the myth of the free warrior equestrians, who had a unique culture and traditions and who served the state but had a high degree of autonomy on internal matters. Even though this myth often contradicted reality throughout history, it has proven to be persistent.[57] Cossacks nowadays maintain traditions of direct democracy, and although the top-rank appointments are usually controlled by the state, the bottom and middle ones are elected at all-male Cossack "circles." The Cossacks also are not limited to men officially registered with the host—even more numerous are the so-called public Cossacks who see themselves as belonging to this group by blood or otherwise; and these "public" Cossacks are a rather diverse group too.[58] Despite all the fluidity of Cossacks as a category, though, they have a very distinct identity within Russian ethnicity, and a good way to think about it may be as "a 'nation' but not a nationality": "We are Russians, only more so!"[59]

In the Russian population of the Rostov region, the Cossacks do not constitute a large share, but they are still very important players in regional politics. Because of the diversity of Cossacks and their simultaneous identification with Russians, estimates of the share of Cossacks vary widely, from 0.7% to 15% of the region's population, with many estimates being about 2%–4%.[60] Unlike non-Russian ethnic groups, though, Cossacks do not concentrate in several villages or city districts; they are dispersed among the Russian population. Unlike the general Russian population, however, the Cossacks are much more institutionalized as a group, which makes them independent political players and contributes to the pluralist dynamics of regional politics.[61]

---

56 Ure, *The Cossacks*; Волков, *Казачество как этносоциальный феномен современной России*.
57 Ure, *The Cossacks*.
58 Interviews Ros-12, Ros-13.
59 Ure, *The Cossacks*, 243.
60 *Итоги Всероссийской переписи населения 2010 года*; Markedonov, "Ethnopolitical Processes in the Rostov Region, the Krasnodar and Stavropol Territories"
61 Interview Ros-13.

The legacy of these regional histories continues to this day: People's views of the state and everyday interactions with state officials, which I observed while doing fieldwork, matched these historical patterns. The view of the state as either a legitimate collective leader or an outsider and potential predator shaped the ways in which grassroots politics worked in these regions. In the Kemerovo region and Tatarstan, it was driven by social norms, conformity, and cooperation with the state, while in the Rostov region and Altai it was based on competition for state resources. The next two chapters will demonstrate how these differences give rise to different structures of public organizations and to the difference in electoral resilience of Putin's regime.

Chapter Summary

The second chapter connected the theory of unity- and division-based authoritarianism to a concrete empirical puzzle and the research design that allowed me to discover it. The puzzle is related to the 2012 presidential election in Russia, which Vladimir Putin won with 64% of the vote despite a historically low approval rating. To understand how that happened, I used a nested analysis research design that combined quantitative analysis of electoral statistics with regional case studies.

The quantitative part of the nested analysis looked at the performance of regional political machines in 2012 compared to 2008 and found that some of these machines were more reliable than others in the situation of decreased regime support. To investigate the causes of this variation, four regions—the Kemerovo region, the Republic of Tatarstan, the Rostov region, and the Republic of Altai—were chosen as case studies. In the first two of these regions, the political machines were much more reliable than I would have expected based on the quantitative data, while in the last two they were much less reliable. It is this contrast between the regions that allowed me to formulate the distinction between statist and antistatist societies.

Before the next chapters delve into the empirical manifestations of statism and antistatism, this chapter also presented brief summaries of the regional political histories, which provide a preliminary answer to the question about the origins of statism in the Kemerovo region and Tatarstan and antistatism in the Rostov region and Altai and show that statism and antistatism are rooted in long-term historical developments rather than recent Soviet and post-Soviet periods.

3

Team State versus Outsider State

Public Organizations in Statist and Antistatist Societies

The four regions I studied had different histories, in which economies, ethnic composition, and the politics of larger powers intertwined to form different views of the proper role of the state in everyday life. This difference can be seen nowadays in the way people talk about state leaders and organizations, in what they feel proud about and what they see as appropriate or inappropriate. State leadership is viewed as a positive and right thing in some regions and as negative and counterproductive in others.

For state rulers—regional authorities in this case—these views of the state determine one very important thing: Are they dealing with a cooperative or noncooperative society? It is much easier to rule when the population expects regional authorities to organize and direct the people than when every state initiative is viewed with suspicion by default. When the population is cooperative, the ruler can build centralized governance structures from the top. When it is noncooperative, this is not an option because of societal resistance, and other ways to govern must be used.

In this and the next chapters, I will use interviews and other fieldwork data from the four Russian regions to demonstrate how the different views of the state ultimately produce different kinds of political machines. This chapter will connect the views of the state to different structures of grassroots public organizations, while the next chapter will explain how these public organizations turn into loyalty-based or clientelistic political machines.

This chapter consists of three parts. First, it juxtaposes the everyday views of the state and state officials in different regions. Second, it uses the examples of residential councils in the Kemerovo region and youth organizations in Tatarstan to show that public organizations form a centralized structure in statist social environments. Third, it uses data from the Rostov region and Altai to demonstrate that a similar centralization is absent in these regions and that competition for state resources takes place instead.

The Team State in the Kemerovo Region and Tatarstan

The Kemerovo region and Tatarstan resemble each other, as people in both regions view the state as their team leader. In both regions, governors cultivated an image of fathers of the nation—wise and fair leaders who put the regional interests first—and many people prided themselves on joining this team state and contributing to state-led projects. The difference between the two regions, though, was in what the state leadership was built around: in the Kemerovo region, it was focused on social security; in Tatarstan—on economic development.

The State as Protector

In Kemerovo City, the fatherly image of Aman Tuleyev was ubiquitous in the public space.[1] Local prime-time TV news was occupied with the messages of how the governor cared for the people. He was the one who provided material help for the poor and opened new daycare centers. He publicly held the bureaucrats and the business accountable for paying decent salaries, running social programs, and generally meeting the needs of the people. In his interviews in newspapers and on TV, he would also give advice on how people could protect themselves from natural disasters or crime: for example, he would explain how to prepare for the spring floods and urge people to buy insurance. The street radio—the speakers placed in public squares and on buildings—talked about summer trips abroad that the governor organized for schoolchildren, and the children standing by the entrance to the regional library discussed who was selected to go on those trips. All these policies and actions combined into the idea of a "socially oriented region," which I often heard in the media and conversations with the people.

This image of Tuleyev as a caring patriarch has been deliberately created by the loyal regional media and journalists.[2] Tuleyev, a pragmatic politician, made social security his political agenda in the 1990s, when the country and the region were in deep economic crisis. This agenda resonated with popular sentiments, and he carried it along throughout his political career while being opportunistic in his relations with political competitors and allies. He started as a member of the Communist Party and used its organizational infrastructure to gain political

---

[1] In the Kemerovo region, the fieldwork was conducted in February and March 2014.
[2] Interview Kem-01. Some of the books written fully or at least partially by the loyal journalists include Голованова, *О времени, о людях, о Тулееве*; Тулеев, *Оставаться самим собой*; Черемнов and Шалакин, *Аман Тулеев—человек, политик, губернатор*; Шатская, *Доверие*. The only independent newspaper that criticized Tuleyev was *Kuznetskii Krai* (*Кузнецкий край*), renamed *Krai* (*Край*) in 2002. It had limited resources and audience and ceased to exist in 2006 after its editor died from cancer.

weight. Once he became the governor, he abruptly turned against his fellow party members, divided their ranks, and eliminated them from the regional parliament. At different points of his career, he both supported and disapproved of labor strikes and took both promarket and proregulation stances on economic policy. At the same time, in his public statements, he was always able to connect his current actions to the theme of social security while addressing concrete grievances. Here is how one of his political opponents explained his success: "He knows exactly what to say to different groups: one thing to miners, another thing to pensioners, a third one to teachers. He knows when to shake hands and when to smile to a woman. When he speaks, the audience's jaws drop. And his explanations are simple, understandable, making use of colorful Russian phrases. He has no problem publicly calling himself an idiot. He is a genius of populism, and there is no one better than him in Russia."[3]

Tuleyev's idea of a socially oriented region determined both the structure and the public framing of regional social policy. The Kemerovo region did not spend significantly more on social policy than other Siberian regions.[4] However, the way it distributed the money made it easy to present these policies as care—the care that one would expect from community or extended family—rather than an impersonal monetary transaction. First, social assistance in the region was explicitly structured around protecting the most vulnerable members of the community demonstrating to the people that everyone had a safety net. Regional authorities used formal and informal means to identify the neediest people. Requiring means testing for receiving many social benefits was the formal way to do it.[5] In addition, through various organizations working with different population groups, state officials collected information on individuals and families who found themselves in difficult circumstances. For example, they regularly reached out to the Russian Orthodox Church in the region asking for the priests' help in identifying the neediest people in their parishes.[6]

Second, more benefits in the Kemerovo region than in other regions were provided in in-kind rather than monetary form, for example, transportation passes, sets of food items, coal for heating houses, kits for newborns, seeds to grow vegetables, or packages to local sanatoria.[7] Even when the benefits were distributed in monetary form, a portion of it might be symbolically designated

---

[3] Лукьянова, "Аман во спасение."
[4] See Figures A3.1 and A3.2 in Appendix 3.
[5] Шипачев, Дерябина, and Шабанов, *Меры социальной поддержки жителей Кемеровской области: Сборник информационных материалов*.
[6] Interview Kem-08.
[7] See Figures A3.5 and A3.6 in Appendix 3. Besides the handbooks published by the Kemerovo regional and municipal governments, I used newspaper publications as a source of information about social benefits in the region. Some of the publications talking about in-kind benefits include: Акимова, "Проезд останется бесплатным;" Горкунов, "Пенсионный проездной;" Васильева, "Сажаем картошку и выращиваем кроликов;" "Главное не лениться."

for a specific material need to show that the regional government has thought through the different aspects of people's lives and wanted to make sure that all the basic needs were covered. For example, low-income pensioners received "bread allowance"—0.8 rubles a day (about ¢3), which was probably equivalent of the cost of two slices of bread.[8] All these efforts of the regional officials to identify the most vulnerable and take care of them were widely advertised in the loyal regional media and in special publications—thick handbooks on social benefits for different population groups.[9]

"Is It Bad to Help the Poor?"

The socially oriented policies in the Kemerovo region did not seem to impact significantly regional inequality, according to the official statistics.[10] Despite of these statistics, though, many people I met talked about their region as socially oriented. When I expressed my interest in social policies, people's usual reaction was: "Oh, yes, we are very proud of our system of social support!"

This pride and approval of the social orientation of the regional government did not depend on whether my respondents benefited from these policies personally. For example, I heard the praise of the governor and his policies from a librarian, who, as I found out later, had to supplement her government-provided medical insurance with a private one. My other respondent, Elena, whom we will meet again later in this chapter, lived in a recently built city neighborhood branded as an upper-middle class housing, and some of the apartments in the neighborhood participated in a heavily subsidized mortgage program for public sector workers. Although Elena's family was not eligible for this program, she spoke very highly about it as an example of a progressive social policy:

---

[8] Шипачев, Дерябина, and Шабанов, *Меры социальной поддержки жителей Кемеровской области: Сборник информационных материалов*, 98.

[9] For examples of such handbooks, see Шипачев, Дерябина, and Шабанов, *Меры социальной поддержки жителей Кемеровской области: Сборник информационных материалов*; Администрация Кемеровской области, Департамент образования и науки, *Основные виды социальной поддержки студентам, учащимся и сотрудникам учреждений образования Кемеровской области*. Detailed information about social benefits for different population categories can also be found on the regional government website (https://ako.ru/obshchestvo/sotsialnaya-podderzhka/mery-sotsialnoy-podderzhki.php, access date June 28, 2019).

[10] The share of the population with incomes below subsistence level has been lower in the Kemerovo region than the national average for most of the 2000s (see Figure A3.3 in Appendix 3). This number, however, was at least partly the consequence of a lower subsistence income level (see Figure A3.4 in Appendix 3), which, in its turn, must have been at least partially the result of price regulation for the basic food items (Шипачев, Дерябина, and Шабанов, *Меры социальной поддержки жителей Кемеровской области: Сборник информационных материалов*, 14). The Gini coefficient in the Kemerovo region was not substantially lower than in other regional cases or the national average (see Figure A3.7 in Appendix 3).

The apartments on the first street that was built there were sold through a subsidized mortgage program to the workers of the social sphere, for example, schoolteachers, doctors, kindergarten teachers. (...) They were given minimal interest rates—only about 5%,[11] so the subsidy from the administration was very significant. And I am just totally excited about it! Unfortunately, my family could not participate in this program as we are not public workers,[12] so we were not allowed to take this mortgage. But as a result, our schoolteachers were able to buy very good, elite housing with minimal interest rate and pay it off in the next 10–15 years.[13]

Why was the idea of a socially oriented region so popular even among the people who did not benefit from it directly? One of my conversations with the librarian who praised the social orientation of the region while buying private health insurance provided me with a good answer to this question. In that conversation, I mentioned that this system legitimized political monopoly and lack of political competition. The librarian looked puzzled and asked, "Is it bad to help the poor?" Political competition did not have an intrinsic value for her but helping the most vulnerable did. She praised the governor not because he provided anything personally to her, but because he did the right and moral thing—took care of those who had less than her. The pride that she and other people expressed about their socially oriented region was not the pride about growing their own fortune; it was the pride of supporting a morally right cause that benefited the larger community. This pride of being good citizens was the basis of people's loyalty to the state in the Kemerovo region, which I discuss later in this chapter.

The Developmental State

The Tatarstan version of state leadership was different from the Kemerovo one: it was focused on spearheading the regional economic development and on raising the symbolic status of the region at the federal and even international arenas. Mintimer Shaimiev, the Tatarstan president in 1991–2010, laid the foundation for this regional leadership in the early post-Soviet years when he used the Tatar nationalist movement to negotiate privileges for the Republic in its relations with Moscow. Together with Tatarstan's oil deposits, these privileges quickly made Tatarstan one of the richest Russian regions.

---

[11] A 5% interest rate on a mortgage is very low for Russia. A usual rate at the time of the interview was about 12%.
[12] "Бюджетники" in Russian.
[13] Interview Kem-13.

The importance of economic modernization for the Tatarstan government is immediately noticeable to anyone who visits the regional capital, Kazan'. For its alleged 1000th anniversary in 2005,[14] the Tatarstan government significantly renovated the center of the city, which now looks similar to many European capitals.[15] The city government demolished unsafe housing in the city center, almost completely wiping out an old neighborhood, and filled the space with new shiny buildings, pedestrian streets, and shopping malls. Using federal and regional money, the authorities also financed the construction of a subway, a large mosque in the Kazan' Kremlin, and several museums, parks, and sports arenas. Together with an effort to develop domestic and international tourism, the modernized city demonstrated the status and prosperity of the region to the rest of Russia and the outside world.

The international status of the region was just as important for the regional authorities as competition with other Russian regions. To strengthen cultural connections of Tatarstan with other countries, especially with Turkey, the Tatarstan government attempted to Latinize the Tatar language in 1999, but the federal government reversed this reform in 2004. In 2013, Kazan' hosted the FISU Summer Universiade—a multisport competition for university athletes from all over the world, which further elevated its domestic and international status.

The efforts of the regional government to make Tatarstan the leader in many areas resonated with the public. Many people to whom I talked in Kazan' viewed the region as a team competing and winning the competition with other regions. One of my interviewees talked about Tatarstan's youth team participating in a national-level competition and emphasized: "We all go with a clear idea that we must win. This is the ideology of the Republic [of Tatarstan] in which the young people are raised: We are Tatarstan! We must be among the leaders!"[16]

This common regional identity and team-like unity—"We are Tatarstan!"—came up in casual conversations a lot. People felt that their region was among the leaders; they also felt that each of them was part of this common project. This regional unity was so strong that it diminished the salience of the internal division between Tatars and Russians in the region.[17] Although the two groups have lived side by side for centuries and share a common identity, some issues continue to spark controversies, for example, the language of school instruction and

---

[14] 1005 as the foundation date of Kazan' is disputed and was probably picked by the regional government for political reasons.
[15] In Tatarstan, the fieldwork was conducted in May 2014.
[16] Interview Kaz-03.
[17] According to public opinion polls in Tatarstan in 2011–2012, over 90% of both Tatars and Russians said that they feel a regional unity. Tatars and Russians were also very similar in other aspects of their identity and political views (Дробижева et al., Консолидирующие идентичности и модернизационный ресурс в Татарстане).

the amount of school time devoted to Tatar and Russian languages.[18] Despite periodic public protests on both sides of the debate, though, this controversy is not strong enough to overpower the regional solidarity that both Russians and Tatars had.

Pride and Loyalty

With all the differences between the socially oriented Kemerovo region and modernization-oriented Tatarstan, the vision of the state as the collective leader was similar in two regions. People did not expect the state to serve their individual interests; rather, they expected it to do what was right for the whole regional community. And since the state was viewed as acting in the public, collective interest, helping the state was viewed as honorable and morally right thing to do. Quite a few people to whom I talked prided themselves on being involved in state-led projects and regarded recognition of their work by the state as an honor. For example, a non-Tatar woman[19] who worked with youth volunteers, compared her work in a Moscow-based NGO and in Tatarstan's regional government and explained why she came back to Kazan':

> There is no such spirit there [in Moscow]. Here I feel, although it may sound high-toned, that the Republic is behind me, that I am valued by the Republic and it is ready to invest in me. When you feel it, you work differently. And there [in Moscow] ... if you did something useful for the society—you're probably a freak, this was not normal.[20]

This sentiment was echoed by an employee at the regional social work department in Kemerovo, who said:

> We all feel the support of the governor. This is one of the main things [motivating people to work well] ... The governor values the work of our social services very highly.... When people feel the care about them, they work [properly].... Whenever we suggested doing something new, we have never heard a no from the governor. Never.[21]

---

[18] This issue is not as clear-cut as it might seem, as Russian is widespread among the urban population, including Tatars, and provides advantages nationwide, while Tatar is the native language of many people in the republican government, and may boost career chances in Tatarstan (Interviews Kaz-14, Kaz-05).

[19] She said she was neither ethnically Russian nor Tatar, but her first name, last name, and patronymic were clearly Slavic and she was probably thought to be Russian by the most people.

[20] Interview Kaz-03.

[21] Interview Kem-12.

The reader might reasonably ask whether this is the loyalty to the state as collective leader or to the charismatic governor. As I will show further in this chapter, people's loyalty was not limited to the governors but rather spread to all state institutions. Governors also changed: for example, in Tatarstan, the president changed in 2010, when Shaimiev's successor, Rustam Minnikhanov, assumed office, and it did not seem to change anything in the narratives of my respondents.[22] Most importantly, if people's loyalty was only related to the personality of the governor, I should have observed governors in other regions trying to use similar strategies of loyalty cultivation, even if some of them were more successful than others. However, the attitudes to the state and group loyalties in the Rostov region and Altai show that state collective leadership is not so easily accepted by the people in all societies.

The Outsider State in the Rostov Region and Altai

In the Rostov region and Altai, the pride of helping the state was almost absent. Although I encountered a lot of manifestations of regional identity, it was not focused on state institutions. People's understanding of who they were as a group stemmed from their belonging to nonstate, usually ethnic, communities and to the land where they lived. These communities regulated many aspects of everyday life, provided social safety net, resolved conflicts—and determined whom people considered a legitimate authority. State officials who did not possess a high status in these communities were seen as outsiders and treated with suspicion.

Social Norms and Safety Net in Nonstate Communities

In both the Rostov region and Altai, the nonstate groups set the most important norms that guided people's lives and served as the institutions that provided social support for individuals. In Altai, the core of these communities were indigenous Altai clans; in the Rostov region, these were ethnic communities and Cossacks, a quasi-ethnic group within the Russian ethnos. Although the regional population was not limited to these groups, they were consolidated and powerful enough to set the tone in the regional social life and politics.

Among the indigenous Altai population, clans (seoks) were the most important social units. There are 36 clans in Altai, and the members of each of them consider

---

[22] In Kemerovo region, the governor changed in 2018, a few years after completion of the fieldwork.

themselves a family. People of the same generation in a clan are considered brothers and sisters, even if they do not know each other personally. When Altaians interact, they usually try to find out each other's clan affiliation, which affects the kind of relations that they can have in the future. For example, marriages between the members of one clan are believed to be incest and are extremely rare.[23]

Clans form a security network for individual members, which often involves sharing material resources. Since the time when Altai tribes were nomadic and anyone could lose their cattle to diseases, sharing material resources with relatives has been a usual practice.[24] I heard in a casual conversation that one of my interviewees, an ethnic Altaian, had relatives in the countryside, so her family received all the meat they ate for free.[25] Another interviewee, also an ethnic Altaian, illustrated the norms of sharing material resources with the observations she made while promoting a subsidized loan program for small businesses. This program often failed to produce the intended results because people treated the loan money as a community resource:

- They come and say: "I need three million [rubles]." What do you think they will do with these three million? They will waste them! This relative will have an anniversary; that one—a wedding; and that one—a funeral. (...) Few people will use this money according to the original purpose. (...) Or I could give some money to Elena, and she would buy a studio apartment in the city, and her daughter and my daughter will live there when they go to college. (...) And she will be grateful to me her whole life. And I will remind her: "Elena, remember the apartment," of course, I will use it to manipulate her. Then, she will do something similar for me, and this is how we get bogged down in these mutual obligations. And when it is time to pay back, I will call my relatives, go visit them and say: "Listen, turns out it is time to repay the loan, but I don't have any money; I gave everything away."
- And will the relatives give the money?
- Yes, they will. Somehow, they find a way to pay back. (...) This is astounding and I still don't understand this mechanism as I was brought up in the European rationality tradition. It does not work here, and it is difficult for me to survive here.[26]

To maintain this network, clans organize family reunions where younger clan members get to know each other and older ones can maintain personal

---

[23] Тюхтенева, "Личность и общество у алтайцев: От родовой принадлежности до общеалтайской идентичности."
[24] Тюхтенева, 75.
[25] Altai fieldnotes.
[26] Interviews Altai-05, Altai-07.

connections. In the future, especially at times of crisis, these connections will serve as a valuable resource.[27]

In the Rostov region, a similar role of creating social order was fulfilled by non-Russian ethnic groups, Cossacks, and local communities, and this was the case in both rural and urban environments. In Rostov, the capital of the region, most ethnic communities, even very small ones, had their own organizations, which are officially registered in the Ministry of Justice. The leaders of ethnic communities are often wealthy businessmen, who are elected by community members and who regularly spend their own resources on charity projects for their less fortunate coethnics. For example, the leader of the Greek community in Rostov provided material help for the elderly community members and sponsored a Greek school and a Greek church, which he had built. Ethnic communities also formed mutual help networks, which provided help for the most vulnerable community members and fundraised to promote their ethnic culture at public events organized by the city and regional governments.[28]

The leaders of ethnic groups also played a major role in conflict resolution. Since many different ethnicities lived side by side in the Rostov region, everyday conflicts occurred regularly between the members of different ethnic groups, especially among the youth. Most ethnic communities in Rostov City had an assistant of the community leader responsible for youth issues, which often means using community authority to calm down the younger men. This is especially important for the Caucasian ethnicities, whose young men often conflict with the young men of other ethnic groups. To resolve such conflicts, ethnic community leaders get together, find a compromise, and then use their authority to convince their youth to back off. Universities in Rostov, which admit a significant number of Caucasian youth, use this ethnic community resource to incentivize these students to study and behave properly. My interviewee shared a story of how she once attended a university meeting with Chechen students, the university administration, faculty, and the leaders of the Chechen community. The university administration and faculty publicly discussed the performance and behavior of every student, one by one. The head of the Chechen diaspora emphasized that the students should be worthy representatives of the Chechen people and took notes about every student to notify their families back in Chechnya. My interviewee said it was a very effective disciplining tool because these students try to avoid bringing shame to their families at all costs.[29]

Among the Russians, informal social order maintenance and conflict resolution are often performed by Cossacks, especially in the rural areas and small towns.

---

[27] Тюхтенева, "Личность и общество у алтайцев: От родовой принадлежности до общеалтайской идентичности," 80.
[28] Interview Ros-11.
[29] Interview Ros-08, Ros-11.

Their authority among the Russian population is not nearly as strong as the authority of non-Russian ethnic leaders in their communities, but the functions they fulfill are often similar. Order maintenance may manifest in the form of Cossacks being included in police patrols. In some villages, Cossack atamans work together with social workers to oversee families in difficult life situations. They involve children from such families in educational activities with other Cossacks to reduce deviant behavior among them. Cossacks are also sometimes called to resolve conflicts to prevent these conflicts from turning into even bigger ones if they occur between different ethnic groups.[30]

One of my interviewees told me a personal story illustrating the way social inclusion, exclusion, and authority work in the region. Her family, ethnic Armenians, relocated to a small town in Rostov region from Grozny, the capital of Chechnya, during the war in the 1990s. Once they moved, her uncle got to know a local Cossack ataman and convinced her father to join Cossacks because he felt that it would help them to integrate in the local community. They applied to become Cossacks, went through the approval process, and obtained official IDs as Cossacks. Her father's ID read "Cossack-electrician." Sometime later, they had a conflict with an alcoholic neighbor, who called Cossacks to help oust "these Black non-Russians."[31] However, when her father showed them the Cossack ID, these men said, "We apologize, brother," and retreated.[32] What mattered in this case was not the essence of the conflict but the social boundaries between "us" and "them."

The Legitimate Authority of Nonstate Community Leaders

In an environment where nonstate groups play a major role in ordering social life, significant community support before assuming any office is crucial for a politician or a state official who wants to be seen as a legitimate authority. For example, in Altai,

> when a person, who has few relatives and, therefore, small support, tries to enter politics, people listen to him and think: "Who is that? Whose is he? How did you even get here? I understand, those people [from larger clans] are powerful, but you?"[33]

---

[30] Interviews Ros-01, Ros-12, Ros-13.
[31] The racialized and derogatory category for the people from the North Caucasus in Russia is "Black."
[32] Interview Ros-01.
[33] Interview Altai-07.

Unlike in statist societies in the Kemerovo region and Tatarstan, in the Rostov region and Altai association with the state did not endow a public figure with legitimate authority and did not guarantee people's cooperation, but status in a nonstate community did. For state governance to be minimally effective, the state in these regions had to recruit the already existing informal leaders because people would cooperate with them but not with someone they saw as an outsider. I heard the most vivid example of this phenomenon, in the Rostov region, in an interview with a former municipal employee with several decades of experience. He said:

> Everything comes down to informal leaders. If such a leader emerges and takes an office, everything works smoothly. Residential committees[34] always speak their own language. The [external] authorities have never been praised regardless of personalities, but it is a different matter when an informal leader is elected—a leader of a homeowners' association, of a small dwelling, of a block or a street—and he gathers a team of like-minded informal leaders.... I can bring many examples from my practice.
>
> In Sovetskii district,[35] where I worked, there is a village Stepanovskaia, 11 thousand people. It was impossible to get their cooperation on anything. Even during the Civil War, Budyonny[36] was extremely surprised that this village was not burned down, he just could not do anything with it. And it remains the same today.
>
> When I started my job, I was sent to oversee this territory. I could not understand what those people wanted and why we couldn't resolve any issues—until I got the main principle of doing things there. They have powerful clans and traditions, and they don't regard as their own even the people who work in sovkhoz across the road, it's very strict there. Cossacks are particularly powerful. I tried to obtain community support on different issues, gathered them in a public hall,[37] it was packed, there weren't enough chairs, and I spoke for a long time trying to convince them until I almost lost my voice. They applauded, I got out, and they said:
>
> - Thank you! Everything you said was right. But we, Stepanovtsy, are not going to do that. We are going to do exactly the opposite.
> - But you just agreed!
> - We simply felt bad for you.

---

[34] The interviewee used the Russian term "ТОС"—territorial public self-governance.
[35] Proper names in this quote have been changed.
[36] A famous Marshall of the Soviet Union who played a major role in Bolsheviks' victory in the Russian Civil War 1917–1922.
[37] В Доме Культуры.

I could not understand what they needed. Then it occurred to me that I should have dealt with informal leaders—it was either an ataman or the head of a block committee.... I began to work through them. They repeated my words exactly, including commas and periods, and were immediately cheered by the people! Everything gets done! And you don't need any gatherings and discussions. I tell him: say in your own words, and everything is done in three seconds. Any issues—social ones and even fundraisers. The [municipal] authorities should not try hard to convince people. You may be a thousand times right and convincing, but they are not going to do it anyway. But if their own person says it, they will go over and above. In this Stepanovka, they repaired the bridge between their village and Alekseyevsk to avoid a long detour. 80% of the necessary funds were collected from the people and only 20% came from the village administration and the municipality. The money was gathered without any order from the top because the informal leaders announced the call. Before that, the issue remained unresolved for decades because the municipality tried to require something from the people, to say that they had to do it. And the situation did not change until the call went through the informal leaders, which was a completely different game.

We underestimate it. We frequently come to power and do not take advantage of this, which is unfortunate.[38]

The message that my interviewee delivered to the villagers in this example did not matter; what mattered was the messenger. When the messenger was one of "us," the message was believed; when the message came from outside of the group, it was distrusted despite any rational arguments. Importantly, the group defining "us" was not the state—it was an informal, nonstate community, of which there were many in the region. This interviewee worked in multiple municipalities across the region and emphasized that what I quoted was only one of the many examples from his practice in both rural and urban settings.

Centralized Public Organizations in the Kemerovo Region and Tatarstan

People's views of the state in the four regions directly influenced the type of grassroots organizations that structured people's everyday life. In statist societies of the Kemerovo region and Tatarstan, people believed it was normal and right that the state took the lead in community development as well as in fixing social problems. It was not a consumerist attitude of expecting "free stuff"—quite the

---

[38] Interview Ros-03.

opposite, people considered it morally right to participate and invest their efforts and resources in common projects. They, however, expected that the state would initiate and direct those projects and appreciated it when state officials lived up to these expectations.

Kemerovo's Aman Tuleyev and Tatarstan's presidents have lived up to them. Since their early days in power, they used the state apparatus to create and maintain grassroots community organizations, continuing or reviving the Soviet tradition.[39] Both regions had multiple organizational hierarches that penetrated society, extended the reach of state apparatus into people's everyday lives, and made the state work as the social glue that connected individuals into a community.[40] Below, I will use the examples of community centers in Kemerovo City and youth organizations in Tatarstan to show how they worked to maintain the role of the state as the community leader.

Community Centers and Residential Councils in Kemerovo

Elena's Residential Council

My first encounter with residential councils in Kemerovo City was through Elena,[41] the owner of the apartment I rented while doing fieldwork whom we already met earlier in this chapter. When she learned about my interest in social policy and community programs in the region, she was clearly pleased and proud that a researcher from outside of the region and even outside of the country noticed that Kemerovo had what she called a developed system of social support. Elena lived in a new residential neighborhood; at the time of our conversation, it had about 3,000 residents, but the plan was to expand it to 30,000. "I can tell you about the social programs in our neighborhood," she said. "We have a residential council that organizes many of them."[42]

The residential council, of which Elena was a member, took care of various local issues and ran community programs. Neighborhood infrastructure was one of them: right after the council was created, it requested extra walkways and storm drains from the construction company. It also developed a set of rules of communal life covering such issues as handling construction garbage, dog walking, or using communal spaces. To organize community events, the council pulled together available community resources. For example, they could ask a resident who worked in the entertainment industry to borrow a life-size

---

[39] Friedgut, *Political Participation in the USSR*, chap. 4.
[40] For a similar account of state-led civil society in Tatarstan, see Brunarska, "Understanding Sociopolitical Engagement of Society in Russia."
[41] The name has been changed.
[42] Interview Kem-13 and fieldnotes.

puppet; or find a volunteer who knew how to do face painting for children; or invite a school band or a dance team to perform at the event. They also looked for sponsors among the local businesses who could provide small prizes for competitions.

The most interesting thing about this residential council, though, was that it was not created by the residents. Its creation was initiated by the city administration, which reached out to the residents as soon as they moved into the first few buildings. The city officials suggested that the residents created a local council, which would help with various aspects of neighborhood development. From the very beginning, this suggestion assumed that the council would include the representatives of the city government as well as the heads of the infrastructure management company and the local school. Besides them, it involved the representatives of each residential building as well as the activists "who wanted the neighborhood to be comfortable, clean, and fun."[43]

In Elena's words, such partnership with the city administration had many advantages. For example, when they requested extra walkways and storm drains from the construction company, the support of the city administration, whose representative was on the council, made communication with the construction company very smooth. When the council worked on the community rules, the city government's staff lawyer helped with legally correct wordings. This partnership made it easy to discuss public safety issues with the local police representative who made sure that residents' safety concerns were resolved in a timely manner. And even for the community events, the city provided a small budget. Although most of the community work was performed by volunteer residents on the council, the council itself was created and closely supervised by the city government.

The Infrastructure of Residential Councils and Community Centers in Kemerovo City

As I learned later, Elena's council was only one of over 7,000 residential councils in Kemerovo City.[44] The city government began to create them in 1997, when Aman Tuleyev became the governor and Vladimir Mikhailov, his long-term political ally, served as Kemerovo City mayor.[45] Since 1997, the development of residential councils has always been present in city development plans with a clear

---

[43] Interview Kem-13.
[44] In Russian they are called TOSes, which stands for *territorial'noe obshchestvennoe samoupravlenie* (territorial public self-governance). For an account of how they work in another region with similar conclusions, see, for example, Polishchuk, Rubin, and Shagalov, "Managing Collective Action."
[45] Тотыш, "С пользой и интересом;" Итоги работы с населением за 2016 г.; Mikhailov had been in office for over 26 years (1986–2013), after which he retired, citing health reasons.

goal to increase the number of councils and activists.[46] By 2001, more than 7,000 people had been enlisted, but it seems that coordination of such a big number of volunteers became too burdensome for the city government and required additional midlevel structures.

To facilitate interactions with residential councils and neighborhood communities, the city government came up with the idea of community centers, which were created using neighborhood police stations as the base. In the city of Kemerovo, whose population in 2002 was 485,000 people,[47] there were 49 such police stations covering the territory of the city. Officers at these stations handled domestic conflicts, watched out for unsupervised children on the streets, and made sure that the neighborhood was clean and its safety infrastructure was functioning properly.

In 2002 the city government named creation of community centers one of its major tasks for the nearest future, and by the end of 2006, all 49 community centers that were still functioning in 2019 were in place.[48] The literal translation of the Russian name of these community centers is "centers for working with the population."[49] The newly organized community centers used the physical infrastructure of police stations as a starting point with subsequent expansion, renovation, and hiring of new personnel. If the area had apartment buildings and dorms, a community center could occupy several restructured apartments or dorm rooms on the ground floor. In some other cases, old buildings that used to be social infrastructure in the Soviet Union (for example, former movie theaters) were renovated to become community centers. In several cases, new buildings were constructed either specifically for community centers or in conjunction with other public organizations (e.g., a local public library).[50]

Like residential councils, community centers were a product of the city administration initiative, limited state resources, and wide input from the community. While the salary of community center inspectors and small funding for operational expenses came from the city budget,[51] the cost of renovation was frequently covered by local businesses. For example, a newspaper publication reports that while the cost of renovation of one of the old movie theaters "Komsomolets" was 8.5 million rubles, the city government only paid 660,000.

---

[46] See, for example, "Город: анализ, успехи, проблемы, перспективы;" Итоги работы с населением за 2015 г.; Итоги работы с населением за 2016 г.; Администрация города Кемерово, Постановление от 16 сентября 2016 года N 2382 "Об утверждении муниципальной программы, 'Развитие общественных инициатив в городе Кемерово' на 2017—2019 годы."
[47] Росстат, *Российский статистический ежегодник. 2014*, Table 4.14.
[48] "Город: анализ, успехи, проблемы, перспективы;" Пресс-служба администрации города, "Пункты стали центрами." Two centers were recently merged with other ones, so there were 47 of them functioning in the early 2020s.
[49] Центры по работе с населением.
[50] "...и много радости;" Логинова, "Шахтерский край города Кемерово."
[51] Фефелова, "Город делится опытом."

The report does not reveal who covered the rest, but the only conceivable option is that local businesses paid for the rest as well as for landscaping of the nearby territory.[52] In another case, a local meat-producing enterprise financed renovation of several dorm rooms where the center would be placed and purchased furniture and appliances for it.[53] In 2009 one municipality in Kemerovo, which turned 65 years old, announced an initiative "A gift to the neighborhood" and managed to get donations from 500 businesses. More than 850,000 rubles of those donations were used to buy equipment for three community centers, a few schools, and a local health center. More than 24 million rubles went to infrastructure renovations and landscaping.[54] In addition to local businesses, the deputies of the city and regional parliaments have helped with their own funds to modernize and equip the centers.[55] Some of these donations might have been driven by a sincere desire to improve community life. Others might have had the goal to demonstrate loyalty to the authorities in order to shield the business from unplanned tax and safety audits, refusal of governmental contracts, and so forth. In either case, though, businesses were responding to the expectation of both society and the state that everyone should contribute what they could to state-led initiatives to improve community life.

In 2006, after the formation of the community center network was completed, the city government intensified the creation of residential councils and brought this work to a new level. This time, it made an effort to standardize the councils' work and introduce the elements of bureaucratic workflow. It issued a decree deliberating the procedures for creating residential councils, including a special registration certificate, IDs for their members, sample charters, and two volumes describing best practices in the work of these organizations.[56] This decree sped up the process of establishing new councils, and by the end of 2006, there were 6,366 of them in the city (Figure 3.1).[57] Given that in 2006, the population of Kemerovo was 520,000 people,[58] every council worked with 82 people on average. Over 10 years later, the number of councils only increased by about 22%, and every council worked with 71 people on average—it seems that the number of councils was at its capacity for the city. The number of listed activists, though,

---

[52] Пресс-служба администрации города, "Центры есть, работа будет."
[53] "Равных нет в рукопашном бою."
[54] "Год юбилея."
[55] "К кемеровчанам—с отчетом."
[56] "ТОС—самая близкая власть."
[57] It is usually unclear how exactly the reported numbers were counted. My best guess is that these statistics summed up TOSes of different levels (say, a TOS in an apartment building and a TOS of the whole street where that apartment building is situated). Since I cannot clearly distinguish the upper-level TOSes from the lower-level ones and the upper-level TOSes probably make up only a small share of the total number of TOSes, I will treat all TOSes as lower-level ones for my approximate calculations of society penetration further in this paragraph.
[58] Росстат, *Российский статистические ежегодник. 2007*, Table 4.14.

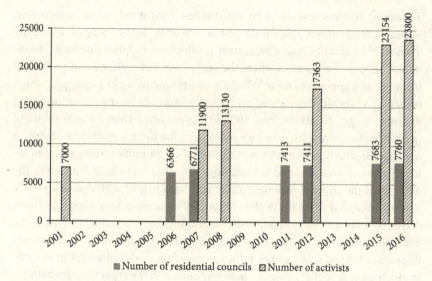

Figure 3.1 Available statistics on the number of residential councils and activists in Kemerovo City.

Sources: Numbers taken from Город: анализ, успехи, проблемы, перспективы. Кемерово. N 23. 2002-06-07; Тотыш, Наталья. С пользой и интересом. Кемерово. N 51. 2006-12-22; ТОС — самая близкая власть. Кемерово. N 4. 2007-01-26; "Кто, если не мы?" Кемерово. N 4. 2009-01-23; Работа с населением. http://www.kemerovo.ru/?page=357, access date April 22, 2016; Итоги работы с населением за 2016 г. http://www.kemerovo.ru/administration/rabota_s_naseleni em_.html, access date March 29, 2017.

has continued to increase throughout the 2000s and 2010s: if in 2001, approximately every 70th person in the city was an activist, by 2016, it was already every 23rd one (see Figure 3.2).[59]

Activities of Community Centers and Residential Councils

When I was in Kemerovo in March 2014, I visited one of the community centers. It was situated on the first floor of a residential building, apparently in a renovated apartment, and had a separate entrance with a porch on the backside of the building right by the children's playground. A police workstation was situated next door and had a similar porch. In a narrow hallway of the community center, there were a couple of side tables with a booklet about citywide competitions of community projects, a printed report about the activities of community centers in 2013, and several books, including a published collection of autographs given to Aman Tuleyev by famous people.

---

[59] Kemerovo population in 2002 was 485,000 (data for 2001 are not available), and in 2016 it was 553,000 (Росстат, *Российский статистические ежегодник. 2016*, Table 4.14).

TEAM STATE VERSUS OUTSIDER STATE   83

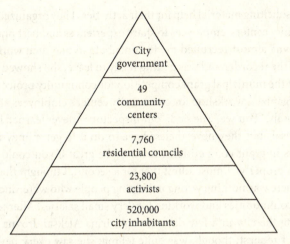

Figure 3.2 The organizational hierarchy of residential councils and community centers in Kemerovo by 2016.

I talked to Irina Aleksandrovna,[60] the director of the center, at her desk in the administrative room. It seemed there was only one room for the employees: it had several desks, and on the other side of the room, a few people were having a heated work meeting. Irina Aleksandrovna offered me a cup of tea, suggested that I ask her questions, and immediately began speaking before I was able to ask anything. She said that there were 48[61] community centers in the city, and they worked with various population groups—the elderly, youth, teenagers, children—by organizing community events as well as providing support for hobby clubs and extracurricular activities. The big drawback of this work, she said, was that the centers' employees did not have any special qualifications for this kind of work. They were only able to do it because the centers attracted enthusiasts who had a passion for crafts, sports, music, and so forth, and were eager to share it with the community. The centers would then provide the room and supplies for these activities and help inform the community about them.

Identifying the activists and community resources that the center could pull together was clearly a big part of Irina Aleksandrovna's job and the job of other community centers' directors. They worked closely with the residential councils on their territories as well as with public schools, libraries, and Veterans' Councils.[62] They reached out to private businesses and state-owned enterprises

---

[60] The name has been changed. Interview Kem-06.
[61] The number of community centers varied slightly in different sources and interviews because at any given moment in time, some centers might have been opening or closing.
[62] Veterans' Councils constitute a network of organizations for the elderly in Russia. This network originated from the popular movement of World War II veterans in the Soviet Union. See Chapter 4 for more information about these organizations.

in the area, soliciting material help for their activities. They organized workshops for community centers' employees to share experiences and best practices. Irina Aleksandrovna almost recruited me to contribute to one such workshop. After I turned off the recorder and was getting ready to leave, she showed me the brochure about the municipal grant competition for community projects and asked if I could organize a workshop for community center's employees about writing grant proposals. "You see," she said, "our inspectors[63] never learned how to write those proposals but they nevertheless have to do it to get money for community projects in grant competitions. It would be great if you could teach them how to do it properly." I must admit that for a second, I thought that I could do that since there was nothing wrong in helping people who were sincerely trying to develop communities and working for very small salaries. After learning that I was leaving the city in a few days, though, Irina Aleksandrovna gave up on the idea. Her request, though, was quite telling: she saw every new encounter as a chance to recruit an activist who might contribute to the work the center had been doing. And my reaction was telling, too: It felt very natural to respond positively to such a request and make a good use of your time and expertise by helping a community cause.

From Irina Aleksandrovna's interview as well as from my later reading of media publications and community centers' websites and casual conversations with the people, I learned that community centers and residential councils did a lot more than handling hobby clubs.[64] They were designed to be an amalgam of community support and social security provided by the state. Are you a pensioner having trouble navigating healthcare services? You can go to your residential council or community center, and someone there will give a call to the hospital and help you sort it out. Are you going through a divorce and have questions about dividing the ownership of your apartment? You can ask your questions at a free legal consultation that your community center organizes every few weeks. Are you a teenager whose parents are addicted to alcohol and do not pay much attention to your life? A community center inspector can help you navigate your way to a community college and help you find a summer job. Community centers together with the residential council activists would regularly mobilize community resources to help those in need: they could call for food and clothes donations or ask local businesses to help pay for school supplies for the children in the poorest families. They would also recruit volunteers among schoolchildren to help the elderly around the house and garden, especially if these people were in poor health and living in private home with little modern infrastructure.

---

[63] Inspectors is the official title of community center employees.
[64] Appendix 3 has the list of sources on Kemerovo City community centers and residential councils, on which the description is based.

Besides facilitating help to the most vulnerable, community centers and residential councils also addressed general community concerns. As Elena's example above illustrates, the issues related to infrastructure or safety were frequently resolved through community centers. Newspaper sources show that the centers regularly organized meetings with local authorities—for example, municipal government officials, the chief of the major utility company, or local police chairman—where residents could voice their concerns directly rather than through bureaucratic channels. Community centers would also call for volunteers to maintain the neighborhood territory: to clean the surrounding areas, help with snow removal, or perform minor landscaping and repairs. The centers would provide volunteers with necessary equipment and might organize a tea party after the job is done.

Finally, a lot of work of community centers was geared to make people's life more fun. They provided space for the already mentioned hobby clubs that ranged from gardening, handcrafting, folk singing, and dancing to chess, poetry, Slavic culture, Orthodox Christians, and mature Internet users. All community centers had sports equipment (volleyball and soccer balls, badminton and ping pong rackets, hockey sticks, pucks, and balls, etc.) that they lent for free to the people from the neighborhood. This equipment was most in demand by schoolchildren from poorer families and pensioners who organized "health groups" that would regularly meet up for a light physical exercise or team sports. Other resources that community centers lent out included fiction books, movies, and board games. Community center inspectors and volunteers also actively organized leisure time of schoolchildren during the school year and holidays. They took children for historical tours around the city, organized trips to theaters, riverboat tours, and meetings with local celebrities (writers, athletes, activists, etc.). Children could participate in sports or art contests with prizes. During the summertime, community centers recruited volunteers among college students to organize game activities. Teaming up with schools, community centers carried out "patriotic education" events, usually related to World War II. They might take place in a school museum, a community center, or some special place in the area—a monument or a memory board with the names of fallen soldiers.

Community centers' activities involved not only children and pensioners, as many holiday celebrations and cultural, educational, artistic, and sports events were organized for the community at large. Celebrations took place on all major holidays, whether state, orthodox religious, or traditional Russian. For example, on the New Year's Eve, the neighborhood residents enjoyed costume parties, performances with traditional Russian characters, potlucks, fireworks, contests with prizes, dancing, and karaoke. Other celebrations were related to national or regional events and initiatives: for example, many community centers organized parties on the Miner's Day, which was widely celebrated in the region, and devoted community events to the Family Year, which was a nation-wide initiative in 2008. An important part of these events was the recognition of outstanding people in the community with presents, certificates, or just special attention of the public. For example, the elderly received signs of recognition on their anniversaries when they turn 85 or older. Military veterans were recognized during patriotic events. Parents with many children received their share of recognition, and the best activists were rewarded with prizes or titles.

Community centers and residential councils were not the only state-led organizations in Kemerovo region that did community work. Another network, no less impressive in size, was the region-wide organization of Veterans' Councils that worked with over 700,000 retirees and had about 1,900 primary territorial organizations.[65] The regional Women's Council had over 400 primary organizations.[66] Student Labor Squads[67] were present in all higher education institutions in the region, and the list goes on. All these organizations were driven by the masses of volunteers who had an "active life stance"—an expression I encountered frequently in Kemerovo—meaning that they were not indifferent to the interests of their communities and the region as a whole and wanted to contribute to the common good. Kemerovo regional authorities either created or actively supported these organizations providing the molds that this grassroots energy could fill.

Youth Organizations in Tatarstan

The Origins of Tatarstan's Youth Organizations
In Tatarstan, the most developed network of state-led community organizations focused its efforts on youth.[68] This orientation stemmed from a specific problem that the regional authorities were initially trying to solve—the problem of youth street gangs. In many cities of the late Soviet Union, informal youth groups gained popularity over the weakening institutions of the Soviet state, and in some of the cities, including Kazan', the capital of Tatarstan, many of these informal groups were street gangs. They started as groups of mostly teenage boys and young men who would socialize on the city streets and form territorial communities. Many of them gathered at informal gyms usually

---

[65] See more information on Veterans' Councils in Chapter 4.
[66] Общественная палата Кемеровской области, "Союз женщин Кузбасса."
[67] In Russian—студотряды, student teams put together for summer work in a particular occupation.
[68] Youth has been an important group targeted by the state at the national level as well; see, for example, Hemment, *Youth Politics in Putin's Russia*.

situated in the basement of apartment buildings where they would build up their bodies, show off their masculinity, and prepare to guard their territory from the members of other gangs. In the 1980s and the 1990s, the clashes between the gangs turned into full-blown "asphalt wars" with multiple fatalities as the gangs tried to take control of the nascent private businesses in the city. The gangs seriously threatened public security and became a problem that the regional government was committed to resolve.[69]

To deal with the problem, Tatarstan authorities created an alternative communal space for children, teenagers, and youth. In the late 1980s, the regional government set up a network of residential teenager clubs with many of them located in major cities. Most of these clubs started as sports groups with different specializations. These clubs occupied the first floors of apartment buildings or their basements. All of them had coaches on staff and sports equipment; some even had access to larger sports facilities.[70] The clubs attracted children and teenagers from the neighborhood, including current gang members, and provided an alternative community and socialization space to keep them off the streets. Some coaches in these clubs were highly respected among the young men and could potentially influence their life choices.[71]

After the dissolution of the Soviet Union, residential teenager clubs were promptly transferred to the jurisdiction of municipalities, which continued supporting and developing them. By the early 2000s, the number of clubs grew to over 200, with 5–6 employees in each. Some of the clubs would still be primarily concentrated on sports but many developed other activities from music, dance, and theater to drug use prevention programs. In addition to the groups with a focus on a certain activity, many clubs had "free attendance groups," which provided space and resources for the children and teenagers to spend their free time. The clubs also organized wider public events of every imaginable kind for children or teenagers: sports competitions, quests, concerts, theater performances, art exhibitions, public lectures, intellectual competitions, environmental campaigns, and so forth. The available statistics shows that 20%–25%

---

[69] Stephenson, "The Kazan Leviathan"; Interviews Kaz-03, Kaz-06.

[70] Interviews Kaz-03, Kaz-06; Министерство по делам молодежи и спорту Республики Татарстан, *Материалы к коллегии "Итоги 2002 года и задачи Министерства по делам молодежи и спорту Республики Татарстан на 2003 год."*

[71] The social network VKontakte has a group "Казанский феномен" (Kazan' phenomenon) (https://vk.com/kazan_opg) that documents the history of youth street gangs in Kazan'. The group has over 5,000 subscribers, and one of the pictures uploaded by users shows a number of young men, many of them topless, in a small gym with a bodybuilder poster on the wall (https://vk.com/kazan_opg?z=photo-164753307_456241087%2Falbum-164753307_259120533, access date January 27, 2020). The caption says that the picture was taken in 1995 in Antei Club—the residential teenager club that still exists in the center of Kazan'—and that the men there belonged to three different street gangs. Together with them there is Gennadii Andreevich, a famous coach from the 1980s and 1990s who trained many "patsans" (gang members).

of the 7- to 18-year-old cohort in the region were attending the regular groups, while virtually everyone of that age participated in at least some public events.[72]

The Infrastructure and Activities of Youth Organizations

Residential teenager clubs were not the only organizational network that worked with youth. Since the early 2000s, Tatarstan authorities created a centralized infrastructure of organizations supported by the regional government and coordinated by the Ministry of Youth Affairs (Figure 3.3). One of the units of the Ministry, the Republican Center of Youth, Innovation, and Prevention Programs, functioned as a think tank for this network, publishing analytic papers, informational booklets, and collections of best practices related to working with children and youth.[73] Other units, such as the Youth Center of the Republic of Tatarstan and the Republican Center for the Recreation and Summer Employment of Children and Teenagers, helped coordinate the regionwide programs and events that involved multiple organizations. Yet others, such as the Centers "Volga" and "Chernomorets," provided physical facilities for summer camps, competitions, and training sessions, which multiple organizations used.[74]

About 20 social work and psychological services specialized on helping children, teenagers, and youth who might already be in a difficult life situation.[75] I attended one such service center situated on the first floor of an apartment building, similar to residential teenager clubs. Shortly after I came in, the center's staff conducted a conflict-resolution workshop for a group of 11- to 13-year-olds, which I was able to observe. The psychologist talked about the types of conflicts among teenagers, the ways to identify conflicting interests, and the strategies of moderation. When I talked to the center's staff later, they told me that they closely worked with schools to identify children who might benefit from such training and that the best moderators are frequently those kids who used to be the biggest troublemakers. They believed it was the effect of social inclusion and responsibility,

---

[72] Министерство по делам молодежи, спорту и туризму РТ, Республиканский центр молодежных, инновационных и профилактических программ, *Деятельность учреждений по месту жительства*; Министерство по делам молодежи, спорту и туризму РТ, *Материалы коллегии "Итоги работы Министерства по делам молодежи, спорту и туризму Республики Татарстан за 2008 год."* Calculating the share of children and youth that participated in regular groups and larger events is difficult because the methods of collecting statistics in governmental reports are unclear. It seems that the number of participants at all the events was summed up without any attempt to understand how many unique individuals were among the participants. Also, the age limits of the events are usually flexible, which creates an uncertainty about the denominator—the size of the corresponding cohort in the population.

[73] See one of the pages on the Center's website titled "The Analysis Hub" (http://rcmipp.tatarstan.ru/rus/analiticheskiy-hab.htm, access date January 27, 2020).

[74] See the list of organizations set up by the Ministry of Youth Affairs on the ministry's website (http://minmol.tatarstan.ru/rus/podvedy.htm, access date June 28, 2019).

[75] The governmental website detitatarstana.ru listed 21 such services (https://www.detitatarstana.ru/-----, access date June 28, 2019). As of January 2020, the website has been taken offline, possibly because of organizational restructuring inside the Ministry for Youth Affairs.

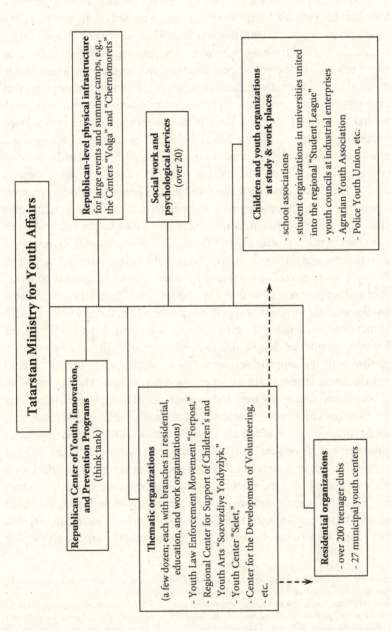

Figure 3.3 Children and youth organizations in Tatarstan in mid-2010s.

which the teenagers felt after they practiced conflict-resolution techniques in their social environment. Besides the program on conflict resolution, the center ran a psychological help service, a legal service, a service on addiction prevention and help, and a program of street work that was focused on unsupervised children.[76]

Community work with the youth beyond school age was less residentially based and more oriented to the young people's study and workplaces. Those young people who decided to continue their education could join student organizations in their institutions. All universities and community colleges had student councils and several student organizations. Some of them matched the themes developed in teenager clubs—sports, music, dance, theater, intellectual competitions, and so forth—while others might be related to the professional skills that the students were developing, such as social work, law clinic, or a service of public opinion polls.[77] For those who completed their studies and joined the workforce, most large industrial enterprises in the region had youth councils that organized events and clubs and helped coordinate some benefits programs for the youth between the management of the enterprises and the regional government.[78] Young people living in rural areas could benefit from the work of the Agrarian Youth Association, which, along with organizing community events, worked to develop entrepreneurship and support new agricultural businesses.[79] Additional residential-based community work for the youth was performed by the 27 municipal youth centers. They functioned much like residential teenager clubs: provided space for various youth interest groups and organized mass public events.[80]

Together with the separate organizations for different age groups, several regionwide thematic organizations cut across different ages. They all had a regional center and frequently used the organizational and physical infrastructure of teenager clubs, youth centers, educational establishments, and even private businesses to support their local branches. For example, the Youth Law Enforcement Movement "Forpost," which was established by the regional authorities in 1998 to counteract the influence of street gangs, worked with schools, community colleges, universities, and large employers. The Republican Center "Forpost" coordinated the movement, which included almost 1,400 squads with 18,000 participants: 1,057 in schools, 93 in colleges and universities, and 243 at employment or residential sites.[81] The squads were mostly helping

---

[76] Interview Kaz-07.

[77] Interview Kaz-09. I checked several websites of universities and community colleges in Tatarstan, and all of them had a similar profile of student organizations.

[78] Министерство по делам молодежи, спорту и туризму РТ, *Материалы коллегии "Итоги работы Министерства по делам молодежи, спорту и туризму Республики Татарстан за 2005 год и задачи на 2006 год"*; Министерство по делам молодежи, спорту и туризму РТ, *Материалы коллегии "Итоги работы Министерства по делам молодежи, спорту и туризму Республики Татарстан за 2008 год."*

[79] Аграрное молодежное объединение Республики Татарстан.

[80] https://www.detitatarstana.ru/--c17oj, access date June 28, 2019.

[81] Государственное бюджетное учреждение Республиканский центр молодежных формирований по охране общественного порядка "Форпост", "Об организации."

the police to maintain public safety and counteract street crime, but they also participated in public patriotic events, sports competitions, and drug prevention or road safety campaigns. Children as young as 10 years old were recruited to the youngest squads, where they were taught the goals of the movement, received physical training, and began participating in squad activities. Older participants had classes of martial arts, shooting, marching, and survival skills, which they practiced at their squads' locations and in summer camps. The Center "Forpost" also regularly presented the most active participants with awards and prizes.[82]

"Forpost" was only one example of a regionwide thematic youth organization in Tatarstan, while there were many others. The Regional Center for Support of Children's and Youth Arts "Sozvezdiye Yoldyzlyk," to take another example, supported popular music, film, and theater. It worked with educational organizations and residential clubs across the region to find the most talented singers, dancers, actors, or filmmakers among children and youth. The organization provided them with additional resources and training, and then promoted their work at the regional and national level. The Youth Center "Selet" was dedicated to intellectual development and the arts. They ran regular groups in some schools and organized competitions and summer camps on topics from programming to poetry. The Center for the Development of Volunteering coordinated and provided instructional support to over 700 volunteer organizations in the region.[83] These are only a few examples of possibly a few dozen thematic organizations that worked with children and youth in Tatarstan.[84]

Although Tatarstan authorities have initially focused their community-building efforts on the young people, later they started to expand this work to involve other age cohorts. For example, psychological services for youth have been recently integrated into a more comprehensive and centralized system of psychological support for all population groups. This system is still managed by the Ministry for Youth Affairs but reaches out to other regional ministries, media, and academic organizations.[85] Since 2012, the regional government has also been building "village clubs," that is, community centers in villages across the region, which may combine club space, a library, a medical care center, a kindergarten, and a school. By the end of 2018, there were 285 such clubs in Tatarstan.[86]

---

[82] The information comes from the official website of the Republican Center "Forpost" (http://rcforpost.tatarstan.ru/rus/index.htm, access date June 28, 2019) and VKontakte Forpost group (https://vk.com/rcforpost, access date June 28, 2019).

[83] Interview Kaz-03; АНО "Информационно-ресурсный центр добровольчества Республики Татарстан."

[84] The total number of these organizations is difficult to determine because some of them were formally state organizations, other were civil society ones, and yet others existed in a dual form—I discuss this issue in the next section of this chapter.

[85] Министерство по делам молодежи Республики Татарстан, "Модель системы психологической помощи населению в Республике Татарстан."

[86] "Число новых сельских клубов в Татарстане к концу года вырастет до 285."

State Leadership beyond the Formal State

Similar to the Kemerovo region, an important characteristic of this organizational infrastructure is that its creation was initiated by state representatives who recruited activists among the public. Such state initiative connected even organizations outside of the formal hierarchy, that is, private or nongovernmental, into one integrated system under the state leadership.

One example of such organizational integration concerns charity donations from large businesses. Similar to the Kemerovo region, where the regional government signed official agreements with big industrial enterprises that specified their social obligations,[87] charity donations in Tatarstan were also regulated at the regional level. The Tatarstan president had a deputy on social issues who put together a list of social projects in need of support, and businesses could choose one from the offered options. Every year, the Tatarstan government organized a competition "The Philanthropist of the Year," where it recognized the businesses that made most significant contributions to social projects.[88]

Another example of organizational integration were NGOs created by state employees. Some of them were created from the top as classic GONGOs; others might be bottom-up initiatives of professionals working for the state, cutting in the middle between a state-initiated program and a grassroots initiative. As one of my interviewees in Tatarstan said, "there are civil society organizations, there are pseudo–civil society organizations, and there are organizations that change their faces once in a while."[89] She herself worked in two organizations, both named "Vybor (Choice)" and having the same legal address. One of them was the municipal center for addiction prevention, the other a public foundation. The public foundation had a few external people among the founders, but most of the foundation staff simultaneously worked in the municipal center. Having two organizational forms allowed this group of professionals to do more for the cause about which they all cared deeply. Through the foundation, they were able to work with different age groups, establish close contacts with medical professionals, and engage in legislative advocacy. At the same time, the status of the municipal center gave them better access to municipal and regional resources and the organizational infrastructure that allowed scaling up their prevention programs. The employees of some other state units established pseudo–civil society organizations because it was a convenient way to obtain additional state resources earmarked as grants for civil society. Pulling together their resources as a governmental unit with those they could receive as an NGO, they were able

---

[87] For example, see "Кузбасское соглашение между Федерацией профсоюзных организаций Кузбасса, Коллегией Администрации Кемеровской области и работодателями Кемеровской области на 2010–2012 годы."
[88] Interview Kaz-04.
[89] Interview Kaz-06.

to do more for the programs they planned and, as an additional bonus, include the interaction with civil society in their reports.

The most vivid example, however, of how the state shaped the activities of private organizations came from a small private university in Kazan'. This university, like many others, had quite a few student organizations, and I asked the university's provost for student affairs who took the initiative to create them. She answered: "No, there is no initiative as such; there is a hierarchy."[90] It turned out that the creation of student organizations was "the functional responsibility of the provost for student affairs." She envisioned student organizations in her institution and her own work as an integral part of the regionwide system of working with youth. Although her institution was a private one and even public universities in Russia are officially in the federal jurisdiction, she attended a monthly meeting of the Coordination Council of Provosts for Student Affairs, which took place at the regional Ministry of Youth Affairs. Besides the provosts, there was usually an assigned coordinator from the Ministry, the deputy minister, and the head of a similar municipal committee participating in the meeting.

During the meeting, ministry officials informed participants about planned regionwide programs and events, allowed them to ask questions, and assigned tasks. For example, every year there is a regional festival called "The Student Spring." Every year, the ministry sets the themes and priorities of the festival. The universities then organize it within the framework set by the ministry while actively involving the student organizations in their institutions. "It is not like I do what I want," my interviewee said, "otherwise there will be no common scheme, no [systematic] work with students as such." For her, the regional integration made a lot of sense because it allowed their students to participate in and benefit from large-scale projects, immediately connected them to many regional organizations, and made sure her own work served a strategic goal that extended beyond her institution.

I also asked her about the motivation of students who joined and led student organizations. In the beginning of every school year, her university had a fair where the organizations presented themselves and recruited freshmen to become their members. She said that the activists who joined the organizations were usually attracted by the opportunity to communicate not only with students from other universities but also with municipal and regional authorities. The leadership positions in the organizations, in their turn, provided an opportunity to become a public figure, a little boss, and this managerial responsibility was appealing. She recognized that occasionally students were reluctant to invest a lot of their time in some large-scale projects such as Universiade,[91] which Kazan'

---

[90] Interview Kaz-09.
[91] A version of Olympiad for university athletes.

hosted in 2013. Generally, however, she found students rather active and appreciative of the opportunities that student organizations provided for them. Just like for her, it was important for the young people to become a part of a wider cause and use their talents in a way that could be seen and appreciated by the wider community.

Decentralized Public Organizations in the Rostov Region and Altai

In the Rostov region and Altai, the structure of the public sphere was very different from that in the Kemerovo region and Tatarstan. In these antistatist societies, people considered it right when their informal leaders rather than state officials took the lead on collective projects, and viewed state initiatives as intrusion in community affairs. For them, the state's interests were different from those of their communities, and in every interaction with the state, they aimed to pursue their own interests rather than work together with the state for the common good.

As a result, no centralized organizational structures emerged in such societies. Instead, grassroots public organizations existed with no direct state involvement in their activities even if they originated from the Soviet community organizations. The organizations considered themselves autonomous entities with their own interests, rather than part of a larger system as was the case in the Kemerovo region and Tatarstan. State officials, in their turn, viewed these organizations at best as independent partners and at worst as potential moochers, not the means to extend state power deeper into society. Below, I will use the examples of youth organizations, NGOs, and labor unions in the Rostov region and Altai to show how social attitudes of resistance to the state shaped decentralized organizational environment.

Organizational Autonomy from the State

The autonomy of public organizations in the Rostov region was most apparent in the case of former Soviet organizations, such as children's and youth associations or sports clubs. After the dissolution of the Soviet Union, many of them found themselves in an uncertain situation as the all-Union organizational infrastructure ceased to exist, and their fate had to be decided by the local authorities. Unlike in Tatarstan, where the regional government immediately took over the teenager clubs, the Soviet youth organizations in Rostov—Young Pioneers and Komsomol—transformed into the Rostov Union of Children's Organizations and the Don Youth Union. These unions gave a start to multiple other initiatives and organizations, which bloomed in the region in the 1990s. The regional government and the Rostov city government continued to allocate a budget to support these organizations, but they did not have a designated state official or governmental unit that would take over their general leadership, as did the Ministry for Youth Affairs in Tatarstan.[92] About the same time, foreign donors began providing substantial financial support to Russian NGOs, which allowed these organizations to supplement limited governmental funds and expand their activities.[93] A governmental unit responsible for youth policy at the regional level appeared only in 1999 and at the municipal level in the regional capital only in 2006, about a decade later than in most Russian regions.[94]

The newly created NGOs also had very limited contacts with the state. Unlike in Tatarstan, where NGOs often shared people and material resources with state organizations working on the same issues, Rostov NGOs might not even know about the governmental resources for which they could apply. For example, I interviewed the director of an NGO "Support,"[95] which provided educational services for children with special needs. "Support" was a grassroots organization that existed for a long time without state funding. It started as a volunteer group of people who worked in different educational organizations and realized the need to have specialized programs for children with special needs. They teamed up with the parents of such children to create a weekend family club. At first, they had trouble finding a free suitable space to meet until a Catholic charity organization connected them to a Catholic church that had a proper room and allowed them to use it free of charge. Later, a priest in this church suggested applying for a grant from an international Catholic charity, which has been providing basic funding for the organization ever since. Only after the organization found this basic funding from a nonstate source, it received several municipal grants for specific projects, while also providing free training for the specialists in state organizations who worked with special needs children.[96]

This disconnect between the NGOs in the region and governmental initiatives came up in interviews as characteristic for the region. A regional state official responsible for the government's relations with civil society organizations told me a story of an NGO that worked with orphanages. Nobody in the regional government knew about it, and the NGO did not know about the government resources that might be available to them either. My interviewee learned about this

---

[92] Interview Ros-04.
[93] Interview Ros-08.
[94] Interview Ros-04.
[95] The name of the organization has been changed.
[96] Interview Ros-07.

NGO accidentally when his own auto club once participated in a charity event that this NGO organized.

I ask them:

- Are you a legal entity?
- Yes.
- Have you existed for a long time?
- Yes.
- Do you have a bank account?
- Yes.
- Do you have an accountant?
- Yes.
- I don't understand, why are you not participating in our grant competition?
- What competition?

And there are a lot of organizations like that. . . . Yes, of course, they have IKEA as a partner, so they are able to work. And the relationship with the state somehow did not happen.[97]

Both the Rostov region and Altai also had rather independent education labor unions, which was not the case in either Tatarstan or the Kemerovo region. The Altai teachers' union had a full-time lawyer who prepared official complaints to different state institutions regarding cases of labor rights violation.[98] The teachers whom I interviewed recollected a case when they received significant sums of money because the labor union was able to defend some benefits that the regional government tried to take away from them.[99] Altai regional authorities even tried to create an alternative labor union for teachers as the existing one was too independent, but their attempt finally failed and even led to a slight increase in membership for the existing union.[100] In the Rostov region, the education labor union used legal means less frequently, but it has protected its members, including students, from pressure of university administrations. The universities created their own student self-governance bodies, which were more dependent on the institutional administration. However, students were still able to organize some protests, which the administrations did not approve, since they were also union members.[101]

[97] Interview Ros-08.
[98] Interview Altai-14.
[99] Interview Altai-08.
[100] Interview Altai-14; Савин, "'Жёлтая' инициатива."
[101] Interview Ros-15.

State Strategy of Minimal Interference

This lack of centralized organizational structures was not the result of lack of initiative and vision on the part of state officials. Rather, it was a deliberate strategy that the regional authorities followed in their relations with NGOs, public-sector organizations such as schools, and businesses that participated in community projects. Multiple state officials to whom I talked expressed reluctance to create overarching structures that would standardize the grassroots work. A municipal official at the Rostov City administration, for example, told me that the possibility of creating an overarching organization for all volunteers in the city was raised several times at the City Public Chamber hearings. Every time, though, he and his colleagues "have fought it off," and the city mayor supported them by saying that things would only be worse if they tried to standardize them.[102] Another municipal official expressed support for temporary ad hoc associations of already existing organizations instead of permanent but inefficient state structures.[103] A regional official responsible for interactions with NGOs was puzzled by my question of whether the state officials ever created youth organizations. The idea that an external party could initiate a youth organization was so foreign to him that he did not understand my question: "If the organization does not exist, how can it initiate itself? We assume that our job is to create the right conditions so that the young people themselves are willing to get together and work on certain issues."[104] His reaction stands in sharp contrast to the reaction of one of my interviewees in Tatarstan, who could not understand how student organizations could be created by students and not the university administration fulfilling the task of the regional ministry.

I asked several of my interviewees directly, why was it that state officials in the Rostov region did not create more state-led organizations that worked with communities, and none of them provided a satisfactory answer. One justified his support for ad hoc associations rather than permanent state organizations by saying that permanent organizations were very expensive and difficult to dissolve, as many people would lose their jobs in this case.[105] Another one said that for the regional authorities, things that did not turn in a profit had never been a priority.[106] Neither of these explanations, though, were useful to understand the contrast with the Kemerovo region and Tatarstan. State organizations were not more expensive or harder to dissolve in the Rostov region, and given that the state-led community organizations provided opportunities to control society

---

[102] Interview Ros-04.
[103] Interview Ros-03.
[104] Interview Ros-08.
[105] Interview Ros-03.
[106] Interview Ros-04.

better, it was unclear why the regional authorities would not see their development as a priority.

The only plausible explanation for this regional difference, which only becomes apparent within side-by-side comparison of the regions, is the different patterns of state–society relations in these societies. The Rostov state officials might not be able to articulate this contrast, but they intuitively knew what kind of society they were dealing with.

First, building centralized organizational structures was not possible there because communities and public organizations resisted state interference. Earlier in this chapter I brought up an example of how the villagers would not trust the words of a state officials but would accept the same exact message from their informal leader and support it with their labor and resources. The same theme came up in other interviews in the Rostov region and Altai. One example was related to attracting business resources for social projects. The reader may remember that in the Kemerovo region and Tatarstan, such donations were managed by state authorities who explicitly asked for help, signed official agreements with businesses, and publicly recognized the donors. In Rostov, though, a regional state official specializing on interactions with NGOs, said that the regional government never directly asked businesses to support social projects because it would be seen as pressure, which is unacceptable:

INTERVIEWEE: First, the regional government cannot even hint at ...
NF: Some governments do that.
INTERVIEWEE: No, no, here is it not allowed. We do not do that because it is seen as pressure. This is not serious.
NF: It does not have to be pressure; it may be a request for help.
INTERVIEWEE: It will be seen as pressure. Imagine that some governor ... gets together with the representatives of the regional big business and says, "Guys, we have this development program and we need to support this socially oriented NGO; I hope you will make responsible choices." They are not naive children; they understand everything. Tomorrow an NGO representative shows up and says that the governor told this, so you should help me. Good luck not supporting them.... This is pressure. We do not even start on this path.[107]

Even the public-sector organizations, which are usually most dependent on the state, guarded their organizational boundaries against state interference. A representative of the educational labor union in Rostov, for example, told me that schools in the region did not allow any state representatives on the school

[107] Interview Ros-08.

boards that made decisions about teacher salaries. He said it might turn into pressure and jeopardize the school's right to distribute the salary budget.[108] In Altai, schools seemed to be too autonomous from the state, which might result in corrupt practices. Both the teachers I interviewed there and the labor union representative said that school principals had too much power in distributing salaries, which resulted in nepotism and manipulations even with the mandatory payments.[109]

Second, trying to involve the informal leaders of different communities into one organization made governance even more difficult for state officials. These informal leaders would be looking for ways to appropriate state resources for their communities and organizations rather than care about common goals of the state or society at large. Take, for example, the leader of the Don Youth Union—one of the organizations that originated from a Soviet predecessor. He actively developed connections with the regional elites and saw his role as the organization's leader primarily in lobbying its interest in external interactions, while the other members of the organization concentrated on the substantive activities. The leaders of other youth organizations, if they obtained a state post or "got close to the state," continued to advance the interests of these organizations, which remained their political base.[110]

A similar thing happened when the initiative came from the federal government. In the mid to late 2000s, especially during Dmitry Medvedev's presidency, the federal government allocated significant budgets for youth policy and youth organizations. At the time, the head of the Rostov regional committee for youth affairs was an ambitious young man who saw the demand of the federal government for youth programs that would counteract the alleged foreign influence on youth, especially the so-called orange threat—the influence of the forces that drove the Orange Revolution in Ukraine in 2004. Using the "fight with the Orange Revolution" as a window-dressing, this man successfully obtained large sums of federal money for regional youth initiatives. According to my interviewee, who is unlikely to understate Putin's regime pressure, as he used to work for an oppositional NGO, the declared goal did not have significant influence on the character of youth initiatives in the region. He said that, although a big part of these funds were stolen, these moneys nevertheless made it possible to set up a system of government support for youth initiatives at all levels, which allowed funding many unique local projects.[111] The money that the federal center meant to work for a particular purpose were, thus, successfully repurposed for grassroots initiatives.

[108] Interview Ros-15.
[109] Interviews Altai-08, Altai-14.
[110] Interview Ros-04.
[111] Interview Ros-04.

This tendency of public organizations to prioritize their own interests over the interests of the state made state officials in Rostov quite defensive about the state budget. They worried that multiple people and organizations had their eye on the budget money and saw their role as ensuring proper use of this money and developing accountability mechanisms of state money recipients. The general condition of satisfying any funding requests, whether for infrastructural or social projects, was that the applicants must find part of the necessary funds on their own, usually by finding a business partner or attracting individual donations.[112] Here is a description of a funding request that would be viewed favorably by the regional government: "Here is the problem, and I have a plan. The overall cost is 1.4 million rubles. 100,000 was raised from the population, 120,000—from businesses and the local administration. I found an additional 80,000. 1.1 million is still needed, but all the funding I mentioned is already in place."[113] The NGOs applying for state funding in Rostov must raise a minimum of 10% of cash required for the project on their own before they file the application. To that end, the state officials organize workshops with NGO leaders to teach them how to approach and talk to businesses. If an application for funding has a support letter from a business, it is a sign for the regional government that this NGO is capable, that their project is needed by society, and that the budget money will be spent well.

> Few state officials talk about it, but, unfortunately, because of the Soviet system of NGO support . . . we inherited many NGOs who are moochers. They asked different state institutions for money, and state officials gave this money just to get rid of them. . . . They all came through the back door of the Soviet system. All these wars, Afghanistan [veterans' organizations], women's councils, labor unions—there are many of them. . . . The money for them were allocated in advance, and we all got used to it. Then the Soviet Union fell apart, and the budget shrank, but in place of the state came Western donors. . . . When the information about the availability of these grants for all the good things—democracy development, civil society, freedom, bla-bla-bla—became available, the number of NGOs suddenly increased, and the big money came. Reporting was very formal. It was free money, for which you had to do something, but mostly just put in your own pocket. As a result, a big cohort of moochers has formed. . . . This description may be a bit emotional, but I was a participant of this process. . . . The sad part was that these free grants created conditions when many people for many years did not have to earn money with their labor, to understand and value money and resources. . . .

[112] Interviews Ros-03, Ros-08.
[113] Interview Ros-03.

In our competition, we are creating conditions so that the applicants do not have a feeling that these are free money. They have to do their homework, prepare the application ... We deliberately created a requirement of 10% co-funding, which I mentioned. If they don't have the money, they should be able to find a business partner, to convince him that his participation in the project is necessary. ... We develop a socially responsible business this way, but not only that. ... Our goal is to teach the NGO leaders to be reliable partners. ... They should not be moochers—they should be partners![114]

As this quote shows, the Soviet community organizations, which were an asset for the governments of the Kemerovo region and Tatarstan, were a burden for the regional government in Rostov. In an antistatist society, state-created organizational structures, such as the Soviet youth organizations, are appropriated by the local communities and interest groups, which use these organizations toward their own interests.

The State, Civil Society, and "Collective Institutions"

The contrasting views of the state—team state and outsider state—that I described in this chapter raise an important question about the boundary between the state and civil society. Although the separation between these two concepts exists in the Russian language, legislation, and to some degree in public discourse, it does not always exist in people's everyday lives. Among the regions I researched, the boundary between the state and society, their interests, and their organizations was rather clear in the Rostov region and Altai. The same conceptual separation, however, did not exist in the Kemerovo region and Tatarstan. In these regions, people would confuse the state and civil society in conversations and even official documents. For example, an interviewee in Tatarstan characterized one of the regional youth organizations as "a civil society organization (in Russian—общественная) that works at the level of the Ministry of Youth Affairs," while the Tatarstan government website listed at least two ministry units under the category of "Youth Civil Society Associations of the Republic of Tatarstan."[115]

What people in the Kemerovo region and Tatarstan had in place of the state and civil society distinction was one general category of what can be called collective institutions—those that worked for the common good regardless of whether they were formally state organizations or civil society ones. In both

---

[114] Interview Ros-08.
[115] Правительство Республики Татарстан, "Молодежные общественные объединения Республики Татарстан."

Kemerovo region and Tatarstan, state organizations and NGOs routinely shared resources—not only in the form of grants from the state budget to NGOs but also through people, physical facilities, organizational ties, or informational support. Their organizational structures largely overlapped and worked as one system. For example, in Kemerovo City, the residential councils and other local organizations thought of themselves as an extension of community centers and, through them, of the city and regional authorities. A member of one of the Veterans' Councils in Kemerovo region—the organization I only mentioned so far, which also has a ramified hierarchy down to the residential level—once proudly said to a journalist: "Our Veteran's Council feels like an authentic unit of the municipal government."[116] In Tatarstan, large regional NGOs working with youth frequently worked on the government property, paid rent back to the government from governmental grants, and had their pages on the website of the Ministry of Youth Affairs, not to mention that they were sometimes run by the people who worked for the government. This arrangement was not considered by the employees of these organizations or the public to be a violation of any norms as long as the activities of these organizations contributed to the collective good. Quite the opposite: pulling together the resources for the common cause was a sign of unity, in which the state and society came together to create that common good.

These "collective institutions" were neither civil society independent from the state nor the state apparatus with the top-down chain of command. A better model to think about them would be a party, except that it represents the whole society, not just a part of it. Party structure is a fusion of centralized leadership and local initiative united by a common cause. Parties have ramified hierarchical structures that reach down to the local level, where they aim to recruit volunteers from among the people who care about the same cause. Finally, even though party leadership is responsible for strategy and coordination, parties do not survive without the energy of the masses who support them and share their values. Even the self-description of some of the organizations I talked about in this chapter tried to capture this party-like unity that combines hierarchy and voluntary participation. For example, the Youth Law Enforcement Movement "Forpost" in Tatarstan described itself as "a state-civil organization with vertical structure, branch offices in every municipality, hierarchy, and voluntary, unselfish performance of one's duties." It defined its work principles as "voluntariness, selflessness, civic consciousness, solidarity, and social romanticism."[117]

---

[116] "Наш совет ветеранов чувствует себя равноправным подразделением администрации района." (Ермакова, "Когда дело ладится.")

[117] Государственное бюджетное учреждение Республиканский центр молодёжных формирований по охране общественного порядка "Форпост," "Наша история."

The lack of distinction between the state and civil society is important for the understanding of how political machines in statist societies differ from those in antistatist ones. The fusion of the state and civil society may seem Panglossian until we realize that it hides the possibility of abusing the state's position as collective leader. In statist societies, autocrats can build political machines based on the power of social norms and the organizational fusion of the state and civil society rather than on personal favors. Such machines are more reliable in the situation of crises as they are resilient to fluctuations of popular support. The next chapter will elaborate on the difference between political machines in statist and antistatist societies.

Chapter Summary

This chapter laid out the evidence highlighting the contrasting views of the state and the different structure of public organizations in the two pairs of regions—Tatarstan and the Kemerovo region, on the one hand, and Altai and the Rostov region, on the other. People in Tatarstan and the Kemerovo region viewed the state and state officials as members of their team and considered cooperation with state officials a part of their civic duty. They took pride in participating in state-led projects as this was their way to contribute to the well-being of their communities. Such logic of teamwork made it easy for state officials to build centralized organizational structures, which united governmental and nongovernmental organizations as well as private businesses under the regional government.

In contrast, for the people in Altai and the Rostov region, the state was largely an outsider. Their teams were clans, ethnic groups, and cultural and local communities whose leaders enjoyed people's default support. Unlike the leaders of nonstate groups, state officials were viewed with suspicion in these regions. They could not count on people's cooperation and, to obtain it, had to either give something to these communities or threaten to take something away. The state for the people was, therefore, a source of perks and punishment, and their goal in relations with the state was to maximize the perks and minimize the punishment. The next chapter will elaborate on how these two logics, teamwork and utility maximization, play out as the driving principles of political machines.

4
The Political and the Civic
Political Machines in Antistatist and Statist Societies

The statist and antistatist regions in this study had different views of the state, different structures of public organizations, and different logics—teamwork and utility maximization—that drove state-society relations. But how exactly would these translate into the different performance of political machines during the 2012 presidential election? Why would political machines in statist regions with teamwork logic demonstrate more stable performance than political machines in antistatist regions with utility maximization logic?

Most research on political machines focuses on how various perks and payments work to induce electoral support regardless of programmatic platforms of the candidates. To distribute those perks and payments, candidates need a network of brokers who can steer their communities to vote for the candidate in exchange for the perks. Utility maximization is the main principle driving the behavior of all parties in this scenario.

In this chapter, I will show that a political machine can also be built on the opposite logic—the teamwork one. In this case, electoral support is not driven by maximizing the financial and other benefits; rather, it is driven by the sense of group solidarity and civic duty, which such machines masterfully blend with political support. These political machines often consist of public sector organizations that already fulfill many public functions. When they blend political functions into the public ones, few individuals recognize it as an unacceptable practice. Most people view political involvement of public organizations as yet another, if unpleasant, facet of their public activities. Blending political action into ongoing civic actions makes achieving stable performance much easier than in clientelistic political machines, where the performance depends on ever-changing brokers and deals.

In this chapter, I will, first, demonstrate that political machines in the Rostov region and Altai worked through brokers and conditional clientelistic exchanges. Then I will turn to the Kemerovo region and Tatarstan to show that their political machines worked by blending the civic and the political. I will demonstrate that, together with providing public goods, public organizations in these regions helped the regional authorities to mobilize the population, co-opt future political leaders, monitor dissent, and control public spaces. Finally, I will use the story of the Veterans' Councils in the Kemerovo region to show how lack of separation between the state and civil society allowed the state to hijack even a mighty grassroots social movement.

Buying Loyalty: Political Machines in Antistatist Societies

The structure of a political machine is significantly influenced by the structure of the society it aims to mobilize as people's identities and group loyalties shape their expectations from politicians. In the Rostov region and Altai, people's group loyalties laid primarily with their nonstate communities. In Altai, it was clans of indigenous Altai peoples; in Rostov, it was local and ethnic communities, including Cossacks—a quasi-ethnic group that has lived in the area for centuries. These communities and their social norms ordered everyday life and set the boundaries between us and them, our team and other teams. Those included in "us" deserved unconditional support through the social safety net; those included in "them" were evaluated pragmatically, depending on the use or harm they might inflict.

The salience of multiple nonstate communities and organizations in the Rostov region and Altai makes the political environment by default pluralist and driven by the pragmatic logic of clientelist exchanges. Separation of society into multiple communities means that no politician is viewed as a group leader by a significant share of the population. No politician, therefore, can rely primarily on group authority to amass the needed level of support. Instead, they must turn to buying loyalty and engaging people's pragmatic interests. While within the communities people still follow the logic of teamwork when interacting and supporting their leaders, the political machines that cut across groups are based on pragmatic clientelist exchanges of material benefits and favors for political support.[1]

Pluralist Political Environment

In Altai, indigenous clans are the most salient example of communities whose members feel an obligation to support their own leaders but treat all other political interactions pragmatically. Clans provide their members with a social safety net in everyday life, and the expectation of community support transfers to the political arena: "No matter how bad Y. is, he is my relative. And no matter

---

[1] For the evidence that competitiveness is connected to such manipulation techniques as vote-buying in other Russian regions, see Harvey, "Changes in the Menu of Manipulation."

how good S. is, I will vote against him because he is not my relative, and I have commitments to my relatives."[2] Even when people realize that their relative might not be the best candidate, they often concede to the pressure of social norms and their community. Although these group loyalties are not the only factor determining political support, they are by far the strongest. One of my interviewees brought up a case when a clan member had been elected as the village head three times despite doing a very poor job. At the fourth election, he finally lost support of his relatives, who voted for an alternative candidate who was not a clan member. That alternative candidate, however, was only in office for one term and, despite a much better performance, had to move out of this village because the hostility of the clan members quickly returned and staying might have been dangerous for his life.[3]

Competition between clans is an old phenomenon that persists over time and sets the tone in regional politics despite Altaians making up only about 35% of the regional population. In the 19th to early 20th century, this competition drove the choice of marriage partners for Altaians; in the 21st century, it moved primarily to the realm of regional politics. As ethnic Russians live with Altaians side by side and are involved in the same governance decisions, they are drawn into the political games that Altaian clans play between themselves. As one of my interviewees said, "The idea of political game is not a metaphor; it is a real game."[4]

In the Rostov region, the competing groups are more diverse. The region has several consolidated ethnic minorities, who often form territorial communities, and Cossacks, who live across the region but have a distinct group identity. Besides them, there are various communities and organizations, many of which also engage in political games to the extent their organizational resources allow. Here is how my interviewee from Rostov described this pluralism at work during the electoral campaign period. In this quote, he refers to the "administrative resource," which, in this context, means using resources of any existing organizations for political purposes:

> I worked in a municipality, and there was an electoral campaign. Ok, we're engaging the administrative resource to work with voters. Everyone who is in the boat must row in one direction. So, we look around and it turns out there are no ordinary voters. They are all in administrative boats, from the municipal administration to all the civil society organizations and residential councils. For example, there are a couple dozen civil society organizations in

---

[2] Interview Altai-07.
[3] Interview Altai-07.
[4] Interview Altai-07.

the municipality (Afghanistan veterans, environmentalists, political parties, etc.). And everyone participates—including schools and teachers—everyone participates, participates, participates in the administrative resource. As civil society, as a party, as bureaucrats, etc., etc. We allocate people responsible for the campaign and then ask ourselves the question: whom are we going to work with? Turns out, only with ourselves. You are the voter and you are the administrative resource. Work on convincing yourself how to vote. There are no ordinary people, no group you can work with. And I am not exaggerating.[5]

As this quote shows, many voters were already involved with some groups and organizations that shaped their political loyalties, and there were barely any neutral voters left who might be the target of an electoral campaign. The only way for a politician who wants to obtain electoral support in this situation is to negotiate with the leaders of these groups and organizations and promise them some perks in exchange for political support.

Utility Maximization as the Driver of Clientelist Political Machines

The negotiations with group leaders, each of whom pursued their own interests and the interests of their groups, add up to clientelist political machines in the Rostov region and Altai. These machines are very similar to the ones described in political science literature. Their primary driver is the direct exchange of votes for material goods, cash payments, or access to services in contrast to politics based on more durable symbolic bonds, whether traditional or modern.[6] Such an exchange is captured well by a model of rational choice action of two autonomous parties, each of which tries to maximize its utility: The voter aims to exchange her vote for as much material resources as possible, potentially even with different politicians, and politicians aim to obtain the largest number of votes with the resources they have.[7]

In the Rostov region and Altai, utility maximization drove clientelistic exchanges between politicians, on the one hand, and group leaders and individual voters, on the other. Group leaders played the role of brokers bargaining with politicians on behalf of their communities. For example, in Altai, one proud head of municipality told my interviewee that their village "won a minivan" at

---

[5] Interview Ros-03.
[6] Scott, "Corruption, Machine Politics, and Political Change," 1151; Piattoni, "Clientelism in Historical and Comparative Perspective," 4; Kitschelt and Wilkinson, *Patrons, Clients, and Policies*, 2; Stokes, *Brokers, Voters, and Clientelism*, 7.
[7] Magaloni, *Voting for Autocracy*; Stokes, *Brokers, Voters, and Clientelism*.

the federal election because they all voted for United Russia.[8] He remembered about this "victory" after complaining about the United Russia's land policies hurting his community, which may seem paradoxical. According to the utility maximization logic, though, it made perfect sense. This village head was too powerless to do anything about the land policy pursued by the predatory state, but by negotiating getting a minivan for the village, he was able to compensate for the harm at least partially.

Another great example of bargaining comes from Rostov, from the same municipal employee who told us about the importance of informal leaders in the previous chapter. Another piece of knowledge, which he proudly shared with me, was the importance of delivering a very high electoral percentage for the governor or the legislature deputies as this provides good leverage over politicians later on:

> At the end of the month, the deputies travel across the regions to meet with their constituencies. So, one is traveling through the Sovetskii[9] district [where the interviewee worked].
>
> - Where are you heading?
> - To Troitsk.
> - Come over to our place.
> - Why? You're doing fine.
> - And what's over there?
> - I'm holding a town hall there, 120 people signed up, they have so many issues.
> - No, come over, have some tea.
> [The deputy comes over, sits down to talk, and asks:]
> - So, how are you doing?
> - We're doing well. One thing: we need to install a water pipe system in Petrovka village, they still don't have a centralized water pipe.
> - How much does it cost?
> - 800 million rubles.
> - What?! Come on! Do you understand what you're asking for?
> - Wait, wait. Vladimir Aleksandrovich, do you remember who elected you to be the deputy? Did Slaviansk fail you? It did. Did three rural municipalities fail you? They did. And how much did Sovetskii rural district give you? 96% Do you want the same in four years?
> - Yes.
> - And how much are you getting in Troitsk?
> - 3–4–5%

---

[8] Interview Altai-09.
[9] Proper names in this quote have been changed.

- So, deliver there for 3–4–5% and here for 96%.
- And how am I supposed to resolve this?
- That's a different question. Let me explain to you if you don't get it yourself. Didn't the governor ask you to attract a billion rubles of investment to Rostov region?
- Yes, he did.
- So, go to the governor, since this is a regional question, not a federal one, and say: "You want a billion ruble investment, and I have to deliver on the mandates from my constituencies. They need 800 million rubles for a water pipe. You resolve my mandate, and I attract that billion for you." The logic is simple. God help you![10]

This quote is describing multiple layers of bargaining. The head of a municipality, namely, my interviewee,[11] is looking for a way to build a water pipe system in one of the villages. He may or may not be the informal leader of that village. If he is, then he is bringing resources to his own community, which makes him stronger as a group leader. If he is not, such material benefit for the community allows him to bargain with the informal leaders in that village for political support. To find the money, he leverages the electoral support that the district provided to one of the deputies at the previous election and encourages him to engage in bargaining with the governor.

Individual voters in these regions also engaged in clientelistic exchanges. As one of my interviewees in Altai said, "People sell themselves with pleasure."[12] They sell and resell their votes, while feeling little obligation to keep their promises if they cannot be held accountable. Another interviewee who was a schoolteacher in the south of Altai recollected how the candidates at the village head election visited their school just a few months ago, before the election day: "We had three or four candidates for the post. The first one came to our school, and one of our teachers was like 'Oh, of course, we are going to vote for you, you are so ... bla-bla-bla.' Ok. In half an hour, another one comes in. [And she says again,] 'Bla-bla-bla.' 'Oh, my god,' I thought to myself. What a chameleon!"[13] The same interviewee also recollected that one winter, some pensioners in their village needed compound feed for the cattle, and a deputy who ran from their district bought it for them. Laughing, she told me how her neighbor ingenuously admitted that he sold his vote: "It's funny, if you think about it. It should be called a bribe, but he is just a simple old man, our neighbor. He comes [to

---

[10] Interview Ros-03.
[11] In fact, my interviewee was the deputy head of municipality who worked in the interests of his boss, but I will omit this detail to simplify the analysis.
[12] Interview Altai-07.
[13] Interview Altai-08.

the polling place] and says 'He just bought some compound feed for my cattle; I guess I should vote for him.'"[14]

The Challenge of Stable Electoral Performance

When politics is based on clientelistic exchanges with multiple brokers and individual voters, it is challenging to achieve stable electoral performance even at the municipal level, let alone at the regional one. First, when all the brokers and individuals are trying to maximize their economic utility, electoral performance becomes very dependent on the amount of economic resources that the governor can distribute. This would make a clientelistic political machine perform well when the economy grows and perform poorly during the economic decline. Second, the performance of such a political machine depends on many independent transactions simultaneously going well, which is rarely the case. Individual voters may break their promise and vote differently; the electoral results in territorial communities are more transparent, but the leaders of those communities may change, creating the need to establish new relationships.

Since it is difficult to build a reliable political machine in a competitive political environment, those municipal heads who manage to do it even at the local level are apparently very proud of their achievement. I learned about it accidentally when I asked a municipal official in Rostov to comment on the unstable performance of the region at the federal election, thinking that I was making a compliment to the regional more democratic and competitive politics. He interpreted my question as a hesitation in the abilities of the municipal heads as politicians. In response, he brought up an example of his former boss who has served as a municipal head for over 20 years and still got elected with 98%–99% support. "Like in the Soviet times!" he said proudly. "And if the result is a bit too high," he continued hinting at the likely falsification, "it is only for one purpose: he celebrates for a day and then works hard for five years."[15]

Reproduction of the Boundary between the Civic and the Political

In the previous chapter, we saw that in the Rostov region and Altai, there was a clear boundary between society and the state. People intuitively viewed the state as a potential adversary and questioned any state interference with the matters of

---

[14] Interview Altai-08.
[15] Interview Ros-03.

their community, such as a village or an ethnic group, or organization, such as a school or an NGO.

Another, related boundary, which is also intuitively clear and successfully reproduced in an antistatist society, is the boundary between the civic and the political. The civic here is the realm of the collective good and impartiality, and the political is the realm of the competition for power and partisanship. For example, civil servants are supposed to make sure that state resources are used in a nonpartisan manner, while politicians are supposed to raise resources for their political organization, and these two roles are clearly in conflict.

The reason why this boundary between the civic and the political is intuitively clear is that it has real consequences for the interests of competing political actors. The competitive political environment both stimulates politicians and state officials to abuse public resources for partisan purposes and constrains such efforts via counterstrategies of other political players. For example, a regional governor may be tempted to use his control of public resources and organizations, such as schools, to make teachers agitate or falsify the vote count in favor of his political allies. But if he does that, his opponents will quickly point it out to the public. Also, they will be compelled to do the same, and in a society with highly fragmented group loyalties, there is no guarantee that the net effect of such political engagement will be in favor of the governor. Involvement of public organizations in politics, thus, may become a double-edged sword.

An example from Altai illustrates this dilemma. Several of my interviewees who worked in education told me a story of an election in one of the rural municipalities where two competing candidates had approximately equal chances of winning. The head of the municipal education department as well as school principals and teachers were involved in agitation, but out of 16 school principals in the municipality, only 8 supported the incumbent together with the current head of education department, while another 8 supported the opponent. The incumbent was the political ally of the regional governor, but he ended up losing the election. After this election, the regional governor publicly prohibited using teachers as agitators in the region, which conveniently looked like enforcing the rule of law.[16]

The presence of political opponents makes it difficult to abuse public resources and organizations even if these opponents do not win the election, as they monitor such abuses and make them public. For example, in Rostov, where the Communist Party of the Russian Federation has a strong branch, the electoral observers from this party managed to prove electoral falsification in court, which convicted the members of the precinct-level electoral commission of a crime. This incident significantly raised the perceived cost of engaging in falsification

---

[16] Interview Altai-08.

for the electoral commission members, and my interviewee said that they had not had issues in that commission ever since.[17]

The political engagement of public workers and organizations in a competitive environment may also have adverse consequences for these workers and organizations, which may limit their desire to engage in clientelistic political transactions. For example, in the earlier example of different school principals supporting different candidates, the principals who supported the loser had their job contracts suspended. The new head of municipality appointed a new head of education department, who refused to renew their job contracts.[18] The leader of the teachers' union in Altai remembered about this episode when I asked about involvement of teachers in politics and expressed his unequivocal negative attitude to that. He admitted that he himself made the mistake of engaging in politics in the past when he actively supported one of the candidates for the governor's post. When that candidate lost, it took him two years to build a relationship with the new governor, who initially refused any negotiations with the teachers' union on the grounds that they supported his political opponent during the election. "It can have big consequences,"—he told me—"This is why I say just do not get involved."[19]

As these examples show, in the Rostov region and Altai, political actors reproduce the boundary between the civic and the political as they discuss and negotiate their strategies in the competitive political process. The intuitive clarity of this boundary for everyone involved distinguishes politics in these regions from the politics in the Kemerovo region and Tatarstan.

Building Unity: Political Machines in Statist Societies

Unlike in antistatist societies, where the boundary between the civic and the political is intuitively clear, in statist societies, this boundary is almost nonexistent. Statist societies, such as those in the Kemerovo region and Tatarstan, are not separated into multiple nonstate communities, which would compete for power. Instead, the dominant social institution organizing life in these regions is the state. It is the primary provider of social order and social safety net and the primary leader of any collective action. It plays the role that was played by nonstate communities in the antistatist Rostov region and Altai, and the same group solidarity, which bonded those communities, bonds the state and society in the statist Kemerovo region and Tatarstan.

---

[17] Interview Ros-17.
[18] Interviews Altai-08, Altai-14. At the time when I left the region, three of the eight school principals were officially fired and the rest were in limbo.
[19] Interview Altai-14.

Accordingly, the political machines in statist societies are driven not by the logic of utility maximization, but by group loyalty and the social pressure to conform. Most people in these environments easily cooperate with the state, which opens wide opportunities for state officials to control society and prevent it from becoming an independent actor. To do that, state officials blend political functions into the work of organizations already providing public goods, and most people do not distinguish between state officials acting in civic capacity and the same officials acting in political capacity. Public organizations, therefore, are involved in politics not by taking a clearly partisan position as they did in the Rostov region and Altai, but by using the veil of the civic to help the current state officials maintain their political monopoly.

The Blurred Boundary between the Civic and the Political

I showed in the previous chapter that in the Kemerovo region and Tatarstan, the realms of the state and civil society existed unseparated in people's minds as one sphere of "collective institutions." The state had a near monopoly on the role of the collective leader, while other social groups and identities were much weaker and had little impact on regional politics. As a result of such monopoly, the realm of the political, that is, competition of different groups for state power, was almost nonexistent, while the realm of the civic, that is, collective action for the common cause, dominated the public space.

An important consequence of such lack of political competition was that the people in these two regions could not easily distinguish between the civic and the political. They confused political with civic organizations and did not differentiate the actions of state officials in their civic capacity from the actions of the same individuals in their political capacity. For example, in Tatarstan, the governmental website, which listed both formally state and civil society organizations under the label of civil society, also included the regional youth wing of the United Russia Party in the same category despite the fact that this party is clearly a political organization competing with other political parties for elected posts.[20] The activities of this "Young Guard of the United Russia" included both preparing the political cadres for the United Russia Party and such civic projects as social volunteering, work with children in orphanages, and help in enforcing parking rules and tobacco sales regulations.[21]

---

[20] Правительство Республики Татарстан, "Молодежные общественные объединения Республики Татарстан."
[21] Interview Kaz-16.

114   THE SOCIAL ROOTS OF AUTHORITARIANISM

Another example of organizational mixture of the civic and the political is Tatarstan's largest "public movement" titled "Tatarstan—The New Age."[22] This organization combines the features of a civil society and political organization with no signs of conflict between the two. It was created in 1999, allegedly by several civil society organizations, including the Council for Youth Organizations, the Council of Businesswomen, the Society for People with Disabilities, and the Theater Union. The initiative of these organizations was supported by Tatarstan's President Shaimiev, while the speaker of Tatarstan's parliament, Farid Mukhametshin, became the leader of the movement. Over the years, the movement participated in multiple electoral campaigns at the federal, regional, and municipal levels and always had a deputy group in the regional and municipal legislative bodies, which in recent years has largely overlapped with that of the United Russia Party. At the same time, the member-organizations of the movement also engaged in nonpolitical public initiatives, such as organizing WorldSkills—the worldwide championship of vocational skills—in Russia.[23] This movement, therefore, works as a joint initiative of civil society and the state and fulfills both civic and political functions.[24]

In both Tatarstan and the Kemerovo region, I found multiple examples of people who worked in the public sector or the state-led community organizations and routinely shared with me the details of their political activities, apparently not seeing any conflict between the two. A woman who worked in the Kemerovo Regional Veterans' Council—the pensioners' regionwide organization whose story I will tell later in this chapter—proudly described how the council organized public forums with activist pensioners and state officials. As she talked about it, she said: "We show that we make an effort and work for [improving] the image of the regional and municipal governments to help them. People cannot see everything, right? We deliver this information in the correct form through public forums."[25] The forums she talked about were townhall-style meetings of the leadership of their organization and state officials with the pensioners, which they organized across the region. These meetings were not a mechanism of holding the state officials accountable to the pensioners. Rather, they worked to involve the pensioners in state-led projects and activities. The head of the regional Veterans' Council was in regular contact with the governor, and she "passed all the governor's initiatives to the heads of local Veterans' Councils, and they passed these initiatives to their members."[26] Among these

[22] Республиканское общественное движение "Татарстан—Новый век"—"Татарстан—Яңа гасыр", "История."
[23] "Мухаметшин"; Антонов, "Депутатскую группу 'Татарстан—новый век' возглавил Артур Абдульзянов."
[24] The Kemerovo region also had a similar movement in 2007–2013; see Гулик, "Вместо блока 'Служу Кузбассу'—общественное движение."
[25] Interview Kem-07.
[26] Interview Kem-07.

initiatives were celebrations of important holidays, e.g., of the Miners' Day or the Victory Day, various support programs for pensioners, e.g., a program helping pensioners' homesteads, or involvement of pensioners in patriotic education activities with schoolchildren. My interviewee saw spreading the information about such projects and activities and improving the image of the regional and local administrations as her civic duty and was proud of her organization's contribution to the common cause.

Another vivid example comes from Tatarstan, from the interview with the provost of a private university whose student organizations were embedded into the regionwide hierarchy of youth organizations, which I also described in the previous chapter. This provost attended monthly meetings in the regional Ministry of Youth Affairs and then passed the information from the Ministry to the students. Talking about the "tasks" for the student organizations in her university, which she was given at these meetings, she mentioned election of regional deputies: "I have some information from the ministry, then I come to the student leaders and say: Ok, guys, we should tell the students this and this. For example, we have an election of a State Council deputy.[27] All student leaders should be saying this and this."[28] For her, this task was no different from, for instance, organizing a regional student art festival and asking students to participate in it. It came through the same channels from the regional ministry and involved the same routine algorithm of engaging student organizations in her institution.

The Distorted Idea of Representation

Lack of political competition and public negotiations between different social groups in a statist society also distorts the idea of political representation. In a pluralist society with politically salient divisions, elections and representative institutions serve as a platform for negotiation between different groups even if these elections are not free and fair. In a society with little to no politically salient divisions, elections become a way to put together the Team State, that is, the group of individuals who will help the state exercise its leadership. These elected individuals are expected by the electorate not so much to represent their constituencies and defend their interests as to link these constituencies to larger state-led initiatives, that is, to reaffirm their belonging to the larger community led by the state.

---

[27] Tatarstan's parliament.
[28] Interview Kaz-09.

I could trace this distorted idea of representation in the governance structures and procedures of the organizations I studied in the Kemerovo region and Tatarstan. One example of that was the residential councils and community centers in Kemerovo City. As I described in the previous chapter, the creation of these councils was initiated by the city administration, which reached out to the activists in neighborhoods asking for their help with routine governance issues. The residential council, however, was not meant to become an independent body representing the residents of the neighborhood in their interactions with the city government, public institutions, or utility companies. Instead, it was the city administration's requirement that, besides the residents, the council would also include city officials, the principal of the public school situated in the neighborhood, and the head of the property management company.[29] The councils, thus, were the extension of the city administration, miniteams led or supervised by the state officials and often fulfilling their agenda.

The example from Tatarstan is even more telling. The private university, whose provost for student affairs I interviewed, had a student council and a student president. My interviewee insisted that the election of the student president followed all the democratic procedures. There were several candidates, a designated campaign term, during which the candidates presented their programs, and a voting procedure, for which they even borrowed ballot boxes from the city administration. However, when she described the voting procedure, it turned out that it was not only students who elected the student president. Faculty and staff voted too. This would not make sense if the student president's mission were to represent students' interests. However, it does make sense if we think of this election as the election of a member of the university leadership team who is responsible for involving students in institutional projects. Since faculty and staff would have to work closely with this person, they also had a say in whom they wanted to see on their team. The student president, in her turn, had the right to change the leaders of all student organizations, which themselves were the creatures of the provost for student affairs in that institution. These organizations needed voluntary participation on the students' end, but their activities were largely directed from above.[30] This governance structure was a fusion of a centralized leadership and bottom-up initiative, which, as I showed in the previous chapter, was characteristic of many organizations in the Kemerovo region and Tatarstan.

[29] Interview Kem-13.
[30] Interview Kaz-09.

Political Functions of Public Organizations

This team-oriented vision of politics and the lack of distinction between the civic and the political produced a very different structure of regional political machines. If in the Rostov region and Altai the machines were based on clientelist exchanges between politicians and community leaders and the logic of utility maximization, in the Kemerovo region and Tatarstan they are based on group loyalty and blending the political functions into the civic activities of various public organizations. These machines were not run by individuals trying to maximize their material or political gain. They were fueled by the energy of the people who were eager to be good citizens and by those who conform with the group to avoid ostracism and social sanctions.

The public organizations united into a state-led network were a crucial component of the political machines in the Kemerovo region and Tatarstan. As I showed in the previous chapter, they extended the reach of the state bureaucracy into people's everyday lives and facilitated popular participation in state-led projects, both civic and political ones. By providing public goods, they placed state agents in close social proximity to most people and used that position to strengthen the state's political monopoly and prevent society from becoming an independent political actor.

The political functions of public organizations in the Kemerovo region and Tatarstan can be divided into three categories: (1) popular mobilization for regime goals and co-optation of activists, (2) working with existing and potential discontent, and (3) control of public space and public discourse.

Mobilization and Co-optation

As I showed in the previous chapter, the social penetration of state-led public and community organizations in the Kemerovo region and Tatarstan has put them in close proximity to almost every individual in both regions. In Kemerovo City, for example, every 23rd person was listed as a residential council activist, which meant that every city inhabitant likely knew at least one community activist personally. In Tatarstan, the network of children's and youth organizations affected almost all families with young children as well as young adults. Besides these two examples, there were other state-led organizational networks in these regions, which penetrated society and enjoyed the population's trust as community-builders and civic activists.

The deep social penetration of the state-led community organizations put them in the position that they could use for proregime popular mobilization and cooptation of activists. For example, the web of personal contacts cultivated by residential councils and community centers in Kemerovo could be easily used for electoral mobilization. Activists who knew people in their neighborhood and were aware of their personal situations were likely to be much better agitators than outsiders would be. Even though the ballot vote is secret, it should not have been difficult for the activists to monitor the turnout of many people in the community and exercise peer pressure to turn their votes as well as selectively mobilize supporters, but not opponents.[31] Community centers and residential councils in Kemerovo have organized meetings of activists with the members of the city-level electoral commission,[32] as well as training and competitions for high school students on knowledge of electoral procedures and "the political field of Russia."[33] They included preparation for electoral campaigns in their reports as one of the areas of work—yet another sign of the absence of the boundary between the civic and the political.[34]

The pensioners community organizations in the Kemerovo region—the Veterans' Councils—have also helped with electoral mobilization. The network of Veterans' Councils is an old organization that existed in the Soviet Union and has polished the skills of patriotic education and propaganda for decades. It has actively engaged in door-to-door electoral agitation not only in Kemerovo but also nationwide, and in the 1990s the Communist Party had greatly benefited from these efforts.[35] In Kemerovo, the Veterans' Councils not only agitated for a particular candidate or party but also increased the turnout on the election day. To do that, they organized "Veterans' Salons" at the polling stations, in which they presented their music and dance ensembles; held arts and crafts exhibits, and master classes; and served tea and baked goods.[36]

The main force driving mobilization is the activists—those members of the community who have the abilities and desire to engage in public politics. State-led community organizations provide these people an avenue for developing their abilities within the framework that would work for the state rather than against it. The state nurtures the engagement desire of these activists with community projects, develops their relations with the state, and later recruits the members of team state from this pool by, for example, having them run for local legislative bodies. Community organizations, including residential committees and Veterans' Councils, have often supplied deputies to local legislatures nationwide, and the Kemerovo region and Tatarstan were not an exception.[37] The

---

[31] For more information about strategies of such selective mobilization see Gans-Morse, Mazzuca, and Nichter, "Varieties of Clientelism."
[32] "В районах города."
[33] Рассказова, "Бой политического значения."
[34] Об итогах деятельности центров по работе с населением в 2013 г.
[35] See the section on pensioners' organizations' involvement in elections in Appendix 4.
[36] "Ветеранские гостиные"; Будяковская, "Были 'ничейные', стали—наши!"
[37] Матвеев, Власть и общество в системе местного самоуправления России в 1993–2003 гг., 179. See also the lists of sources in Appendices 3 and 4.

activists, who did not run for an elected office, supplied reserve work force for other political tasks, for example, for serving as members of precinct-level electoral commissions, where most falsifications take place.[38]

In Tatarstan, the state-led youth organizations have explicitly engaged in training the future politicians who would become the members of the team state. For example, the Tatarstan's Union of Youth Organizations and the Agrarian Youth Union have published a manual for candidates in municipal elections. This manual explains how to run a campaign in a city and rural areas, what kind of information to collect, how to interact with the media, how to organize agitation, and how to be an effective public speaker. It was put together by the leaders of these two organizations in coauthorship with a state official and published as a part of the regional governmental program, "Rural Youth in the Republic of Tatarstan in 2011–2015."[39] "Politicians" in Tatarstan and Kemerovo, therefore, are raised by the state itself, and their political career depends on how good of a team member they will show themselves to be.

Management of Existing and Potential Discontent

Besides mobilization of society for state-led projects and coopting activists, public organizations also helped control grassroots politics by identifying people's grievances and addressing them before they become the basis for self-organization. Since state-led community organizations were in personal contact with a large number of people, they could easily gather the necessary information and deliver it to the state.

In my fieldwork, this function of community organizations was most apparent in the Kemerovo region—the region with poorer population and the history of social unrest. The community centers and residential councils, which covered the city territory, regularly helped the city government with various information needs. For example, they took an active part in the 2010 National Census[40] and

---

[38] I downloaded and analyzed a list of precinct-level electoral commissions in Kemerovo City in 2008. The file was downloaded from the Kemerovo regional government website but was later moved from its original location (it is available from the author). The occupation of the heads of local electoral commissions was identified in the list, but their involvement in community organizations was unclear. As elsewhere in Russia, the majority of electoral commission heads in 2008 were teachers (45%), but the directors of community centers and nonworking pensioners added another 10%. It is very possible that other people on the list have also been involved in either community organizations or labor unions at the industrial enterprises, which were also controlled by the governor.

[39] Сафиуллин, Мухамадеева, and Тухватова, *Применение избирательных технологий в условиях города и сельской местности. Методические рекомендации для кандидатов в депутаты в органы местного самоуправления*.

[40] Кикиой, "Решаем вместе"; see also Фефелова, "Готовимся к переписи."

assisted the city government in surveying the population on specific issues, such as knowledge about social benefits or preferences about community activities.[41]

Besides the ad hoc surveys, the city government used the network of community centers and residential councils for regular monitoring of the situation on the ground. When it created these organizations, it introduced standardized paperwork for the residential councils and treated each community center as "a database" of information about the population of the particular city territory. This information was later used by the City Council deputies, the city administration, the police, and other community organizations.[42]

The work of community organizations helped the city and regional governments not only receive the information about potential sources of discontent but also alleviate at least some of them before they grew into larger social concerns. Community centers and Veterans' Councils with their local knowledge helped the state direct its resources to those in need, especially if they brought their concerns directly to these organizations. Basic livelihood needs such as food, clothes, or medical care could be handled by community center inspectors or activists through donations or administrative help. Grievances that could not be resolved easily could often be alleviated by making people feel listened to and heard.[43]

Some issues, however, were so serious and potentially disruptive that they required an intervention of the regional government. In this case, the monitoring system allowed adjusting regional policies quickly before civil society mobilized. In an interview with the head of an NGO for people with disabilities in the Kemerovo region, I heard a story about such policy correction that deemed civic action unnecessary: "Our governor sometimes just amazes me. I will give you a simple example. Once there was a time when we started to have problems with [free] medicines. That was it—the end of the world! People with diabetes started dying; it was horrible! We started having this problem in January, and while we, the activists, had still been thinking what to do, the governor issued an order in early February saying that the regional budget would compensate all the expenses for medicines, that is, if we paid cash, we could get the money back! What a graceful move! I was truly shocked."[44]

On the surface, such attention to people's grievances may seem to be a practice of good governance, and such impression makes it easy to convince people to supply the information for the state. The message that the activists are receiving

---

[41] Зинчук, "Что знаете о льготах?"; Сваровский, "Заслужили всей жизнью."

[42] "ТОС—самая близкая власть"; "Итоги работы с населением за 2016 год."

[43] The regional administration sometimes publishes a report about citizens' complaints, analyzing its dynamic and informing about the steps taken to improve the situation (see, for example, "Барометр общественных нужд"). The main message of such reports to the population is, "We hear you."

[44] Interview Kem-10.

is: "Let us know about the issues people have and we will try to resolve them." Indeed, the critical issues, those that may place the population on the verge of a riot, are provided at least temporary solutions. Minor issues, which do not require a significant effort on the part of the state, also get resolved. Such a signaling system, however, still leaves the decision power with the state and cannot work as a true accountability mechanism. It helps alleviate the information problem in autocracies and protects the state from a spontaneous protest of those population groups, which have nothing to lose.[45] At the same time, it takes away the opportunities for society to practice self-organization independent of the state. When the state has co-opted the potential activists and cultivated an image of a caring parent who decides which population's needs are worth its attention, society has few opportunities to raise its own leaders who could truly hold the state accountable.

Control of Public Space and Discourse

In addition to co-opting activists as potential agents of social mobilization and managing grievances, around which mobilization may occur, the state-led community organizations also help control the means of mobilization—the usage of physical space as well as information flows and public discussions.

All politicians must use public spaces to build political support among the population, and controlling that space provides the state and its team with a significant advantage over any potential challenger. Many community organizations that I studied in the Kemerovo region and Tatarstan, had a designated physical space, usually provided by the regional or city government. Community centers in Kemerovo had several renovated apartments or parts of stand-alone buildings. The Veteran's Councils had rooms in governmental buildings. Youth organizations in Tatarstan had a network of residential clubs and youth centers as well as several larger facilities for big events.

This physical space as well as the logistical help of community organizations was often used by the current state officials or the deputies of the ruling party for town halls and engaging with voters during public events. During campaigns and between election cycles, the deputies of the municipal and regional legislative bodies in Kemerovo, the vast majority of whom represented the United Russia Party,[46] met with their constituencies, informed them about their work,

---

[45] Dimitrov, "Vertical Accountability in Communist Regimes."
[46] I was not able to find a single mention of a representative of another party holding a meeting with the constituency in a community center.

and collected concerns to bring them up in the city or regional council.[47] Some community centers ran youth voter clubs ("Clubs of Young Voters," "The Choice of the Young") giving the opportunity to the youth wing of the United Russia, the Young Guard, to target the youth audience before elections.[48] Youth organizations in Tatarstan provided the same opportunities to state-supported politicians: For example, the Tatarstan Student League runs a Political Club, which organizes meetings of students with state officials and regional deputies.[49]

Besides the meeting sites, community organizations also helped control the physical space of a neighborhood, which is another venue where a potential opposition might try to run information campaigns. In the Kemerovo region, residential councils, community centers, and the Veterans' Councils, often with the volunteer help of the larger community, attend to the physical space of their neighborhoods by organizing meeting spaces with benches and tables, planting flowers and trees, and keeping them clean. The city government regularly holds competitions for the best courtyard or apartment hallway, encouraging such engagement. In both Kemerovo and Tatarstan, community organizations also kept many neighborhoods under surveillance by organizing volunteer patrols, which helped the police to prevent violence and find the places selling drugs or illegal alcohol. In Kemerovo, these squads included adult local activists, university students, and even adolescents.[50] In Tatarstan, the regionwide organization "Forpost" focused mostly on youth and had its squads in many territories and educational establishments.[51]

Although controlling grassroots politics might not be the primary reason why community organizations took care of the neighborhood territory, it further reduced the opportunities for any social mobilization independent of the state. For example, people and organizations who control the neighborhood physical space are able to influence the display of visual political ads, which is one of the most effective ways to increase a politician's recognition and popularity. Such ads are placed on boards, walls, and other visible places in the neighborhood. Many apartment buildings have special plastic-covered boards by each building entrance, half of which is used for announcements from utility companies and another half for ads. Such boards are guaranteed the attention of everyone living in the building, and access to such boards is very important during electoral

---

[47] On using public events for agitation purposes outside of Kemerovo see also Бузин, *Административные избирательные технологии*, 154–55.
[48] Пресс-служба Горсовета народных депутатов, "'Молодая гвардия' укрепляет тылы."
[49] "Участники политического клуба студентов РТ встретились с депутатом Госсовета Татарстана."
[50] Брежнева, "На добровольных началах"; "Слово активистов."
[51] "Республиканский центр молодежных (студенческих) формирований по охране общественного порядка 'Форпост'"; Министерство внутренних дел по республике Татарстан, "'Форпост' подвел итоги работы и наметил планы на будущий год."

campaigns.[52] The ads placed on such boards are often the last thing voters see before casting their ballot.[53] If state-led community organizations control access to these boards, as is the case in Kemerovo,[54] politicians not endorsed by the state have little chance of displaying their agitation materials in these popular places.

Visual ads can also be placed on leaflets, which are then disseminated around the neighborhood, and here state-led community organizations have an advantage as well, since they often use leaflets even beyond the scope of political campaigns. For example, in Kemerovo, residential council activists, sometimes with the help of schoolchildren, use leaflets to inform the population about traffic and fire safety rules, the need to keep the neighborhood clean, or changes in government regulations regarding public order or benefits.[55] A known political trick, though, is using leaflets that are allegedly unrelated to elections but still contain information about election candidates, and community organizations are in the best position to do that.[56] At the same time, constant surveillance of the neighborhood and maintaining its "cleanliness" guarantees prompt removal of any unsanctioned agitation materials.

Even beyond the scope of electoral campaigns, community organizations, along with the state-controlled media, help to shape public discourse. Some of that influence goes through personal contacts with activists who can spread the word to other people on the ground. In Tatarstan, for example, the Ministry of Youth Affairs used the hierarchy of youth organizations to deliver publicly important information to students and other young adults.[57] In Kemerovo, the city administration has community activists for similar purposes. One instance of that documented in the media was related to the implementation of one of the most controversial social reforms in Russia in the 2000s—the so-called monetization.[58] The municipal social security department worked together with community activists, who knew the population of their territories and were trusted by it, to explain the details of the reform.[59]

Another way state-led community organizations can shape the public discourse, is by saturating the state-controlled media with positive and politically benign topics and activities and pushing away the undesirable content.[60] Such

[52] Бузин, *Административные избирательные технологии*, 143–44.
[53] Бузин, 144.
[54] "Коротко." Кемерово, February 8, 2008.
[55] See, for example, "Коротко." Кемерово, August 24, 2007; Зинчук, "Что знаете о льготах?"; Брежнева, "На добровольных началах"; "Ни дня без дела."
[56] Бузин, *Административные избирательные технологии*, 145.
[57] Interview Kaz-09.
[58] The replacement of in-kind benefits for certain population groups with monetary compensations, which started in 2005.
[59] Шилова, "Хорошее настроение делаем сами"; Ильина, Надежда. "Дойти до каждого."
[60] The "cheerleading"—celebrations and community events—in which community organizations engage is similar to what bots do on the Chinese Internet. Instead of engaging in political discussions and taking the side of the government, they fill online discussion with benign positive information

stories usually revolve around helping those in need, strengthening community ties, developing people's creativity, or working together with the state to help the people.[61] The general emphasis of such messages on practical improvements and community values makes it easy to dismiss alternative political opinions from public discussions because they allegedly only criticize instead of helping. Such avoidance of political discussion is not entirely imposed by the state, but it is actively supported and reproduced by state-led community organizations.[62]

Stability of Electoral Performance

Controlling public space and discourse, monitoring and managing potential discontent as well as social mobilization and co-optation of activists by state-led community organizations are the internal mechanisms of unity-based political machines. Unlike the clientelist political machines in the Rostov region and Altai, the unity-based ones in the Kemerovo region and Tatarstan were more stable performers. As I showed in Chapter 2, they were able to increase the electoral percentage for Vladimir Putin in 2012 compared with the electoral percentage of Dmitry Medvedev in 2008 despite the fact that popular support of the regime had significantly decreased during those years. The internal mechanisms of unity-based political machines that I described in this chapter, help us understand why this was the case.

Unlike clientelist political machines based on multiple interpersonal contacts between politicians, brokers, and individuals, unity-based political machines have impersonal bureaucratic structures. These structures are not renegotiated every time they need to be used for political gain and do not change because of constant political competition at the local level as was the case in the Rostov region and Altai. Rather, they have stable, official hierarchies, which are maintained in working condition via daily engagement in civic projects and public goods provision. Be it schools, community centers, women's organizations, youth clubs, or pensioners' councils, they work on politically neutral projects and initiatives on a regular basis and use the same organizational channels for routine monitoring of discontent, co-optation of activists and other political functions. The position of these organizations in the community

about life in general, successfully distracting the attention of the audience from political issues (King, Pan, and Roberts, "How the Chinese Government Fabricates Social Media Posts for Strategic Distraction, Not Engaged Argument").

[61] Some community organizations even had their own media, for instance the Veterans' Councils in the Kemerovo region published a newspaper, *Zemlyaki*.
[62] Avoidance of political discussions and actions while concentrating on community issues is certainly not unique to Russia: see, for example, Eliasoph, *Avoiding Politics*, for the analysis of the US case.

and contact with the population depends very little on the personalities of the people who run them, which makes it easier to achieve stable performance in any sphere, including electoral manipulations.

Blending the political into the civic is the way authoritarianism thrives in a statist society. When the state is viewed as the only legitimate leader, that is, the only institution possessing group authority, nothing stops state officials from abusing people's desire to belong to a community and be good citizens. Using their monopoly on group authority, they prevent the emergence of political actors who would be independent of the state and able to control it. Moreover, even if, despite all odds, such actors emerge, they will be vulnerable to being hijacked by the state, as the next section shows.

How the State Hijacked a Social Movement: The Story of the Kemerovo Veterans' Councils

Several times, this book has mentioned pensioners' organizations in the Kemerovo region but never told their whole story. In many ways, their role in the regional politics is similar to that of residential councils and community centers: the regionwide network of Veterans' Councils is a community organization for pensioners that is tightly coupled with the state apparatus. There is, though, one important difference: The state did not create the Veterans' Councils but rather successfully hijacked the already existing social movement.

The Kemerovo Veterans' Councils is a regional branch of the nationwide network of the Veterans' Councils—an organization that is widely seen as an extension of state-controlled labor unions and, thus, as a part of state-controlled social infrastructure. Few observers these days realize, though, that this organization originated in the social movement of World War II Soviet veterans. Unlike many social movements that fight for equal rights of different population groups, this movement had a different message. It sought not equal rights but privileges for the veterans that would recognize their sacrifice for the country. This idea of a special privileged status based on one's selfless service to the country continued to inspire the movement even after the Soviet state turned the Veterans' Councils into a pensioners' organization in 1986. The same idea continues to be the key for understanding the activities of the Veterans' Councils in contemporary Russia.

In the section below, I will first present a brief history of the veterans' movement in the Soviet Union and then turn to its history in the Kemerovo region, where Aman Tuleyev, the Kemerovo governor, successfully took control over the regional Veterans' Councils and made them yet another community organization that worked to strengthen his regime.

A Short History of Veterans' Councils in the Soviet Union and Post-Soviet Russia

The Russian Veterans' Councils originated from the social movement of World War II veterans in the USSR, which emerged right after their demobilization in the late 1940s. The key characteristic of this large group that shaped its political agenda was a strong sense of entitlement: veterans shared a conviction that their battlefield sacrifice for the country earned them a right to a special treatment after the war. They demanded economic entitlements as well as recognition of war veterans as a group and creation of their own nationwide organization.[63]

The Soviet government was generally reluctant to satisfy these demands. It provided veterans with some privileges during the war but abolished them in 1947 for economic reasons. Only in the late 1970s, the state finally yielded to veterans' requests and brought some of the entitlements back.[64] The organizational recognition was equally controversial. The Soviet government needed veterans' support for propaganda work, which was the primary mission of the Soviet Committee of War Veterans created in 1956.[65] At the same time, any political organization independent of the party-state would threaten its political monopoly. Several times during the post–World War II decades, the Soviet government allowed the creation of limited organizational infrastructure and then scaled it back.

Even though the Soviet government stymied the veterans' efforts for decades, it could not eliminate the grassroots movement. Veterans kept gathering to celebrate the Victory Day, organized clubs and assistance committees associated with museums, Komsomol cells, or local military enlistment offices, where they worked to preserve the memory of the war and to advocate for their economic needs. All these diverse organizational forms were finally standardized and organized into a hierarchical structure of the Veterans' Councils only in 1986, when Mikhail Gorbachev allowed the institutionalization of the veterans' movement at the national level.[66] By January 1991, the veterans' organization, "The All-Union Public Organization of Veterans (Pensioners) of War, Labor, Army and Law Enforcement Agencies," consisted of more than 180 regional-level units, about 5,000 municipal-level ones, and about 180,000 local organizations.[67]

Ironically, starting with the creation of the designated organization for veterans in 1986, the term "Veterans' Councils" became increasingly misleading.

---

[63] For a comprehensive source on the veterans' movement in the USSR, see Edele, *Soviet Veterans of the Second World War*.
[64] Edele, chap. 8.
[65] Edele, 161–64.
[66] Edele, chap. 7.
[67] Edele, 183.

This new organization united war veterans with the so-called labor veterans, that is, people who devoted a large part of their career to a particular occupation or enterprise, and labor pensioners in general.[68] This unification was not completely artificial, as all these people shared the sense of earned retirement after a lifelong service to the country. However, instead of being an association of military veterans, the Veterans' Councils gradually became the organization for all pensioners regardless of their war or labor veteran status.[69] As World War II veterans have been passing away, the Veterans' Councils have been successfully sustained by the new retirees and the mission of advocating for the needs of the older generation.

In contemporary Russia, the Veterans' Councils[70] is probably the largest civil society organization in the country.[71] It has survived the hectic 1990s and currently represents the constituency of about 28 million retirees.[72] Its organizational structure consists of a hierarchy of branches from the national to the local level with over 70,000 primary organizations and about 2.5 million activists.[73] This big organization is held together by the common cause—serving the needs of the elderly who have earned their right for support and respect with their lifelong labor. The organization generally lacks strict formal subordination, even though the activists in the local Veterans' Councils often look up to the regional and national level ones for guidance.

---

[68] The official title of a labor veteran was a form of moral encouragement in the Soviet Union. Starting in 1995, a Russian federal law "On Veterans" ("О ветеранах") established a number of in-kind benefits for labor veterans.

[69] See Interview Altai-15.

[70] I am talking here only about the Veterans' Councils affiliated with the "The National Public Organization of Veterans (Pensioners) of War, Labor, Army and Law Enforcement Agencies," which is the largest pensioners' organization in Russia. Although it is the largest, it is not the only one. The main competitor organization is the Pensioners' Union, which was created in 1994, almost ceased to exist in the following years, and was revived in 2006. This organization, being formally a civil society one, functions in most regions as a branch of the Pension Fund of the Russian Federation: the heads of the regional branches of the Pensioners' Union are frequently current employees of the Pension Fund and their offices are usually situated in the Pensions Fund building (the list of regional branches of the Pensioners' Union can be found at http://www.rospensioner.ru/regions; simple Internet search confirms that many heads of the regional branches currently work in the Pensions Fund; see also Interview Altai-16).

[71] A lot of information about the activities of the post-Soviet Veterans' Councils and public discussions in these organizations has been obtained from the publications in the national newspaper *Veteran* (Ветеран), Kemerovo regional newspaper *Zemliaki* (Земляки), and other media sources. The structured list of these sources is available as Appendix 4. I will give references to particular sources from this list as appropriate, but some general statements based on this body of publications will be made only with a reference to the list as a whole.

[72] The Veterans' Councils claim all retirees in Russia as members of the organization. This number, therefore, should be treated as an estimate of the constituency size rather than the number of active members.

[73] "Основа успеха—в первичных организациях!"; Всероссийская общественная организация ветеранов (пенсионеров) войны и труда, "Об организации."

In the three post-Soviet decades, the Russian governments did not engage closely with the Veterans' Councils at the national level, while the regional governments took different routes. In some regions, the state officials limited their contacts with the Veterans' Councils to so-called patriotic education and targeted help for the neediest pensioners. In other regions, including Kemerovo, governments developed a much closer relationship with the pensioners' organizations in order to use their full political potential.

Aman Tuleyev's Takeover of the Veterans' Councils in the Kemerovo Region

Aman Tuleyev was the governor of Kemerovo in 1997–2018, which is one of the longest governor terms in post-Soviet Russia. Boris Yeltsin appointed Tuleyev as Kemerovo governor hoping that his political experience and popularity in the region would help to alleviate the political tensions created by a mighty workers' movement in the 1990s.[74] Over the next years, Tuleyev managed to monopolize the power in the region by getting rid of his political opponents, putting big business under his control, and developing organizational structures that helped him control the grassroots politics.

The regional Veterans' Councils was one of the organizations Tuleyev used for the latter task. Their relationship spanned almost three decades, during which Tuleyev gradually turned the organization from an independent political player to an organization fully controlled by the regional government. During the 1990s, when he was affiliated with the Communist Party, Tuleyev allied with it to oppose the market-oriented "democrats" in the Kemerovo region. After he became the governor in 1997, he managed to steer the Veterans' Councils away from the Communist Party and toward supporting him personally, until he completely took over control of the organization in 2003.

Tuleyev's relationship with the Veterans' Councils dates back to at least April 1989, when the Presidium of the regional Veterans' Council nominated Tuleyev as a deputy secretary of the regional Communist Party Committee.[75] In the early to mid-1990s, when Tuleyev was the head of the regional parliament, he actively developed his alliance with the Veterans' Councils by advocating for various veterans' privileges and developing organizational and symbolic connections with them. He often raised the issues of veterans' and pensioners' benefits in the regional parliament,[76] attended Veterans' Council

---

[74] Лукьянова, "Аман во спасение"; Лопатин, *История рабочего движения Кузбасса (1989–1991 гг.)*.

[75] Неворотова, Кушникова, and Тогулев, *Отдать свой опыт людям . . .*, 2:28.

[76] Неворотова, Кушникова, and Тогулев, 2:25–32, 149–51.

conventions,[77] participated in commemorative events related to World War II,[78] and made an effort to recognize veterans' special status publicly.[79] In doing that, Tuleyev not only developed his political agenda of social security and vocally opposed the actions of Mikhail Kisliuk, the current Kemerovo governor and the former workers' movement leader.[80] He also criticized the Veterans' Council and the labor unions for political weakness and willingness to compromise with the regional administration, thus sending a message to the pensioners and the public was that he was an even more principled advocate for them than their own organizations.[81]

Despite a close relationship with Tuleyev, the Kemerovo region Veterans' Councils remained a politically independent organization in the late 1980s and the 1990s. They often supported Tuleyev at various elections at the regional and federal level, agitated for him,[82] organized town halls, helped him collect signatures,[83] and worked in electoral commissions.[84] Their support, however, was not always unified and unequivocal. For example, in 1996, while most members of the Veterans' Council Presidium supported Tuleyev's bid for the Russian president,[85] the deputy chair of the regional Veteran's Council, V. I. Mil'sitov, called for support of Boris Yeltsin in that race.[86] The organization also did not automatically support all Tuleyev's allies, thus reserving the final judgement for itself.[87]

This situation began to change after Tuleyev assumed the governor's post in 1997. During the 1999 parliamentary election, he suddenly broke away from the Communist Party and announced this call at the veterans' convention.[88] He accused the party leadership of a lack of real political progress during the years when they controlled the parliament, and of establishing privileges for themselves while forgetting about the ordinary people, including veterans. He also criticized their lack of desire to work with noncommunists and stressed the need for professionals in the government rather than people of a particular political orientation.[89] Tuleyev's move split the regional Veterans' Council, whose

[77] Неворотова, Кушникова, and Тогулев, 2:91, 6:50–51, 97.
[78] Неворотова, Кушникова, and Тогулев, 3:33, 6:7–8, 35.
[79] Неворотова, Кушникова, and Тогулев, 5:29.
[80] Неворотова, Кушникова, and Тогулев, 3:72.
[81] Неворотова, Кушникова, and Тогулев, 5:32–33.
[82] Неворотова, Кушникова, and Тогулев, 2:147–48.
[83] Неворотова, Кушникова, and Тогулев, 7:6.
[84] Неворотова, Кушникова, and Тогулев, 6:97–119.
[85] Неворотова, Кушникова, and Тогулев, 7:58.
[86] Неворотова, Кушникова, and Тогулев, 7:96.
[87] Неворотова, Кушникова, and Тогулев, 6:5. T. G. Avaliani, a communist deputy from Kemerovo in the 1996–1999 State Duma, tells how Tuleyev unsuccessfully tried to get the Veteran's Councils to support a candidate from the Agrarian Party instead of communist Avaliani at the 1995 federal parliamentary election (see Авалиани, "Наглость правит бал").
[88] Старожилов, "Кузбасс прильнул к 'Медведю.'"
[89] Иванов, "Аман Тулеев: 'Наберу больше голосов—Кузбассу будет легче жить.'"

members were forced to choose between Tuleyev and the communists.[90] In the next few years, the tension between the communist-oriented part of veterans' leadership and Tuleyev was building up. The head of the Veteran's Council, Vladislav Galkin, publicly spoke against Vladimir Putin and the United Russia Party, but in 2003, he ultimately resigned, citing health reasons and the inability to handle the conflict with the regional government.[91]

After Galkin's resignation, Tuleyev took over control of the regional Veterans' Council when the now-loyal members of its presidium elected Nina Nevorotova, Tuleyev's former deputy who had just turned pension age, as the head of the organization. A former schoolteacher, who later served in the city and regional governments, Nevorotova was an experienced and reliable cadre who could cope with an independent and therefore potentially dangerous organization and turn its power to Tuleyev's benefit. She has been heading the Veterans' Council since 2003 while continuing her affiliation with the regional government as the governor's advisor on social policy.[92]

The Expansion of the Veterans' Councils in the Kemerovo Region after 2003

Once Nevorotova took over the Veterans' Council, she began to expand the organizational network and build its capacity for mobilizing, monitoring discontent, and controlling public discourse—much like the mayor of Kemerovo City was expanding the network of residential councils at the same time. She increased the number of primary organizations by more than 20% from 2005 to 2009 (from 1491 to 1827)[93] and created additional Veterans' Councils by occupation, paying particular attention to the retirees of the coal mining industry. Their regional-level Veterans' Council was created in 2006, and it included the miners retired from the enterprises that went out of business.[94] In 2014, when I visited Kemerovo, the main regional veterans' organization had 13 Veterans' Councils by occupation with their own primary organizations and 34 municipal-level Councils that united 1,892 of their "primary cells."[95] All the major Councils had

[90] Старожилов, "Кузбасс прильнул к 'Медведю.'"
[91] Сорокин, "Коммунисты не станут угождать властям."
[92] See the list of sources in Appendix 5.
[93] "В поле зрения—800 тысяч судеб"; "Главное внимание первичкам."
[94] Чурпита, "Бывших шахтеров не бывает"; Ермакова, "Преграды на пути первопроходцев." Including the miners retired from the enterprises that ceased to exist was important because they were the people who would otherwise fall through the cracks. Currently existing enterprises, frequently under pressure from Tuleyev, provided their retirees with support and benefits, but if the enterprise did not exist anymore the pensioners were left without this kind of support. Since quite a few coal mines in Kemerovo region went bankrupt in the 1990s, the number of such people was significant.
[95] Interview Kem-07.

THE POLITICAL AND THE CIVIC   131

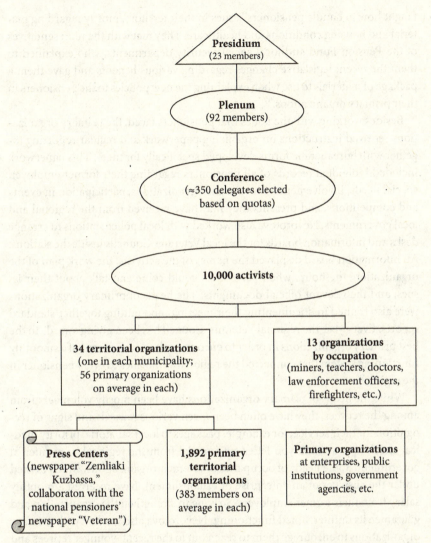

Figure 4.1 Structure of the Veterans' Councils in the Kemerovo region, March 2014.
Sources: Interview Kem-07; "Tochki prilozheniia usilii"; "Glavnoe vnimanie pervichkam."

offices equipped with phones and computers.[96] About 10,000 activists were involved in these organizations throughout the region (see Figure 4.1).

For the heads of primary organizations, Nevorotova developed a special training system. During group workshops and individual interviews, they were

---

[96] Старцев, "Ступенька в завтра."

taught how to handle pensioners' issues in their territory, mostly regarding material and housing conditions and healthcare. They met with the representatives of the Pension Fund and local social security departments, who explained to them the recent legislative changes regarding various benefits and gave them a package of materials to use when explaining the new policies to the pensioners in their primary organizations.[97]

Besides working with the issues that pensioners faced, the primary organizations received instructions on organizing paperwork and regular reporting together with bureaucratic forms developed specifically for them. This paperwork included individual records of all pensioners regarding their former employer, special needs, involvement with veterans' organizations, participation in events and competitions, and presents they may have received from the regional and local governments. Nevorotova also worked with local police stations to arrange desks and information boards for the local Veterans' Councils inside the stations. An information board displayed the names of the activists, the work plan of the organization, the hours when pensioners could come and talk about their issues, and the relevant official documents. The heads of primary organizations were also trained in documenting their meetings and putting together standard reports. Every year the regional Veterans' Council has been giving awards to the best primary organizations in order to encourage the development of a smoothly functioning system that connected the regional authorities to every pensioner in the region.[98]

While the heads of primary organizations have been mostly volunteers from among the retirees, they have often been given various rewards and signs of recognition for their service, for example, packages to local sanatoria, priority medical check-ups, a thank-you letter, or a medal from the regional or municipal government. Some heads of occupational veterans' organizations, which existed under the auspices of an enterprise or establishment, have received a monthly salary from their former employers. Striving to strengthen the organization and guarantee its uninterrupted functioning, Nevorotova also worked with primary organizations to encourage them to reach out to the recent, younger retirees and involve them in the organizations' activities in order to have a trained reserve of cadres that can take over the organization from the current leaders.[99]

To ensure better communication between the different levels of the organization and in particular a better familiarity of the regional Veterans' Council with the local ones, Nevorotova actively traveled across the region[100] and

---

[97] "Центр работы—первички"; Ермакова, "Когда дело ладится."
[98] "Центр работы—первички"; Микельсон, "Знать каждого—по паспорту"; Ермакова, "О чем скажут 'незабудки'"; Федорова and Ермакова, "Инициативы, продиктованные жизнью."
[99] "Центр работы—первички"; Белоусова, "Вписаны в Золотую летопись города."
[100] Неворотова, "И с бедой и с радостью идут к нам…."

quickly introduced a practice of holding veterans' conventions in different municipalities. These conventions were attended not only by pensioners but also by local authorities and representatives of public sector organizations who participated in discussions of pensioners' problems and development of their solutions.[101] Right after taking over the organization in 2003, Nevorotova also introduced a regional program of no-interest loans for pensioners,[102] which were given out by the regional Veterans' Council members during their visits to different municipalities.[103] As one of the members of the regional Veterans' Council told me, they did not simply give out the money to the pensioners—they always talk to each of them during the process, listen to their complaints, and provide information about the activities of the Veterans' Council that can help them.[104]

Another important development that happened under Nevorotova's leadership was a significant expansion of the "media complex."[105] The regional Veteran's Council had had its own newspaper, *Zemliaki*,[106] since 1990. At different points in time, it was funded by the Communist Party,[107] the regional administration under Mikhail Kisliuk,[108] and personally by Tuleyev.[109] The newspaper had been disseminated through the lower-level Veterans' Councils, which subscribed themselves and recruited pensioners to subscribe.[110] In addition to this newspaper, Nevorotova created press centers in all 34 municipal-level Veterans' Councils. Activists in those press centers have worked closely with the local media and with the regional veterans' newspaper "Zemliaki." They have reported on pensioners' issues and the policies of the regional government that address them, written about local history, and participated in "patriotic" education. They have also gathered in Kemerovo to share their experiences and report on the work completed.[111]

Finally, through Nevorotova, Tuleyev took control not only over the regional Veterans' Council but also over the regional branches of alternative national organizations and political parties that could potentially attract dissenters from among the pensioners. The regional branches of Russian Pensioners' Union and Russian Pensioners' Party were established in Kemerovo in 2006, and

---

[101] Бальзанова, "Хороших дел немало"; Ермакова, "Вместе в добрый путь!"; "Нина Павловна Неворотова."
[102] The loans of up to two monthly pensions were given for a year with repayments made through the Pension Fund.
[103] Бальзанова, "Хороших дел немало"; Милютина, "Предназначение защищать"; "Нина Павловна Неворотова."
[104] Interview Kem-07.
[105] "Голос старшего поколения."
[106] An approximate translation is "fellow countrymen," people from the same land.
[107] Неворотова, Кушникова, and Тогулев, *Отдать свой опыт людям*..., 2:170–71, 3:133.
[108] Неворотова, Кушникова, and Тогулев, 5:7–8.
[109] Неворотова, Кушникова, and Тогулев, 5:60.
[110] Неворотова, Кушникова, and Тогулев, 3:136.
[111] Милютина, "Ни дня без строчки."

Nevorotova became the head of both of them.[112] During the same year, the Just Russia Party, which also attracts some supporters from among the pensioners, also created a regional branch in Kemerovo. Not surprisingly, Nevorotova was put in charge of this organization too.[113] As a member of the regional Veterans' Council told me in the interview, "The policy in our region is such that all pensioners should be in one fist, so that they don't disperse."[114]

How Social Statism Makes Social Movements Vulnerable

Why was Tuleyev able to hijack the regional branch of the social movement that survived for decades in the Soviet Union and post-Soviet Russia? I argue that he was successful because he correctly identified the basic sentiment that sustained the movement for decades: *veterans and later pensioners wanted to be recognized and valued by the state*. The benefits that they demanded did not stem only from economic needs—they were a call for respect and recognition of the pensioners' lifetime contribution to their communities, regions, and the whole country. Respect from ordinary people did not carry the same sense of official, legitimate recognition as respect from the state, and the state official who provided this respect could easily put the organization under control.

Tuleyev understood this need for recognition and used it to undermine the Veterans' Council organizational independence. In the 1990s, he criticized its leadership for not doing enough for the veterans. Later, when he was already the governor, he bet on this sentiment again when he forced the leadership of the Veterans' Council to choose between him, the governor who allegedly prioritized the well-being of the veterans over party lines, and their loyalty to the Communist Party. The fact that the loyal communists failed to get enough support in the Veterans' Council, which ultimately voted to elect Nevorotova as the leader of the organization, shows that Tuleyev's bet was right. Once he provided the pensioners with the recognition and respect, few were able to see political interest behind it and resist the state taking over the organization.

The Achilles' Heel of State-Led Unity

The political monopoly of the state not only makes the political machines more reliable and social movements vulnerable to being hijacked by the state but also

---
[112] Союз пенсионеров России; "В Кемеровской области появилось региональное отделение 'Российской партии пенсионеров.'"
[113] Неворотова and Ермакова, "Милосердие нацелено в завтра."
[114] Interview Kem-07.

creates unique vulnerabilities. The universal psychological need to belong, on which group authority of the state rests, has its counterpart, which is no less universal—the need for individual autonomy. Even in most collectivist cultures, people prefer to act out of their own volition rather than be forced by external pressures, including the pressure of social norms. Lack of political space for individual choice does not eliminate the need for autonomy and individual freedom; it does, though, channel this need into the actions sabotaging the otherwise solidary political system from within.

In a political environment where people cannot exercise their freedom by choosing to join an oppositional force, they channel their need for autonomy into skepticism and hypocrisy about the current system. In other words, when there are no other politically salient groups nearby, which they could choose to join, they exercise their freedom by denying the value of their current group—the state—and of the collective action as such. As a result, society divides not along the lines of race, class, or political preferences, but rather into the activists who have faith in the state as a leader and the skeptics, most of whom reluctantly conform but do not express much enthusiasm.

Both in my conversations with the people in the Kemerovo region and Tatarstan and in my readings of secondary sources about them, I observed such instances of people's skepticism. In response to the pressure to join state-led projects, some people would fake participation, falsify statistics in their reports to state officials, and express general discontent about their life and work conditions. This skepticism did not make them more likely to organize against the state, as they still lacked an alternative center of group authority. However, such foot-dragging diminished the effectiveness of political control that the state exercised over society. The fact that in both Tatarstan and the Kemerovo region the regional authorities had to arrange large-scale electoral falsifications indicates that unity-based authoritarianism, while successful in preventing the rise of political opposition, fails to produce a high level of genuine support for the regime.

Chapter Summary

This chapter argued that political machines in statist societies are based on the opposite principle compared to antistatist societies and supported this argument with data from the four studied regions. While the literature on political machines focuses on clientelistic exchanges driven by utility maximization, in statist societies, political machines are based on group unity, the sense of civic duty, and the logic of teamwork. They blend the political into the civic, working through the organizations that already perform many public functions. The chapter showed how in the Kemerovo region and Tatarstan, centralized organizational structures worked smoothly to fulfill various public projects, but also turned into a political machine during election time by blending their political functions with the civic ones. In contrast, in the Rostov region and Altai, the political machines followed the classic principles of clientelism and utility maximization. Leaders of nonstate communities bargained with the state on behalf of their groups, creating bottom-up clientelistic structures with multiple layers of brokers, who used votes as their currency.

The different organizational principle makes the performance of unity-based political machines more stable over time compared to clientelist machines in antistatist societies, in which state officials must constantly negotiate and renegotiate deals. Blending of the civic and the political also allows the state to highjack grassroots movements, and the chapter illustrated this using the story of the Veterans Councils—a grassroots movement of the World War II veterans. State-led unity, however, has a weak spot: By suppressing individual autonomy with group pressure, it induces compliance but also breeds hypocrisy rather than genuine regime support.

The next chapter, which applies the theory of social statism to Russia as a whole, will explore the phenomenon of hypocrisy in statist societies in more detail. The chapter will look at Russia's history through the lens of social statism and present a dynamic model that explains the historical pattern of state oppression and societal resistance, including the political trajectory of Putin's regime, the resistance that has been growing in Russian society in the last decade, and the swings of the public opinion before and after the full-scale invasion of Ukraine in 2022.

5
The Riddle of Russian Authoritarianism

Over the course of its history, Russia continues reviving authoritarianism. Why it happens has been the subject of scholarly debate for a long time. Some scholars and political commentators argue that Russia is a country with a hopelessly authoritarian political culture and the population craves a tsar. Others say that politics in any country can be explained perfectly well by the level of economic development and the default desire of any political leader to monopolize power, which means that Russian authoritarianism is mostly a product of unfortunate historical circumstances. The 2022 Russian invasion of Ukraine intensified the debate about whether Russia is uniquely defined by its imperial past and doomed to remain authoritarian, or whether it resembles other countries, for example, Germany, in similar circumstances and has a tangible chance to democratize in the future.

The theory of authoritarian power developed in this book provides a novel perspective that reconciles some of the existing explanations of Russian authoritarianism. It recognizes the importance of political culture, especially its statist component, and the imperial past that shaped it. At the same time, it interprets this culture in terms of universal motivations of human action, making Russia easily comparable to countries with other political systems. It explains why it may be more difficult for Russia to develop democratic institutions while also showing that there is nothing in its political culture that makes it impossible.

The chapter, first, looks at the different existing explanations of Vladimir Putin's popularity and highlights how the theory of social statism deepens and connects these explanations. Second, it argues that the main tension that has been driving state–society relations in Russia over the course of its history has been the tension between the ideal of a just state and the reality of an oppressive state. It outlines three possible reactions to this conflict—active resistance, passive resistance, and compliant activism. Third, it traces this tension and reactions to it over the course of Russian history, including the most recent period since Russia's full-scale invasion of Ukraine in 2022.

Russian Statism:
The Case of Vladimir Putin's Regime

In the previous chapters, I used the empirical material from different Russian regions to show how unity and division serve as the social roots of authoritarianism in statist and antistatist societies. Despite this territorial variation, however, there is a lot of evidence that Russia as a whole is much closer to the statist society pole than to the antistatist one. Scholars have argued that in Russia, the state is more than just an institution responsible for security, social order, and public goods. It is a "metaphysical entity," which must be protected and served.[1] Some citizens are proud of it; others are ashamed of it; but for all of them, no other social institution has a comparable symbolic power in the Russian political space.

I would also argue that the statism of Russian society has been an important factor of Vladimir Putin's success in consolidating his regime. Researchers often characterize Vladimir Putin as a statist, that is, as someone who believes in the virtue of a strong state and its supreme authority in society, which guarantees order and protection.[2] Putin himself often addressed this issue in his speeches throughout his time in power, starting with his "Millenium message," published two days before Boris Yeltsin handed power over to him on December 31, 1999.[3] Over the years, statism allowed Putin to transcend political and ideological contradictions inside the country, to appeal to different constituencies simultaneously and to pursue economic policies that utilized both market tools and state intervention.[4] His public image has been deliberately built around state institutions and the role of the personal guarantor that those institutions function properly.[5] For over two decades by now, this public image has been well received by the Russian public, and Putin not only stayed in power but has also been a rather popular autocrat.[6]

Scholars have used different concepts to describe and explain Putin's popularity, including personalism, nationalism, performance legitimacy, and social contract. Statism does not contradict any of these explanations but introduces important distinctions and a better understanding of how exactly these different power mechanisms work.

---

[1] The quote is from the interview of Fiona Hill at the Brookings Institute (*Vladimir Putin as Statist*), which is based on Hill and Gaddy, *Mr. Putin*.
[2] Sakwa, "Putin's Leadership"; Hill and Gaddy, *Mr. Putin*.
[3] Hill and Gaddy, chap. 3.
[4] Sakwa, "Putin's Leadership"; Miller, *Putinomics*.
[5] Wengle and Evans, "Symbolic State-Building in Contemporary Russia."
[6] Greene and Robertson, *Putin v. the People*.

Personalism

Putin's regime is often called personalist by academic researchers and political commentators alike. Putin's political ratings are consistently much higher than those of other politicians or political institutions in Russia. With his macho image in the media and the statement by the speaker of the Russian State Duma that "if there is no Putin, there is no Russia," it seems indeed that Putin has created a cult of personality.[7] Putin, however, is not the first personalist ruler of Russia; there seems to be a pattern of personalist rule, which existed before him. The figure of supreme leader—the tsar—has been important in Russia for centuries, and Joseph Stalin also created a cult of personality, which the Communist Party had to debunk.

Recent research in psychology of leadership convincingly shows that successful leadership does not depend on the qualities of the leader's personality but rather on his ability to articulate the collective identity—the "we-ness"—of her followers and to become the embodiment of that collective identity.[8] Personalist leadership, thus, is rooted in group membership and group authority, and the important question is which group or groups have this power in society.

In Russia, this group seems to be the state, which explains why Russia is prone to personalist rule of state leaders and why Putin was able to capitalize on that. Since Russians view the state as their group, the state leader who embraces the same identity and successfully demonstrates that he cares about state collective interests above all else resonates with such popular expectations. Putin was lucky to begin his first term during the economic boom in Russia, which made it easy to claim credit for the people's collective interests. He has also deliberately constructed his image as the personal guarantor of smooth functioning of state institutions inside the country and the defender of state interests outside of it.[9] His political intuition and, quite possibly sincere, belief in the supremacy of the state matched the preexisting societal views in the same way as had happened for other personalist rulers in Russia.

---

[7] Smyth, "The Putin Factor"; Sperling, "Putin's Macho Personality Cult"; Cassiday and Johnson, "Putin, Putiniana and the Question of a Post-Soviet Cult of Personality"; Trudolyubov, "Drop the Corruption, Keep the Authoritarianism"; Frye, "What's Vladimir Putin's End Game?"; Хамраев, Нагорных, Корченкова, and Самохина, "Валдайский клуб убедили в безальтернативности Владимира Путина."

[8] Haslam, Reicher, and Platow, *The New Psychology of Leadership*; Hogg, "A Social Identity Theory of Leadership."

[9] Wengle and Evans, "Symbolic State-Building in Contemporary Russia"; Greene and Robertson, *Putin v. the People*; Sharafutdinova, *The Red Mirror*. See also Slater, "Iron Cage in an Iron Fist," on the compatibility of personalized rule with strong state institutions.

Nationalism

"Nationalism" is another term often associated with Putin's regime by some scholars and, more often, political observers.[10] This association is not surprising, given Putin's aggressive foreign policy and warm relationships with some far-right Western politicians as well as the domestic turn to conservative family and religious values. In trying to understand these trends in Russian politics, however, it is important to delineate the concepts of nationalism, patriotism, conservatism, and even fascism[11] or to understand whether these ideological trends are orchestrated or merely adopted by the Kremlin. Nationalism provides a simple lens for explaining multiple complicated phenomena all at once but may obscure important distinctions.[12]

One important trend that the concept of nationalism does capture in the case of Russia is the growth of national unity. Unlike Russia of the 1990s, Russia in the 2010–20s is a country with a more capable state, pronounced collective identity, and widespread national pride. The growth of this national unity is the result of the collective trauma of the 1990s and the subsequent recovery of national self-worth. It both resonates with and is formed by the state-media propaganda, and it also served as the basis of the post-Crimea euphoria among the Russian population as well as popular support of the 2022 invasion of Ukraine.[13] This ideology and sentiment of national unity is usually referred to in the Russian public space as "patriotism" rather than nationalism, and the tendency of the state to monopolize the discourse of patriotism is one of the manifestations of the statist political environment discussed in this book.[14]

The term "Russian nationalism," however, refers to two very different phenomena: Russian ethnic nationalism and Russian official nationalism.[15] If the Russian official nationalism is, by definition, the political agenda of the state, Russian ethnic nationalism can be found both in the actions of some Russian officials and among the political opposition.[16] Ethnic and official nationalisms in Russia often work at cross purposes, since they represent competing political forces. Groups of ethnic Russian nationalists have been rather independent from

---

[10] See, for example, Marten, "Vladimir Putin"; Clover, "The Return of Russian Nationalism"; Sipher, "Vladimir Putin Isn't as Russian as He Seems"; Foer, "It's Putin's World."
[11] Motyl, "Putin's Russia as a Fascist Political System."
[12] Laruelle, *Russian Nationalism*, 4, 7.
[13] Галямина, "Мы-они"; Matovsky, "The Logic of Vladimir Putin's Popular Appeal"; Sharafutdinova, *The Red Mirror*; "Далекая близкая война."
[14] Goode, "Love for the Motherland"; Goode, "Becoming Banal."
[15] Many chapters in this volume discuss the different interactions between official and ethnic nationalisms in Russia: Kolstø and Blakkisrud, *The New Russian Nationalism*.
[16] Laruelle, *Russian Nationalism*, pt. 3; Greene and Robertson, *Putin v. the People*, 59–64.

the state and often prosecuted by it on the charges of extremism.[17] At the same time, the rise of national pride in the Russian public opinion after the Crimea annexation has not been accompanied by the rise of ethnic nationalism or xenophobia, as one might expect. Multiple empirical studies found that ethnic nationalist attitudes and xenophobia have remained stable or declined after 2014, and, if anything, Russians came to view their national identity as more ethnically inclusive.[18] The agenda of this inclusive—and sometimes aggressively inclusive—official nationalism is advanced by the Russian state, and the theory of social statism explains why this statist kind of nationalism is appealing to the Russian population.

The concept of statism, thus, makes it possible to distinguish between statist and antistatist kinds of nationalism. Historically, the rise of nationalism in Europe was a rebellion against multiethnic empires and was based on the idea that "people who spoke for coherent nations—and they alone—had the right to rule sovereign states."[19] As a reaction to that, the imperial rulers tried to turn their subjects into "coherent nations" by promoting what different authors called state-led or official nationalism.[20] The term "nationalism," thus, emphasizes the ideas of citizen equality and their belonging to the nation, but it does not imply that people must place state institutions at the center of their national identity, since it is only required for official nationalism. Nationalism may be successfully built in an antistatist society through the efforts of private actors, as it happens in the United States.[21]

Since nationalism can be statist or antistatist, I would argue that the term "statism" captures the Russian national unity more precisely than "nationalism." The Russian statist unity is better understood as the successor of the Russian imperial past than as a version of European nationalism or nationalism in the United States.[22] The inclusive character of Russian statism parallels the long imperial tradition of gathering different peoples under the umbrella of the Russian state and allowing the local cultures and institutions to exist in parallel with the Russian statist identity as long as they recognize its supremacy.[23] This inclusivity is at the core of the conflicts between Russian ethnic nationalists and Putin. His

---

[17] Verkhovsky and Kozhevnikova, "The Phantom of Manezhnaya Square"; Yudina and Alperovich, "Summer 2011"; Yudina, "In the Absence of the Familiar Article"; Arnold, *Russian Nationalism and Ethnic Violence*.

[18] Alexseev and Hale, "Rallying 'round the Leader More than the Flag"; Chapman et al., "Xenophobia on the Rise?"

[19] Tilly, "States and Nationalism in Europe 1492–1992," 133.

[20] Seton-Watson, *Nations and States*; Tilly, "States and Nationalism in Europe 1492–1992"; Anderson, *Imagined Communities*, chap. 6.

[21] Clemens, *Civic Gifts*.

[22] Понарин and Комин, "Дилемма русского национализма"; Pain, "The Imperial Syndrome and Its Influence on Russian Nationalism."

[23] Kivelson and Suny, *Russia's Empires*.

interest lies in maintaining an inclusive national unity in which the state reigns supreme, while the nationalists want "Russia for (ethnic) Russians," in which the state serves their ethnic group.

Performance Legitimacy and the Social Contract

The last explanation for Putin's popularity with which I will engage is related to so-called performance legitimacy. Its argument connects Putin's popularity with the rapid growth of Russia's economy during Putin's first two terms in the 2000s, which was a long-awaited relief for the Russian population after the deep economic crisis of the 1990s. This argument uses a very intuitive idea that people care about their material well-being and will support the government on whose clock the economy does well.[24]

Although there is a lot of truth to this argument, especially if we look at the period between 2000 and 2009, seeing Putin's popularity as directly connected to people's pocketbook considerations would leave too many things unexplained. The dynamic of Putin's approval index has not always followed economic performance and reacted even more strongly to the second Chechen war in 1999, the benefits reform in 2005, the annexation of Crimea in 2014, and the pension reform in 2018.[25] In addition to that, Putin's support across demographic and economic groups does not vary much, even if the justification for that support does.[26]

Statism, however, explains how these facts can be reconciled with the performance legitimacy argument. The Russian population views the state as the dominant collective providing the security net, and economic security is part of it. Putin was the state ruler who initially fulfilled people's expectations of not just economic growth but also security and stability. The Chechen war was a collective security issue; the public framing of the Crimea annexation and the 2022 invasion of Ukraine as a demonstration of the Russian state's decisiveness in defending an ethnically Russian population connected to the same theme. The benefits and pension reforms, on the other hand, were seen by the people as an attack on the collective security net, which resulted in a decline in Putin's support. Economic factors, thus, are viewed within the framework of collective security rather than of individual material well-being.

---

[24] Treisman, "Presidential Popularity in a Hybrid Regime"; Treisman, "Putin's Popularity since 2010."

[25] For a more detailed analysis of the dynamic of Putin's approval, see Matovski, "The Logic of Vladimir Putin's Popular Appeal," 229.

[26] Matovski, "The Logic of Vladimir Putin's Popular Appeal"; Левинсон, "Внуки против бабушек"; Гудков, "Доверие политикам и президентское голосование."

This economic aspect of collective security is captured rather well by the concept of "social contract" although the very term "contract" may be misleading. Scholars use this term to refer to an arrangement between an authoritarian political regime and the population, in which the regime provides the population with stable employment and a social security net, while the population agrees to give up their political rights and remain quiescent.[27] The term "contract," though, may obscure the nature of this arrangement, as it is not an agreement of two independent parties, exchanging favors. Rather than being a contract, it is an institution.[28] It involves a common identity, group belonging, social norms, and an expectation that the group will provide a security net for its members and the leader will commit to this goal on behalf of the group. Material well-being is important, but within this material well-being, the state is held responsible for the safety net rather than for the size of one's income. Violation of this responsibility hurts the ruler's support stronger than declining economic performance.

The Search for a Just State and the Russian Political Culture

Vladimir Putin's regime is only one instance of authoritarianism in Russia. There is a historical pattern of reproducing authoritarianism, and scholars have debated the best explanation for it. As mentioned earlier, some scholars say it is the result of authoritarian political culture. One of the most famous contributors to this tradition was Richard Pipes, who famously argued that state domination has formed the Russian authoritarian political system and culture.[29] This system, he said, is inherently hostile to freedom, participatory public sphere, individualism, property rights, and the rule of law, all of which served as the basis of European politics and public life. What Russia had instead of these European freedoms was a patrimonial system, in which the despotic power of the tsar governed all the people and property as his own, leaving no space for public initiatives or decision-making. The tsarist regime has formed this political culture of obedience, which later resulted in the lack of individual freedoms in the Soviet Union, and the subsequent failure of democracy to take root in Russia. According to this tradition, liberal democracy is alien to the Russian culture, and Russia is doomed to remain authoritarian.

---

[27] See, for example, Cook, *The Soviet Social Contract and Why It Failed*.
[28] For a discussion of this term along the same lines, see Heydemann, "Social Pacts and the Persistence of Authoritarianism in the Middle East," 25.
[29] Pipes, *Russia under the Old Regime*; Pipes, *Russian Conservatism and Its Critics*. For another example of research explaining Russian history through the lens of political culture, see Obolonskiĭ, *The Drama of Russian Political History*.

Many researchers disagreed with this line of thought, and the existing counterarguments roughly follow two approaches. The first approach is taken by some social scientists who argue that Russia is a perfectly "normal" country. It does not exhibit any abnormal sympathy to authoritarianism, these researchers say, if you compare it with the countries at a similar level of socioeconomic development rather than with Western liberal democracies with much higher living standards.[30] A version of this approach are the studies that link the authoritarian turn under Vladimir Putin to the country's bitter experience of the 1990s and a combination of historical circumstances during the postcommunist transition.[31] These researchers also argue that basic people's desire for economic prosperity and political stability can explain Putin's success without recourse to authoritarian political culture formed centuries ago.[32]

The second approach is used primarily by other historians who do not deny the importance of historical legacy and culture but argue that the Russian political tradition is not simply a negative of the liberal democratic one.[33] This tradition must be understood in its own terms rather than through the lens of Western categories. These researchers argue that although the Russian political system did not have formal representative institutions for most of its history, in practice, the power of the Russian tsar was limited by the societal expectation that the tsar must be pious and must listen to the advice of his subjects.[34] Although resistance to the tsar's authority was almost absent from this worldview, disagreement and disobedience were acceptable if the tsar's morality was corrupted by evil.[35] The very status of subjects ("slaves") of the tsar not only underscored his power but also claimed the subjects' membership right—the right to participation in the political universe.[36] Such participation did not come in the form of representation, but had other forms, such as petitioning, which institutionalized the individual's direct connection with the tsar.[37] In general, this political system was

---

[30] Colton and McFaul, "Are Russians Undemocratic?"; Shleifer and Treisman, "A Normal Country"; Fish, *Democracy Derailed in Russia*.

[31] Gel'man, *Authoritarian Russia*; Matovski, "The Logic of Vladimir Putin's Popular Appeal."

[32] Treisman, "Presidential Popularity in a Hybrid Regime"; Treisman, "Putin's Popularity since 2010."

[33] One exception to this disciplinary boundary is political scientist Andrei Tsygankov (see, for example, Tsygankov, *The Strong State in Russia*). He argues not only that Russia has a tradition of a strong state, which had been successful in counteracting external threats, but also that autocracy, which is not equal to despotism, rather than Western-style democracy is the best political system for Russia. He is one example of whom Richard Pipes called the Russian conservatives, while Tsygankov believes that Pipes's views are driven by Russophobia and lack of respect for the choices of the Russian people.

[34] Shields Kollmann, "Muscovite Political Culture," 95.

[35] Shields Kollmann, 92.

[36] Shields Kollmann, 96; Poe, "What Did Russians Mean When They Called Themselves 'Slaves of the Tsar'?"; Kivelson, "Muscovite 'Citizenship': Rights without Freedom."

[37] Shields Kollmann, "Muscovite Political Culture," 98.

based on societal consensus, and symbols and rituals told more about the crux of this political arrangement than formal institutions and explicit rules.[38]

How does the theory of social statism developed in this book contribute to this debate? It agrees with historians in saying that state dominance has had a major lasting impact on Russian politics by forming a set of societal preferences about the political sphere. However, I understand the nature of these statist preferences differently than Richard Pipes and other researchers in this tradition and more in line with his opponents. Pipes's theory implies that centuries of state dominance have made Russian people hostile to individual freedoms. In contrast, I argue that the historical domination of the Russian state did not eliminate people's desire for freedom but rather created *a political tension between the ideal of a just state that respects individual freedoms and the reality of the repressive state that does not*. While it is true that the Russian people never sought a weak state,[39] they never enjoyed being oppressed by the state either.

This tension is different from what most scholars imagine as contentious politics, which is concerned with power-sharing among different groups. In contrast to that, this tension is internal, that is, it happens not between groups, but inside the group that shares an identity. To a large degree, this is the tension inside the mind of each individual who feels both attached to the state and oppressed by it. Even in most collectivist societies, people prefer to choose to follow social norms rather than be forced into it.[40] If they choose to do it, their belonging is authentic, that is, their own interests and the interests of their group match. If they are forced rather than given a choice, it undermines the moral authority of the group and breeds hypocrisy: Are the norms of, say, the socialist society indeed so good if the state must force people to follow them? Belonging to the state provides people with a sense of identity, security, and pride. However, the lack of choice that comes with it violates the fundamental psychological need for autonomy and creates internal conflict between group authority and the demand for individual freedom.

This in-group conflict is not exclusive to statist societies, but only there does it become the main driver of domestic politics. Nonstate groups, for example, religious ones, may also be very restrictive toward their members. However, the state is the only institution that controls the territory and has a dedicated coercive apparatus. It uses these powers to persecute disloyal individuals and groups with alternative identities that threaten the state monopoly. Lack or weakness of alternative identities in the public space make it very difficult to resist state oppression. If in antistatist societies, resistance to the state often grows around

---

[38] Shields Kollmann, 100; Kivelson and Suny, *Russia's Empires*, 8.
[39] Tsygankov, *The Strong State in Russia*.
[40] Kasser and Sheldon, "Autonomy Is No Illusion."

146   THE SOCIAL ROOTS OF AUTHORITARIANISM

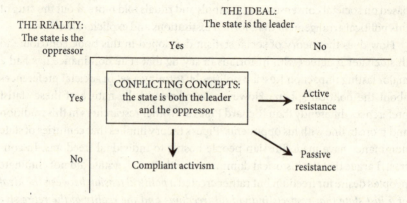

Figure 5.1 Societal reactions to the conflict between the ideal and the reality of state–society relations.

nonstate identity groups and their elites,[41] people in statist societies do not have such options. Their legitimate leader is the state, and the tragedy of their situation is that *their leader is simultaneously their oppressor*. The Russian state is cheered by the Russian people for its leadership in economic modernization campaigns, the war with Nazi Germany, and the development of science that helped to send the first man to space. The same Russian state, however, is resented by the Russian people for systematic lack of concern for the needs of those who remain loyal to the state and make all its achievements possible. The people want to have a state that respects them, and all they have is a state that oppresses them.[42]

This mismatch between the desired ideal and reality presents the Russian people with a cognitive and emotional conflict that is difficult to resolve, and the reactions to this conflict can be roughly separated into three types (see Figure 5.1). Some people choose to stick with the ideal image of the state and justify the incidents of state repression in different ways.[43] Other people choose to condemn state repression and deny any value to the ideal of a just state. Yet others refuse to resolve this conflict altogether by shielding themselves with a wall of skepticism and moral relativism, distancing from the public life, and cherishing private relationships with family and friends instead. These reactions can be activated in the mind of the same individual in different circumstances as they are

---

[41] Slater, "Revolutions, Crackdowns, and Quiescence," 2009.

[42] As one Russian respondent interviewed for Paul Goode's research put it, "patriotism is love for the motherland, but it would be nice if it were mutual" (see Goode, "Becoming Banal," 12).

[43] Compliant activism should not be conflated with rightful resistance (O'Brien and Li, *Rightful Resistance in Rural China*). Compliant activism is not resistance: it is an enthusiastic support of the state and often a denial of any wrongdoing by the state.

all reactions to the same basic conflict—the conflict between the ideal of a just state and the reality of a repressive one.[44]

The rest of the chapter will trace this conflict and reactions to it throughout Russian history. It will describe the circumstances in which the Russian state established its authority, and then show the structural similarity of state–society relations in different historical eras. Despite all the economic, social, and political transformations that Russia has gone through over the centuries, the interaction between state repression and people's search for a just state remains the core issue framing Russian domestic and foreign politics.

The Foundations of State Authority in Russia

When and how did the Russian state build up its authority? Most historians studying Russia agree that it happened gradually in the 15th–18th centuries, when the Muscovy state united Russian principalities under its rule, claimed independence from the Golden Horde, and subsequently weakened the rival institutions—the Russian hereditary aristocracy and the Orthodox Church—that could limit state power. It was during that time that the idea of a just and pious state leader who should be followed by their subjects grew roots in the Russian political culture.

In large part, the process of building group authority by the early Russian state was driven by external threats from multiple directions—the East, South, and West—although historical contingencies might have played a role too.[45] In the 15th century, the Muscovite grand princes united different principalities of the Early Rus' under their rule. After that, they claimed independence from the weakening Golden Horde, which used to tax the population of Russian principalities and approve the rights of the Russian princes for their thrones. Ivan III, the Muscovite grand prince, began calling himself "Tsar of All Rus" and "autocrat" to underscore this newly acquired sovereignty.[46] The large new Muscovite state was often seen as a threat by its neighbors, but it also remained vulnerable

---

[44] These reactions bear a similarity to Hirschman's exit, voice, and loyalty (Hirschman, *Exit, Voice, and Loyalty*), but I do not share Hirschman's methodological individualism, in which individuals remain group members only as long as it benefits their individual interests. In contrast, I treat the need to belong as one of the main motivators of human behavior, which often conflicts with individual autonomous needs.

[45] Sergei Sharov-Delone (Сергей Шаров-Делоне), for example, in his 2013 lecture "Alternative pathways in 1400 and the Autocracy Choice" ("Развилка 1400 г. и самодержавный выбор,") has argued that in the late 14th–early 15th centuries, Russian political development was very similar to that in Europe, but in the early 15th century, a combination of several random historical circumstances primarily related to the relative power of elite actors with different ideals of political order in mind, set the country on the path of consolidated centralized power.

[46] Bushkovitch, *A Concise History of Russia*, 39.

to multiple external threats: early on, by Lithuania and, in later centuries, by Poland, Sweden, and the Tatars as well as the Ottoman and Habsburg empires.[47]

The persistent external threats created favorable conditions for strengthening centralized authority and weakening the Russian hereditary aristocracy—boyars—and the Orthodox Church. In the early days of the Russian state, the tsar needed boyars' support to rule, and it was not always easy to obtain, as feuds between boyar clans were common.[48] However, as defending themselves from powerful external actors required unity, boyars ultimately accepted the tsar's rule as the lesser evil. Over the next two centuries, the institution of boyars was gradually weakened and replaced with nobility, whose defining feature was service to the tsar.[49]

The Orthodox Church, which was an important unifying institution in the Muscovy state, also conceded its independent authority to the tsar. The key moment for that was the church schism of the mid-17th century. Patriarch Nikon, the head of the Russian Orthodox Church at the time, initiated reforms for faith purity in order to make the Russian Orthodox Church the new ecumenical center of the Orthodox world, the role Constantinople used to play before it fell to the Ottomans. The reforms divided the church community, and Nikon needed the tsar's support to strengthen his position. Tsar Aleksei, who reigned at the time, supported the reforms but not Nikon's ambition to turn the Moscow Patriarchate into an ecumenical one, which would dominate not only the other Orthodox Churches but also the tsar. Aleksei's position offended Nikon, who dramatically resigned from his post in response. To reaffirm his own legitimacy, Aleksei invited Greek prelates from Constantinople to the church council, where they happily endorsed the reforms that followed Greek rather than the old Russian norms. This endorsement further weakened the clergy that opposed the reforms and strengthened the position of the tsar as the God-appointed ruler of the people.[50]

According to historians, the symbolic role of the tsar as a ruler having a direct relationship to God and embodying the common good is key to understanding political and public life in the Muscovy state and the Russian Empire. In the 16th century, as political documents demonstrate, observers already had a rather uniform vision of the tsar as leading his people to salvation. He was assumed to act benevolently, and the people were to follow him.[51] By obeying the tsar, people signified themselves as "slaves" of God and joined his journey to salvation. In front of God, the tsar was one of them—the best and most virtuous one. The

---

[47] Kivelson and Suny, *Russia's Empires*, 8.
[48] Bushkovitch, *A Concise History of Russia*, chap. 3.
[49] Hosking, *Russian History*, chap. 2.
[50] Hosking, chap. 2.
[51] Shields Kollmann, "Muscovite Political Culture," 92; Rowland, *God, Tsar, and People*.

tsar's direct connection to God legitimized his power and made the Russian state an existential institution, the metaphysical entity that must be protected and served.[52]

This ideal model of power, however, was not completely unidirectional and assumed that the interests of the people are incorporated into the interests of the state. One obligation expected from the virtuous tsar was taking advice from his subjects, that is, taking into account their needs, desires, and opinions.[53] The tradition of petitions to the supreme authority, which is alive and well even in contemporary Russia, is based on this expectation, as is the tradition of advisory boards. Through such mechanisms, people's needs and preferences were supposed to be incorporated into state policies, so that the state could lead the team efforts to solve these problems in society.

Starting in the 17th century, the state increasingly assumed the role of the civil society leader, that is, the leader of people's collective efforts to solve internal social problems. At that time, the idea emerged that it was one of tsar's duties to inspire individual voluntaristic contributions to the common good.[54] Catherine II was driven by a similar idea in the late 18th century, when she encouraged the development of the educated class by instituting press freedoms, allowing free associations, and expanding education opportunities. In her vision, these associations were supposed to work together with the state on various developmental goals.[55] As we will see later, this idea of teamwork spearheaded by the state was often behind the different forms of compliant activism in Russian society.

This ideal model of a just state, which leads the people's collective pursuit of happiness, however, has never become a reality. The Russian monarchs were not caricature despots; they modernized the country, developed its culture, and sometimes even implemented liberalizing reforms. However, most of them continued to hold a patronizing view of society, take steps to strengthen the state's control over it, weaken the authority of other groups and institutions, and ignore the need to develop effective mechanisms of society's input to state policies.[56] For the greater part of its history, the Russian state, including the state bureaucracy, has used its symbolic power to prioritize its own interests over the interests of its subjects and citizens. Although some feedback institutions such as petitions, local self-governance, and advisory bodies existed, none of them was powerful enough to turn the Russian autocracy into a political system where the population could have a say in state policies on a regular basis.

---

[52] Brookings Institution, *Vladimir Putin as Statist*.
[53] Shields Kollmann, "Muscovite Political Culture," 95.
[54] Shields Kollmann, 99.
[55] Ely, "The Question of Civil Society in Late Imperial Russia," 231.
[56] Ely, 231. On the lack of publicly influential elites independent from the state, see also Гудков, Дубин, and Зоркая, *Постсоветский человек и гражданское общество*, 22–24.

Resistance and Compliance in Tsarist Russia

Throughout history, the reactions of Russian society to the lack of political feedback mechanisms ranged from active resistance to compliant activism. Historians still debate where exactly the boundaries between the different reactions lie and how it is best to categorize them.[57] What looked like active resistance, for example, peasant uprisings, were often fueled by a rather conservative idea of politics, while the compliant activism of the intelligentsia often aimed to transform the system from below and from within.

These resistance and transformation attempts existed side-by-side with the apathy and fatalism of the majority of the population, who dealt with the abusive state by lowering their expectations and adjusting to the reality, which they did not believe they could change.[58] Even nowadays, this fatalism is often regarded as one of the main elements of the Russian culture.[59] However, it is important not to overestimate its significance. Historically, the Russian state increased repressions and developed political police not because the majority of the population was passive and fatalist, but because of the persistent active attempts of different groups in Russian society to transform its political system.

During the eras of the Muscovy state and the Russian empire, societal resistance came from two main sources: the peasants often led by Cossacks and the intelligentsia influenced by Western ideas and eager to reform the Russian autocracy. Peasant riots against worsening conditions of serfdom happened in the Muscovy Tsardom and the Russian Empire fairly often, but most of them were short in time and small in scale. There were two larger peasant uprisings, though—the ones led by Stepan Razin (1667–1671) and Yemelyan Pugachev (1773–1775)—whose common features illustrate the people's quest for a just state.[60]

Both leaders of these uprisings were Cossacks—a quasi-ethnos that lived in the Russian frontier. Although Cossacks thought of themselves as loyal allies

---

[57] David-Fox, "Whither Resistance?" The authors in this volume discuss the Soviet period, but the same conceptual issues apply to other historical periods too.

[58] See, for example, Howell, College, and Wenzel, "Rationality in a Fatalistic World."

[59] Wierzbicka, *Semantics, Culture, and Cognition*, 396; Nemtsova, "Russia's Fatalism Has Fatal Consequences against COVID-19."

[60] I will not discuss here two other major uprisings that are often mentioned together with Razin's and Pugachev's ones—the uprisings led by Ivan Bolotnikov in 1606–1607 and Kondratiy Bulavin in 1707–1708. Bolotnikov's uprising took place during the Time of Troubles, between the two dynasties of Russian tsars when state authority did not firmly belong to any of them, and involved not only peasants but also nobility as participants. Bulavin's uprising was driven by Cossacks, a group with a distinct identity of their own, and did not coordinate with peasants who staged a series of uprisings at the same time. Although some of the features that I discuss in relation to Razin's and Pugachev's uprisings were present here too, there were enough differences not to lump them together for the purposes of current discussion. For more information about these uprisings, see, for example, Glinski, "Peasant Uprisings"; Avrich, *Russian Rebels, 1600–1800*.

of Russian tsars, they had a distinct identity, which emerged before the consolidation of the Muscovy state, and strong traditions of self-governance.[61] In fact, the Cossacks' independence and privileges was one of the institutions that the Russian state aimed to weaken, but it only partially succeeded. This distinct identity together with the specialization in warfare made it easier for Cossacks to stage an uprising against the state.[62]

To gain legitimacy among the peasant masses, though, the leaders of the uprisings had to speak to the ideal of a just state that existed in the minds of most peasants. Both Razin and Pugachev framed their uprisings as aimed at defending the virtuous tsar against enemies. Razin called for fighting the boyars, who allegedly had a bad influence on Tsar Aleksei Mikhailovich.[63] Pugachev himself claimed to be Tsar Peter III, who allegedly escaped murder a decade earlier and was now leading a rebellion to give the peasants back the freedoms taken away by his treacherous wife, Catherine II.[64] In both cases, disobedience to the current authorities was justified by the monarch's behavior, which did not fit the image of a pious leader who cared about her subjects, and people's duty in this situation was to put in place the right, virtuous tsar.

The second source of resistance, intelligentsia, that is, the educated elite, played a key role in the state–society tensions of the 19th century. The intelligentsia positioned itself as a moral alternative to the state, as everything it did was for the good of the whole society rather than any of its parts. Ironically, the Russian intelligentsia grew from the reforms by Catherine II mentioned earlier in this chapter. She imagined that the new educated class would work together with the state to develop the country rather than become a moral alternative to the state. However, as the young noblemen began traveling abroad for their education in the next few decades, they started absorbing Western ideas of alternative political orders. It was these people who staged the poorly timed and organized Decembrist revolt in 1825, during the interregnum after the sudden death of Alexander I. Influenced by Western ideas, they planned to turn Russia into a constitutional monarchy or even a republic.[65] After the Decembrists' defeat, Nicholas I further strengthened the control of the political opposition by moving the political police from the Ministry of Internal Affairs to his personal chancellery.[66]

This increased control, however, did not stop the intelligentsia's demand for expanding political participation. In large part, this demand for

---

[61] Buchanan, "Cossacks"; Plokhy, *The Cossack Myth*.
[62] Avrich, *Russian Rebels, 1600–1800*, 59.
[63] Avrich, 78–79.
[64] Stearns, "Pugachev, Emelyan Ivanovich (1742–1775)"; Avrich, *Russian Rebels, 1600–1800*, 183.
[65] Bushkovitch, *A Concise History of Russia*, 153.
[66] Bushkovitch, 156.

participation was driven by the emerging sense of national identity in urban society, which developed over the course of the 19th century. As the number of voluntary associations grew, the press and literature developed, and educational opportunities expanded, "educated Russians came in one way or another to conceive of Russia not merely as the domain of the tsar but as a government created by its people and for its people."[67] The intelligentsia debated the political fate of the country with Slavophiles and Westernizers being the main opposing camps, assisted the state when Alexander II implemented his liberalizing reforms, created charitable associations, and developed local self-governance through the *zemstvo* network, which brought over 70,000 technical specialists to modernize agriculture and the countryside.[68] The Russian state did not resist such contributions from the intelligentsia, as they fit well into the existing tradition of state leadership. However, attempts to go beyond developmental issues and restrict the political power of the state did not fit into the statist political framework nearly as well, as the Russian monarchs continued to dismiss the idea of people's direct participation in political decision-making.

By the early 20th century, Russian civil society became an important enough moral alternative to the state to unite enough participants for the protests and the general strike in 1905, which pushed Nicholas II to form a legislative body and grant civil liberties.[69] Unfortunately, this alternative was not strong enough to maintain the legislative institution until it could grow roots. By that time, the continued state resistance to political reform throughout the 19th century convinced part of Russian intelligentsia to reject liberalism and constitutionalism in favor of Marxist ideology as a more radical theory and practice. Instead of creating and maintaining alternative institutions that would balance the power of the state, the radicals' quest for justice led to the creation of a state that was even more oppressive than the tsarist one.

The Search for a Just State in the Soviet Union

In many ways, the Soviet Union was a rupture with the past, as the 1917 revolution and the civil war shattered society's structure. Rather quickly, however, the state resurrected as the main institution ordering social life, now under a different name and with a different ideological basis. The preexisting ideal of a just state, which made the tsar such a powerful political symbol, eventually provided a mold for the Marxist doctrine, originally unfavorable to the idea

---

[67] Ely, "The Question of Civil Society in Late Imperial Russia," 232.
[68] Ely, 234.
[69] Ely, 235.

of a strong state. The result was a state that exercised a much tighter control of social, economic, and political life for the sake of a modern atheist version of salvation—communism.

Similar to the tsar in the Russian Empire, the Communist party-state claimed to stand for the common good, to act benevolently, that is, in the interests of the people, and take advice ("soviet" in Russian) from them. The Soviet propaganda encouraged voluntary work for the collective good, while also benevolently claiming that the party always had people's interests and well-being in mind. Just like the attitude of Russian tsars toward society, the attitude of the Communist party was also patronizing, as it claimed that "[t]he party knows better than the people itself what the people's interest demands."[70] Similar to petitions to the tsar, it had an institutionalized system of complaints to the party, which followed the same model of political inclusion via vertical, direct connection to the central authority.[71] In general, the ideal model of political order in the Soviet Union reproduced the same logic of teamwork under state leadership in seeking a better life, which had been present in the Russian political culture for a long time.[72]

Just as in the Russian Empire, this ideal model of political order never became reality in the Soviet Union. By now, volumes have been written about the repressive practices of the Soviet state, which had even more tools to assert its authority than the Russian monarchs. The Soviet state did whatever it took to eliminate any alternative centers of authority and become the only social institution to order social life. It repressed the Orthodox priests and blew up churches.[73] It removed political opponents through purges.[74] It shook up social structure through dekulakization and collectivization and got rid of "socially destructive elements" to "order" society.[75] It repressed and displaced ethnic communities before and during World War II, accusing them of various anti-Soviet activities and collaboration with Nazi Germany.[76] After Stalin's death, overt repression significantly decreased, but the Soviet regime remained intolerant to even a hint of political pluralism and became more sophisticated in dealing with it through surveillance and censorship.[77]

In the modernized Soviet Union, the societal reactions to the mismatch between the Soviet ideal and reality can be traced even more clearly than in previous historical periods when the masses did not actively participate in politics.

---

[70] Kornai, *The Socialist System*, 55.
[71] Friedgut, *Political Participation in the USSR*, 224–34; Dimitrov, "Tracking Public Opinion under Authoritarianism."
[72] For more on the empirical evidence about the political ideal during the Soviet and post-Soviet time, see Lukin, "Russia's New Authoritarianism and the Post-Soviet Political Ideal."
[73] Стецовский, *История советских репрессий*, 34–37.
[74] Harris, *The Great Fear*.
[75] Shearer, *Policing Stalin's Socialism*.
[76] Стецовский, *История советских репрессий*, 453–514.
[77] Hornsby, *Protest, Reform and Repression in Khrushchev's Soviet Union*.

Once again, we can talk about compliant activism, active resistance, and passive resistance as representing the different ways of how the Soviet people dealt with the cognitive and emotional conflict between the ideal just state and the real oppressive one.

Compliant Activism

Compliant activists were the people who often sincerely believed in the ideal of socialism, minimized the flaws of the Soviet system, and actively engaged in state-directed political activities. Counter to the stereotype, political participation in the USSR was not universal or mandatory except for several forms such as voting or membership in youth organizations. Other forms of political and civic participation involved a much smaller share of the population, and a significant number of people did not participate in any such activities. The most politically active citizens, who also identified more with the Soviet values, were party members, deputies in the local councils ("soviety"), members of various commissions at work, and participants of people's militias. The less politically active group engaged in government-supported neighborhood associations, school councils, and housing commissions, which provided them a sense of communal identity and social influence.[78] Such organizations were very similar to the ones I observed in the Kemerovo region and Tatarstan, the two statist regions in my study, as they also blended the civic and the political. The activists involved in them were not forced to do it; neither were they motivated by the prospect of particularistic favors or services.[79] Rather, they were driven by the team logic of achieving a common goal—to better the lives of their communities within the political framework set by the Soviet state.

This state-led team spirit is also captured by a set of concepts, such as "welfare state authoritarianism" and "social contract," which I already mentioned above when discussing Putin's regime. These concepts point at the commitment of the Soviet state to provide "minimal and rising levels of material and social security"[80] in exchange for acceptance of its political monopoly. The researchers who studied these phenomena did not explicitly distinguish the teamwork logic

---

[78] Friedgut, *Political Participation in the USSR*; Bahry and Silver, "Soviet Citizen Participation on the Eve of Democratization." See also Libman and Kozlov, "The Legacy of Compliant Activism in Autocracies" for the study of long-term effects of compliant activism.

[79] Bahry and Silver ("Soviet Citizen Participation on the Eve of Democratization.") point out that individual contacts of public officials were a form of political participation that is empirically and analytically distinct from compliant and social activism.

[80] Breslauer, "On the Adaptability of Soviet Welfare-State Authoritarianism," 4.

in statist societies from the utility maximization logic in antistatist societies—the distinction that is fundamental for my argument. However, they described many features that are characteristic of the statist political environment, such as viewing the state as a leader and public goods provider, popular desire for egalitarianism and justice, and giving up autonomous political agency in favor of direct contact with the central authority through the system of complaints.[81] Such a statist vision of politics was not uniform across the Soviet Union, but the concept of social contract explains well the logic of that part of the population that complied with the regime on the basis that it at least attempted to fulfill their ideal of the just state.

There are no comprehensive studies about how these compliant activists explained the reality of state coercion to themselves, but anecdotal evidence suggests that they justified it in different ways. Some of them believed that state coercion, including Stalin's repressions, were harsh but fair.[82] This view was well captured in the superpopular 1979 Soviet movie *The Meeting Place Cannot Be Changed*, in which Gleb Zheglov, a charismatic police investigator, famously said, "There is no punishment without guilt" and "The thief must be in prison," when he justified his violations of investigation procedures and the presumption of innocence. Even those people who were repressed during Stalin's purges and knew that they were innocent tried to preserve their faith in the system and constructed a narrative that their arrests were mistakes, isolated malfunctions of what was generally the right political order:

- Shockingly, people who worked for the good of their homeland, went through the labor camps and somehow managed to survive in these camps, after their release, continued to work for the state that subjected them to these terrible repressions. Do you have an explanation for this?

- Yes, none of them got embittered. I have talked to many people. Both my father and everyone else thought it was a mistake.... When Stalin died in 1953, my father was struck by his death. In his letter he wrote: "Our comrade Stalin has died." He was sure that Stalin had nothing to do with it. Maybe he changed his mind later, I don't know. But we all grieved Stalin's death: both my mother and I, a university freshman at the time. The whole country. Everyone was crying. All these repressed people believed that someone else had falsely accused them, but Stalin was not to blame.

---

[81] Cook, *The Soviet Social Contract and Why It Failed*; Dimitrov, *Why Communism Did Not Collapse*; Cook and Dimitrov, "The Social Contract Revisited"; Dimitrov, "The Functions of Letters to the Editor in Reform-Era Cuba."

[82] For example, in Gerber and van Landingham, "Ties That Remind," some respondents whose family members were repressed, say that their punishment was fair.

(Interview with Natalia Koroleva, daughter of Sergei Korolev, a lead Soviet rocket engineer and spacecraft designer involved in the launches of Sputnik 1 and Yuri Gagarin into space, who spent six years in labor camps.)[83]

Only recently, researchers and public intellectuals started investigating this issue and paying attention to the psychological aspects of this phenomenon, and specifically to the importance of people's emotional connection to the Soviet epoch and the difficulties of condemning state violence, even when it broke their lives.[84]

Active Resistance

Some of the sources of active resistance to the Soviet rule were similar to the Russian Empire, such as the peasants and intelligentsia, and others emerged from the 1917 Russian Revolution, such as workers.[85] The peasants' resistance was particularly strong during and after the collectivization, and, as in the Russian Empire, it was the strongest on the periphery, for example, in Siberia and in the Cossack areas in the south of Russia and Ukraine.[86] The symbolic framework that accompanied that resistance reflected the ideal of the just state and the duty to resist the unjust one. Collectivization was viewed by the peasants as the beginning of the apocalypse and the mark of Antichrist, and some of them demanded to bring back the tsar—the virtuous ruler who would not mistreat them.[87] The workers, from the beginning of the Soviet Union through the Khrushchev's era, often protested low and worsening living standards, while calling on the state to be true to its values of being a workers' state: "Lenin taught us how to fight, so now we must fight and look after our own well-being."[88] These unrests were likely an important factor in the emergence of a consumerist Soviet social contract between the industrial workers and the Soviet state.[89]

---

[83] Королева and Хрусталева, "Интервью с дочерью легендарного конструктора Сергея Королева."

[84] Эппле, *Неудобное прошлое: Память о государственных преступлениях в России и других странах*, sec. Appendix to Part III.

[85] I will not discuss here in detail the many resistance practices of the non-Russian ethnic groups, which never fully recognized the Soviet state as their collective leader. This resistance was very important, especially toward the end of the Soviet Union (see, for example, Beissinger, *Nationalist Mobilization and the Collapse of the Soviet State*; Hornsby, *Protest, Reform and Repression in Khrushchev's Soviet Union*, chap. 6), but it is much less indicative of the state–society tension in the statist political environment, which I am analyzing in this chapter.

[86] Fitzpatrick, *Stalin's Peasants*, 65.

[87] Viola, *Peasant Rebels under Stalin*; Fitzpatrick, *Stalin's Peasants*, 66.

[88] Viola, *Contending with Stalinism*, 50.

[89] Hornsby, *Protest, Reform and Repression in Khrushchev's Soviet Union*, 180; Cook, *The Soviet Social Contract and Why It Failed*.

The resistance of the Soviet intelligentsia—the critically thinking educated class—became particularly noticeable with the dissident movement born of Khrushchev's Thaw.[90] Similar to the intelligentsia in the Russian Empire, these people were often inspired by Western liberal ideals, which they now acquired by listening to foreign radio. Some of them organized underground groups where they discussed politics and criticized the Soviet regime.[91] Others disapproved of underground activities and opted for public advocacy for human rights.[92] Generally, this group followed the traditional aspiration of the Russian intelligentsia to serve "the people," to speak for the whole society. But as it was small and mostly Moscow-based, it was viewed by ordinary Soviet citizens as part of a Westernized, privileged elite at best or as the traitors of the country at worst.[93]

Passive Resistance

The third reaction to the conflict between the Soviet political ideal and reality was passive resistance. The hypocrisy and skepticism directed at the state and the propaganda machine in the late Soviet Union, which many observers and participants noticed, was the symptom of such passive resistance. People who reacted this way did not buy into the state propaganda about socialism and did not try to justify the problems they encountered as compliant activists did. At the same time, they felt too powerless and helpless against the state, which prevented them from engaging in active resistance. They dealt with the situation by shielding themselves from the state that did not live up to the proclaimed moral ideal with skepticism and hypocrisy, by putting up a show of compliance in the public setting and using all the informal means available to improve the lives of their own families and friends.

The scholarly work that studied this phenomenon in most detail is the project of the Soviet and Russian sociologist Yurii Levada called "the Soviet simple person," or *Homo soveticus*, as it is often referred to in the Western tradition. Levada started this study in 1989 to investigate the processes of totalitarian regime erosion by looking at the link between the Soviet institutions and the values and behaviors of the Soviet people. Through public opinion polls, the sociologists examined people's identities, life aspirations, understandings of moral and social obligations, psychological preferences, and views of historical

---

[90] Kozlov and Fitzpatrick, *Sedition*, 22; Reddaway, *The Dissidents*.
[91] Kozlov and Fitzpatrick, *Sedition*; Hornsby, *Protest, Reform and Repression in Khrushchev's Soviet Union*.
[92] Kozlov and Fitzpatrick, *Sedition*, 26.
[93] Kozlov and Fitzpatrick, 22–23; Hornsby, *Protest, Reform and Repression in Khrushchev's Soviet Union*.

events. Levada and his colleagues continued to trace the transformations of these characteristics of public opinion after the Soviet Union collapsed.[94]

The main theme in the analysis of "the Soviet simple person" is the conflict between the coercive state, with which the person identifies, and the private, autonomous interests of individuals. "The Soviet person is the state person. This is not only because the state was the only employer, but also because it was the institution that provided the safety net. Lack of alternatives to the paternalistic state makes that state a monopolistic holder and interpreter of all collective values, of the meaning of the social whole."[95] This monopoly made people share the meanings and values set by the state—even when it contradicted their own needs and desires—and develop adaptation mechanisms of living within the framework of the repressive state. One such mechanism was compensating for the feeling of inferiority in relations with the state by the feeling of superiority over other countries. These people felt proud that they were part of a world superpower while also being convinced that this superpower would never truly care about them.[96]

Levada's concept of *Homo soveticus* is valuable in this discussion of the role of state–society tension in Russian politics, as it problematizes and systematically examines the conflict between the Soviet political ideal and the Soviet reality in the minds of Soviet citizens. At the same time, critics point at several important drawbacks of this tradition. Gulnaz Sharafutdinova, for example, argues that the concept of *Homo soveticus* has ideological baggage as it was constructed in contrast to liberal democratic values, which the authors of the theory shared.[97] Similar to Richard Pipes's work, *Homo soveticus* highlights the incompatibility of the Russian political culture with liberal democracy, which resonates with the Russian intelligentsia's frustrations about the obedience and lack of protest potential of the majority of the Russian people. A less ideologically driven view, however, presents a different picture of a Soviet person. Authors who studied primary sources about the everyday life of the Soviet people presented their private worlds as the ones filled with agency rather than passivity, resourcefulness rather than helplessness, and value of human relations among family and friends rather than social atomization, distrust, and hypocrisy. These authors argue that the Soviet people found ways to express their agency and humanity even though the public space for individual choice was severely limited.[98]

---

[94] Левада, *Простой советский человек: опыт социального портрета на рубеже 90-х*; Гудков, *Абортивная модернизация*; Гудков, "'Советский человек' сквозь все режимы."
[95] Гудков, "'Советский человек' сквозь все режимы."
[96] Гудков, Дубин, and Зоркая, *Постсоветский человек и гражданское общество*, 5–6; Гудков, "'Советский человек' сквозь все режимы."
[97] Sharafutdinova, "Was There a 'Simple Soviet' Person?"
[98] Козлова, *Советские люди*; Yurchak, *Everything Was Forever, until It Was No More*. See Sharafutdinova, "Was There a 'Simple Soviet' Person?" for more references and examples.

This critique highlights an important point developed in this book as well: the statism of Russian society and its unitary political environment do not stem from different values that the Russian people have. They are the result of the universal human nature playing out in different historical circumstances. Compliant activism, passive resistance, and active resistance are all reactions to the persistent abuse by the trusted party—the state, which is the center of people's collective identity and is viewed as the only legitimate leader of collective action. This pattern emerged long before the Soviet Union and continues to exist to this day, long after the Soviet Union has been gone.

The Search for a Just State in Post-Soviet Russia

The tension between society's desire for justice and respect and the state's desire to maintain its unconstrained political monopoly continued to drive Russian politics in the post-Soviet period, but there were also important changes. If during the Russian revolution of 1917 the vast majority of the country was still rural, with many peasants being illiterate and spending most of their lives within their rural commune, society in the late Soviet Union was urbanized, educated, and consumerist. Population's standards of material well-being substantially increased in the 1970s, when high world oil prices drove the imports of consumer goods to the Soviet Union. The Soviet workers at the time enjoyed particularly generous salaries and benefits as well as the pride of contributing to the greatness of the country and being valued by it. People still envisioned the state as the only legitimate leader, but it was becoming more and more difficult for the Soviet state to meet the rising expectations of the population.[99]

By the late 1980s, the inefficient economic system weighed down by the gigantic military sector together with plummeting oil prices exposed the failure of the Soviet state leadership.[100] Perestroika and glasnost' accelerated the erosion of state authority already damaged by the decades of subtle cultural resistance and grassroots sabotage. Economic and symbolic weakening of the central authority led to a series of nationalist mobilizations in the Soviet republics as well as the workers' movement of Soviet miners whose participants demanded political and economic reforms.[101] The Soviet state stopped living up to even the minimal expectations of society from its leader.

---

[99] For more details on the raising societal expectations, see, for example, Cook, *The Soviet Social Contract and Why It Failed*; Dimitrov, *Why Communism Did Not Collapse*; Cook and Dimitrov, "The Social Contract Revisited."

[100] Miller, *The Struggle to Save the Soviet Economy*.

[101] Beissinger, *Nationalist Mobilization and the Collapse of the Soviet State*.

The crisis of state authority in the late Soviet Union highlights an important property of statist societies: even if people envision the state as the only legitimate leader, it does not mean that any state and any state ruler automatically meet their expectations. A statist society tends to be loyal to the regime that has already established its authority and proved to be a true leader. But the advantage of group authority does not mean that society's loyalty is unconditional. People want a leader who is both strong and respectful toward them, and violation of either of these expectations breeds discontent.[102]

Evidence of Social Statism in Public Opinion Polls

Public opinion polls conducted in the late 1980s to early 1990s as well as in later decades demonstrated exactly that kind of demanding statism. They show that what most Russian people wanted throughout the post-Soviet period has been a fair system that would both protect the vulnerable and provide people with the space to realize their potential as well as have a say in public matters, which was severely limited in the Soviet Union. For example, a survey conducted in mid-1991 showed that people in postcommunist states, including Russia, most wanted a socialism with a more humane face rather than a completely free-market arrangement.[103] Another poll of 1996 demonstrated that despite some population groups being more promarket than others, there was "a remarkable level of agreement on some of the key ideological issues: that the government should continue to provide basic minimums, in terms of both jobs and a standard of living; but that the society should abandon radical egalitarianism in favor of a more meritocratic system where rewards and incentives matter."[104]

Further development of public opinion polls in post-Soviet Russia provided more evidence of social statism in people's opinions. Three-quarters of respondents in a 2005 nationwide poll, for example, said their political ideal was indeed a system in which the state and the people have common goals and respect each other.[105] In another poll, Russians were clear that they want a strong leader who would not be constrained by institutions and would be able to get things done, but they were just as clear that they desire to elect that leader through free and fair elections and be able to remove them from power if the problems are not

---

[102] Lukin, "Russia's New Authoritarianism and the Post-Soviet Political Ideal."
[103] Mason, "Attitudes towards the Market and Political Participation in the Post-Communist States."
[104] Mason and Sidorenko-Stephenson, "Public Opinion and the 1996 Elections in Russia."
[105] Гудков, Дубин, and Зоркая, *Постсоветский человек и гражданское общество*, 23. Recent polls show a very similar picture; see, for example, Мухаметшина, "Три четверти россиян говорят о необходимости сильной руки в руководстве страны."

resolved.[106] Such electoral accountability connecting the people directly to the state ruler is the only one that Russian society intuitively understands. It fits well the statist model that connected the people directly to the tsar earlier and does not provide any legitimacy to societal elites, who could maintain the institutions limiting the state leader's power.[107] Institutions that could limit state power are not trusted, while the state is viewed as a necessary component of any civic action that benefits society as a whole.[108]

Together with recognizing the state as the only legitimate leader, Russians also consistently expressed their dissatisfaction with how the state treated them. While they tended to pride themselves on the country's history, its art and literature, advancements in science, and sports victories, they were ashamed of the conditions in which ordinary people live, and this contrast is stronger in Russia than in many other countries.[109] People often felt like the state was not fulfilling its obligations and that the elected officials quickly forgot about the needs of ordinary people after elections. Paradoxically, the development of nonstate charities has been partially impeded by this shame for state failure: during focus groups, people said that they felt ashamed to give money to charities because "the state must fulfil its obligations rather than shift them onto the ordinary people."[110]

This societal demand for the state to fulfill its obligations as leader has been reciprocated by the statist ideas that were present among the Russian elites even in the 1990s. Just as there was a consensus in society that it wanted the state to get things done, there was also a consensus among elites that the state should restore the social order.[111] The 1990s did not differ much from the 2000s in terms of societal expectations from the state or the intentions of state elites, but they differed a lot by the circumstances in which the post-Soviet state had to re-establish its authority.

Yeltsin versus Putin

Boris Yeltsin and Vladimir Putin were very different leaders operating in different circumstances, and yet, they dealt with the same society and had to respond to similar demands. Both Yeltsin and Putin during his early years in power

---

[106] Hale, "The Myth of Mass Russian Support for Autocracy," 1371.
[107] Гудков, Дубин, and Зоркая, Постсоветский человек и гражданское общество, 24.
[108] Hale, "Civil Society from Above?"; Гудков, Дубин, and Зоркая, Постсоветский человек и гражданское общество, 28. See also Gans-Morse et al., "Self-Selection into Public Service When Corruption Is Widespread," for the evidence that Russian college students with higher levels of altruism tend to self-select into the civil service.
[109] Магун and Магун, "Идентификация граждан со своей страной: российские данные в контексте международных сравнений." See also Левада-Центр, "Гордость и идентичность."
[110] Волков, "Почему россияне боятся активизма и благотворительности."
[111] Hill and Gaddy, Mr. Putin, 38.

tried to balance order and freedom. Although Yeltsin's support was stronger among the urbanites and those working in the private sector,[112] he tried to capitalize on the societal consensus about the ideal political system promising both more freedom through market reforms and protection of the most vulnerable members of society.[113] Likewise, Putin implemented several liberalizing economic reforms during his first presidential term while also strengthening state domination in Russian politics.

Scholars and political commentators disagree on whether Yeltsin was personally a more democratic leader than Putin, but regardless of their personal preferences, the historical situation in which Yeltsin found himself made it very difficult for him to meet the societal demand for a just state. His support peaked in 1990, when only 2%–9% of poll respondents disapproved of him.[114] At that time, he was both a state official—the chairman of the Supreme Soviet of the Russian Soviet Federative Socialist Republic—and the main political figure opposing the central state apparatus of the USSR. For many people, he was the symbol of change, of a different state that would be much closer to the political ideal they had in mind. However, the many challenges that Yeltsin's government had to handle after the USSR's collapse and the mistakes it made along the way prevented him from building a state that would match the societal ideal.

The challenges were present on both material and symbolic fronts. During Yeltsin's time in power, Russia underwent a painful transition from command to market economy, which opened new opportunities for some people and made others vulnerable and resentful. The weak economy made it impossible to maintain strong centralized power; it led to the rise of regional powers and an increase in regional inequality, which contributed to the general sense of state weakness and injustice. The state also did not suggest a clear symbolic framework that would resonate with society and validate people's grievances. Public opinion on how to achieve the ideal of a just state—through a more socialist or a more capitalist path—divided Russian society into different camps with a significant number of people who were rather disoriented and did not firmly belong to either of them. The war in Chechnya, which exposed the weakness of Moscow, significantly contributed to the feelings of insecurity and the failure of state leadership. Yeltsin's support fluctuated over the years, and although his contention with the Communist Party continued to energize his core supporters, he

---

[112] ВЦИОМ (Всероссийский центр изучения общественного мнения), "Информационный бюллетень мониторинга," 15.

[113] Mason and Sidorenko-Stephenson, "Public Opinion and the 1996 Elections in Russia."

[114] ВЦИОМ (Всероссийский центр изучения общественного мнения), "Информационный бюллетень мониторинга," 14.

continued to be a controversial figure who did not fit the role of the state leader in the eyes of many Russians.[115]

Putin, on the other hand, was well positioned to fit into that role from the very start. He did not belong to the world of contentious electoral politics when Yeltsin chose him as his successor. He was director of the Federal Security Bureau, a position firmly associated with strong centralized state power. He was appointed prime minister in August 1999 and immediately launched an "antiterrorist campaign" in Chechnya, which established his claim of being a law and order leader, the state leader for which a large part of the public had craved throughout much of the 1990s. Public trust in him skyrocketed from about 5% in September 1999 to about 45% in November 1999, which demonstrates how much his figure resonated with societal expectations.[116]

In the next decade, the match between the societal ideal of a strong, just state and Putin's figure became even clearer.[117] He benefited from the rise of oil prices, which gave a boost to the Russian economy and state revenue. Throughout most of the 2000s, people's real incomes increased, because of both increasing salaries and increasing social assistance, including pensions.[118] At the same time, most ordinary people did not feel much infringement of their freedoms. They were free to change jobs, buy property, or travel abroad, which all became possible in the booming economy. For many people who resented the power of the oligarchs in the 1990s, Putin's crackdown of the Russian oligarchs, which culminated in the arrest of Mikhail Khodorkovsky in 2003, was a sign of restoring justice rather than an attack on private property. And Putin's increasingly aggressive rhetoric in the international arena starting in 2007 was seen as restoration of state strength.

Putin's public image also gradually came in sync with the societal idea of the state as a team leader. If in his early years in power Putin spoke on behalf of his government, later on he adopted the rhetoric of the representative of the whole nation.[119] During his carefully orchestrated "Direct lines"—a kind of press-conferences for the ordinary people—he presented himself as the supreme arbiter who always stays above the battle and personally guarantees stability and proper functioning of state institutions.[120] He never directly participated in any political battles, never debated his official opponents at the presidential elections, and never put forward a political platform with any concrete details

---

[115] See, for example, the poll results in ВЦИОМ (Всероссийский центр изучения общественного мнения), "Мониторинг перемен: основные тенденции," fig. 7.

[116] ВЦИОМ (Всероссийский центр изучения общественного мнения), fig. 7.

[117] Lukin, "Russia's New Authoritarianism and the Post-Soviet Political Ideal."

[118] On the motivation of Putin's regime to increase pension payments, see, for example, McCullaugh, "From Well to Welfare."

[119] Галямина, "Мы-они."

[120] White and McAllistar, "Putin and His Supporters," 387; Wengle and Evans, "Symbolic State-Building in Contemporary Russia."

that could spark controversies. For many people, he became the symbol of stability and an indivisible Russia, to which people could belong.[121] This symbolic side of his power, maintained through state-controlled media, played a bigger role in his regime's durability than direct repression of the opposition, which is usually associated with authoritarian regimes.[122]

Compliant Activism and the Social Roots of Putin's Support

Putin's image as a team leader tapped right into the socially accepted statism—the expectation that the state unites the people and leads them in solving problems. This resonance has been traced by researchers at the level of individual views and attitudes as well as at the level of community organizations, similar to the ones I observed in the Kemerovo region and Tatarstan and described in earlier chapters.

At the individual level, Putin's supporters are the people who want to feel that they are part of a team. They are not very different from nonsupporters by their sociodemographic characteristics. Even though among the middle class, public-sector employees support him more than private-sector ones, his overall support is rather evenly distributed in society.[123] His supporters are different from nonsupporters, however, in that they are more psychologically agreeable, that is, they value social harmony and avoid contradictions. They feel uncomfortable in a contentious environment and seek social unity by following social norms.[124] Since the social norm is that the state is your team, these people perceive successes of the state as their own. This explains why "the shared experience of the Crimean 'moment'" in 2014 has improved "people's evaluation of their social, political, and economic surroundings in the present, the future—and even the past."[125] The more people felt that social unity, the less important the internal tensions, such as ethnic xenophobia, became to them.[126] The same unity with the team state explains a less enthusiastic, but still widespread support for the 2022 invasion of Ukraine, which will be discussed later in the chapter.[127]

[121] Matovski, "The Logic of Vladimir Putin's Popular Appeal." It is interesting that a better translation of *Единая Россия* into English would be not *United Russia* but *Indivisible Russia*. The word "единая" communicates the idea of a monolith, of an entity that has never been apart rather than a union of several formerly autonomous entities, such as in "the United States" or "the United Kingdom." On the connection between the power of Putin's regime and collective belonging, see, for example, Гудков, "Механизмы кризисной консолидации," 7.
[122] Treisman, *The New Autocracy*.
[123] White and McAllistar, "Putin and His Supporters," 384; Rosenfeld, "Reevaluating the Middle-Class Protest Paradigm."
[124] Greene and Robertson, *Putin v. the People*.
[125] Greene and Robertson, "Affect and Autocracy."
[126] Chapman et al., "Xenophobia on the Rise?"
[127] "Далекая близкая война."

At the organizational level, both the federal government and the authorities in different regions have capitalized on the value of social unity for the population to maintain state presence in people's everyday lives. During Putin's time in power, they made an effort to build or take control of community organizations to place the state at the center of community-oriented projects.[128] Examples of organizations created by the state at the federal level include the youth movements Nashi and Yunarimia, the "civic" movement the All-Russia People's Front, and the Russian Pensioners' Union, closely affiliated with the Pension Fund of Russia. Regional and local authorities have participated in these federal initiatives and developed their own networks of loyal civil society organizations.[129] Both regional and federal authorities have also attempted to take control of the organizations that initially emerged as grassroots movements. For example, the Immortal Regiment movement, which aims at maintaining the private family memory about the generation who lived through the World War II and emerged as a grassroots initiative in 2012 in Tomsk, now has a government-created twin, the Immortal Regiment of Russia, which substituted the family memory aspect of the original mission with glorification of the nation's victory in World War II.[130]

The community organizations supported by the state helped practice the idea of the state as the leader and society as the team. State officials viewed these organizations as "an auxiliary of the state . . . activating citizens to assist the state in governance."[131] Many researchers have connected such views with the Soviet tradition, but, as I showed earlier in this chapter, the idea of the Russian state encouraging voluntary contributions to the common good dates back to the pre-Soviet time. In the Soviet Union, participation of ordinary citizens in public projects was justified by the communist ideology; during Putin's time, such involvement of citizens in everyday governance resonates with the international norms of a "small state," outsourcing state functions, and public–private collaboration.[132]

The practice of compliant activism benefited Putin's regime politically in several ways. First, the very fact that participatory forms of engagement existed increased Putin's genuine popularity and made people feel that they had more voice in politics.[133] Second, they reproduced the idea of politics as direct connection between the state leader and the people who work together on solving

---

[128] On how the state unites the otherwise atomized society, see, for example, Гудков, "Механизмы кризисной консолидации," 9.
[129] Salmenniemi, "Struggling for Citizenship."
[130] The website of the original grassroots movement is www.moypolk.ru; the website of the government-created twin is www.polkrf.ru.
[131] Salmenniemi, "Struggling for Citizenship."
[132] Owen, "A Genealogy of Kontrol' in Russia."
[133] Chapman, "Shoring Up Autocracy."

problems as opposed to a system where representative political institutions voice population's interests and place restrictions on the state leader's power. These practices of direct communication of grievances to the government were widespread in the Soviet Union and have been likewise encouraged by Putin's regime.[134] Research shows that societal knowledge and acceptance of these practices last over long periods of time, which is another piece of evidence that Putin's regime capitalizes on statism that has been accepted by Russian society for a long while.[135]

The third way in which community and public organizations helped Putin's regime politically is that they helped it win elections and counteract the growing societal resistance. As I showed in the previous chapters using the examples of the Kemerovo region and Tatarstan, state-controlled community and public organizations influenced elections by blending their civic and political functions. Every election cycle local authorities were provided with target numbers of turnout and proregime vote on their territories, and these numbers functioned as another set of performance indicators for regional governors and bureaucracies.[136] The civic and political functions of state bureaucracies were so blended in the minds of state officials that they sometimes issued official orders about instituting campaign headquarters of the United Russia right in the city hall, even though it was against the law.[137] These local authorities then used public sector and community organizations to deliver the vote. Volumes of evidence from social networks as well as systematic research shows that public sector employers, state-owned enterprises, and various community organizations mobilized their employees and constituencies to turn out to the elections and to vote for Vladimir Putin or the United Russia Party.[138] The authorities also worked through community organizations, such as pensioners' organizations or residential councils, to increase the turnout of loyal voters or used schoolteachers

---

[134] Lussier, "Contacting and Complaining."
[135] Libman and Kozlov, "The Legacy of Compliant Activism in Autocracies."
[136] Reisinger and Moraski, "Russia's Governors under Presidential Control, 2005–2012"; Галимова, "В Кремле обсудили получение 70% голосов за своего кандидата на выборах"; *Радио Свобода*, "Кремль определил явку на голосовании по поправкам к Конституции."
[137] Движение "Голос," " 'Голос' обнаружил незаконный штаб 'по организации выборов' в Краснознаменске"; Melkonyants, "Очередная 'бомба' с незаконным штабом при администрации." For other examples of blending civic and political functions, see Корня and Козлов, "Партия власти агитирует за себя с помощью неполитических мероприятий"; Движение "Голос," "Уговоры и шантаж."
[138] For systematic studies, see Frye, Reuter, and Szakonyi, "Political Machines at Work"; Forrat, "Shock-Resistant Authoritarianism." For a few more recent examples from the media, see Полыгаева, " 'Соцработники часто настраивают пенсионеров голосовать за партию власти' "; *Радио Свобода*, " 'Голос' "; Лукьянова, " 'Коллеги, регистрируемся, скриншот в личку!' "; Канкия, "Как медики во время эпидемии коронавируса будут за поправки в Конституцию агитировать."

as agitators.[139] The ability to mobilize turnout of the otherwise passive voters has played a major role in the regime's electoral victories.[140]

Passive Resistance

The fact that Putin's regime needed to use the capability of community and public organizations to mobilize the vote is the sign that the tension between the state and society that had driven protest in the previous era was still in place. On the one hand, the Russian state rebuilt a lot of its capacity in the 21st century compared to the 1990s, when informality governed people's lives. In the 2020s, it has functioning courts, a working tax system, uneven but functional education and healthcare, and other elements of a modern state that increase the efficiency of state performance. On the other hand, the dominance of the resurrected state in the public sphere created other problems also not unheard of in Russian history. State officials, and especially the part of the state apparatus that deals with security—the so-called siloviki—increased their influence in all spheres of public life facing few restrictions of their ambition to make the state serve them rather than society as a whole. The growth of unrestricted power of the state led to lost economic opportunities and stagnating incomes as well as the quickly deteriorating situation with human rights and the increased fears of mass repressions among the population.[141]

Societal resistance to the state during Putin's era mirrors the patterns we observed in the Soviet Union. Although many people periodically engaged in activities that fell under the label of compliant activism described above, the same exact people easily turned into passive resisters of state authority when it came to state influence on their individual lives.[142] They sabotaged state policies and tried to use informal mechanisms to make the situation work in their favor, thus counteracting state power at the national level with their own power at the local one.[143]

Similar to the Soviet times, this passive resistance has been a strategy of individual adjustment, not collective action against the state. People still largely

---

[139] Gans-Morse, Mazzuca, and Nichter, "Varieties of Clientelism"; "Выборы: уроки для проигравших"; Forrat, "Shock-Resistant Authoritarianism."

[140] Tkacheva and Golosov, "United Russia's Primaries and the Strength of Political Machines in the Regions of Russia."

[141] Taylor, *State Building in Putin's Russia*; Gel'man, *Authoritarian Russia*; Гудков, "Механизмы кризисной консолидации," 9; Гудков, "Характер и структура массовой тревожности в России."

[142] Kalinin, "Exploring Putin's Approval Ratings during the Ukrainian Crisis 2014"; Snegovaya, "Guns to Butter"; Greene, *Moscow in Movement*.

[143] Krupets et al., "Imagining Young Adults' Citizenship in Russia"; Greene, "Running to Stand Still"; Greene, "Homo Post-Sovieticus"; Morris, Semenov, and Smyth, *Varieties of Russian Activism*.

view any nonstate parties who advocate for collective action as illegitimate. One of the illustrations of such attitudes is the public attitude toward charitable organizations. At the focus groups conducted by Levada-Center, respondents expressed a lot of skepticism about charities and NGOs. Even though focus-group participants generally recognized that the work of these organizations is important, they doubted whether the actual motivation of the leaders of these organizations and their activists was to serve the common good or to use these organizations for corruption and personal enrichment.[144] The accusations of corruption and inefficient use of public funds, which in antistatist societies are often directed at the governments, are expressed in relation to grassroots nonstate initiatives in the statist Russian society. This distrust of nonstate parties as potential leaders of collective action is the main obstacle faced by the politicians who oppose Putin's regime.

Active Resistance

The inertia of the Russian people, who have hard time believing that a politician opposing the state is not driven by the motives of personal enrichment, has been strong in the post-Soviet Russia. But from the early 2010s through the early 2020s, there were also signs of growing demands of the state and a growing ability to hold the state accountable to these demands and expectations.

During the first two presidential terms of Vladimir Putin, it seemed that the Russian state approached the ideal that the Russian people had in their mind closer than ever before. The economy was on the rise, oil prices were high, individual incomes grew for several years in a row, and the government invested in education and healthcare. Most people at the time genuinely approved of Vladimir Putin as the leader, and active resistance to his regime was confined primarily to professional politicians from officially existing opposition parties such as Yabloko, human rights organizations, journalists from the liberal media, and a relatively small share of the general population. They protested the growing restrictions of political freedoms that most ordinary people rarely thought about. Although there were a few larger grievances, such as education reforms or the reform on monetization of in-kind benefits, Putin skillfully neutralized their protest potential early on by restructuring incentives of the elite actors who could potentially lead the protests.[145] To that end, he demonstrated the price of disloyalty to the oligarchs by arresting Mikhail Khodorkovsky, the CEO of the

---

[144] Волков, "Почему россияне боятся активизма и благотворительности."
[145] Wengle and Rasell, "The Monetisation of l'goty."

Yukos Oil Company, and made regional governors and the leaders of the largest universities much more economically dependent on the Kremlin.[146]

After the first two Putin's terms, however, it became more difficult for his regime to satisfy the growing societal expectations of the state. The world financial crisis of 2008–2009 together with the growing monopolization and state domination of the Russian economy led to stagnation and the decrease of real incomes. Putin's approval ratings began to decline, and the feelings that the people are not given proper respect increased among the population.[147] The "castling" of Dmitry Medvedev and Vladimir Putin in September 2011 only contributed to the crisis, as it demonstrated that the state-led modernization declared by Medvedev was a hoax, and radicalized the already present societal resentment.[148]

As a result, the 2011–2012 electoral cycle was accompanied by an unprecedented antiregime mobilization and postelection protests. During this electoral cycle, the civil society and the opposition were able to mobilize enough protest voters and cover many precincts with independent observers, primarily in Moscow and St. Petersburg. The revelation of electoral falsifications together with the accumulated grievances led to the largest political protests since the fall of the Soviet Union in the two capital cities and a series of smaller ones across the country.

That electoral cycle was very important for the development of active resistance to Putin's regime even though the leaders of the opposition failed to unite, and Putin's regime stopped the protest wave using targeted repression. It was during the 2011–2012 mobilization that the political narrative of holding the state accountable expanded beyond the circles of professional politicians and civic activists into the masses. This narrative was about the need for the people to put the state and the ruling party under control. It resonated with the growing public demand for respect and justice from the state and competed with the image of the state as the team leader and supreme arbiter.[149]

The main manifestation of this narrative was the campaign advanced by Alexey Navalny "Vote for any party except the United Russia." At the time, Navalny was an activist who had already launched several anticorruption projects, such as "Rospil" and "Rosyama," and just pulled them together in his "Anti-Corruption Foundation" (Фонд борьбы с коррупцией, ФБК) registered

---

[146] Robertson, *The Politics of Protest in Hybrid Regimes*; Forrat, "The Political Economy of Russian Higher Education."

[147] In focus groups, participants frequently said that "People are treated as *bydlo* (a Russian word for lower class, despised people)"—see Белановский and Дмитриев, "Политический кризис в России и возможные механизмы его развития," 10.

[148] Белановский et al., "Движущие силы и перспективы политической трансформации России."

[149] Owen, "The Struggle for Meaning of *Obshchestvennyi Kontrol'* in Contemporary Russia."

in September 2011. Navalny's qualification of the United Party as "the party of crooks and thieves" became a known meme by the time of the parliamentary election in December, and the theme of Putin's regime corruption that he developed in the public space for years contributed to the poor electoral performance of the ruling party and the protest wave of 2011–2012.

The less visible but no less important sign of the strengthening accountability narrative was the rise of civic initiatives aimed at counteracting the abuse of power by the state. Unlike many other Russian NGOs that dealt with social issues and often used state support to benefit their causes, these initiatives aimed specifically at limiting the power of state officials and law enforcement agencies to restrict individuals' rights and political freedoms for the benefit of Putin's regime. One such initiative was the association "Voice" (Голос), which united civic activists who tracked and reported violations of free and fair election procedures. The association existed since the early 2000s, but it was in the 2011–2012 elections that it launched its crowdsourcing projects "The Violations Map" and the alternative system of vote count.[150] These projects made it possible to scale up the efforts of civil society on electoral observation and create pressure on the officials trying to falsify the results. Another notable initiative was "OVD-info"—an independent human rights group that helped the victims of political persecution. The group came together in December 2011 during the protests against electoral falsifications and over the years grew into a project with dozens of employees and several hundred volunteers. This group provides resources and coordinates legal help in cases of political persecution, monitors the violation of political freedoms, and informs the public about the situation in this sphere. Both of these initiatives, which emerged during the 2011–2012 electoral cycle, drew at least a part of its funding from crowdsourcing and attracted hundreds to thousands of volunteers, which had never been the case before for the civic initiatives aimed at state accountability.

The demand for state accountability, which resonated in the 2011–2012 elections, slowly grew over the next decade. Throughout the 2010s, national public opinion polls showed that most Russians continued to view the state as their leader, but they also had higher expectations from that leader regarding their individual well-being and political freedoms.[151] Between 2017 and 2019, as the Crimean euphoria wound down, incomes continued to fall, and authorities implemented the unpopular pension reform, the demand for political freedoms and human rights significantly increased. The share of respondents saying that freedom of speech was important increased by 24%, freedom of conscience

---

[150] Движение "Голос," "Голос—за честные выборы. История 'Голоса.'"
[151] Гудков and Сеньшин, "'На первом месте—армия, на втором—президент, на третьем—ФСБ'."

by 18%, freedom of assembly by 15%, and the right for fair trial and information by 14% each.[152] The share of respondents feeling personal responsibility for what was happening in the country increased by about 20% in 2018–2019 compared with previous years.[153] In parallel, the number of people who believed that they could influence the decisions the state makes also increased.[154] These increased demands began eroding the relatively uniform support that Putin had across population groups. In 2020, the younger and mid-age urbanites, including students, entrepreneurs, and workers, expressed a clear dissatisfaction with Putin's regime compared with the less educated, older generation and those living in rural areas.[155] This declining support of Putin's regime did not necessarily mean that society was becoming less statist; in fact, the view that the state must take care of its citizens and make sure their living standards are decent was on the rise.[156] This meant, however, that certain population groups increased their expectations of individual well-being and freedom. There was also evidence that these expectations significantly undermined the effect of state media propaganda exploiting the theme of national unity.[157]

Growing societal demands increased active resistance to Putin's regime at the regional and local levels. In 2012–2018, a number of oppositional candidates were elected as governors and city mayors and many more as deputies of local representative bodies, despite the increasingly restrictive electoral laws and the dominance of the state media. In 2012, Evgenii Urlashov won the mayor elections in Yaroslavl. In 2013, Evgenii Roizman became the mayor of Ekaterinburg and Galina Shirshina the mayor of Petrozavodsk. In 2015, Sergei Levchenko won the governor's election in Irkutsk region, and in 2018, oppositional governors were elected in three regions (Khabarovsk region, Vladimir region, and the Republic of Khakassia), in addition to an oppositional mayor, Sardana Avksent'eva, in Yakutsk. At the 2017 municipal election in Moscow, United Russia failed to gain a majority in more than 30 city districts, in some of which it failed to place a single deputy to the municipal council. This electoral dynamic was also accompanied by regional protests, some of which demonstrated a growing grassroots support for independent elected officials. For example, the protests in Khabarovsk against the arrest of the Khabarovsk governor Sergei Furgal lasted for months and consolidated the grassroots groups who were ready to actively resist the state. The environmental protest at the Shiyes Train Station against the construction of a vast landfill resulted, beyond other things, in the leader of the

---

[152] Левада-Центр, "Права человека."
[153] Левада-Центр, "Ответственность и влияние."
[154] Гудков, "Политическое участие и отношения с государством в России."
[155] Левинсон, "Внуки против бабушек."
[156] Гудков, "Политическое участие и отношения с государством в России."
[157] Группа Белановского, "Новый спектр политических настроений в российском обществе в 2020 году"; Snegovaya, "Guns to Butter."

activists trying to run for the regional governor and a parliamentary deputy.[158] Emergence of oppositional leaders with grassroots support in multiple regions showed that growing societal demands not only increased discontent but also resulted in concrete acts of active resistance.

Another important development of active resistance in the late 2010s was that it became more coordinated and institutionalized at the national scale. Alexey Navalny's presidential bid, which he announced in December 2016, allowed him to create a regional organizational network, which united his supporters and directed their collective actions.[159] The nationwide anticorruption protests in March 2017, which happened after Navalny released his investigation about Dmitry Medvedev's properties, were largely driven by that network channeling the grassroots discontent into concrete protest actions. These organizations supported not only protest activities and Navalny's presidential bid but also the local activists running for municipal councils.[160] Similar support networks that streamlined the recruitment and campaign help for local activists were organized by a Moscow politician and former parliamentary Dmitry Gudkov and an NGO "Open Russia" led by Andrei Pivovarov and supported by Mikhail Khodorkovsky, an exiled businessman and the former CEO of Yukos Oil Company.[161] Yulia Galiamina, another Moscow politician and former municipal deputy, also led a wealth of initiatives supporting activists working to increase transparency and accountability of state institutions at the local level.[162] All these organizations and initiatives have connected and helped thousands of activists, which was a clear sign of the grassroots demand for state accountability.

Repression, Resistance, and Compliance Shortly before and after the 2022 Invasion of Ukraine

These growing popular demands and the organizational structures that began forming around them were in the way of Vladimir Putin's authoritarian and imperial ambition. Until 2020, his regime had been moderately repressive compared to other authoritarian regimes. But starting in 2020, it intensified the

---

[158] "Архангельск"; "Лидер 'Стоп-Шиес' Олег Мандрыкин собрался в Госдуму от партии 'Яблоко.'"

[159] See, for example, Dollbaum, Semenov, and Sirotkina, "A Top-Down Movement with Grass-Roots Effects?"

[160] Штаб Навального в Санкт-Петербурге, "Муниципальные выборы 2019"; "Главы штабов Навального побеждают на муниципальных выборах в Томске и Новосибирске."

[161] Фохт, Горяшко, and Козлов, "Независимые кандидаты назвали успехом выборы в Москве"; "Дмитрий Гудков запустил 'политический Uber' в Петербурге"; Гармоненко, "Структуры Ходорковского помогут штабам Навального"; Сатановский, "О чем говорили на форуме муниципальных депутатов в Clubhouse."

[162] Команда Юлии Галяминой, "Проекты."

attacks on the political opposition, civil society, and independent media. These attacks significantly undermined the ability of nascent civil society structures to build an antiwar resistance movement after Russia invaded Ukraine in February 2022.

The repression campaigns that took place in 2020–2021 targeted all the main networks that fostered and institutionalized the growing societal demand for state accountability. Alexey Navalny and his supporters constituted a large number of those repressed. In August 2020, Russian secret services attempted to murder Alexey Navalny by poisoning him with the nerve agent Novichok. After his recovery and return to Russia in January 2021, he was immediately jailed, kept in torture conditions, and murdered in prison in February 2024. Thousands of his supporters were detained at the street protests in January–February and April 2021, which started on the day of Navalny's return to Russia and continued to demand his release and proper treatment. Several members of Navalny's team were prosecuted for allegedly breaking COVID-19 protocols prohibiting mass gatherings. They were kept under house arrest for several months, and then sentenced to probation. Several of them subsequently left the country fearing further repression. Over 20 of Navalny's supporters without widely recognized public profiles were sentenced to jail time for allegedly resisting the police while participating in pro-Navalny protests, and more were prosecuted on various other grounds. Navalny's Anti-Corruption Foundation was labeled an extremist organization by the Russian court and disbanded by its organizers to protect their personnel. Several leaders of the organization, including the leaders of its regional branches, were accused of extremism; many of them left Russia to avoid imprisonment.[163]

Besides Navalny and his supporters, other groups and individuals who were part of active resistance to the regime were targeted as well. Mikhail Khodorkovsky's "Open Russia" was disbanded, several of its activists, including its leader Andrei Pivovarov, have been jailed, and its Internet media have been blocked in Russia.[164] Many independent journalists and human rights defenders have been included in the lists of "foreign agents" and repressed in other ways.[165] Opposition candidates in the 2021 parliamentary and local elections, especially those who had significant support among their constituencies, including Yulia Galiamina and Dmitry Gudkov mentioned earlier, have been prosecuted on various grounds as well.[166]

As a result of these repressions, by the time of Russia's invasion of Ukraine on February 24, 2022, the *active resistance* inside the country, which had been

---

[163] "Политзаключённые и политические репрессии в России в 2021 году," 14–40.
[164] "Политзаключённые и политические репрессии в России в 2021 году," 41–46.
[165] "Политзаключённые и политические репрессии в России в 2021 году," 46–54.
[166] "Политзаключённые и политические репрессии в России в 2021 году," 54–60.

growing over the previous decade, was almost completely demolished with most of their leaders being either in jail or in exile. In the absence of clear leadership, the antiwar resistance that emerged immediately after the start of the invasion was very decentralized and much less coordinated than previous protest campaigns.[167] A wave of street protests and petitions that took place in the first few weeks was put down by restrictive legislation criminalizing "the discreditation of the Russian armed forces." Repressions and subsequent military draft pushed out of the country hundreds of thousands of the most liberal-minded and well-off citizens.[168]

Those who stayed and wanted to resist had to organize underground depersonalized networks coordinating primarily through Telegram channels. By June 2022, there were an estimated 55 channels with 250,000 subscribers across them.[169] Their members often concealed their names for security reasons. Some of them focused on reducing harm done by the war by helping Ukrainians who fled or were deported to Russia to leave for Europe, helping Russian men to flee the country to avoid the draft, and engaging in various acts of sabotage that would make the war logistics more difficult. Others worked to maintain the antiwar agenda in the public space via leaflets, stickers, graffiti, and other means that are more difficult to repress than street protests.[170]

As during previous historical periods, only a small share of the Russian population engaged in active resistance, while the rest chose passive resistance (ranging from unenthusiastic support of the war to disengagement) or compliant activism. According to public opinion polls, 70%–80% of the population declared their support of the invasion—a figure that had not significantly changed one year into the invasion.[171] Scholars debate the degree to which these numbers can be trusted given intensified repression of dissenting political opinions. But multiple experiments and detailed analysis of polling procedures generally agree that these numbers have not been significantly distorted by fear or social desirability bias, particularly in the first months of the war.[172]

What exactly stands behind these numbers is an important question, though. The rally around the flag effect and trusting the country leaders during wars, whether aggressive or defensive, are not unique to Russia and would not

---

[167] Драбкин and ОВД-Инфо, *Как теперь протестовать и защищать себя, оставаясь в России*, pt. 9:00.
[168] Камалов et al., "Большой исход."
[169] Antiwarriors, "За 100 дней войны в России появилось низовое антивоенное движение."
[170] Olimpieva, Olimpieva, and Galenko, "Russia's Antiwar Movement Goes Far beyond Street Protests."
[171] Levada-Center, "Conflict with Ukraine."
[172] Rosenfeld, "Survey Research in Russia"; Frye et al., "Is Putin's Popularity (Still) Real?"; Zavadskaya, "On the Harmfulness of Russian Polls"; Козеренко, "О недостижимости и прерванных интервью."

be too surprising.[173] A more surprising fact is that public opinion in Russia demonstrated a gigantic swing in support of the military invasion. In December 2021, when the tension was growing but the messaged transmitted by Russian state-controlled media was that Russia had no intent of attacking Ukraine, only 8% of the Russian population supported military action.[174] In March 2022, this figure skyrocketed to about 80%, together with the changed rhetoric of state-controlled media.[175]

This swing of the Russian public opinion can be only partially explained by the intensified attack on independent media prior to the invasion and lack of alternative information. Even before this attack, the independent media only reached a smaller share of the liberally minded population, while state-controlled television remained the main information source for the majority.[176] The more important factor seems to be the inclination of the Russian population to perceive state narratives uncritically when they concern external threats and the default compliance with the state characteristic of a statist society. Research investigating the different state narratives in the early days of the invasion found that the narrative about the existential NATO threat and the need to defend Russia from it resonated most with the population.[177] The Russian population can be extremely skeptical about the government's messages related to domestic policies, such as COVID vaccination, as it always expects the state to mistreat the people. However, an external threat to the country, whether a real or imaginary one, easily elicits default compliance.

Unlike after the annexation of Crimea, this default compliance came with intensified internal conflict between group loyalty to the state and resistance to abuse by the same state—the conflict that unraveled in the minds of many Russians. Russians suddenly faced loads of conflicting information about violence, death, and suffering that the Russian army brought to Ukraine, on the one hand, and the statements of Russian state-controlled media that all these images are fake and part of the information war of the West, on the other. Extremely disturbing and directly contradicting messages from the two sides of the war made it difficult to maintain a distanced skeptical stance characteristic of passive resistance. However, direct opposition to the state in the situation of potentially an existential external threat was too radical for many Russians to take, pushing the majority to unenthusiastic default support of the invasion reflected in poll figures.[178]

---

[173] Larson, "Public Support for U.S. Military Operations."
[174] Hale et al., "Russia May Be About to Invade Ukraine. Russians Don't Want It to."
[175] Levada-Center, "Conflict with Ukraine."
[176] Левада-Центр, "Основные источники информации и популярные журналисты."
[177] Alyukov, Kunilovskaya, and Semenov, "Mobilizing for War."
[178] See, for example, "Далекая близкая война," 128–40.

Detailed qualitative interviews with the *hesitating* people (i.e., those unenthusiastically supporting the war) show a range of reactions characteristic of *passive resistance* and highlighting the conflict between the desired ideal of the just state and the reality of the oppressive state. In the beginning of the invasion, the future unenthusiastic supporters' reaction to it was very similar to the reaction of active resisters: shock, disbelief, disorientation, and shame. Months into the invasion, many such respondents continued to express disapproval of war as a method of resolving any conflicts but also employed multiple strategies to reconcile it with their own loyalty to the country. Some explicitly recognized that even if their country is wrong, they could not wish for a defeat for it. Others went to great length to look for reasons why the war they disapproved of might have been inevitable. Many unenthusiastic supporters demonstrated reactions characteristic of passive resistance in general, for example, refusal to engage in matters going beyond their private lives, helplessness to change the situation, and skepticism. They cited their lack of knowledge about politics and lack of ability to distinguish between reliable sources of information and unreliable ones. They also expressed a general skepticism that any sources of information about the war might be objective.[179] Yet another time in Russian history, a large share of the population disliked the Russian state committing violence, this time primarily against another nation, but still accepted it because it was unable to break the bond with the state and act collectively against it.

Finally, the last part of society opted for *compliant activism*, which accepted the Russian state narratives of the invasion and rejected any conflicting information. In public opinion polls, these people expressed consistent support not only of the decision to invade Ukraine but also of continuation of the war.[180] Some of these people signed up as volunteer soldiers in the early days of the invasion. Others drove public initiatives to support Russian troops in Ukraine.[181] Those education officials and schoolteachers who chose compliant activism quickly adjusted historical narratives to match the Russian state narratives about the war.[182] Unlike the public that hesitates or supports the war unenthusiastically, compliant activists do not experience any internal conflicts. They either hold long-standing imperialist views or, more often, repeat the statements of Russian state-controlled media about liberation of

---

[179] "Далекая близкая война"; "Смириться с неизбежностью"; Morris, "What Do Ordinary Russians Think about the Invasion of Ukraine?"; "Россия полностью и необратимо втянулась в войну."
[180] "Россия полностью и необратимо втянулась в войну."
[181] Затари, "'Во-первых, они не воюют.'"
[182] "'Мы чужое не берем, а свое назад вернем.'"; "'Ощущение, что школьников уже давно готовят к войне.'"

Ukraine from the American-controlled government. And similar to compliant activists in previous eras, these people very easily initiated and engaged in collective action, as long as it was in line with the state-approved course of actions.

The invasion of Ukraine amplified all the reactions—active resistance, passive resistance, and compliant activism—that the Russian people had to the fundamental conflict between the ideal of a just state and the reality of the oppressive state. Ironically, the cleavage between compliant activists and active resisters, which became deeper than ever in recent Russian history, contributed to an increased sense of responsibility for the country in 2022, as both camps likely felt the urgency for action.[183] The cleavage broke many families, often running along generational lines with older people being loyal to the Russian state and the younger generation taking positions of resistance.[184]

By deepening the cleavage between compliant activists and active resisters, the invasion of Ukraine also strengthened Putin's regime. The opposition that had been growing during the previous decade in response to the social demand for state accountability was undermined by a large number of activists leaving the country under the threat of repression. As the invasion forced many people to take a stance, the compliant activists became personally invested into state propaganda narratives of external threat, which made it even more difficult for the opposition agenda to develop inside the country. The social demand for state accountability is unlikely to disappear, and a significant share of the population inside the country still opposes the war. However, organizing collective action around it will be extremely difficult if not impossible until the Russian state, including its propaganda machine and the economic basis, weakens.

Chapter Summary

This chapter applied the theory developed in the book to Russia as a country and argued that Russia has a statist society, and its authoritarianism is a unity-based one. While there are other popular explanations of Russian authoritarianism, including personalism, nationalism, and performance legitimacy, statism of Russian society often makes it possible to look deeper into the mechanisms of social support for Russian autocrats.

The chapter also argues that the main driver of Russian domestic politics is the tension between the ideal of a just state that respects individual freedoms and

---

[183] Левада-Центр, "Чувство ответственности и возможности влиять на ситуацию."
[184] *Broken Ties.*

the reality of the repressive state that does not. It outlines three reactions to this internal conflict—compliant activism, active resistance, and passive resistance—and briefly traces them throughout Russian history, starting with the early imperial period and ending with the reaction of Russian society to the invasion of Ukraine in February 2022.

Conclusion

The theory of authoritarianism in statist and antistatist societies developed in this book can be applied to other countries beyond Russia. The political logic characterizing divided (pluralist) and unitary environments can help understand different phenomena, from popular support of parties to social policy to democratization pathways. Before applying this theory, however, researchers must consider what the ideal types mean and how to use them as an analytical tool.

Statist and Antistatist Societies around the World

Statist and antistatist societies described in the first chapter of the book are ideal, or pure, types.[1] This means that their characteristics have been exaggerated and purified to highlight the contrast of the opposite logics driving politics in unitary and pluralist settings. In actual societies, these logics coexist and interact with each other, following patterns shaped by the local history. Disentangling how these logics work in individual behavior and where the group authority lies helps explain the political dynamics in very different societies using a common theoretical framework.

The prevalence of teamwork and utility maximization logics, which correspond to unitary and divided environments, may vary depending on location, societal level, and time. As I showed in the book, different logics may dominate in different geographic regions where the regional histories of state–society relations have created different political traditions. The different logics can also coexist at different societal levels. For example, local lineages in China have been very competitive between themselves, but their relationship with the state follows the team logic much more than the utility maximization one.[2] The two logics may also activate at different times in the minds of the same individuals as external circumstances make some of their group identities more or less salient. A clear external threat to the country often has an effect of rallying around the

---

[1] Weber, *The Methodology of the Social Sciences*, 90.
[2] On how the Chinese state limited competitiveness to the lower level of governance, see, for example, Wang, "China's State Development in Comparative Historical Perspective."

flag even in divided societies: for example, the terrorist attacks on September 11, 2001, in the United States activated unifying feelings in the nation, even though the country's politics had been polarizing for some time.

It is also important to remember that the ideal types of statist and antistatist societies are static categories, while the reality is always dynamic. States, especially authoritarian ones, are often trying to strengthen their group authority and establish themselves as sole legitimate leaders of collective action while weakening competing centers of authority. The nonstate groups, in their turn, try to take over the states, use the state apparatus for their own benefit, and possibly merge with the state one day.

For example, the 1979 Islamic revolution in Iran is the case of a religious institution taking over the state. Before the revolution, the state and religion in Iran were competing group authorities that balanced each other, preventing the creation of a political monopoly. The revolution subjugated the state to religion and moved Iran closer to a unitary society, but the legacy of state–religion competition survived in the form of conservative and reformist forces in Iranian politics.

In another example, the legitimacy of the current Vietnamese regime comes from a nationalist movement that has taken over the state from the colonial authorities. The country's tradition of nationalism had been coined for many centuries through popular resistance to the Chinese and the French rule. Vietnam had its own monarchy for several centuries, which likely strengthened the authority of the state during that period. However, yet another colonization by the French undermined state authority again while strengthening nonstate nationalist elites who established the current regime.

Neither Iran nor Vietnam fit the statist–antistatist ideal types perfectly well. These are not divided societies with a strong resistance of different population groups to the state; these are unitary environments, which are not perfectly statist either.[3] Each of them has seeds of resistance to state authority embedded in their history. Now, it is an open empirical question whether and when their group authority completely blends with the state or they may separate again in the future, that is, whether the Iranian state can become secular again and whether the nationalist agenda in Vietnam can be taken over by nonstate actors. The growing discontent in Iran in the late 2010s to early 2020s suggests that the separation of the state and religion may be supported by a large share of the population there, while in Vietnam, we do not see a similar dynamic about the state and nationalism. The ideal types developed in this book help identify key

---

[3] On how the Iranian authorities have been building a unitary political environment, see Harris, "The Martyrs Welfare State." On the origins of the Vietnamese regime legitimacy, see Slater, "Revolutions, Crackdowns, and Quiescence."

developmental alternatives such as these and understand how they might impact the authoritarian regimes.

The concepts of statist and antistatist societies also help conceptualize the differences between some countries that may seem culturally similar but have a very different history of state–society relations. One example from the post-Soviet space is Ukraine and Russia. Unlike in Russia, where the state successfully suppressed nonstate identities upon its consolidation in the 16th to 17th centuries, the Ukrainian identity continued to grow largely in resistance to the state—the Lithuanian, Polish, Austrian, and Russian ones during different historical periods. The post-Soviet political trajectory of Ukraine demonstrated typical characteristics of an antistatist political environment: a high level of political competitiveness that did not always follow democratic norms, the importance of business tycoons in politics (since money is more powerful than state authority in this environment), and a strong societal potential of organizing against the state, which fueled both the Orange Revolution in 2004 and the Revolution of Dignity in 2014. Despite a large part of shared cultural heritage, the political components of Russian and Ukrainian cultures fall on the different ends of the statist–antistatist scale.

The statist and antistatist environments are sometimes characteristic of whole regions that share the history of state formation. For example, most societies in Latin America are antistatist.[4] Historically, caste identities structured these societies to a much larger degree than national identities. The region experienced few and limited interstate wars as the internal elite divisions have been stronger than the disputes between states.[5] As the countries democratized, grassroots-level clientelism driven by the utility maximization logic became one of the main electoral tools.[6] Similarly, the colonial history of Africa contributed to the relative weakness of state authority there.[7]

Explaining Politics, Society, and Democratization through the Statist/Antistatist Lens

The opposite logics of statist and antistatist environments may also explain some contradictory empirical observations made by researchers so far. These contradictions arose partially because research was done in different contexts

---

[4] With a partial exception of Uruguay. I thank Michael Coppedge for pointing this out at a Kellogg Institute workshop at the University of Notre Dame.
[5] Centeno, *Blood and Debt*.
[6] The literature on clientelism in Latin America is vast. For a couple of examples, see Hilgers, *Clientelism in Everyday Latin American Politics*; Nichter, *Votes for Survival*.
[7] See, for example, Jackson and Rosberg, "Why Africa's Weak States Persist"; Bratton, "Beyond the State."

rather than across them. Researchers may have intuitively treated statist and antistatist environments as too different to compare since there was no theory spelling out the differences between them and making it possible to craft explanations for the opposite outcomes.

One example of such a challenging question about authoritarian regimes is the question about public goods provision and political competition. Some research shows that political competition increases the provision of public goods, while other research shows that it decreases the provision of public goods.[8] When cases with contradictory results are present in the same study, authors struggle with developing an explanation for both. For example, in their cross-regional study of welfare systems, Haggard and Kaufman admit that socialist welfare states do not fit into their model connecting democracy and a higher redistribution level. They say this is because these welfare states originated not from "constraints operating through formal political institutions but as a component of a larger socialist economic project," thus switching the explanation from political economy to ideology.[9] The theory developed in this book, though, would explain the opposite effects of political competition by whether it took place in a statist or an antistatist society. In a statist society, which is already solidary and favorable to provision of public goods, increased competition may lead to an increase in public goods provision as it helps reduce corruption and inefficiencies through effective accountability mechanisms or simply by winning more votes.[10] In an antistatist society, where multiple groups expect politicians to serve their constituency rather than that of their neighbors, high competition increases the demand for exclusive, private goods and, thus, reduces public goods provision.[11]

Another example of a question in which the distinction between statist and antistatist contexts may help, is the link between state institutions and democracy. Part of existing scholarship links democratic backsliding to institutional weakness. It argues that when weak states fail to deliver good governance, people follow personalist dictators and populists who promise to deliver concrete benefits defying poorly functioning institutions.[12] Another strand of research argues that it is the strong states and institutions that benefit autocrats, who learned to abuse them for their own purposes.[13]

Definitions of institutions in disciplines other than political science do not help clarify the issue. Sociologists understand institutions as sets of social norms

---

[8] Haggard and Kaufman, *Development, Democracy, and Welfare States*; Driscoll, "Why Political Competition Can Increase Patronage."
[9] Haggard and Kaufman, *Development, Democracy, and Welfare States*, 16.
[10] Haggard and Kaufman, 16.
[11] Driscoll, "Why Political Competition Can Increase Patronage."
[12] See, for example, Levitsky and Murillo, "Variation in Institutional Strength"; Levitsky, "Latin America's Shifting Politics"; Foa, "Why Strongmen Win in Weak States."
[13] See, for example, Slater, "Iron Cage in an Iron Fist."

that guide and constrain individual behavior.[14] Such understanding connects weak institutionalization not to political regimes but to sweeping historical transformations, such as modernization, during which the old norms weaken, while the new ones are only being formed. The economic understanding of institutions as enforced rules that reduce transaction costs emphasizes stability of those rules and of the enforcement rather than their democratic character.[15] Neither of these understandings assumes a conceptual contradiction between authoritarianism and institutions.

The intuition connecting democratization and institution-building, however, has value, which the theory developed in this book helps clarify. The implication of this theory is that democratization is linked not to institutions in general, but to different kinds of institutions that counteract the different sources of authoritarian power in statist and antistatist societies. In the case of antistatist societies, where authoritarian regimes exploit social divisions, the institutions that are missing are those of equal representation and power-sharing. These societies are pluralist and competitive by default, which is why they are often classified as more democratic.[16] But power in such societies is not distributed according to impartial and mutually agreed on rules. It usually goes to the faction that has the most resources at the moment. Democratization in this context means not so much increasing competitiveness but setting and *enforcing* fair rules for political competition. Building more societal support for the impartial state authority that can enforce these rules is crucial for democratization of an antistatist society.

In the case of a statist society, however, strengthening the impartial state authority would only make the authoritarian regime more durable. In such a society, the main problem is not that the state favors some societal groups over others but that the power of the impartial state is unrestricted. The state has formed a separate corporation, which oppresses all societal groups while benefiting itself.[17] Its power is based on societal norms that view the state as the only legitimate leader of collective action, which makes it very difficult to grow a political opposition with a strong social base that would be able to keep the state accountable. Breaking the political monopoly of the state, increasing political competitiveness, and building accountability institutions that limit state power is crucial for democratization of a statist society.

As I mentioned in the introduction, the idea that democracy needs both a strong state authority and the institutions that restrict it is not new. The contribution of this book is in spelling out what exactly happens when either of these

---

[14] Durkheim, *The Rules of Sociological Method*, 50–59; Parsons, *The Social System*; Powell and DiMaggio, *The New Institutionalism in Organizational Analysis*.
[15] North, *Institutions, Institutional Change, and Economic Performance*.
[16] Way, *Pluralism by Default*.
[17] Восленский, *Номенклатура*.

two sides of democracy is missing and how these omissions produce authoritarianism with opposite qualities. The next step that future research should take is to explore the different paths of democratization, through building different types of institutions, and identify its likely sources and scenarios. Such research would help policymakers and democracy activists develop the course of action that would move countries closer to a stable, fair, and inclusive democracy.

APPENDIX 1
Quantitative Analysis

This appendix contains information about the regression model from the author's article "Shock-Resistant Authoritarianism: Schoolteachers and Infrastructural State Capacity in Putin's Russia" published in *Comparative Politics*.[1] Case selection in this book is based on the finding from this article. The Appendix has two parts: (1) model specification and (2) information about data sources and notes on the regression analysis.

Model Specification

The model estimates the influence of different factors on the electoral resilience of Putin's regime during the 2012 presidential election. Table A1.1 presents the variables included in the model and the corresponding hypotheses. See also the next section of this Appendix for more details on data sources and variable transformations.

I used an ordinary least squares (OLS) regression to estimate the systematic effect of each variable on the outcome. Table A1.2 shows regression coefficients of three models. Model 1 tests the factors that could impact the dynamic of genuine regime support and includes the predictors related to economic performance or public goods provision. Model 2 adds the variables related to infrastructural state power. The number of variables (17) in Model 2 is large for the number of cases (79), which may impact the clarity of the effects. Model 3 reduces the number of independent variables in half, using the eight predictors that showed the most systematic relationship to the outcome in Model 2.

Note on Interpretation of a Population Rather than a Sample Model

Researchers frequently report statistical significance of the quantitative results of subnational unit analysis even when all or nearly all units in a country are included. By doing that, they treat these units as a random sample from a hypothetical population, whose parameters the model estimates. This assumption is rarely explicitly justified, and it provides researchers with conventional cutoff α levels, which are frequently deployed as indicators of substantive rather than only statistical significance.

In contrast, I treat my models as population models. Statistical significance is irrelevant in this case, since all regression coefficients are population parameters, not their sample estimates. Standard error in this case does not measure estimator reliability, but rather "the variability of the observed effect size (β), subject to model misspecification, autocorrelation, heteroscedasticity, and measurement error."[2] In a population model, a regression coefficient represents a systematic effect, while standard error represents stochastic

---

[1] Forrat, "Shock-Resistant Authoritarianism."
[2] Gill, "Whose Variance Is It Anyway?," 327.

Table A1.1 Variables and Hypotheses in the Regression Model

OLS Regression Model	Explanations and Hypotheses
Putin 2012 = b_1 * Medvedev2008 +	These two variables work together to capture Putin's electoral resilience in 2012.
	The following predictors test whether the change in regime support, i.e., Putin's electoral resilience in 2012, is related to …
b_2 * Δ income $_{2011-2007}$ + b_3 * Δ inflation $_{2011-2007}$ + b_4 * Δ unemployment $_{2011-2007}$ +	… the change in economic performance.[a]
b_5 * Δ education_exp $_{2011-2007}$ + b_6 * Δ healthcare_exp $_{2011-2007}$ + b_7 * Δ social_security_exp $_{2011-2007}$ +	… the change in social policy expenditures.
b_8 * Δ teacher_density $_{2011-2007}$ + b_9 * Δ doctor_density $_{2011-2007}$ + b_{10} * Δ civil_servant_density $_{2011-2007}$ + b_{11} * Δ pensioner_density $_{2011-2007}$ +	… the change in the number of state-dependent population groups.[b]
b_{12} * Δ federal_transfer_share $_{2011-2007}$ +	… the change in the share of federal transfers in regional budget incomes.[c]
b_{13} * unemployment $_{2011}$ b_{14} * teacher_density $_{2011}$ + b_{15} * doctor_density $_{2011}$ + b_{16} * civil_servant_density $_{2011}$ +	… infrastructural state power, i.e., the density of state-controlled organizations, and population's dependency on employment in these organizations.[d]
b_{17} * urban_population $_{2011}$ + b_{18} * non-Russian region + e	… the level of urbanization or titular status of the region.

[a] McAllister and White, "'It's the Economy, Comrade!'"; Treisman, "Presidential Popularity in a Hybrid Regime"; Treisman, "Putin's Popularity since 2010."

[b] Rosenfeld, "Reevaluating the Middle-Class Protest Paradigm"; Rosenfeld, "State Dependency and the Limits of Middle Class Support for Democracy." Note, however, that the size of the public sector workforce has also been found not to affect regime's electoral performance—see, e.g., Reuter, "Regional Patrons and Hegemonic Party Electoral Performance in Russia."

[c] Kalinin, "Signaling Games of Election Fraud"; Starodubtsev, *Federalism and Regional Policy in Contemporary Russia*.

[d] Frye, Reuter, and Szakonyi, "Vote Brokers, Clientelist Appeals, and Voter Turnout."

effect. Rather than discussing statistical significance of the coefficients, I use t-values as a measure of the clarity of the systematic effect of a particular factor relative to the stochastic effect. I compare t-values of the variables related to competing hypotheses to see which factors are more systematically related to the outcome.

Regression Results

First, none of the variables related to the different versions of economic voting, urbanization, or the titular status of the region had a systematic effect on the resilience of Putin's electoral support in 2012 (see Model 1). After controlling for infrastructural state power

Table A1.2 OLS Regression Coefficients† (t-values in parentheses)

Outcome: Electoral Support for Putin in 2012	Model 1	Model 2	Model 3
Electoral support for Medvedev in 2008	*0.779*	*0.709*	*0.753*
	(7.996)	*(7.435)*	*(8.812)*
Change from 2007 to 2011 in:			
– income per person	−0.016	−0.027	
	(−0.282)	(−0.506)	
– yearly inflation rate	−0.373	−0.375	
	(−0.980)	(−1.033)	
– unemployment rate	−0.014	−0.027	−0.018
	(−0.846)	(−1.673)	(−1.193)
– regional budget expenditures on education	0.024	0.000	
	(0.451)	(−0.002)	
– regional budget expenditures on healthcare	0.055	0.071	0.024
	(1.303)	(1.805)	(0.751)
– regional budget expenditures on social security	−0.043	−0.042	
	(−1.628)	(−1.564)	
– teacher density	−0.057	*−0.193*	*−0.174*
	(−0.558)	*(−2.009)*	*(−2.003)*
– doctor density	0.021	0.080	
	(0.446)	(1.532)	
– civil servant density	−0.105	−0.144	
	(−1.012)	(−1.399)	
– pensioner density	0.092	††	
	(0.700)		
– the share of federal transfers in the total income of regional budgets	0.032	*0.047*	*0.047*
	(1.680)	*(2.485)*	*(2.684)*
Unemployment rate in 2011		0.004	*0.004*
		(1.794)	*(2.227)*
Teacher density in 2011		*0.001*	*0.001*
		(2.573)	*(2.173)*
Doctor density in 2011		−0.001	−0.0002
		(−1.605)	(−0.359)
Civil servant density in 2011		0.000	
		(−1.015)	

(*continued*)

Table A1.2 Continued

Outcome: Electoral Support for Putin in 2012	Model 1	Model 2	Model 3
Share of urban population in the region at the end of 2011	−0.098	0.091	
	(−1.611)	(1.199)	
Non-Russian region	0.024	0.003	
	(1.278)	(0.150)	

[†] N = 79. Cells with t-values more than 2 are marked in bold italic. This marking is introduced for readability purposes and does not imply any statistical or substantive thresholds.

[††] Pensioner density was dropped from this model due to high correlation with unemployment rate in 2011.

variables, two of the economic voting variables revealed a systematic effect (see Model 2). I will discuss below that both of these effects may be speaking more to the infrastructural state power hypothesis than to the economic voting one.

Second, only one of the indicators of infrastructural state power—teacher density, i.e., the number of teachers per 10,000 population—had a systematic effect on the outcome. The more teachers a region had relative to its population, the higher was Putin's electoral resilience in 2012. This effect of teacher density was robust to different model specifications, i.e., it stayed in place under various combinations of predictors in the model. The effect size is also nontrivial: For every standard deviation increase in teacher density, Putin's electoral percentage increased by 2.6%. For a comparison, the same number for the Medvedev's 2008 electoral percentage, which is a strong but trivial predictor, is 5.6%.

Third, other indicators of infrastructural state power—doctor and civil servant density—did not have the same effect on the outcome. This may mean that not all public organizations are equally involved in electoral mobilization or orchestrating voter fraud. Teachers may be especially well positioned to impact Putin's electoral performance, while doctors and civil servants do not have the same structural advantage.

Fourth, the other variables that had a systematic effect on the outcome in Models 2 and 3 may be adding more details to the connection between teacher density and Putin's electoral resilience in 2012. The resilience was higher in the regions that (1) had more teachers, (2) laid off more teachers between 2007 and 2011, (3) had higher unemployment at the end of 2011, and (4) became more dependent on federal transfers between 2007 and 2011.

The connection of these four variables to the electoral outcome highlights one of the mechanisms of Putin's 2012 victory, which is corroborated by qualitative evidence from the media. Teachers indeed occupy a special position in society: Unlike doctors or civil servants, they contact families of their students on a regular basis and are generally trusted by them, which puts them in a convenient position for political agitation. In addition, teachers are often part of precinct-level electoral commissions at the polling stations situated mostly in schools. Serving on these commissions gives them access to the process of voting, including vote count, and makes them the single professional group most targeted by state officials facilitating electoral fraud.[3]

---

[3] Forrat, "Shock-Resistant Authoritarianism."

The results of the regression analysis presented above are likely capturing the work of the political machine that made teachers boost Putin's electoral resilience in 2012 through agitation and fraud. This machine worked through explicit or implicit threats to teachers that they might lose jobs and benefits unless they agitate and falsify the vote count.[4] Three of the variables with systematic effects in Model 3 speak in favor of this explanation by highlighting teachers' vulnerability on the regional job market. The more teachers a region had, the larger share of the workforce they constituted and the fewer opportunities of alternative employment existed in the region. Higher unemployment made it more difficult to find a new job, and a higher number of teachers laid off in the last few years made the threat of losing a job more credible. Existing qualitative evidence suggests that teachers and school principals in Russia are highly dependent on municipal authorities, who can easily fire them or cut school funding.[5] The pressure on municipalities, in turn, comes from the regional governors—the last part of the political machine that the regression model traced. The fact that regions with increased dependence on federal transfers demonstrated higher electoral resilience likely speaks to the motivation of the regional governors to put more pressure on the organizational mechanisms at their disposal, including schoolteachers, rather than to the increased sympathies of the population to Putin as a presidential candidate in poorer regions.[6]

Information about Data Sources and Notes on the Regression Analysis

Regression Analysis Notes

Value Change for the Moscow Case

The value of the variable measuring the change of federal transfer share in regional budgets for the case of Moscow City has been changed from -1.29 to variable minimum of -0.48. The reason for this is that the value -1.29 is a statistical artifact produced by the low base effect and the direction change of the transfer flow between the Moscow regional budget and the federal budget in 2007–2011. The correction makes it possible to bring this value in line with the phenomenon for which the variable is used as a proxy—the financial incentive for the governors to deliver the electoral percentage for Putin.

In 2007 Moscow City was the only region that, according to the treasury data, was giving rather than receiving money from the federal budget. By 2011, it was receiving money. Both figures constitute rather small shares of the regional budget, especially the 2007 one that serves as a base. When calculating the change of the share of federal transfers in the regional budget for Moscow, not only is the sign wrong but also the value is very high because of the low base. The sign could be fixed to reflect the fact that Moscow has become more dependent on federal transfers, but then the value (1.29, which means

---

[4] Forrat.
[5] Forrat.
[6] An analysis of the United Russia performance at the 2011 parliamentary election using similar conceptual categories (governor's dependence on the federal center, governor's capacity to organize fraud, and vulnerability of the population) but very different empirical indicators can be found in Bader and Ham, "What Explains Regional Variation in Election Fraud?"

Table A1.3 Information about Variables and Data Sources (all variables measured at the regional level)

Original Variables	Time of Measurement (day/month/year)	Short Name (see Table A1.4)	Description	Source
Electoral support for Putin	04/03/2012	Putin12	Share of votes received by Vladimir Putin in the election of the president of the Russian Federation	Central Election Commission of the Russian Federation (http://www.cikrf.ru/; access date October 9, 2014)
Electoral support for Medvedev	02/03/2008	Medvedev08	Share of votes received by Dmitry Medvedev in the election of the president of the Russian Federation	
Income per person	2007 2011	PIncome07 PIncome11	Average monetary income per person	Росстат, *Регионы России*. 2012. Pp. 168–169. Table 5.2.
Number of schoolteachers in the region	2007 2011	Teach07 Teach11	Number of teachers in the organizations providing general (i.e., secondary) education	Unified Interdepartmental Statistical Information System / Ministry of Education and Science of the Russia Federation / Information on the number and structure of employees in the organizations of general education / Number of teachers (http://www.fedstat.ru/; access date October 9, 2014)
Number of doctors in the region	2007 2011	Doc07 Doc11	Number of doctors per 10,000 population	Росстат, *Российский статистические ежегодник*. 2012. Pp. 271–272. Table 8.6.
Number of executive government employees (including municipal ones) in the region	12/2007	Gov07	Number of employees of executive government bodies and municipal bodies with executive functions	Росстат, *Российский статистические ежегодник*. 2008 Pp. 48–50. Table 2.4.
	12/2011	Gov11	Number of employees of executive government and municipal bodies	Росстат, *Российский статистические ежегодник*. 2012. Pp. 48–49. Table 2.4.

Original Variables	Time of Measurement (day/month/year)	Short Name (see Table A1.4)	Description	Source
Number of pensioners in the region	12/2007	Pens07	Number of pensioners registered in the Pension Fund of the Russian Federation	Росстат, *Регионы России. 2012*. Pp. 163–164. Table 5.5.
	12/2011	Pens11		Росстат, *Регионы России. 2012*. Pp. 174–175. Table 5.5.
Regional budget expenditures on education	01/01/2008	EducExp07	Yearly expenditures on education (budgetary code 0700)	Russian Federal Treasury, Reports on the Execution of Regional and Local Budgets of the Russian Federation (http://www.roskazna.ru/byudzhetov-subektov-rf-i-mestnykh-byudzhetov/; access date March 27, 2015); all numbers taken from the column referring to "Executed: Consolidated regional budget and territorial state non-budgetary fund."
	01/01/2012	EducExp11		
Regional budget expenditures on healthcare	01/01/2008	HealthExp07	Yearly expenditures on healthcare (budgetary code 0900); for the year 2007 expenditures on sports (budgetary code 0902) are subtracted from healthcare expenditures to make them comparable to the year 2011, when sports became a separate category	
	01/01/2012	HealthExp11		
Regional budget expenditures on social security	01/01/2008	SocSecExp07	Yearly expenditures on social security (budgetary code 1000)	
	01/01/2012	SocSecExp11		
Federal transfers to regional budgets	12/2007	Trans07	Yearly interbudgetary transfers (budgetary code 000 202)	
	12/2011	Trans11		
Total income of regional budgets	12/2007	RIncome07	Yearly total income of regional budgets (budgetary code 850)	
	12/2011	RIncome11	Yearly total income of regional budgets (no budgetary code for this year; number located in column 14, row code 010)	

(*continued*)

Table A1.3 Continued

Original Variables	Time of Measurement (day/month/year)	Short Name (see Table A1.4)	Description	Source
Non-Russian region			Indicates whether a non-Russian ethnicity is titular in the region	Coding by the author
Regional population	01/01/2008	Pop07	Regional population estimate on January 1 (Information almost identical to the referenced sources can be found in Regiony Rossii. 2012. Pp. 54–55. Table 3.1.)	Росстат, *Российский статистические ежегодник*. 2008. Pp. 84–85. Table 4.3.
	01/01/2012	Pop11		Росстат, *Российский статистические ежегодник*. 2012. Pp. 76–77. Table 4.3
Purchasing power index	12/2007	Infl07	Change in consumer prices to December of the previous year	Росстат, *Регионы России*. 2012. Pp. 953–954. Table 25.1.
	12/2008	Infl08		
	12/2009	Infl09		
	12/2010	Infl10		
	12/2011	Infl11		
Purchasing power index December 2007 to December 2011		InflAdj	Change in consumer prices from December 2007 to December 2011	(Infl08/100)*(Infl09/100)*(Infl10/100)*(Infl11/100)
Urban population in the region	12/2011	Urban11	Urban population in the Russian regions	Росстат, *Демографический ежегодник России*. 2012. P. 28. Table 1.7.
Unemployment rate	2007	Unempl07	Unemployment rate (International Labor Organization standard)—ratio of the number of unemployed to the number of economically active in the certain age group	Росстат, *Регионы России*. 2012. Pp. 134–135. Table 4.15.
	2011	Unempl11		

Table A1.4 Variable Generation for Models

Generated Variables Included in the Models	Formulae (components correspond to the Original Variables in Table 1)
Change from 2007 to 2011 in:	
– income per person ‡	((PIncome11 / InflAdj) – PIncome07) / PIncome07
– yearly inflation rate	(Infl11 – Infl07) / Infl07
– unemployment rate	(Unempl11 – Unempl07) / Unempl07
– regional budget expenditures on education per capita ‡	((EducExp11 / InflAdj / Pop11) – EducExp07 / Pop07) / (EducExp07 / Pop07)
– regional budget expenditures on healthcare per capita ‡	((HealthExp11 / InflAdj / Pop11) – HealthExp07 / Pop07) / (HealthExp07 / Pop07)
– regional budget expenditures on social security per capita ‡	((SocSecExp11 / InflAdj / Pop11) – SocSecExp07 / Pop07) / (SocSecExp07 / Pop07)
– teacher density	(Teach11/Pop11 – Teach07/Pop07) / Teach07/Pop07
– doctor density	(Doc11/Pop11 – Doc07/Pop07) / Doc07/Pop07
– executive government employee density	(Gov11/Pop11 – Gov07/Pop07) / Gov07/Pop07
– pensioner density	(Pens11/Pop11 – Pens07/Pop07) / Pens07/Pop07
– the share of federal transfers in the total income of regional budgets	(Trans11/RIncome11 – Trans07/RIncome07) / (Trans07/RIncome07) ‡‡
Teacher density at the end of 2011	Teach11 / Pop11 * 10,000
Government employee density at the end of 2011	Gov11 / Pop11 * 10,000
Share of urban population in the region at the end of 2011	Urban11 / Pop11
Non-Russian region	binary variable: 1 = non-Russian, 0 = Russian

‡ Inflation adjusted to December 2007.

‡‡ Value of transfers to Moscow has been changed from -1.29 to variable minimum of -0.48 (see "Regression Analysis Notes" in this Appendix for explanation). In addition, the resulting variable was trimmed to remedy the effect of extreme values resulting from the low base. Values more than 1.5 were recoded to exactly 1.5. This trimming affected two cases: Tiumenskaia oblast' (original value 3.02) and Iamalo-Nenetskii avtonomnyi okrug (original value 4.86).

129% increase) would create a wrong impression that Moscow came to be very dependent on the federal budget.

This value would also ignore the fact that Moscow was the region where the largest protests against electoral falsifications at the 2011 parliamentary election took place. The fear of a new wave of protests led to significantly reduced, almost nonexistent pressure for falsifications in Moscow, which can be verified by normalized turnout distribution at

Table A1.5 Descriptive Statistics of the Variables Included in the Models

	Unit	N	min	max	median	mean	SD
Electoral support for Putin in 2012	vote share	79	0.469	0.928	0.616	0.639	0.097
Electoral support for Medvedev in 2008	vote share	79	0.593	0.919	0.673	0.696	0.081
Change from 2007 to 2011 in							
– monetary income per person, inflation adjusted to December 2007	share of personal income in 2007	79	−0.14	0.69	0.24	0.23	0.15
– yearly inflation rate	share of yearly inflation rate in December 2007	79	−0.09	−0.02	−0.06	−0.06	0.02
– unemployment rate	share of unemployment rate in 2007	79	−0.48	1.71	0.11	0.20	0.41
– regional budget expenditures per capita on education, inflation adjusted to December 2007	share of 2007 per capita expenditures	79	−0.31	0.95	0.18	0.18	0.17
– regional budget expenditures per capita on healthcare, inflation adjusted to December 2007	share of 2007 per capita expenditures	79	−0.34	0.65	−0.04	−0.01	0.19
– regional budget expenditures per capita on social security, inflation adjusted to December 2007	share of 2007 per capita expenditures	79	−0.13	1.21	0.48	0.48	0.28
– teacher density	share of the number of teachers per population unit in 2007	79	−0.49	0.35	−0.13	−0.14	0.09
– doctor density	share of the number of doctors per population unit in 2007	79	−0.23	1.02	0.02	0.04	0.14
– government employee density	share of the number of executive government employees per population unit in 2007	79	−0.17	0.34	−0.05	−0.04	0.07

	Unit	N	min	max	median	mean	SD
– pensioner density	share of the number of pensioners per population unit in 2007	79	−0.07	0.61	0.05	0.06	0.08
– the share of federal transfers in the total income of regional budgets	share of the share of federal transfers in regional budgets' income in 2007	79	−0.48	1.5	0.11	0.18	0.34
Teacher density	number of schoolteachers per 10,000 population in 2007	79	48.1	155.8	75.7	79.2	21.7
Doctor density	number of doctors per 10,000 population in 2007	79	30.2	87.2	49.1	49.2	11.7
Government employee density	number of executive government employees (including municipal ones) per 10,000 population in 2007	79	56.2	300.6	104.2	110.6	37.9
Unemployment rate at the end of 2011	% unemployed	79	1.4	48.8	7.0	7.8	5.3
Share of urban population in the region	share of urban population in the region in 2011	79	0.29	1.00	0.71	0.70	0.13
Ethnic (non-Russian) region	binary variable	79	0	1		0.291	

Table A1.6 Correlations between the Predictors Included in the Models (absolute values less than 0.2 are shaded; larger than 0.4 are marked in bold italic)

	elect%$_{t-1}$	Δinc	Δinfl	Δunempl	unempl	teachD	docD	govD	Δeduc_exp	Δhealth_exp	Δsoc_exp	ΔteachD	ΔdocD	ΔgovD	pensD	Δfed_trans	urban	non-Rus
elect%$_{t-1}$	1																	
Δinc	0.24	1																
Δinfl	−0.01	−0.29	1															
Δunempl	−0.26	−0.16	−0.13	1														
unempl	*0.40*	0.34	0.06	−0.09	1													
teachD	0.39	0.33	0.11	−0.22	*0.56*	1												
docD	−0.20	−0.31	0.15	−0.14	−0.22	−0.20	1											
govD	−0.10	−0.07	0.27	−0.04	0.08	0.34	−0.05	1										
Δeduc_exp	0.03	0.39	−0.03	−0.14	*0.42*	0.14	−0.05	−0.09	1									
Δhealth_exp	0.01	0.10	0.08	−0.11	0.25	0.19	0.00	0.22	*0.57*	1								
Δsoc_exp	−0.24	0.11	−0.15	−0.09	−0.24	−0.01	0.01	0.04	0.31	0.32	1							
ΔteachD	−0.08	0.04	0.22	0.14	0.53	0.20	−0.05	0.16	*0.43*	0.37	−0.07	1						
ΔdocD	−0.05	0.01	0.18	−0.11	0.09	−0.06	*0.42*	−0.01	−0.02	−0.08	0.08	0.05	1					
ΔgovD	0.19	0.17	0.08	−0.05	*0.57*	0.24	−0.13	0.21	0.38	0.36	−0.06	*0.43*	0.06	1				

	elect%$_{t-1}$	Δinc	Δinfl	Δunempl	unempl	teachD	docD	govD	Δeduc_exp	Δhealth_exp	Δsoc_exp	ΔteachD	ΔdocD	ΔgovD	ΔpensD	Δfed_trans	urban	non-Rus
ΔpensD	0.18	0.07	0.25	−0.06	0.75	0.3	−0.05	0.22	0.37	0.39	−0.20	0.66	0.17	0.58				
Δfed_trans	0.12	−0.16	0.05	0.14	−0.16	−0.02	−0.07	0.02	−0.23	−0.13	−0.25	−0.01	−0.1	0.05	0.08	1		
urban	−0.44	−0.52	0.10	0.28	−0.50	−0.63	0.40	−0.04	−0.10	−0.02	0.01	0.09	−0.01	−0.15	−0.09	0.04	1	
non-Rus	0.57	0.16	0.19	−0.34	0.36	0.59	−0.06	0.15	−0.11	−0.02	−0.20	−0.05	0.16	0.20	0.28	0.07	−0.45	1

Variable description

elect%$_{t-1}$—Medvedev's electoral percentage in March 2008

Δinc—change in personal income from 2007 to 2011

Δinfl—change in inflation from 2007 to 2011

Δunempl—change in unemployment rate from 2007 to 2011

Δeduc_exp—change in regional expenditures on education from 2007 to 2011

Δhealth_exp—change in regional expenditures on health care from 2007 to 2011

Δsoc_exp—change in regional expenditures on social security from 2007 to 2011

ΔteachD—change in teacher density from 2007 to 2011

ΔdocD—change in doctor density from 2007 to 2011

ΔgovD—change in government employee density from 2007 to 2011

ΔpensD—change in pensioner density from 2007 to 2011

Moscow precincts in 2012 presidential election.[7] Changing the Moscow value of transfer dynamic to the minimum one reflects this reduced pressure from state officials and, therefore, seems preferable to excluding the case, both because the number of cases is limited and because Moscow is a very important region where the hypothesized mechanism should be tested.

Cases Excluded Because of Missing Data

Chitinskaia oblast'/Zabaikal'skii krai—missing budget data for 2011
Chechnya—missing data on income per person in 2007

Model 2 Diagnostics

Multicollinearity

Variance inflation factor (VIF) was calculated for each variable and did not detect problems with multicollinearity (maximum VIF = 4.9).

Influential Observations

Cook's distances were calculated for each observation. Two of them had Cook's distances larger than 10/79 (10/n). They were:

1. the Republic of Ingushetiia (Cook's distance = 0.28),
2. Moscow City (Cook's distance = 0.15).

Data for these cases were checked for possible errors, but no errors were detected. Cases were kept in the analysis.

Residuals

1. The distribution of regression residuals is very close to normal.
2. The mean of residuals is very close to zero.
3. Residuals are uncorrelated with predicted values and predictors.
4. The Studentized Breusch-Pagan test was performed to detect possible heteroscedasticity. The results (BP = 18, df = 17, p-value = 0.3616) indicate no problem with heteroscedasticity.

---

[7] Байдакова, "'Реально "Единую Россию" поддержали 15% избирателей'. Интервью физика Сергея Шпилькина;" Орешкин, "Гибридные выборы. Предварительный отчет 'Народного избиркома."

APPENDIX 2

Fieldwork Data Collection and Analysis

This appendix lays out the structure of the fieldwork, the choices encountered during the fieldwork, and the emergence of the main argument of this book from fieldwork data.

The focus of my fieldwork was the question of why the political machines in the Kemerovo regions and Tatarstan turned out to be more reliable than in the Rostov region and Altai according to the results of the quantitative analysis. To identify the patterns that the statistical analysis might have missed, I expanded my investigation beyond the impact of the school system, which the quantitative analysis demonstrated, to include other organizations at the border between the state and society. At the same time, I was looking for the common features across these organizational types, which could explain the regional disparity.

I conducted the fieldwork in the four selected regions from December 2013 through June 2014, focusing on the regional capitals—Gorno-Altaisk, Kemerovo, Rostov, and Kazan'—and spending about four weeks in each of them. Using different methods and data sources allowed me to cross-check the information I received from each of them. I split the four weeks in each city into two parts: I spent about two weeks doing research in the main regional library and two weeks conducting interviews. During my whole time at the site, I also conducted observation and wrote fieldnotes about the structure of public space in the city, the interactions with the people, and the organizations that I visited. After I came back from the field, I continued working with secondary sources available in libraries or online in the process of interpreting my data.

Local Library Research

The goal of the first stage of my fieldwork in every region was to get a better idea of the main players and recent events in regional politics, including those related to social policy and the organizations that might work with social issues. Besides being generally valuable for the purposes of studying the case, this information subsequently helped me to decide whom to interview and ask these people informed questions.

In the libraries, I primarily concentrated on the catalogs of newspaper and magazine articles created by the departments of local history, which exist in the main public library in every Russian region. Librarians in these departments catalog not only books but also articles about the region from newspapers and periodicals, which the library receives. Each article in the local history catalogs was accompanied by a short annotation, which made it feasible to look through thousands of annotations before selecting a few hundred articles from several major sources to order from the library depository.

Besides the articles in newspapers and periodicals, I also checked the categories of book catalogs related to local history. Although books related to the post-Soviet period of regional history were rare, these catalogs had records of books and brochures published either by governmental bodies or other organizations that were of interest to me. I looked through and took pictures of the most relevant of these sources as well.

Interviews

As with the other parts of the qualitative stage of this project, the goal I pursued when selecting the interviewees and designing the interview guides was to maximize the qualitative variation of the data. This goal is best served by a selection strategy called "corpus construction," which "typifies unknown attributes, while statistical random sampling describes the distribution of already known attributes."[1] Corpus construction starts with a few known categories that structure the data and aims at maximizing the coverage of the unknown ones. It does so via a cyclical process of collecting small portions of data and adjusting the next selection in a way that maximizes qualitative variation. Corpus data cannot be used to study the distribution of attributes across categories, but they are very valuable for identifying the variables and patterns that are a priori unknown. In my case, I aimed to identify the patterns related to the role that state-controlled organizations played in social life in each region and then use the regional comparison to explain the variance I found in my quantitative analysis.

When selecting my interviewees, I initially targeted at least two categories of people in each locale: the representatives of the public sector organizations in education, healthcare, and social services and the officials dealing with these spheres in the regional government. Besides these groups, I also included nongovernmental organizations (NGOs), but their profiles were different in different regions. Early on, I stopped pursuing interviewees in healthcare organizations because the library research and the first interviews showed that healthcare organizations were not actively involved in the political and community activities, in which I was interested. Instead, I concentrated my energy on youth and pensioners' organizations, whose role in projecting state power quickly became apparent.

Across the four cases, I interviewed 60 people. Most interviews lasted between 40 min and an hour, while a few of them took more than 2 hours. Table A2.1 shows the distribution of interviewees across different types of organizations. Some interviewees have changed affiliation in the course of their careers, and in such cases, I asked them questions about both their current and former organization. This table reflects the official status of the organization with which the interviewee was affiliated at the time of the interview. As I show in Chapter 3, however, in Tatarstan and Kemerovo, the boundaries between some of these types of organizations are blurred.

To identify potential interviewees, I used several approaches. First, as I was doing research in local libraries, I paid attention to the mentions of organizations and people that could be potentially interesting to me. Library research helped me to identify those organizations that had been active and visible in the public space rather than only satisfying my formal criteria. Sometimes I consulted with the librarians in the local history departments about the significance of some organizations to double check the impression I had from reading newspaper articles.

---

[1] Bauer and Aarts, "Corpus Construction."

Table A2.1 The Composition of the Interviews

	Number of Interviewees				Total
	Altai	Kemerovo	Rostov	Tatarstan	
Regional government	6	2	6	2	16
Regional parliament and parties	3	-	1	1	4
Public-sector organizations (education, healthcare, social services)	4	4	1	3	12
Nongovernmental organizations, government-organized nongovernmental organizations (GONGOs), religious organizations	3	5	3	3	14
local academic researchers	3	1	5	6	14
Total number of interviewees (not a sum of lines above; a few interviewees combined two professional affiliations)	19	12	16	15	60

Second, I used the academic contacts that I had in the region to identify the local experts on the topics close to my interest. These experts, in their turn, would connect me to some of the organizations in which I was interested.

Third, as I walked around the city, I paid attention to the offices of organizations situated in the city center and in other convenient locations easily accessible to the public. This is how I stumbled on the pensioners' organizations in my first case, Altai. An interview I conducted there was so interesting that in all other cases I deliberately looked for these organizations and tried to conduct at least one interview with them. In another case, I walked by the office of the Council of Municipalities of the Rostov Region, which also resulted in one of the most interesting interviews in that case.

Finally, at least twice I was lucky to interview people whom I did not seek specifically but rather encountered almost randomly in the process of fieldwork. The first time, it was three schoolteachers from different Altai municipalities, who came for a training course to the university in Gorno-Altaisk. The interview with these teachers was a great opportunity to check how schools worked across the region, as I would not be able to travel to the remote villages myself. The second time, a woman who owned the apartment that I rented during fieldwork in Kemerovo volunteered to give me an interview after she learned about the topic of my research. Her experience as a member of a residential committee in her neighborhood was very valuable for understanding the activities of the community organizations in the city.

In all interviews, I tried to obtain insights into the work of the interviewees' organizations, including their relations with the different state structures and the population as well as their involvement in grassroots political activities. I developed tailored guides for every interview, taking into account the position of the person I was interviewing, the information about the organization that I learned from the library and available Internet resources, and sometimes the information I received from previous interviews. When interviewees began answering my questions, they would usually raise new topics, which I would probe with new questions. Sometimes, however, even after the probes, I could not understand what exactly my interviewees were talking about or why they thought some information was relevant and important. In these cases, I would let them speak about what they thought was relevant rather than continue asking the questions I prepared for them. Much later, when I was writing the first drafts about my cases, the information I could not interpret on the spot sometimes became the source of some of the most fascinating discoveries.

When I coded my interviews, I was looking for the common themes that would be addressed by, for example, both the people working in the government and those working in other public sector organizations, or both public sector organizations and NGOs. I checked these themes against other information that I collected about the cases and used them as guides for further exploration of primary and secondary sources. Such triangulation together with the targeted choice of interviewees ensured that I captured valid data about my topic of interest while covering enough cases and types of organizations that would give me a comparative analytic leverage.

Developing the Argument

My case studies could have resulted in several potential outcomes. I could, for example, have discovered that, in concert with the assumptions of existing research, the political machines across the four cases were driven primarily by economic payoffs to those who run them. The variation between the cases would then be explained by the amount of resources regional governors were willing and able to provide for these machines, which was not captured by the variables I included in the preliminary quantitative analysis. Alternatively, I could have discovered that it was not the money that explained the difference but the level of intimidation and repression. Or I could have seen a different picture in titular regions compared to nontitular ones, or even up to four different patterns among my case studies.

As I was collecting fieldwork data, it became apparent that I observed only two types of the organizational infrastructure, which connected the state and society: one type in the Kemerovo region and Tatarstan, the cases above the regression line (see Figure 2.2 in Chapter 2), and another type in the Rostov region and the Republic of Altai, the cases below the regression line. In Tatarstan and, especially, in Kemerovo, these organizations tended to form a region-wide hierarchy with a government official at the top. The most vivid evidence of that came not from the organizations that were officially a part of the public sector, such as schools or social services, but from those that were legally civil society ones but were nevertheless created and run by state officials, i.e., GONGOs (government-organized NGOs). In Kemerovo the most vivid examples were the Veterans' Councils, i.e., the pensioners' organizations, and a network of community centers and residential councils. In Tatarstan, youth organizations presented a very similar picture.

In contrast to Kemerovo and Tatarstan, in Rostov and Altai I could not find anything that looked similar. Governmental organizations at the regional level would not interact smoothly even with the municipal ones, let alone impose themselves on civil society. Some

NGOs functioned having almost no communication with state officials apart from registration as a legal entity and minimal formal reporting for tax purposes. Regional politics in general looked a lot more competitive and governance looked a lot more decentralized, and the organizational infrastructure reflected this difference.

This contrast between the two pairs of regions was not easy to capture with official statistics. A Tatarstan NGO, registered with the Russian Ministry of Justice and employing three people, might in fact be a center that tops a network of 700 smaller organizations across the region, which engage tens of thousands of volunteers while leaving no trace in the federal-level statistics. This NGO would be located in the building of one of the regional ministries and run by a former government official, who would still participate in most internal meetings in that ministry. A Rostov NGO, also registered with the Russian Ministry of Justice and employing three people, is likely to be a local organization working on a well-defined cause, developing some partnerships with a few other local NGOs and businesses, having a couple dozen volunteers and limited contacts with regional-level officials. We can also imagine many shades in between these two extremes, and no statistical indicator captures these differences well.

Meanwhile, these differences mattered a lot when it came to Putin's electoral resilience. If the regional officials sit on top of well-functioning organizational hierarchies, their capacity to mobilize the population for elections or rallies, monitor the grievances, and co-opt the nascent opposition leaders is a lot stronger than in a region with decentralized governance, where even the formal hierarchies malfunction. I read and heard about multiple instances of how state officials used these organizational networks for political mobilization in Tatarstan and Kemerovo as well as about their struggles to do the same in Rostov and Altai. In the latter cases, the state officials would use clientelistic exchanges to obtain electoral support more frequently exactly because they lacked the region-wide organizational leverage. Clientelistic deals, though, might be expensive and short-lived, which was the likely reason why regime support was not resilient in Rostov and Altai. In a sense, the fieldwork confirmed both the existing understanding of political machines driven by clientelistic economic payoffs and my hypothesis about the importance of organizational hierarchies by showing that both of these mechanisms worked but in different regions.

Observing the two patterns of public organization involvement in politics immediately raised the next question: Why was it that organizational hierarchies dominated in the Kemerovo region and Tatarstan while clientelistic deals were prevalent in the Rostov region and Altai? If centralized organizational infrastructure were so beneficial for electoral resilience, why would not all governors build it up in order to strengthen their power? Why would not the state officials in the low-resilience regions do the same as their colleagues did in the high-resilience ones? I struggled with this question during the fieldwork and asked the regional and municipal officials in Rostov directly about it. Neither of them gave me an answer that would explain the regional differences. They would say, for example, that creating more organizations takes resources and it will be difficult to fire people once you hire them. This, however, was no different in Kemerovo and Tatarstan. Sometimes they would just say that creating more organizations would only make the situation worse without giving a good reason why. Based on my data, I could not even say that state officials in Rostov and Altai wanted to create the organizational infrastructure but lacked resources to do that. Quite the opposite: They seemed to be actively avoiding increasing their infrastructural power, and this made the question even more puzzling.

I found the answer to this question when I was rereading an interview with a former municipal official in Rostov. I initially did not consider this interview very informative. It was long, over two hours, one of those interviews in which I did not completely understand why my interviewee considered some information relevant and important, but I let them talk anyway. This interviewee clearly thought a lot about municipal and regional governance and enjoyed sharing his ideas with me. Once, I was rereading the interview yet another time, and my attention was drawn to an episode he described when he as a municipal official tried to obtain cooperation of the people in one of the villages in the region. He said that he was failing until he understood that people refused to cooperate not because they disagreed with his suggestions but because they did not trust him. Once he asked the village's informal leader to put forward the same suggestions, the problem was solved.

At this point I realized that the question of why the state officials would not create more state-run organization misleadingly focused on state officials' motives and resources, while it was not up to them whether such organizations could be created. The municipal and regional officials in Rostov and Altai were dealing with a different kind of society—one that distrusted the state and resisted its intervention in community matters. Even if state officials would try to create more state-controlled organizations, these organizations would not help them monitor and mobilize society, as people would distrust them and would not cooperate with them. Worse than that, the informal leaders whom the people did trust would use these organizations to redirect public resources toward their communities. The reason why state officials in Rostov and Altai did not even try to create the organizational infrastructure was that they intuitively knew it would not work in their regions. It would indeed make the situation worse by draining their resources while not helping much with social control. They could not explain it to me because they took it for granted; it was natural for them that the world worked this way. Similarly, it was very natural for the people in Kemerovo and Tatarstan to live in a world where the state actively manages their lives. Once I started paying attention to the role of the state that people took for granted in different regions, the strategies of the state officials became easy to explain.

These taken-for-granted social norms, which ultimately became the basis of my theory of social statism, could not be derived directly from interviews, let alone quantitative analysis. It took a comparative framework—a careful selection of cases and a parallel analysis of them—to obtain evidence that these social norms exist and that they matter for how authoritarian regimes reproduce their power at the grassroots level. Understanding of the connection between social norms and the structure of public organizations also allowed me to see the common denominator of statist and antistatist societies—group authority—which helped to pull the theory of statist and antistatist societies together.

APPENDIX 3

Data on Social Policy in the Kemerovo Region

All graphs are author's calculations based on data from the Russian Federal Treasury (http://www.roskazna.ru/) and Russian Federal State Statistics Service (http://www.gks.ru/).

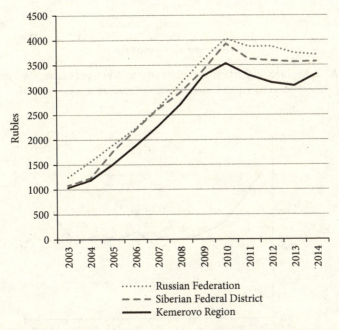

Figure A3.1 Regional budget expenditures of on social security, per capita, 2003 prices (author's calculations based on Russian Federal Treasury data).

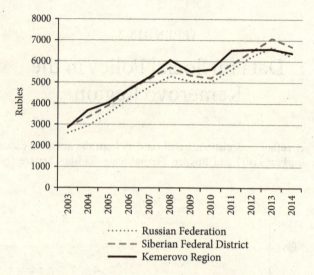

Figure A3.2 Regional budget expenditures on education, per capita, 2003 prices (author's calculations based on Russian Federal Treasury data).

Figure A3.3 Share of population with per capita income below subsistence level.

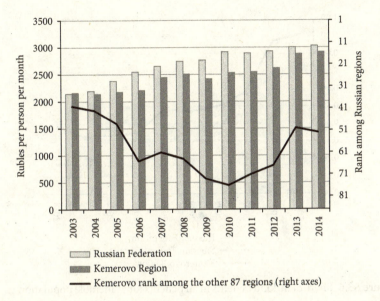

Figure A3.4 Subsistence income level.

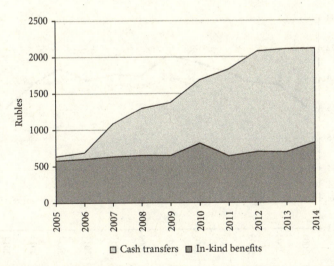

Figure A3.5 Kemerovo region budget expenditures on benefits for vulnerable population groups, per capita, 2005 prices.

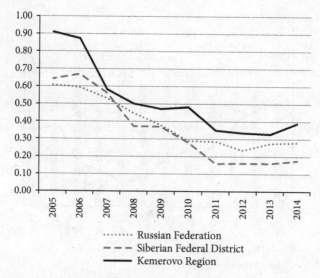

Figure A3.6 Share of in-kind benefits in all benefits for vulnerable population groups.

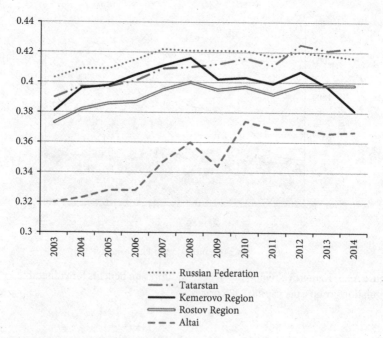

Figure A3.7 Gini coefficient.

APPENDIX 4

Newspaper Publications Related to Residential Committees and Community Centers in Kemerovo and to Their Role in Politics

This list was compiled from three sources: (1) documents about residential committees and community centers copied in Kemerovo regional library and one of the community centers; (2) searches of articles related to Kemerovo residential committees and community centers in the Integrum database; and (3) Kemerovo City Government website. Most entries are articles in the local government-controlled newspaper *Kemerovo (Кемерово)*, which have been downloaded from Integrum. Sources are sorted by date. All texts are available from the author on request.

2002-06-07. "Город: анализ, успехи, проблемы, перспективы." *Кемерово.* N 23.
2004-07-09. "Новости в районах города." *Кемерово.* N 28.
2004-11-19. Акуленко, Татьяна. "Совместными усилиями." *Кемерово.* N 47.
2005-06-01. "Коротко." *Кузбасс.* N 95.
2005-06-01. "Равных нет в рукопашном бою." *Кузбасс.* N 95.
2005-06-10. Акуленко, Татьяна. "Приходите стар и млад." *Кемерово.* N 24.
2005-07-22. "Будет где отдохнуть." *Кемерово.* N 30.
2005-07-29. Логинова, Екатерина. "Шахтерский край города Кемерово." *Кемерово.* N 31.
2005-08-10. "Новая жизнь 'Комсомольца.'" *Кузбасс.* N 144.
2005-08-12. Пресс-служба Администрации города. "Центры есть, работа будет." *Кемерово.* N 33.
2005-12-16. "Фильм—детям." *Кемерово.* N 51.
2005-12-30. "С Новым годом!" *Кемерово.* N 53.
2006-01-27. "Всем дело нашлось." *Кемерово.* N 4.
2006-05-19. Пресс-служба Администрации города. "Подарки городу." *Кемерово.* N 20.
2006-06-02. "Депутатский контроль." *Кемерово.* N 22.
2006-06-23. Пресс-служба Администрации города. "Всем найдется дело по душе." *Кемерово.* N 25.
2006-09-08. Акуленко, Татьяна. "Дружба и понимание." *Кемерово.* N 36.
2006-09-22. Акуленко, Татьяна. "Новое содержание старого названия." *Кемерово.* N 38.
2006-09-22. "Томичи приехали учиться." *Кемерово.* N 38.
2006-10-06. Тотыш, Наталья. "Центр, в котором все есть." *Кемерово.* N 40.
2006-11-24. Пресс-служба Администрации города. "Помощь придет вовремя." *Кемерово.* N 47.
2006-12-22. Тотыш, Наталья. "С пользой и интересом." *Кемерово.* N 51.
2006-12-23. "Кому—враг, кому—стройматериал." *Кузбасс.* N 241.

2006-12-29. Пресс-служба Администрации города. "Пункты стали центрами." *Кемерово*. N 52.

2006-12-29. "Чтобы мы не скучали." *Кемерово*. N 52.

2007-01-12. Матющенко, Юлия. "К себе, на ёлку." *Кузбасс*. N 4.

2007-01-12. Пресс-служба Администрации города. "В гостях, как дома." *Кемерово*. N 2.

2007-01-26. Кошкина, Елена. "Уют семейного гнезда." *Кемерово*. N 4.

2007-01-26. "ТОС—самая близкая власть." *Кемерово*. N 4.

2007-02-02. "В районах города." *Кемерово*. N 6.

2007-02-09. Корогод, Ирина. "Как появляются народные библиотеки." *Кемерово*. N 6.

2007-02-16. "За совет плату не берут." *Кемерово*. N 7.

2007-02-16. Пресс-служба Горсовета народных депутатов. "'Молодая гвардия' укрепляет тылы." *Кемерово*. N 7.

2007-03-30. "В районах города." *Кемерово*. N 13.

2007-04-06. "Постановление Администрации города N 36 от 02.04.2007 г. 'О Положении о смотре-конкурсе социальных проектов центров по работе с населением.'" *Кемерово*. N 14.

2007-04-13. "В районах города." *Кемерово*. N 15.

2007-04-20. "Поделись с другим . . ." *Кемерово*. N 16.

2007-04-20. "Слово и дело депутата." *Кемерово*. N 16.

2007-05-11. Ковшова, Галина. "'Здоровье' для всех." *Кемерово*. N 19.

2007-05-11. Любимов, А. Г. "Концепция развития города Кемерово до 2021 года." *Кемерово*. N 19.

2007-05-11. "Поздравление ветеранам." *Кемерово*. N 19.

2007-05-25. "Победила дружба." *Кемерово*. N 21.

2007-05-25. Шилова, Мария. "С обновой!" *Кемерово*. N 21.

2007-05-25. Шилова, Наталья. "Праздник всех объединил." *Кемерово*. N 21.

2007-06-08. "Вопрос участковому." *Кемерово*. N 23.

2007-06-08. "Заботы общие." *Кемерово*. N 23.

2007-06-08. Зинчук, Валентина. "Что знаете о льготах?" *Кемерово*. N 23.

2007-06-08. "Из века в век." *Кемерово*. N 23.

2007-06-08. "Коротко." *Кемерово*. N 23.

2007-06-08. Костина, Галина. "Максимыч." *Кемерово*. N 23.

2007-06-08. Нораева, Надежда. "На примерах учимся." *Кемерово*. N 23.

2007-06-08. "Трудовые династии." *Кемерово*. N 23.

2007-06-15. "Заявка на проект." *Кемерово*. N 24.

2007-06-19. "Даже в городе скучать им не придется!" *Комсомольская правда–Кемерово*. N 86.

2007-07-06. Брежнева, Нина. "На добровольных началах." *Кемерово*. N 27.

2007-07-06. "Дело общее." *Кемерово*. N 27.

2007-07-06. "И работа, и отдых." *Кемерово*. N 27.

2007-07-06. "Игрушки наших мам." *Кемерово*. N 27.

2007-07-06. Каретина, Маргарита. "Тянутся к небу сирени." *Кемерово*. N 27.

2007-07-06. "Когда смеются дети." *Кемерово*. N 27.

2007-07-06. "Коротко." *Кемерово*. N 27.

2007-07-06. "Красиво и уютно." *Кемерово*. N 27.

2007-07-20. Волков, Андрей. "Коротко." *Кемерово*. N 29.

2007-07-20. "Есть дело для всех." *Кемерово*. N 29.
2007-07-20. Зайцева, Ирина Константиновна. "От чистого сердца." *Кемерово*. N 29.
2007-07-20. Каретина, Маргарита. "Всегда помогут." *Кемерово*. N 29.
2007-07-20. "Коротко." *Кемерово*. N 29.
2007-07-20. "Повеселились от души." *Кемерово*. N 29.
2007-07-20. "Правила знаем." *Кемерово*. N 29.
2007-07-20. "Работа для людей." *Кемерово*. N 29.
2007-07-27. "Летние путешествия." *Кемерово*. N 30.
2007-07-27. Тотыш, Наталья. "Как одна семья." *Кемерово*. N 30.
2007-08-10. "Выбирают власть жильцы." *Кемерово*. N 32.
2007-08-10. "Добрые дела." *Кемерово*. N 32.
2007-08-10. Иноземцева, Елена. "С соседями в мире." *Кемерово*. N 32.
2007-08-10. "Коротко." *Кемерово*. N 32.
2007-08-10. "Коротко." *Кемерово*. N 32.
2007-08-24. Зонова, Любовь. "Есть что вспомнить." *Кемерово*. N 34.
2007-08-24. Каретина, Маргарита. "Счастливое число—13." *Кемерово*. N 34.
2007-08-24. Корогод, Ирина. "Как у хорошей хозяйки." *Кемерово*. N 34.
2007-08-24. "Коротко." *Кемерово*. N 34.
2007-08-24. "Матч дружбы." *Кемерово*. N 34.
2007-08-24. "Музей семейных ценностей." *Кемерово*. N 34.
2007-08-24. Сабельников, Максим, Андрей Работин, Евгений Величко et al. "Благодарим друзей." *Кемерово*. N 34.
2007-08-24. Ткаченко, Ольга. "Красота, которая спасет." *Кемерово*. N 34.
2007-08-24. "Юбилею посвящается." *Кемерово*. N 34.
2007-09-07. "Коротко." *Кемерово*. N 36.
2007-09-14. "…и много радости." *Кемерово*. N 37.
2007-09-21. "Улыбнись!" *Кемерово*. N 38.
2007-10-12. "Надежные люди." *Кемерово*. N 41.
2007-10-12. "Осень в нашем бору." *Кемерово*. N 41.
2007-10-12. "Скажите учителю спасибо." *Кемерово*. N 41.
2007-10-26. "Коротко." *Кемерово*. N 43.
2007-10-26. "Первый паспорт." *Кемерово*. N 43.
2007-10-26. Рассказова, Ирина. "Бой политического значения." *Кемерово*. N 43.
2007-11-02. Пресс-служба Горсовета народных депутатов. "Сход спрашивает—депутат отвечает." *Кемерово*. N 44.
2007-11-16. Пресс-служба Горсовета народных депутатов. "На прием к депутату." *Кемерово*. N 46.
2007-11-22. Красносельская, Татьяна. "Пробудить инициативу." *Кузбасс*. N 217.
2007-12-07. Пресс-служба Горсовета народных депутатов. "Материнское тепло." *Кемерово*. N 49.
2007-12-21. Кемерова, Валентина Алексеевна. "Скучать не давали." *Кемерово*. N 51.
2008-01-08. "Проблемы на контроле." *Кемерово*. N 6.
2008-01-11. "Вместе веселей." *Кемерово*. N 2.
2008-01-11. "Слово и дело депутата: признание по делам." *Кемерово*. N 2.
2008-01-25. Лисицина, Ирина. "30-летию района—30 добрых дел." *Кемерово*. N 4.
2008-02-08. Акуленко, Татьяна. "Счастье общения." *Кемерово*. N 6.
2008-02-08. "Коротко." *Кемерово*. N 6.
2008-02-08. Некрасова, Наталья. "Песня о районе." *Кемерово*. N 6.

2008-02-08. "Постановление Администрации города N 11 от 01.02.2008 г. 'О проведении смотра-конкурса социальных проектов центров по работе с населением'." *Кемерово*. N 6.
2008-02-08. "Постановление Администрации города N 18 от 05.02.2008 г. 'О проведении смотра-конкурса 'Центр по работе с населением.' " *Кемерово*. N 6.
2008-02-08. "Ровесники области." *Кемерово*. N 6.
2008-02-08. Седых, Вера Петровна. "Чтобы старость была в радость." *Кемерово*. N 6.
2008-02-08. Сыватко, Татьяна. "Уроки истории." *Кемерово*. N 6.
2008-02-15. "Слово и дело депутата: Если обещала—сделает." *Кемерово*. N 7.
2008-02-22. "Умом и смекалкой сильны." *Кемерово*. N 8.
2008-04-04. Ильина, Надежда. "Субботник наперегонки." *Кемерово*. N 14.
2008-04-04. "Коротко." *Кемерово*. N 14.
2008-04-04. "Слово активистов." *Кемерово*. N 14.
2008-04-18. "В комитетах горсовета." *Кемерово*. N 16.
2008-04-18. "Коротко." *Кемерово*. N 16.
2008-04-18. "Они работают на Кузбасс." *Кузбасс*. N 69.
2008-05-08. "Центр микрорайона." *Кемерово*. N 19.
2008-06-11. "Для бабушек, внуков и философов." *Кемерово*. N 24.
2008-06-11. Полякова, Ксения. "Поздравляем с юбилеем." *Кемерово*. N 24.
2008-06-11. "С любовью к Кемерово." *Кемерово*. N 24.
2008-07-04. "Спасибо за праздник!" *Кемерово*. N 27.
2008-07-04. Лисицина, Ирина. "На контроле." *Кемерово*. N 27.
2008-07-11. Акуленко, Татьяна. "Памятная экскурсия." *Кемерово*. N 28.
2008-07-11. Ключарева, Раиса. "Работу себе всегда находила." *Кемерово*. N 28.
2008-07-11. Подольская, Тамара. "Чей палисадник лучше." *Кемерово*. N 28.
2008-07-18. "Среди лучших." *Кемерово*. N 29.
2008-09-12. "История—это интересно." *Кемерово*. N 37.
2008-10-24. Воробьева, Жанна. "Проекты для жизни." *Кемерово*. N 43.
2008-10-24. Макарова, Т. "Такой у нас депутат." *Кемерово*. N 43.
2008-11-28. "В гости—с подарком." *Кемерово*. N 48.
2008-11-28. Пресс-служба городского Совета народных депутатов. "Работа в комитетах." *Кемерово*. N 48.
2008-12-12. "А проблемы общие." *Кемерово*. N 50.
2008-12-12. Ильина, Надежда. "Дойти до каждого." *Кемерово*. N 50.
2008-12-12. Сыроватко, Татьяна. "Начало начал." *Кемерово*. N 50.
2008-12-12. Шилова, Мария. "Хорошее настроение делаем сами." *Кемерово*. N 50.
2009-01-23. "Кто, если не мы?" *Кемерово*. N 4.
2009-01-23. "Телефоны и адреса центров по работе с населением." *Кемерово*. N 4.
2009-01-23. Фефелова, Елена. "Жизнь в творчестве." *Кемерово*. N 4.
2009-01-30. Фефелова, Елена. "Здесь всегда интересно." *Кемерово*. N 5.
2009-01-30. "Хорошей, родной район!" *Кемерово*. N 5.
2009-02-27. Ильина, Надежда. "С любой проблемой." *Кемерово*. N 9.
2009-05-15. Кикиой, Татьяна. "Решаем вместе." *Кемерово*. N 20.
2009-05-15. Козлова, Наталья. "Лучший, потому что необычный . . ." *Кемерово*. N 20.
2009-05-29. Пресс-служба Администрации города. "Всегда рядом." *Кемерово*. N 22.
2009-06-19. "Платить по счетам." *Кемерово*. N 25.
2009-06-26. Фефелова, Елена. "Город делится опытом." *Кемерово*. N 26.

2009-07-03. Фефелова, Елена. "Готовимся к переписи." *Кемерово*. N 27.
2009-07-31. Козлова, Наталья. "Люди с блеском в глазах." *Кемерово*. N 31.
2009-09-04. Летов, Андрей. "Важный разговор." *Кемерово*. N 36.
2009-10-02. Спиридова, Светлана. "Оказаться рядом." *Кемерово*. N 40.
2009-10-09. Летов, Андрей. "На свежем воздухе." *Кемерово*. N 41.
2009-10-16. Ткаченко, Ольга. "Всегда вместе." *Кемерово*. N 42.
2009-11-03. "Здесь нескучно и взрослым, и детям." *Комсомольская правда–Кемерово*. N 165.
2010-01-22. "Год юбилея." *Кемерово*. N 4.
2010-01-29. Фефелова, Елена. "В гости на блины." *Кемерово*. N 5.
2010-02-05. Панфилова, Татьяна. "Подготовка к юбилею объединила всех." *Кемерово*. N 6.
2010-02-19. "Результат совместных действий." *Кемерово*. N 8.
2010-04-16. "За консультацией к юристу." *Кемерово*. N 16.
2010-05-14. "Это—Родина моя." *Кемерово*. N 20.
2010-06-11. "Слово и дело депутата." *Кемерово*. N 24.
2010-06-18. "Действовать логично." *Кемерово*. N 25.
2010-09-10. Ершова, Светлана. "Душа Искитимки." *Кузбасс*. N 167.
2010-09-17. Шмайкова, Анна. "С юбилеем, Анна Петровна!" *Кемерово*. N 38.
2010-10-29. Глушакова, Ксения. "Добрый пример." *Кемерово*. N 44.
2010-10-29. "На все вопросы." *Кемерово*. N 44.
2010-11-19. Гусельникова, Надежда Дмитриевна. "У нас в 'Меридиане.'" *Кемерово*. N 47.
2010-12-17. "К кемеровчанам—с отчетом." *Кемерово*. N 51.
2010-12-17. "Ни дня без дела." *Кемерово*. N 51.
2010-12-24. "Снежные волонтеры." *Кемерово*. N 52.
2011-01-28. Жидкова, З. В. "От жителей Южного." *Кемерово*. N 4.
2011-02-11. "Депутат ведет прием." *Кемерово*. N 6.
2011-02-22. "Фестиваль здоровья и радости." *Комсомольская правда—Кемерово*. N 25.
2011-05-27. "Уютный дворик—ветеранам." *Кемерово*. N 21.
2011-07-16. "Теперь не одиноки." *Кузбасс*. N 128.
2011-08-26. "График приема граждан общественной приемной губернатора в центрах по работе с населением района." *Кемерово*. N 34.
2011-08-31. "Помощь в рюкзачке." *Кузбасс*. N 160.
2011-11-30. "Доброе дело—своими руками." *Комсомольская правда—Кемерово*. N 179.
2011-12-20. "Праздник сделай сам." *Кузбасс*. N 237.
2012-02-17. "'Родничок' вдохновения и бодрости." *Кузбасс*. N 29.
2012-03-15. "Выход с лопатами и метлами." *Кузбасс*. N 43.
2012-05-31. Доронина, Мария. "'Скорая помощь' для подростков." *Библиотека*. N 5.
2012-06-01. "За городом и во дворе." *Кемерово*. N 22.
2012-07-06. Прокопьева, Елена. "В тесном контакте." *Кемерово*. N 27.
2012-08-01. "Вместе мы полезней!" *Кузбасс*. N 135.
2012-12-21. Шмидт, Екатерина. "Общественники подвели итоги." *Кемерово*. N 51.
2013-03-22. Чиненова, Наталья, and Татьяна Щавина. "К людям с открытой душой." *Кемерово*. N 11.

2013-07-02. Кошкина, Е. "Участковым нужна опора." *Ветеран*. N 25.

Администрация г. Кемерово, Управление делами. *Итоги городского конкурса "Чистый, уютный город" и муниципального грантового конкурса социально-значимых проектов окружных комитетов ТОС*. Кемерово, 2013.

Информация о комитетах территориального общественного самоуправления г. Кемерово. http://www.kemerovo.ru/?page=273. Accessed April 22, 2016.

Конкурсы по работе с населением. http://www.kemerovo.ru/konkurs/rabota_s_naseleniem_.html. Accessed April 22, 2016.

Об итогах деятельности центров по работе с населением в 2013 г. (printed brochure at a community center; copied during fieldwork).

Работа с населением. http://www.kemerovo.ru/?page=357. Accessed April 22, 2016.

Итоги работы с населением за 2015 г. http://www.kemerovo.ru/administration/rabota_s_naseleniem_.html. Accessed April 22, 2016.

Итоги работы с населением за 2016 г. http://www.kemerovo.ru/administration/rabota_s_naseleniem_.html. Accessed March 29, 2017.

Администрация города Кемерово. "Постановление от 16 сентября 2016 года N 2382 'Об утверждении муниципальной программы 'Развитие общественных инициатив в городе Кемерово' на 2017-2019 годы." http://docs.cntd.ru/document/441678836. Accessed March 29, 2017.

APPENDIX 5

Newspaper Publications Related to Veterans' (Pensioners') Organizations and Their Role in Politics

This list was compiled from two sources: (1) the local history catalog in the Kemerovo regional library and (2) searches of articles in *Veteran* (*Ветеран*) newspaper in the Integrum database. Most entries are articles in two newspapers published by veterans' (pensioners') organizations: the nationwide *Veteran* and the regional *Zemliaki* (*Земляки*). Texts from *Veteran* have been downloaded from Integrum; texts from *Zemliaki* have been photographed in Kemerovo regional library, along with a few articles from other sources unavailable in digitalized databases. Sources are sorted by topic and date.[1] All texts are available from the author on request.

Publications on Veterans' (Pensioners') organizations across Russia, Including Kemerovo Region

Political Positions

Against the Current President (Yeltsin, Putin, or Medvedev), His Government, the United Russia Party, and Current Policies

1998-08-25. Дорофеев, В. "Виновен в наших бедах." *Ветеран*. N 32.
2003-04-22. "'Забот' о пожилых много, достойной жизни нет." *Ветеран*. N 16.
2004-07-15. "Льгот лишенье—это преступление!" *Ветеран*. N 26.
2005-04-05. "Гримасы власти." *Ветеран*. N 13.
2006-10-03. "Истину определяет жизнь." *Ветеран*. N 37.
2006-03-14. "В каждой строке—тревога и боль." *Ветеран*. N 11.
2006-09-05. "Не отдавайте душу Бушу." *Ветеран*. N 33.
2006-10-31. "Народ о жизни трудной пишет, но президент его не слышит!" *Ветеран*. N 41.
2007-02-06. "Нам с 'Единой Россией' не по пути." *Ветеран*. N 5.
2007-06-05. "Народ о жизни трудной пишет, но президент его не слышит." *Ветеран*. N 21.
2008-10-21. "Все решают деньги." *Ветеран*. N 40.
2009-05-12. "Народ о жизни трудовой пишет, надеясь, власть его услышит!" *Ветеран*. N 18.
2010-08-31. "Чинуши." *Ветеран*. N 33.

---

[1] A few sources are listed several times under different topics.

2011-08-23. "Предвыборная лихорадка." *Ветеран.* N 31.
2011-10-25. "Административный ресурс." *Ветеран.* N 40.
2012-01-24. "Вокруг президентской кампании." *Ветеран.* N 4.
2012-12-04. "Тревога нарастает." *Ветеран.* N 46.
2013-10-22. "Без кодекса морали." *Ветеран.* N 40.

In Support of the Communist Party of the Russian Federation or Other Left Political Forces

2003-10-21. "Основа успеха—в первичных организациях!" *Ветеран.* N 40.
2003-11-18. "Подумаем о детях и внуках." *Ветеран.* N 44.
2003-11-25. "Предвыборному пиару—отпор." *Ветеран.* N 45.
2004-01-01. Печенин, И. И. "Мы вас поддержим!" *Ветеран.* N 1.
2007-09-11. "За кого отдадим свои голоса?" *Ветеран.* N 34.

In Support of Putin, Medvedev, the United Russia Party, or the People's National Front

2007-03-06. "Не ошибиться бы!" *Ветеран.* N 9.
2010-12-14. "Ценить прошлое, думать о будущем!" *Ветеран.* N 47.

Organizational Development, Activities, and Involvement in Politics

Embeddedness of Veterans' (Pensioners') Organizations, Their Ability to Reach a Large Number of People

2003-10-21. "Основа успеха—в первичных организациях!" *Ветеран.* N 40.
2009-04-21. "Второе дыхание." *Ветеран.* N 16.
2013-05-28. "Инициатива дает плоды." *Ветеран.* N 20.

Connections of Veterans' (Pensioners') Organizations and the State Apparatus

2006-10-24. "В одной упряжке." *Ветеран.* N 40.
2010-09-21. "Авторитет возрос—ответственность повысилась." *Ветеран.* N 35.

Political Involvement of Veterans (Pensioners) as Agitators, Election Observers, Electoral Commission Members, or Candidates for Elected Offices (Nationwide, Including in Kemerovo Region)

2003-02-07. Ермакова, Нелли. "Когда дело ладится." *Земляки.* N 6 (639).
2003-03-04. "Конкретный вклад." *Ветеран.* N 9.
2003-09-23. "Перед новым испытанием." *Ветеран.* N 36.
2003-11-11. "Народный депутат." *Ветеран.* N 43.
2004-02-12. "Голоса—достойным." *Ветеран.* N 06.
2007-03-30. Будяковская, И. "Были 'ничейные', стали—наши!" *Земляки.* N 13.

2007-04-10. "Пустые посулы." *Ветеран*. N 14.
2007-04-24. "Письма президенту В. В. Путину." *Ветеран*. N 16.
2007-09-18. "Больше инициативы!" *Ветеран*. N 35.
2007-10-02. "Агитатор по зову сердца." *Ветеран*. N 37.
2007-10-30. "Неразрывная связь." *Ветеран*. N 41.
2008-06-17. "Делам ветеранским—богатства души." *Ветеран*. N 23.
2008-10-10. Старцев, П. А. "Ступенька в завтра." *Земляки*. N 41.
2008-12-26. Милютина, Наталья, and Нина Павловна Неворотова. "Нам многое по плечу…" *Земляки*. N 52.
2010-08-10. "Лечение по-сердюковски." *Ветеран*. N 30.
2011-04-15. "Характер лидера." *Ветеран*. N 15.
2011-06-21. "Клуб ветеранов-избирателей." *Ветеран*. N 23.
2011-11-29. "Верить не обещаниям, а делам." *Ветеран*. N 45.
2012-02-28. "'Дети войны', объединяйтесь!" *Ветеран*. N 8.
2012-04-24. "Для дела, для души." *Ветеран*. N 16.
2013-04-02. "Ветеранские гостиные." *Ветеран*. N 13.
2013-09-03. "Больше внимания выборам." *Ветеран*. N 33.
2014-01-28. "Не стареем сердцами…" *Ветеран*. N 4.
2014-02-25. "Памятный юбилей." *Ветеран*. N 8.
2014-05-27. "Николай Григорьевич Игнатов." *Ветеран*. N 20.

Participation of Veterans' Councils in Patriotic Education (Nationwide, Including the Kemerovo Region)

2006-01-10. "Уроки города." *Ветеран*. N 2.
2006-12-05. "Сибиряки чтят героев." *Ветеран*. N 46.
2007-10-02. "Агитатор по зову сердца." *Ветеран*. N 37.
2011-10-04. "Память годы не остудит." *Ветеран*. N 37.
2013-08-06. "Становление патриотов." *Ветеран*. N 29.

Other Bottom-Level Activities of Veterans' (Pensioners') Organizations

2003-10-21. "Основа успеха—в первичных организациях!" *Ветеран*. N 40.
2009-04-21. "Второе дыхание." *Ветеран*. N 16.
2010-09-21. "Авторитет возрос—ответственность повысилась." *Ветеран*. N 35.
2012-01-10. "На пленуме—о первичках." *Ветеран*. N 2.
2013-04-16. "Выступление председателя Всероссийской общественной организации ветеранов (пенсионеров) войны, труда, вооруженных сил и правоохранительных органов Д. И. Карабанова." *Ветеран*. N 15.
2014-09-16. "Как живет первичка?" *Ветеран*. N 35.

Trust and Sympathy to the Newspaper *Veteran*

2003-01-14. "15 строк к 15-летию." *Ветеран*. N 2.
2004-07-08. "Громче звучи, 'Ветеран'!" *Ветеран*. N 25.
2013-04-16. "Газету 'Ветеран'—в каждую первичку!" *Ветеран*. N 15.
2013-06-11. "Слово читателей газеты." *Ветеран*. N 22.

Opposition to the Creation of Alternative Veterans' (Pensioners') Organizations

2004-08-26. "Ответ раскольникам." *Ветеран*. N 32.
2004-11-04. "Раскол, диктуемый сверху." *Ветеран*. N 41.

Publications on Veterans' (Pensioners') Organizations Specifically in the Kemerovo Region

Political Positions

In Support of Tuleyev, His Policies, and His Political Alliances; Tuleyev's Use of Veterans' Newspaper to Voice His Position

1999-11-29. Старожилов, Антон. "Кузбасс прильнул к 'Медведю.'" *Эксперт*. N 45(208).
2000-05-25. Тулеев, А. Г. "Инфарктное это дело." *Земляки*. N 22. С. 2.
2000-10-20. Лавренков, Игорь. "Кемеровчане хотят Тулеева переизбрать на полгода раньше." *Коммерсантъ*. N 197.
2003-04-11. Тулеев, Аман Гумирович. "Такую систему социальной защиты надо беречь!" *Земляки*. N 18.
2003-04-18. "Открытое письмо жителей Центрального района жителям Ленинского района." *Земляки*. N 20.
2003-04-18. Тулеев, А. Г. "'20 апреля—все на выборы!' Обращение А. Г. Тулеева к избирателям." *Земляки*. N 20.
2003-11-28. Авалиани, Т. Г. "Наглость правит бал." *Патриот*. N 49.
2005-04-08. Гришин, Валентин. "Звоните и приходите: поможем." *Земляки*. N 15.
2005-08-19. Останина, Нина. "Пришло время выбора." *Земляки*. N 34 (782).
2006-05-05. Гришин, В. Г. "Ручеек могучей реки." *Земляки*. N 18.
2007-07-06. Гришин, Валентин, and Татьяна Владимирова. "Рука помощи." *Земляки*. N 27.
2007-10-26. Областной совет ветеранов. "Не ошибемся на этот раз." *Земляки*. N 43 (895).
2007-11-30. Тулеев, Аман Гумирович, and Светлана Сергеева. "Определять курс будем вместе." *Земляки*. N 48. С. 5, 6.
2007-12-07. "Рассудит суд." *Земляки*. N 49 (901).
2008-07-18. Колоколова, Татьяна. "Пятилетка доверия." *Земляки*. N 29.
2008-07-25. Чурпита, В. М. "Бывших шахтеров не бывает." *Земляки*. N 30.
2008-09-12. Чех, Людмила. "Мы забыть того не вправе…" *Земляки*. N 37.
2012-11-06. "Перемены в Кузбассе." *Ветеран*. N 42.
2012-07-24. "Кузбасским пенсионерам завидуют." *Ветеран*. N 28.

In Support of the Communists, Including Nina Ostanina

2002-06-21. Останина, Нина. "Закон в поддержку экстремизма власти." *Земляки*. N 25.
2005-09-09. Ермакова, Нелли. "Мы за референдум!" *Земляки*. N 37.

2004-04-09. Останина, Нина. "Куда не ступит нога демонстранта." *Земляки*. N 15.
2006-01-13. Останина, Нина. "Лицом к каждому." *Земляки*. N 2.
2006-12-01. Останина, Нина. "Думские бутафории: продолжение следует." *Земляки*. N 48.
2007-05-18. Останина, Нина. "Год семьи, как мало в этом слове…" *Земляки*. N 20.

Critique of Tuleyev and Politics and Policies in the Kemerovo Region

2000-12-15. Кузнецов, Н. С. "Место назначения—коту под хвост." *Наша газета*. N 130.
2005-04-05. "Гримасы власти." *Ветеран*. N 13.
2007-11-09. Квятковская, Татьяна. "Пренебрежение совестью." *Земляки*. N 45 (897).
2008-10-21. "Все решают деньги." *Ветеран*. N 40.
2011-08-23. "Предвыборная лихорадка." *Ветеран*. N 31.
2011-12-20. "На 'паровозной' тяге." *Ветеран*. N 48.
2012-01-24. "Вокруг президентской кампании." *Ветеран*. N 4.
2012-12-04. "Тревога нарастает." *Ветеран*. N 46.
2013-10-01. "Верните поликлинику и кафе…" *Ветеран*. N 37.
2013-07-02. "Власть дряхлее стариков." *Ветеран*. N 25.
2013-03-26. "По страницам писем." *Ветеран*. N 12.

Concerns about Miners' Pensions

2006-04-28. Ермакова, Нелли. "Нас слышат, но не хотят понимать." *Земляки*. N 17.
2007-01-26. Попок, Василий. "Про шахтерские пенсии и достойную жизнь." *Земляки*. N 4.
2007-02-16. Засадная, Нина. "У печки я и грусть моя." *Земляки*. N 7.

Discredit of Тулеев's Political Opponents

2002-05-04. Кузьмин, Пётр. "Ненависть олигарха." *Земляки*. N 18.
2002-06-07. Тулеев, Аман Гумирович, and Александр Иванов. "КПРФ: всем остыть и крепко подумать." *Земляки*. N 23.
2003-11-28. Владимирова, И. "Стиральный порошок против изнасилования, или еще одна тайна семьи Приставки." *Земляки*. N 52.
2004-12-24. Попок, Василий Борисович. "Палаточный лагерь и его председатель." *Земляки*. N 52.
2006-03-10. Попок, Василий. "Палату проверили и нашли, что там бардак." *Земляки*. N 10.
2007-11-16. Бугаев, Пётр. "О чем не пишут в 'Нашем Кузбассе.'" *Земляки*. N 46 (898).
2007-11-16. "Перешагнув порог допустимого. Открытое письмо первому секретарю обкома КПРФ Н. Останиной." *Земляки*. N 46 (898).
2008-09-19. Привалов, К. А. "Кто под красным знаменем?" *Земляки*. N 38.
2010-10-15. Попок, Василий. "Голосуй правильно, а не то—проиграешь!" *Земляки*. № 42.

Organizational Development, Activities, and Involvement in Politics

General Articles on History and Organizational Development

2000-08-24. Коновалова, Н. "Ветеранскому движению в Новокузнецке—25 лет." *Земляки*. N 35.

2003-02-21. Ермакова, Нелли. "Мы за настоящих патриотов!" *Земляки*. N 8 (641).

2003-10-21. "Сообщение." *Ветеран*. N 40.

2004-03-12. Сорокин, Александр. "'Коммунисты не станут угождать властям…'" *Край*. N 11.

2004-04-30. Ильященко, М. "Дел через край." *Земляки*. N 18.

2005-10-11. "Подход—комплексный." *Ветеран*. N 38.

2005-10-14. "В поле зрения—800 тысяч судеб." *Земляки*. N 42.

2006-08-17. "В Кемеровской области появилось региональное отделение 'Российской партии пенсионеров.'" *Кузнецкий край*. N 89.

2006-10-13. Ермакова, Нелли. "Есть такая партия!" *Земляки*. N 41.

2006-11-03. Ермакова, Нелли. "Преграды на пути первопроходцев." *Земляки*. N 44.

2006-12-29. Неворотова, Нина Павловна, and Нелли Ермакова. "Милосердие нацелено в завтра." *Земляки*. N 52.

2007-01-12. Ермакова, Нелли. "О чем скажут 'незабудки.'" *Земляки*. N 2.

2007-01-26. Майоров. "Вчера—ничьи, сегодня—наши." *Земляки*. N 4.

2007-03-16. Гончарова. "Значит—мы не одни!" *Земляки*. N 11.

2007-05-18. Тихомирова, В. П. "Огни альма-матер." *Земляки*. N 20.

2007-06-01. Ивачев, Антон. "Банкротство не коснулось 'седин.'" *Земляки*. N 22.

2008-03-07. Старцев, П. А. "В шахтерском крае и улицы шахтерские." *Земляки*. N 10.

2008-03-28. Милютина, Наталья. "Ни дня без строчки." *Земляки*. N 13.

2008-05-23. Милютина, Наталья. "Со временем на 'ты.'" *Земляки*. N 21.

2008-07-25. Чурпита, В. М. "Бывших шахтеров не бывает." *Земляки*. N 30.

2008-10-10. Старцев, П. А. "Ступенька в завтра." *Земляки*. N 41.

2008-10-17. Милютина, Наталья. "Языком экспонатов о жизни и датах." *Земляки*. N 42.

2008-11-14. Коновалова, Н. С. "День расписан по минутам." *Земляки*. N 46.

2010-11-30. "Точки приложения усилий." *Ветеран*. N 45.

2014-07-08. "Лидер ветеранов Кузбасса." *Ветеран*. N 26.

Connections of Veterans' (Pensioners') Organizations and the State Apparatus

2005-01-16. "Кузбассовцам льготы сохранены." *С тобой*. N 3.

2006-10-13. Федорова, Галина Федоровна, and Нелли Ермакова. "Инициативы, продиктованные жизнью." *Земляки*. N 41.

2008-05-23. Милютина, Наталья. "Со временем на 'ты.'" *Земляки*. N 21.

2008-09-19. Чурпита, В. М. "Не привыкли сдаваться трудностям." *Земляки*. N 38.

2008-10-10. Старцев, П. А. "Ступенька в завтра." *Земляки*. N 41.

2011-10-25. "Шахтер—звание высокое." *Ветеран*. N 40.

2011-11-15. "Советы непосторонних." *Ветеран*. N 43.

2013-01-22. "Заботу труженикам села." *Ветеран*. N 3.

Activities of Veterans' Councils in Kemerovo Region beyond Patriotic Education

2003-02-07. Ермакова, Нелли. "Когда дело ладится." *Земляки*. N 6 (639).
2003-09-26. Неворотова, Нина Павловна. "И с бедой и с радостью идут к нам…" *Земляки*. N 43.
2005-07-29. Ермакова, Нелли. "Когда служишь людям…" *Земляки*. N 31.
2005-08-12. Бальзанова, В. З. "Хороших дел немало." *Земляки*. N 33.
2005-08-19. Михайлов, В. Д. "Энергия опыта." *Земляки*. N 34.
2005-09-23. Писарева, Н. "Разве может быть оценка выше?" *Земляки*. N 39.
2005-10-11. "Подход—комплексный." *Ветеран*. N 38.
2006-06-06. "И книга, и музей." *Ветеран*. N 21.
2006-06-09. Ермакова, Нелли. "Вместе в добрый путь!" *Земляки*. N 23.
2007-03-27. "Центр работы—первички." *Ветеран*. N 12.
2007-12-04. "Третий возраст." *Ветеран*. N 46.
2007-12-04. "Подворье людей кормит." *Ветеран*. N 46.
2007-12-04. "Город семьей славен." *Ветеран*. N 46.
2007-06-15. Белоусова, Татьяна. "Вписаны в Золотую летопись города." *Земляки*. N 24.
2007-08-24. Пресс-центр Кемеровского областного совета ветеранов войны и труда. "Дед напутствует внука, провожая в забой." *Земляки*. N 34.
2007-11-09. Микельсон, Татьяна. "Знать каждого—по паспорту." *Земляки*. N 45 (897).
2007-12-14. Милютина, Наталья. "Предназначение защищать." *Земляки*. N 50.
2008-07-01. "Две презентации." *Ветеран*. N 25.
2008-04-04. Милютина, Наталья. "Помощь фонда 'Шахтерская память'." *Земляки*. N 14.
2008-05-23. Милютина, Наталья. "Со временем на 'ты'." *Земляки*. N 21.
2008-09-19. Чурпита, В. М. "Не привыкли сдаваться трудностям." *Земляки*. N 38.
2008-10-03. Сваровский, И. В. "Заслужили всей жизнью." *Земляки*. N 40.
2008-10-17. Милютина, Наталья. "Языком экспонатов о жизни и датах." *Земляки*. N 42.
2008-10-28. "Сибиряки в боях не подвели." *Ветеран*. N 41.
2008-11-14. Коновалова, Н. С. "День расписан по минутам." *Земляки*. N 46.
2009-10-06. "Главное внимание первичкам." *Ветеран*. N 37.
2010-01-26. "Голос старшего поколения." *Ветеран*. N 4.
2012-09-25. "Для творчества нет границ." *Ветеран*. N 36.
2012-12-02. Потапова, Юлия. "Придут и помогут." *Российская газета—неделя*. N 273 (5352).
2013-05-21. "Юбилей делами красен." *Ветеран*. N 19.
2013-10-15. "Нина Павловна Неворотова." *Ветеран*. N 39.
2014-02-04. "Город—семья дружная." *Ветеран*. N 5.

Information about Benefits and Welfare Programs for Pensioners and Veterans in the Kemerovo Region

2001-09-27. Неворотова, Нина. "Права и интересы пожилых людей под защиту Федерального закона 'О ветеранах'." *Земляки*. N 40.
2002-10-01. Муравьева, Галина. "Ты этого достоин, ветеран!" *Кузнецкий край*. N 109.

2003-04-08. "В Кузбассе расширяется система социальной защиты ветеранов." *Земляки*. N 17.

2004-11-24. Чистякова, Олеся. "Монетизация социального пакета льгот." *С тобой*. N 93.

2005-01-14. "Колеса диктуют вагонные…" *Земляки*. N 3.

2005-02-25. Ермакова, Нелли. "Помогите сегодня. Завтра будет поздно!" *Земляки*. N 9.

2005-05-11. Филиппов, Сергей. "Ветеранов остеклят и телефонизируют." *Московский комсомолец в Кузбассе*. N 19.

2006-08-25. Величко, Вячеслав. "Связисты расставляют приоритеты." *Кузбасс*. N 157.

2007-05-06. Федорова, Ф. "Парад и праздничный салют для ветеранов." *С тобой*. N 35.

2007-09-12. Ивачев, Константин. "Жизнь продолжается." *С тобой*. N 72.

2007-09-30. Туманова, Марина. "Качество жизни пожилых людей … улучшают." *С тобой*. N 77.

2007-10-07. Туманова, Марина. "Ветеран—всегда у нас в почете…" *С тобой*. N 79.

2007-12-03. Гостев, Константин. "В Кузбассе поддержали ветеранов." *Независимая газета*. N 259 (4219).

2008-04-16. "Поддержка ветеранов—священный долг." *С тобой*. N 30.

2008-04-17. Кемеровская область. Администрация. Пресс-служба. "Льготы для ветеранов." *Кузнецкий край*. N 16.

2008-11-06. Панарина. "Наедине со старостью." *Кузбасс*. N 203.

2008-10-12. "Забота о ветеранах—наш священный долг." *С тобой*. N 81.

2008-12-13. Щербакова, Елена. "О пенсиях и соцподдержке ветеранов." *Кузбасс*. N 230.

2010-02-18. Потапова, Юлия. "Санаторий на дому." *Российская газета—неделя*. N 35 (5114).

2012-02-05. Ивачев, К. "Доплаты пенсионерам." *С тобой*. N 9.

2012-04-11. "День Победы." *С тобой*. N 28.

2012-09-29. "Забота, льготы и поддержка." *С тобой*. N 77.

Business Donations to Veterans' (Pensioners') Organizations or Programs

2003-01-22. "Обновление 'Кузбассфармы.'" *Кузбасс*. N 11.

2005-09-30. Кирикова, Лидия Тимофеевна. "Теплая осень." *Земляки*. N 40.

2005-09-30. Ковылина, В. А. "Не изменяя традициям." *Земляки*. N 40.

2005-11-25. "Без бюджетных средств." *Кемерово*. N 48.

2006-05-05. Максимлюк, Константин. "Когда поддерживает родной завод." *Земляки*. N 18.

2006-09-29. Владимирова, Татьяна. "За дружеским столом с 'коксовым пирогом.'" *Земляки*. N 39.

2007-01-12. Ермакова, Нелли. "О чем скажут 'незабудки.'" *Земляки*. N 2.

2007-06-01. Ивачев, Антон. "Банкротство не коснулось 'седин.'" *Земляки*. N 22.

2007-08-24. Кладчихин. "Узел ответственности." *Земляки*. N 34.

2007-09-28. Шабанов, Валерий Алексеевич, and Татьяна Квятковская. "Партнерство ради милосердия." *Земляки*. N 39.

2007-09-28. Белоусова, Татьяна. "Ступени согласия." *Земляки*. N 39.

2008-07-25. Чурпита, В. М. "Бывших шахтеров не бывает." *Земляки*. N 30.

2008-09-26. Бабарыкина, С. В. "Ваше здоровье—наше богатство!" *Земляки*. N 39.

2008-10-03. "С домом, машиной и не без денег." *Земляки*. N 40.

APPENDIX 6

List of Interviews

Republic of Altai (November–December 2013)

Altai-01	Department head in the regional parliament
Altai-02	Policy specialist of the regional Ministry of Education
Altai-03	Policy specialist of the Budget Department in the regional government
Altai-04	Policy specialist of the Budget Department in the regional government
Altai-05	Faculty member in economics at a local university
Altai-06	Staff member of the Social Services Department at the regional Ministry of Labor and Human Development
Altai-07	Ethnographer who studied rural population in the region and a former faculty member in economics at the local university who traveled extensively across the region delivering workshops for local entrepreneurs
Altai-08	Three schoolteachers from different rural municipalities of the region
Altai-09	An oppositional deputy of the regional parliament, who simultaneously served as the editor of the local oppositional newspaper
Altai-10	Deputy of the regional parliament from the Communist Party of the Russian Federation
Altai-11	Former faculty member in economics at the local university who traveled extensively across the region delivering workshops for local entrepreneurs
Altai-12	Senior government official at the regional Ministry of Health Care
Altai-13	Lawyer-consultant, office of the regional human rights ombudsman
Altai-14	A leader of the regional Education Labor Union
Altai-15	A leader of the municipal Veterans' Council
Altai-16	A leader of the regional branch of the Pensioners' Union
Altai-17	Senior government official at the regional Ministry of Education

Kemerovo Region (February–March 2014)

Kem-01	Faculty member in political science at a local university
Kem-02	Staff member of the regional public library
Kem-03	Staff member of the regional public library
Kem-04	A leader of Orthodox scouts organization
Kem-06	A senior specialist at a community center

Kem-07	A leader of the regional Veterans' Council
Kem-08	Senior member of the Social Services Department in the Kemerovo eparchy of the Russian Orthodox church
Kem-09	Policy specialist at the regional Department of Education
Kem-10	A leader of the regional Association of People with Disabilities
Kem-11	Senior official at the Teacher Training Institute
Kem-12	Division head at the regional Department of Social Security
Kem-13	TOS member

Rostov Region (April 2014)

Ros-01	Faculty member in sociology at a local university
Ros-03	A leader of the Association of Municipalities
Ros-04	Senior official at the Youth Affairs Department in the city government of Rostov-on-Don
Ros-05	Senior government officials at the regional Cossacks Affairs Department
Ros-06	Department head at a local university
Ros-07	A leader at the Center for Children with Disabilities "Sodeistvie" ("Cooperation")
Ros-08	Senior government official at the regional Department of Civil Affairs (the department deals with civil society organizations)
Ros-10	Senior official at the Social Security Department in the city government of Rostov-on-Don
Ros-11	Policy specialist at the Committee for Ethnic and Religious Affairs in the city government of Rostov-on-Don
Ros-12	Faculty member at a local university
Ros-13	Faculty member at a local university
Ros-15	A leader of the regional Education Labor Union
Ros-16	Policy specialists at the Education Department in the city government of Rostov-on-Don
Ros-17	Deputy of the regional parliament from the Communist Party of the Russian Federation

Republic of Tatarstan (May 2014)

Kaz-02	Policy specialist at the regional Ministry of labor and social security
Kaz-03	A leader of the regional Volunteer Center
Kaz-04	Department head at the Ministry of Labor and Social Security
Kaz-05	Faculty member at a local university
Kaz-06	A leader of the Foundation "Vybor" ("Choice")

Kaz-07	Senior specialist at the municipal Center for Children and Youth, the city of Kazan'
Kaz-08	Two leaders of the regional Veterans' Council
Kaz-09	Provost of a small private university
Kaz-11	Provost of a large public university
Kaz-12	Faculty dean at a local university
Kaz-13	Policy specialist at a municipal Center for Social Services, the city of Kazan'
Kaz-14	Researcher at a center for cultural studies, a specialist in Islam
Kaz-16	A leader of the regional youth branch of the United Russia Party

References

Acemoglu, Daron, and James A. Robinson. "Weak, Despotic, or Inclusive? How State Type Emerges from State versus Civil Society Competition." *American Political Science Review* 117, no. 2 (May 2023): 407–20. https://doi.org/10.1017/S0003055422000740.

Albertus, Michael, Sofia Fenner, and Dan Slater. *Coercive Distribution*. Cambridge: Cambridge University Press, 2018.

Albertus, Michael, and Victor A. Menaldo. "Coercive Capacity and the Prospects for Democratization." *Comparative Politics* 44, no. 2 (2012): 151–69.

Alexseev, Mikhail A., and Henry E. Hale. "Rallying 'round the Leader More than the Flag: Changes in Russian Nationalist Public Opinion 2013–14." In *The New Russian Nationalism: Imperialism, Ethnicity and Authoritarianism 2000–15*, edited by Pål Kolstø and Helge Blakkisrud, 192–220. Edinburgh: Edinburgh University Press, 2016.

Altemeyer, Bob. *Enemies of Freedom: Understanding Right-Wing Authoritarianism*. 1st ed. Jossey-Bass Social and Behavioral Science Series. San Francisco: Jossey-Bass, 1988.

Alyukov, Maxim, Maria Kunilovskaya, and Andrei Semenov. "Mobilizing for War: State-Controlled Networks and War Propaganda on Russian Social Media." *Russia.Post*, October 18, 2022. https://russiapost.info/society/mobilizing.

Amsden, Alice H. "The State and Taiwan's Economic Development." In *Bringing the State Back In*, 1st ed., edited by Peter B. Evans, Dietrich Rueschemeyer, and Theda Skocpol, 78–106. Cambridge: Cambridge University Press, 1985. https://doi.org/10.1017/CBO9780511628283.005.

Anderson, Benedict R. O'G. *Imagined Communities: Reflections on the Origin and Spread of Nationalism*. Rev. ed. London; New York: Verso, 2016.

Antiwarriors. "За 100 дней войны в России появилось низовое антивоенное движение." June 5, 2022. https://t.me/antiwarriors_main/135.

Arendt, Hannah. *The Origins of Totalitarianism*. New ed. New York: Harcourt Brace Jovanovich, 1973.

Arnold, Richard. *Russian Nationalism and Ethnic Violence: Symbolic Violence, Lynching, Pogrom and Massacre*, New York: Routledge, 2016.

Avrich, Paul. *Russian Rebels, 1600–1800*. New York: Schocken Books, 1972.

Azarya, Victor, and Naomi Chazan. "Disengagement from the State in Africa: Reflections on the Experience of Ghana and Guinea." *Comparative Studies in Society and History* 29, no. 1 (1987): 106–31.

Bader, Max, and Carolien van Ham. "What Explains Regional Variation in Election Fraud? Evidence from Russia: A Research Note." *Post-Soviet Affairs* 31, no. 6 (2015): 514–28. https://doi.org/10.1080/1060586X.2014.969023.

Bahry, Donna, and Brian D. Silver. "Soviet Citizen Participation on the Eve of Democratization." *American Political Science Review* 84, no. 3 (September 1990): 821. https://doi.org/10.2307/1962768.

Baldwin, Kate. *The Paradox of Traditional Chiefs in Democratic Africa*. Cambridge Studies in Comparative Politics. New York: Cambridge University Press, 2016.

Barkey, Henri J. *The State and the Industrialization Crisis in Turkey*. Westview Special Studies on the Middle East. Boulder, CO: Westview Press, 1990.

Barkey, Karen, and Sunita Parikh. "Comparative Perspectives on the State." *Annual Review of Sociology* 17 (1991): 523–49.

Bauer, Martin W., and Bas Aarts. "Corpus Construction: A Principle for Qualitative Data Collection." In *Qualitative Researching with Text, Image and Sound*, edited by Martin Bauer and George Gaskell, 20–37. London: SAGE, 2000. https://doi.org/10.4135/9781849209731.n2.

Baumeister, Roy F., and Mark R. Leary. "The Need to Belong: Desire for Interpersonal Attachments as a Fundamental Human Motivation." *Psychological Bulletin* 117, no. 3 (1995): 497–529. https://doi.org/10.1037/0033-2909.117.3.497.

Beck, Hermann. *The Origins of the Authoritarian Welfare State in Prussia: Conservatives, Bureaucracy, and the Social Question, 1815–70*. Social History, Popular Culture, and Politics in Germany. Ann Arbor: University of Michigan Press, 1995.

Beissinger, Mark. *Nationalist Mobilization and the Collapse of the Soviet State*. Cambridge; New York: Cambridge University Press, 2002.

Belge, Ceren. "State Building and the Limits of Legibility: Kinship Networks and Kurdish Resistance in Turkey." *International Journal of Middle East Studies* 43, no. 1 (February 2011): 95–114. https://doi.org/10.1017/S0020743810001212.

Bellin, Eva. "The Robustness of Authoritarianism in the Middle East: Exceptionalism in Comparative Perspective." *Comparative Politics* 36, no. 2 (2004): 139–57.

Blake, Charles H., and Stephen D. Morris, eds. *Corruption and Democracy in Latin America*. Pitt Latin American Series. Pittsburgh: University of Pittsburgh Press, 2009.

Blaydes, Lisa. "State Building in the Middle East." *Annual Review of Political Science* 20, no. 1 (May 11, 2017): 487–504. https://doi.org/10.1146/annurev-polisci-051215-023141.

Bratton, Michael. "Beyond the State: Civil Society and Associational Life in Africa." *World Politics* 41, no. 3 (April 1989): 407–30. https://doi.org/10.2307/2010506.

Breeden, Aurelien. "Why So Many People in France Are Protesting over Pensions." *New York Times*, March 23, 2023, sec. World. https://www.nytimes.com/article/france-pension-strikes-macron-explainer.html.

Breslauer, George. "On the Adaptability of Soviet Welfare-State Authoritarianism." In *Soviet Society and the Communist Party*, edited by Karl W. Ryavec, 3–25. Amherst: University of Massachusetts Press, 1978.

Brookings Institution. *Vladimir Putin as Statist: Restoring the Greatness of Russia*, 2013. https://www.youtube.com/watch?v=2_RL3RfQxmY&ab_channel=BrookingsInstitution.

Brooks, Clem, and Jeff Manza. *Why Welfare States Persist: The Importance of Public Opinion in Democracies*. Chicago: University of Chicago Press, 2008.

Brownlee, Jason. *Authoritarianism in an Age of Democratization*. Cambridge: Cambridge University Press, 2007.

Brunarska, Zuzanna. "Understanding Sociopolitical Engagement of Society in Russia: A View from Yaroslavl Oblast and Tatarstan." *Problems of Post-Communism*, 65, no. 5 March 16, 2017: 315–26. https://doi.org/10.1080/10758216.2017.1291309.

Buchanan, Heather. "Cossacks." In *Native Peoples of the World: An Encyclopedia of Groups, Cultures, and Contemporary Issues*, edited by Steven Danver, 218–19. Armonk, NY: Sharpe Reference, 2013.

Burbidge, Dominic. *The Shadow of Kenyan Democracy: Widespread Expectations of Widespread Corruption*. Burlington, VT: Ashgate, 2015.

Burgoon, Brian, and Matthijs Rooduijn. "'Immigrationization' of Welfare Politics? Anti-Immigration and Welfare Attitudes in Context." *West European Politics* 44, no. 2 (February 23, 2021): 177–203. https://doi.org/10.1080/01402382.2019.1702297.

Bushkovitch, Paul. *A Concise History of Russia*. Cambridge Concise Histories. New York: Cambridge University Press, 2012.

Callaghy, Thomas M. *The State-Society Struggle: Zaire in Comparative Perspective*. New York: Columbia University Press, 1984.

Cammett, Melani Claire. *Compassionate Communalism: Welfare and Sectarianism in Lebanon*. Ithaca, NY: Cornell University Press, 2014.

Cannady, Sean, and Paul Kubicek. "Nationalism and Legitimation for Authoritarianism: A Comparison of Nicholas I and Vladimir Putin." *Journal of Eurasian Studies* 5, no. 1 (January 1, 2014): 1–9. https://doi.org/10.1016/j.euras.2013.11.001.

Case, Trevor I., and Kipling D. Williams. "Ostracism: A Metaphor for Death." In *Handbook of Experimental Existential Psychology*, edited by Jeff Greenberg, Sander Leon Koole, and Thomas A. Pyszczynski, 336–51. New York: Guilford Press, 2004.

Cassiday, Julie A., and Emily D. Johnson. "Putin, Putiniana and the Question of a Post-Soviet Cult of Personality." *Slavonic and East European Review* 88, no. 4 (2010): 681–707.

Castano, Emanuele, Bernhard Leidner, Alain Bonacossa, John Nikkah, Rachel Perrulli, Bettina Spencer, and Nicholas Humphrey. "Ideology, Fear of Death, and Death Anxiety." *Political Psychology* 32, no. 4 (August 2011): 601–21. https://doi.org/10.1111/j.1467-9221.2011.00822.x.

Castano, Emanuele, Vincent Yzerbyt, and Maria-Paola Paladino. "Transcending Oneself through Social Identification." In *Handbook of Experimental Existential Psychology*, edited by Jeff Greenberg, Sander Leon Koole, and Thomas A. Pyszczynski, 305–21. New York: Guilford Press, 2004.

Centeno, Miguel Angel. *Blood and Debt: War and the Nation-State in Latin America*. University Park: Pennsylvania State University Press, 2002.

Chapman, Hannah S. "Shoring Up Autocracy: Participatory Technologies and Regime Support in Putin's Russia." *Comparative Political Studies* 54, no. 8 (January 31, 2021): 1459–89. https://doi.org/10.1177/0010414021989759.

Chapman, Hannah S., Kyle L. Marquardt, Yoshiko M. Herrera, and Theodore P. Gerber. "Xenophobia on the Rise? Temporal and Regional Trends in Xenophobic Attitudes in Russia." *Comparative Politics* 50, no. 3 (April 1, 2018): 381–94. https://doi.org/10.5129/001041518822704944.

Clemens, Elisabeth Stephanie. *Civic Gifts: Voluntarism and the Making of the American Nation-State*. Chicago: University of Chicago Press, 2020.

Clover, Charles. "The Return of Russian Nationalism." *Financial Times*, October 13, 2017. https://www.ft.com/content/edb595d8-aeba-11e7-beba-5521c713abf4.

Colton, Timothy J., and Michael McFaul. "Are Russians Undemocratic?" *Post-Soviet Affairs* 18, no. 2 (June 2002): 91–121.

Cook, Linda J. *The Soviet Social Contract and Why It Failed: Welfare Policy and Workers' Politics from Brezhnev to Yeltsin*. Cambridge, MA: Harvard University Press, 1993.

Cook, Linda J., and Martin K. Dimitrov. "The Social Contract Revisited: Evidence from Communist and State Capitalist Economies." *Europe-Asia Studies* 69, no. 1 (January 2, 2017): 8–26. https://doi.org/10.1080/09668136.2016.1267714.

Crowley, Stephen. *Hot Coal, Cold Steel: Russian and Ukrainian Workers from the End of the Soviet Union to the Post-Communist Transformations*. Ann Arbor: University of Michigan Press, 1997.

Crummey, Robert O. *Aristocrats and Servitors*. Princeton, NJ: Princeton University Press, 2016.

Dahlström, Carl, Victor Lapuente, and Jan Teorell. "The Merit of Meritocratization: Politics, Bureaucracy, and the Institutional Deterrents of Corruption." *Political Research Quarterly* 65, no. 3 (September 2012): 656–68. https://doi.org/10.1177/1065912911408109.

David-Fox, Michael. "Whither Resistance?" In *The Resistance Debate in Russian and Soviet History*, edited by Michael David-Fox, Peter Holquist, and Marshall Poe, 230–36. Kritika Historical Studies 1. Bloomington, IN: Slavica Publishers, 2003.

Diamond, Larry Jay. "Thinking about Hybrid Regimes." *Journal of Democracy* 13, no. 2 (April 2002): 21–35.

Dimitrov, Martin K. "The Functions of Letters to the Editor in Reform-Era Cuba." *Latin American Research Review* 54, no. 1 (April 10, 2019): 1–15. https://doi.org/10.25222/larr.232.

Dimitrov, Martin K. "Tracking Public Opinion under Authoritarianism: The Case of the Soviet Union during the Brezhnev Era." *Russian History* 41, no. 3 (2014): 329–53.

Dimitrov, Martin K. "Understanding Communist Collapse and Resilience." In *Why Communism Did Not Collapse: Understanding Authoritarian Regime Resilience in Asia and Europe*, edited by Martin K. Dimitrov, 3–39. New York: Cambridge University Press, 2013.

Dimitrov, Martin K. "Vertical Accountability in Communist Regimes: The Role of Citizen Complaints in Bulgaria and China." In *Why Communism Did Not Collapse: Understanding*

Authoritarian Regime Resilience in Asia and Europe, edited by Martin K. Dimitrov, 276–302. New York: Cambridge University Press, 2013.

Dimitrov, Martin K., ed. *Why Communism Did Not Collapse: Understanding Authoritarian Regime Resilience in Asia and Europe*. New York: Cambridge University Press, 2013.

Dincecco, Mark, and Yuhua Wang. "Violent Conflict and Political Development over the Long Run: China versus Europe." *Annual Review of Political Science* 21, no. 1 (May 11, 2018): 341–58. https://doi.org/10.1146/annurev-polisci-050317-064428.

Dobbin, Frank. *Forging Industrial Policy: The United States, Britain, and France in the Railway Age*. New York: Cambridge University Press, 1994.

Dollbaum, Jan Matti, Andrey Semenov, and Elena Sirotkina. "A Top-Down Movement with Grass-Roots Effects? Alexei Navalny's Electoral Campaign." *Social Movement Studies* 17, no. 5 (September 3, 2018): 618–25. https://doi.org/10.1080/14742837.2018.1483228.

Downing, Brian M. *The Military Revolution and Political Change: Origins of Democracy and Autocracy in Early Modern Europe*. 1st Princeton paperback. Princeton, NJ: Princeton University Press, 1993.

Driscoll, Barry. "Why Political Competition Can Increase Patronage." *Studies in Comparative International Development*, 53, no. 4 (March 18, 2017): 404–27. https://doi.org/10.1007/s12116-017-9238-x.

Durkheim, Emile. *The Rules of Sociological Method*. Edited by Steven Lukes. 1st American ed. New York: Free Press, 1982.

Edele, Mark. *Soviet Veterans of the Second World War: A Popular Movement in an Authoritarian Society 1941–1991*. Oxford; New York: Oxford University Press, 2008.

Eger, Maureen A, and Nate Breznau. "Immigration and the Welfare State: A Cross-Regional Analysis of European Welfare Attitudes." *International Journal of Comparative Sociology* 58, no. 5 (October 1, 2017): 440–63. https://doi.org/10.1177/0020715217690796.

Ekiert, Grzegorz, Elizabeth J. Perry, and Xiaojun Yan, eds. *Ruling by Other Means: State-Mobilized Movements*. Cambridge: Cambridge University Press, 2020.

Eliasoph, Nina. *Avoiding Politics: How Americans Produce Apathy in Everyday Life*. New York: Cambridge University Press, 1998.

Ely, Christopher. "The Question of Civil Society in Late Imperial Russia." In *A Companion to Russian History*, edited by Abbott Gleason, 225–42. Blackwell Companions to World History. Chichester, UK; Malden, MA: Wiley-Blackwell, 2009.

Ent, Michael R., and Roy F. Baumeister. "Obedience, Self-Control, and the Voice of Culture." *Journal of Social Issues* 70, no. 3 (September 2014): 574–86. https://doi.org/10.1111/josi.12079.

Ertman, Thomas. *Birth of the Leviathan: Building States and Regimes in Medieval and Early Modern Europe*. Cambridge: Cambridge University Press, 2010.

Evans, Peter, Dietrich Rueschemeyer, and Theda Skocpol, eds. *Bringing the State Back In*. Cambridge; New York: Cambridge University Press, 1985.

Evans, Peter B. *Embedded Autonomy: States and Industrial Transformation*. Princeton, NJ: Princeton University Press, 1995.

Feldman, Stanley. "Enforcing Social Conformity: A Theory of Authoritarianism." *Political Psychology* 24, no. 1 (March 2003): 41–74. https://doi.org/10.1111/0162-895X.00316.

Fish, M. *Democracy Derailed in Russia: The Failure of Open Politics*. New York: Cambridge University Press, 2005.

Fitzpatrick, Sheila. *Stalin's Peasants: Resistance and Survival in the Russian Village after Collectivization*. New York: Oxford University Press, 1996.

Foa, Roberto Stefan. "Why Strongmen Win in Weak States." *Journal of Democracy* 32, no. 1 (January 2021): 52–65.

Foer, Franklin. "It's Putin's World." *Atlantic*, March 2017. https://www.theatlantic.com/magazine/archive/2017/03/its-putins-world/513848/.

Forrat, Natalia. "The Political Economy of Russian Higher Education: Why Does Putin Support Research Universities?" *Post-Soviet Affairs* 32, no. 4 (2016): 299–337. https://doi.org/10.1080/1060586X.2015.1051749.

Forrat, Natalia. "Shock-Resistant Authoritarianism: Schoolteachers and Infrastructural State Capacity in Putin's Russia." *Comparative Politics* 50, no. 3 (April 1, 2018): 417–49. https://doi.org/10.5129/001041518822704908.

Fourcade, Marion. *Economists and Societies: Discipline and Profession in the United States, Britain, and France, 1890s to 1990s*. Princeton, NJ: Princeton University Press, 2010.

"Freedom in the World 2023: Marking 50 Years in the Struggle for Democracy." Freedom House, 2023. https://freedomhouse.org/sites/default/files/2023-03/FIW_World_2023_DigtalPDF.pdf.

Friedgut, Theodore H. *Political Participation in the USSR*. Princeton, NJ: Princeton University Press, 1979.

Frolic, B. Michael. "State-Led Civil Society." In *Civil Society in China*, edited by Timothy Brook and B. Michael Frolic, 46–67. Studies on Contemporary China. Armonk, NY: M. E. Sharpe, 1997.

Frye, Timothy. "What's Vladimir Putin's End Game? Other Post-Soviet Autocrats Give a Few Clues." *Washington Post*, July 3, 2020. https://www.washingtonpost.com/politics/2020/07/03/whats-vladimir-putins-end-game-other-post-soviet-autocrats-give-few-clues/.

Frye, Timothy, Scott Gehlbach, Kyle L. Marquardt, and Ora John Reuter. "Is Putin's Popularity (Still) Real? A Cautionary Note on Using List Experiments to Measure Popularity in Authoritarian Regimes." *Post-Soviet Affairs* 39, no. 3 (March 15, 2023): 213–22. https://doi.org/10.1080/1060586X.2023.2187195.

Frye, Timothy, Ora John Reuter, and David Szakonyi. "Political Machines at Work: Voter Mobilization and Electoral Subversion in the Workplace." *World Politics* 66, no. 2 (April 2014): 195–228. https://doi.org/10.1017/S004388711400001X.

Frye, Timothy, Ora John Reuter, and David Szakonyi. "Vote Brokers, Clientelist Appeals, and Voter Turnout: Evidence from Russia and Venezuela." *World Politics* 71, no. 4 (October 2019): 710–46. https://doi.org/10.1017/S0043887119000078.

Fukuyama, Francis. *The Origins of Political Order: From Prehuman Times to the French Revolution*. 1st paperback ed. New York: Farrar, Straus and Giroux, 2012.

Fukuyama, Francis. *Political Order and Political Decay: From the Industrial Revolution to the Globalization of Democracy*. 1st ed. New York: Farrar, Straus and Giroux, 2014.

Fukuyama, Francis. *State-Building: Governance and World Order in the 21st Century*. Ithaca, NY: Cornell University Press, 2004.

Gandhi, Jennifer. *Political Institutions under Dictatorship*. New York: Cambridge University Press, 2008.

Gans-Morse, Jordan, Alexander Kalgin, Andrei Klimenko, Dmitriy Vorobyev, and Andrei Yakovlev. "Self-Selection into Public Service When Corruption Is Widespread: The Anomalous Russian Case." *Comparative Political Studies*, 56, no. 6 (October 26, 2020): 1086–128. https://doi.org/10.1177/0010414020957669.

Gans-Morse, Jordan, Sebastián Mazzuca, and Simeon Nichter. "Varieties of Clientelism: Machine Politics during Elections." *American Journal of Political Science* 58, no. 2 (April 2014): 415–32. https://doi.org/10.1111/ajps.12058.

Gao, Eleanor. "Tribal Mobilization, Fragmented Groups, and Public Goods Provision in Jordan." *Comparative Political Studies* 49, no. 10 (2016): 1372–403. https://doi.org/10.1177/0010414015621075.

Geddes, Barbara, Joseph Wright, and Erica Frantz. *How Dictatorships Work: Power, Personalization, and Collapse*. Cambridge; New York: Cambridge University Press, 2018.

Gel'man, Vladimir. *Authoritarian Russia: Analyzing Post-Soviet Regime Changes*. Pittsburg, PA: University of Pittsburg Press, 2015.

Gel'man, Vladimir. "Politics, Governance, and the Zigzags of the Power Vertical: Toward a Framework for Analyzing Russia's Local Regimes." In *Russia's Regions and Comparative Subnational Politics*, edited by William M. Reisinger, 25–39. Routledge Research in Comparative Politics. New York: Routledge, 2013.

Gel'man, Vladimir. "The Politics of Fear: How the Russian Regime Confronts Its Opponents." *Russian Politics and Law* 53, no. 5–6 (November 2, 2015): 6–26. https://doi.org/10.1080/10611940.2015.1146058.

Gerber, Theodore P., and Michael E. van Landingham. "Ties That Remind: Known Family Connections to Past Events as Salience Cues and Collective Memory of Stalin's Repressions of the 1930s in Contemporary Russia." *American Sociological Review* 86, no. 4 (July 9, 2021): 639–69. https://doi.org/10.1177/00031224211023798.

Gerschewski, Johannes. "Legitimacy in Autocracies: Oxymoron or Essential Feature?" *Perspectives on Politics* 16, no. 3 (September 2018): 652–65. https://doi.org/10.1017/S1537592717002183.

Gerschewski, Johannes. *The Two Logics of Autocratic Rule*. Cambridge; New York: Cambridge University Press, 2023.

Gill, Jeff. "Whose Variance Is It Anyway? Interpreting Empirical Models with State-Level Data." *State Politics and Policy Quarterly* 1, no. 3 (October 1, 2001): 318–38. https://doi.org/10.2307/40421434.

Gilley, Bruce. *The Right to Rule: How States Win and Lose Legitimacy*. New York: Columbia University Press, 2009.

Glinski, Dmitri. "Peasant Uprisings." In *Encyclopedia of Russian History*, edited by James R. Millar, 3:1155–56. New York: Macmillan Reference USA, 2004.

Golosov, Grigorii V. "The Last Resort of Political Regionalism: Electoral Blocs in Russia's Regional Legislative Elections, 2003–2005." *East European Politics* 30, no. 1 (January 2, 2014): 71–85. https://doi.org/10.1080/21599165.2013.819467.

Goode, J. Paul. "Becoming Banal: Incentivizing and Monopolizing the Nation in Post-Soviet Russia." *Ethnic and Racial Studies* 44, no. 4 (April 8, 2020): 679–97. https://doi.org/10.1080/01419870.2020.1749687.

Goode, J. Paul. "Love for the Motherland: (Or Why Cheese Is More Patriotic than Crimea)." *Russian Politics* 1, no. 4 (December 30, 2016): 418–49. https://doi.org/10.1163/2451-8921-00104005.

Gottlieb, Jessica, and Katrina Kosec. "The Countervailing Effects of Competition on Public Goods Provision: When Bargaining Inefficiencies Lead to Bad Outcomes." *American Political Science Review* 113, no. 1 (February 2019): 88–107. https://doi.org/10.1017/S0003055418000667.

Gramsci, Antonio. *Selections from the Prison Notebooks of Antonio Gramsci*. Edited by Quintin Hoare. New York: International Publishers, 1985.

Graney, Katherine E. *Of Khans and Kremlins: Tatarstan and the Future of Ethno-Federalism in Russia*. Lanham, MD: Lexington Books, 2009.

Granovetter, Mark. "The Social Construction of Corruption." In *On Capitalism*, edited by Victor Nee and Richard Swedberg, 152–72. Stanford, CA: Stanford University Press, 2007.

Greenberg, Jeff, Sander Leon Koole, and Thomas A. Pyszczynski. "Experimental Existential Psychology: Exploring the Human Confrontation with Reality." In *Handbook of Experimental Existential Psychology*, edited by Jeff Greenberg, Sander Leon Koole, and Thomas A. Pyszczynski, 3–9. New York: Guilford Press, 2004.

Greene, Samuel A. "Homo Post-Sovieticus: Reconstructing Citizenship in Russia." *Social Research: An International Quarterly* 86, no. 1 (2019): 181–202.

Greene, Samuel A. *Moscow in Movement: Power and Opposition in Putin's Russia*. Stanford, CA: Stanford University Press, 2014.

Greene, Samuel A. "Running to Stand Still: Aggressive Immobility and the Limits of Power in Russia." *Post-Soviet Affairs* 34, no. 5 (September 3, 2018): 333–47. https://doi.org/10.1080/1060586X.2018.1500095.

Greene, Samuel A., and Graeme Robertson. "Affect and Autocracy: Emotions and Attitudes in Russia after Crimea." *Perspectives on Politics* 20, no. 1 (September 14, 2020): 38–52. https://doi.org/10.1017/S1537592720002339.

Greene, Samuel A., and Graeme B. Robertson. *Putin v. the People: The Perilous Politics of a Divided Russia*. New Haven, CT: Yale University Press, 2019.

Grzymala-Busse, Anna. *Nations under God: How Churches Use Moral Authority to Influence Policy*. Princeton, NJ: Princeton University Press, 2015. https://doi.org/10.1515/9781400866458.

Guriev, S. M., and Daniel Treisman. *Spin Dictators: The Changing Face of Tyranny in the 21st Century*. Princeton, NJ; Oxford: Princeton University Press, 2022.

Haggard, Stephan, and Robert R. Kaufman. *Development, Democracy, and Welfare States: Latin America, East Asia, and Eastern Europe*. Princeton, NJ: Princeton University Press, 2008.

Haidt, Jonathan. *The Righteous Mind: Why Good People Are Divided by Politics and Religion*. 1st ed. New York: Pantheon Books, 2012.

Hale, Henry E. "Civil Society from Above? Statist and Liberal Models of State-Building in Russia." *Demokratizatsiya: The Journal of Post-Soviet Democratization* 10, no. 3 (2002): 306–21.

Hale, Henry E. "Explaining Machine Politics in Russia's Regions: Economy, Ethnicity, and Legacy." *Post-Soviet Affairs* 19, no. 3 (January 1, 2003): 228–63. https://doi.org/10.2747/1060-586X.19.3.228.

Hale, Henry E. "The Myth of Mass Russian Support for Autocracy: The Public Opinion Foundations of a Hybrid Regime." *Europe-Asia Studies* 63, no. 8 (September 2011): 1357–75. https://doi.org/10.1080/09668136.2011.601106.

Hale, Henry E., Ora John Reuter, Bryn Rosenfeld, David Szakonyi, and Katerina Tertytchnaya. "Russia May Be About to Invade Ukraine: Russians Don't Want It To." *Washington Post*, February 14, 2022. https://www.washingtonpost.com/politics/2022/02/11/russia-may-be-about-invade-ukraine-russians-dont-want-it/.

Hamilton, Nora. *The Limits of State Autonomy: Post-Revolutionary Mexico*. Princeton, NJ: Princeton University Press, 1982.

Harris, James R. *The Great Fear: Stalin's Terror of the 1930s*. 1st ed. Oxford: Oxford University Press, 2016.

Harris, Kevan. "The Martyrs Welfare State: Politics of Social Policy in the Islamic Republic of Iran." Johns Hopkins University, 2012.

Harris, Kevan. *A Social Revolution: Politics and the Welfare State in Iran*. Oakland: University of California Press, 2017.

Harvey, Cole J. "Changes in the Menu of Manipulation: Electoral Fraud, Ballot Stuffing, and Voter Pressure in the 2011 Russian Election." *Electoral Studies* 41 (March 1, 2016): 105–17. https://doi.org/10.1016/j.electstud.2015.11.004.

Haslam, S. Alexander, Stephen Reicher, and Michael Platow. *The New Psychology of Leadership: Identity, Influence, and Power*. Hove, East Sussex; New York: Psychology Press, 2011.

Hasmath, Reza, and Jennifer Y. J. Hsu. *NGO Governance and Management in China*. London: Routledge, 2016.

Heberer, Thomas. "Relegitimation through New Patterns of Social Security: Neighbourhood Communities as Legitimating Institutions." *China Review* 9, no. 2 (2009): 99–128.

Hemment, Julie. *Youth Politics in Putin's Russia: Producing Patriots and Entrepreneurs*. Bloomington: Indiana University Press, 2015.

Heydemann, Steven. "Rethinking Social Contracts in the MENA Region: Economic Governance, Contingent Citizenship, and State-Society Relations after the Arab Uprisings." *World Development* 135 (November 2020): 105019. https://doi.org/10.1016/j.worlddev.2020.105019.

Heydemann, Steven. "Social Pacts and the Persistence of Authoritarianism in the Middle East." In *Debating Arab Authoritarianism: Dynamics and Durability in Nondemocratic Regimes*, edited by Oliver Schlumberger, 21–38. Stanford, CA: Stanford University Press, 2007.

Hilgers, Tina. "Clientelism and Conceptual Stretching: Differentiating among Concepts and among Analytical Levels." *Theory and Society* 40, no. 5 (2011): 567–88. https://doi.org/10.1007/s11186-011-9152-6.

Hilgers, Tina. *Clientelism in Everyday Latin American Politics*. New York, NY: Palgrave Macmillan, 2012.

Hill, Fiona, and Clifford G. Gaddy. *Mr. Putin: Operative in the Kremlin*. Washington, DC: Brookings Institution Press, 2013.

Hirschman, Albert O. *Exit, Voice, and Loyalty: Responses to Decline in Firms, Organizations, and States.* Cambridge, MA: Harvard University Press, 1972.

Hogg, Michael A. "A Social Identity Theory of Leadership." *Personality and Social Psychology Review* 5, no. 3 (August 2001): 184–200. https://doi.org/10.1207/S15327957PSPR0503_1.

Hornsby, Rob. *Protest, Reform and Repression in Khrushchev's Soviet Union.* New Studies in European History. Cambridge; New York: Cambridge University Press, 2013.

Hosking, Geoffrey A. *Russian History: A Very Short Introduction.* Very Short Introductions 308. Oxford; New York: Oxford University Press, 2012.

Howell, Jessica, Flagler College, and Nikolai G. Wenzel. "Rationality in a Fatalistic World: Explaining Revolutionary Apathy in Pre-Soviet Peasants." *Mind and Society* 18, no. 1 (June 2019): 125–37. http://dx.doi.org.proxy.lib.umich.edu/10.1007/s11299-019-00215-2.

Hsu, Jennifer, and Reza Hasmath, eds. *The Chinese Corporatist State: Adaption, Survival and Resistance.* Routledge Contemporary China Series 92. London; New York: Routledge, 2013.

Hui, Victoria Tin-bor. *War and State Formation in Ancient China and Early Modern Europe.* New York: Cambridge University Press, 2005.

Inglehart, Ronald. "From Authoritarian Personality to Authoritarian Reflex: Evolving Views of an Enduring Phenomenon." University of Michigan, 2019.

Jackson, Robert H., and Carl G. Rosberg. "Why Africa's Weak States Persist: The Empirical and the Juridical in Statehood." *World Politics* 35, no. 1 (1982): 1–24. https://doi.org/10.2307/2010277.

Johnston, Michael. *Corruption, Contention, and Reform: The Power of Deep Democratization.* Cambridge: Cambridge University Press, 2013.

Juhl, Jacob, and Clay Routledge. "Putting the Terror in Terror Management Theory: Evidence That the Awareness of Death Does Cause Anxiety and Undermine Psychological Well-Being." *Current Directions in Psychological Science* 25, no. 2 (April 2016): 99–103. https://doi.org/10.1177/0963721415625218.

Kalinin, Kirill. "Exploring Putin's Approval Ratings during the Ukrainian Crisis 2014." San Francisco, CA, 2015.

Kalinin, Kirill. "Signaling Games of Election Fraud." *SSRN Electronic Journal*, 2016. https://doi.org/10.2139/ssrn.2836775.

Kalinin, Kirill. "Validation of the Finite Mixture Model Using Quasi-Experimental Data and Geography." *Electoral Studies* 1 (March 26, 2019): 6. http://electoralpolitics.org/en/articles/validatsiia-konechnoi-smeshannoi-modeli-s-ispolzovaniem-kvaziieksperimentalnykh-i-geograficheskikh-dannykh/.

Kasser, Tim, and Kennon M. Sheldon. "Autonomy Is No Illusion: Self-Determination Theory and the Empirical Study of Authenticity, Awareness, and Will." In *Handbook of Experimental Existential Psychology*, edited by Jeff Greenberg, Sander Leon Koole, and Thomas A. Pyszczynski, 480–93. New York: Guilford Press, 2004.

Kharkhordin, Oleg. *The Collective and the Individual in Russia: A Study of Practices.* Studies on the History of Society and Culture 32. Berkeley: University of California Press, 1999.

King, Gary, Jennifer Pan, and Margaret E. Roberts. "How the Chinese Government Fabricates Social Media Posts for Strategic Distraction, Not Engaged Argument." *American Political Science Review* 111, no. 3 (August 2017): 484–501. https://doi.org/10.1017/S0003055417000144.

Kitschelt, Herbert, and Steven Wilkinson, eds. *Patrons, Clients, and Policies: Patterns of Democratic Accountability and Political Competition.* Cambridge; New York: Cambridge University Press, 2007.

Kivelson, Valerie. "Muscovite 'Citizenship': Rights without Freedom." *Journal of Modern History* 74, no. 3 (2002): 465–89. https://doi.org/10.1086/345109.

Kivelson, Valerie A., and Ronald Grigor Suny. *Russia's Empires.* New York: Oxford University Press, 2017.

Kolstø, Pål, and Helge Blakkisrud, eds. *The New Russian Nationalism: Imperialism, Ethnicity and Authoritarianism 2000–15.* Edinburgh: Edinburgh University Press, 2016.

Kondrashov, Sergei. *Nationalism and the Drive for Sovereignty in Tatarstan, 1988–92: Origins and Development*. New York: St. Martin's Press, 2000.
Kornai, János. *The Socialist System: The Political Economy of Communism*. Princeton, NJ: Princeton University Press, 1992.
Kozlov, Vladimir Aleksandrovič, and Sheila Fitzpatrick, eds. *Sedition: Everyday Resistance in the Soviet Union under Khrushchev and Brezhnev*. Annals of Communism. New Haven, CT: Yale University Press, 2011.
Krupets, Yana, Jeremy Morris, Nadya Nartova, Elena Omelchenko, and Guzel Sabirova. "Imagining Young Adults' Citizenship in Russia: From Fatalism to Affective Ideas of Belonging." *Journal of Youth Studies* 20, no. 2 (February 7, 2017): 252–67. https://doi.org/10.1080/13676261.2016.1206862.
Kulyk, Volodymyr. "National Identity in Ukraine: Impact of Euromaidan and the War." *Europe-Asia Studies* 68, no. 4 (April 20, 2016): 588–608. https://doi.org/10.1080/09668136.2016.1174980.
Kupatadze, A. "Political Corruption in Eurasia: Understanding Collusion between States, Organized Crime and Business." *Theoretical Criminology* 19, no. 2 (May 1, 2015): 198–215. https://doi.org/10.1177/1362480615574404.
Kuran, Timur. "Now Out of Never: The Element of Surprise in the East European Revolution of 1989." *World Politics* 44, no. 1 (1991): 7–48.
Kuran, Timur. *Private Truths, Public Lies: The Social Consequences of Preference Falsification*. 1st Harvard University Press paperback ed. Cambridge, MA: Harvard University Press, 1997.
Lankina, Tomila. *The Estate Origins of Democracy in Russia: From Imperial Bourgeoisie to Post-Communist Middle Class*. Cambridge; New York: Cambridge University Press, 2022.
Larson, Eric V. "Public Support for U.S. Military Operations." RAND Corporation, January 1, 1996. https://www.rand.org/pubs/research_briefs/RB2502.html.
Laruelle, Marlène. *Russian Nationalism: Imaginaries, Doctrines, and Political Battlefields*. Media, Culture and Social Change in Asia, Volume 61. Abingdon, Oxon; New York: Routledge, 2019.
Leitch, Duncan. "Society in Motion: Russia's Emerging Voluntary Sector." *Nonprofit Management and Leadership* 7, no. 4 (1996): 421–33. https://doi.org/10.1002/nml.4130070407.
Leung, Joe C. B., and Richard C. Nann. *Authority and Benevolence: Social Welfare in China*. Hong Kong: Chinese University Press, 1995.
Levada-Center. "Conflict with Ukraine: Assessments for March 2023." April 7, 2023. https://www.levada.ru/en/2023/04/07/conflict-with-ukraine-assessments-for-march-2023/.
Levada-Center. "Indicators." Accessed June 21, 2023. https://www.levada.ru/en/ratings/.
Levi, Margaret. *Consent, Dissent, and Patriotism*. Political Economy of Institutions and Decisions. Cambridge; New York: Cambridge University Press, 1997.
Levitsky, Steven. "Latin America's Shifting Politics: Democratic Survival and Weakness." *Journal of Democracy* 29, no. 4 (October 2018): 102–13.
Levitsky, Steven, and María Victoria Murillo. "Variation in Institutional Strength." *Annual Review of Political Science* 12, no. 1 (June 2009): 115–33. https://doi.org/10.1146/annurev.polisci.11.091106.121756.
Levitsky, Steven, and Lucan A. Way. *Competitive Authoritarianism: Hybrid Regimes after the Cold War*. Cambridge: Cambridge University Press, 2010.
Libman, Alexander, and Vladimir Kozlov. "The Legacy of Compliant Activism in Autocracies: Post-Communist Experience." *Contemporary Politics* 23, no. 2 (July 8, 2016): 195–213. https://doi.org/10.1080/13569775.2016.1206275.
Lieberman, Evan S. "Nested Analysis as a Mixed-Method Strategy for Comparative Research." *American Political Science Review* 99, no. 3 (2005): 435–52.
Lukes, Steven. *Power: A Radical View*. 2nd ed. Palgrave Macmillan, NY, 2005.

Lukin, Alexander. "Russia's New Authoritarianism and the Post-Soviet Political Ideal." *Post-Soviet Affairs* 25, no. 1 (January 2009): 66–92. https://doi.org/10.2747/1060-586X.24.1.66.

Lussier, Danielle N. "Contacting and Complaining: Political Participation and the Failure of Democracy in Russia." *Post-Soviet Affairs* 27, no. 3 (July 1, 2011): 289–325. https://doi.org/10.2747/1060-586X.27.3.289.

Magaloni, Beatriz. *Voting for Autocracy: Hegemonic Party Survival and Its Demise in Mexico*. 1st paperback ed. Cambridge Studies in Comparative Politics. Cambridge: Cambridge University Press, 2006.

Mann, Michael. "The Autonomous Power of the State." *European Journal of Sociology* 25 (1985): 185–213.

Mann, Michael. "Infrastructural Power Revisited." *Studies in Comparative International Development* 43, no. 3–4 (December 1, 2008): 355–65. https://doi.org/10.1007/s12116-008-9027-7.

Marchetti, Raffaele, and Nathalie Tocci, eds. *Civil Society, Conflicts and the Politicization of Human Rights*. Tokyo; New York; Paris: United Nations University Press, 2011.

Mares, Isabela, and Matthew E. Carnes. "Social Policy in Developing Countries." *Annual Review of Political Science* 12, no. 1 (2009): 93–113. https://doi.org/10.1146/annurev.polisci.12.071207.093504.

Markedonov, Sergey. "Ethnopolitical Processes in the Rostov Region, the Krasnodar and Stavropol Territories: Problems, Contradictions, and Prospects." *Central Asia and the Caucasus*, no. 2 (2005). https://www.ca-c.org/journal/2005/journal_eng/cac-02/17.mareng.shtml.

Marten, Kimberly. "Vladimir Putin: Ethnic Russian Nationalist." *Washington Post*, March 19, 2014. https://www.washingtonpost.com/news/monkey-cage/wp/2014/03/19/vladimir-putin-ethnic-russian-nationalist/.

Mason, David S. "Attitudes towards the Market and Political Participation in the Post-Communist States." *Slavic Review* 54 (1995): 385–406.

Mason, David S., and Svetlana Sidorenko-Stephenson. "Public Opinion and the 1996 Elections in Russia: Nostalgic and Statist, yet Pro-Market and Pro-Yeltsin." *Slavic Review* 56, no. 4 (1997): 698–717.

Matovski, Aleksandar. "The Logic of Vladimir Putin's Popular Appeal." In *Citizens and the State in Authoritarian Regimes: Comparing China and Russia*, edited by Karrie J. Koesel, Valerie Bunce, and Jessica Chen Weiss, 217–49. New York: Oxford University Press, 2020.

McAllister, Ian, and Stephen White. "'It's the Economy, Comrade!' Parties and Voters in the 2007 Russian Duma Election." *Europe-Asia Studies* 60, no. 6 (August 2008): 931–57. https://doi.org/10.1080/09668130802180959.

McCullaugh, Marcy E. "From Well to Welfare: Social Spending in Mineral-Rich Post-Soviet States." University of California, Berkeley, 2013.

McGregor, Ian. "Zeal, Identity, and Meaning: Going to Extremes to Be One Self." In *Handbook of Experimental Existential Psychology*, edited by Jeff Greenberg, Sander Leon Koole, and Tom Pyszczynski, 182–99. New York: Guilford Press, 2004.

McLellan, Rachael. "Delivering the Vote: Community Politicians and the Credibility of Punishment Regimes in Electoral Autocracies." *Comparative Politics* 55, no. 3 (April 1, 2023): 449–72. https://doi.org/10.5129/001041523X16601556495592.

Migdal, Joel S. *Strong Societies and Weak States: State-Society Relations and State Capabilities in the Third World*. Princeton, NJ: Princeton University Press, 1988.

Miller, Chris. *Putinomics: Power and Money in Resurgent Russia*. Chapel Hill: University of North Carolina Press, 2018.

Miller, Chris. *The Struggle to Save the Soviet Economy: Mikhail Gorbachev and the Collapse of the USSR*. The New Cold War History. Chapel Hill: University of North Carolina Press, 2016.

Minaeva, Eleonora, and Petr Panov. "Localization of Ethnic Groups in the Regions as a Factor in Cross-Regional Variations in Voting for United Russia." *Russian Politics* 5, no. 2 (June 16, 2020): 131–53. https://doi.org/10.30965/24518921-00502001.

Moore, Barrington. *Social Origins of Dictatorship and Democracy: Lord and Peasant in the Making of the Modern World*. Boston: Beacon Press, 1993. http://books.google.com/books?id=Ip9W0yWtVO0C.

Morgan, Kimberly J., and Ann Shola Orloff, eds. *The Many Hands of the State: Theorizing Political Authority and Social Control*. New York: Cambridge University Press, 2017.

Morris, Jeremy. "What Do Ordinary Russians Think about the Invasion of Ukraine?" *OpenDemocracy* (blog), March 7, 2022. https://www.opendemocracy.net/en/odr/what-do-ordinary-russians-think-about-the-invasion-of-ukraine/.

Morris, Jeremy, Andrei Semenov, and Regina Smyth, eds. *Varieties of Russian Activism: State-Society Contestation in Everyday Life*. Bloomington: Indiana University Press, 2023.

Moser, Robert G., and Allison C. White. "Does Electoral Fraud Spread? The Expansion of Electoral Manipulation in Russia." *Post-Soviet Affairs* 33, no. 2 (March 4, 2016): 85–99. https://doi.org/10.1080/1060586X.2016.1153884.

Motyl, Alexander J. "Putin's Russia as a Fascist Political System." *Communist and Post-Communist Studies* 49, no. 1 (March 1, 2016): 25–36. https://doi.org/10.1016/j.postcomstud.2016.01.002.

Nichter, Simeon. *Votes for Survival: Relational Clientelism in Latin America*. Cambridge: Cambridge University Press, 2018.

North, Douglass Cecil. *Institutions, Institutional Change, and Economic Performance*. Cambridge; New York: Cambridge University Press, 1990.

Obolonskiĭ, A. V. *The Drama of Russian Political History: System against Individuality*. 1st ed. Eastern European Studies, no. 19. College Station: Texas A&M University Press, 2003.

O'Brien, Kevin J., and Lianjiang Li. *Rightful Resistance in Rural China*. Cambridge Studies in Contentious Politics. Cambridge; New York: Cambridge University Press, 2006.

O'Donnell, Guillermo. *Bureaucratic Authoritarianism: Argentina, 1966–1973, in Comparative Perspective*. Berkeley: University of California Press, 1988.

O'Donnell, Guillermo. "Reflections on the Patterns of Change in the Bureaucratic-Authoritarian State." *Latin American Research Review* 13, no. 1 (1978): 3–38.

Olimpieva, Evgenia, Irina Olimpieva, and Masha Galenko. "Russia's Antiwar Movement Goes Far beyond Street Protests." *Washington Post*, October 18, 2022. https://www.washingtonpost.com/politics/2022/10/18/russian-dissent-protest-ukraine-war/.

Owen, Catherine. "A Genealogy of Kontrol' in Russia: From Leninist to Neoliberal Governance." *Slavic Review* 75, no. 2 (2016): 331–53.

Owen, Catherine. "Participatory Authoritarianism: From Bureaucratic Transformation to Civic Participation in Russia and China." *Review of International Studies* 46, no. 4 (October 2020): 415–34. https://doi.org/10.1017/S0260210520000248.

Owen, Catherine. "The Struggle for Meaning of *Obshchestvennyi Kontrol'* in Contemporary Russia: Civic Participation between Resistance and Compliance after the 2011–2012 Elections." *Europe-Asia Studies* 69, no. 3 (April 18, 2017): 379–400. https://doi.org/10.1080/09668136.2017.1301882.

Paget, Dan. "Again, Making Tanzania Great: Magufuli's Restorationist Developmental Nationalism." *Democratization* 27, no. 7 (October 2, 2020): 1240–60. https://doi.org/10.1080/13510347.2020.1779223.

Pain, Emil. "The Imperial Syndrome and Its Influence on Russian Nationalism." In *The New Russian Nationalism: Imperialism, Ethnicity and Authoritarianism 2000–15*, edited by Pål Kolstø and Helge Blakkisrud, 46–74. Edinburgh: Edinburgh University Press, 2016.

Parsons, Talcott. *The Social System*. New York: Free Press, 1951.

Pearlman, Wendy. "Moral Identity and Protest Cascades in Syria." *British Journal of Political Science* 48, no. 4 (October 2018): 877–901. https://doi.org/10.1017/S0007123416000235.

Piattoni, Simona. "Clientelism in Historical and Comparative Perspective." In *Clientelism, Interests, and Democratic Representation: The European Experience in Historical and Comparative Perspective*, edited by Simona Piattoni, 1–30. Cambridge Studies in Comparative Politics. Cambridge; New York: Cambridge University Press, 2001.

Pipes, Richard. *Russian Conservatism and Its Critics: A Study in Political Culture.* New Haven, CT: Yale University Press, 2005.

Pipes, Richard. *Russia under the Old Regime.* 2nd ed. New York: Penguin Books, 1995.

Pitcher, Anne, Mary H. Moran, and Michael Johnston. "Rethinking Patrimonialism and Neopatrimonialism in Africa." *African Studies Review* 52, no. 1 (April 2009): 125–56. https://doi.org/10.1353/arw.0.0163.

Plets, Gertjan. "Exceptions to Authoritarianism? Variegated Sovereignty and Ethno-Nationalism in a Siberian Resource Frontier." *Post-Soviet Affairs* 35, no. 4 (July 4, 2019): 308–22. https://doi.org/10.1080/1060586X.2019.1617574.

Plokhy, Serhii. *The Cossack Myth: History and Nationhood in the Age of Empires.* New Studies in European History. Cambridge: Cambridge University Press, 2012.

Poe, Marshall. "What Did Russians Mean When They Called Themselves 'Slaves of the Tsar'?" *Slavic Review* 57, no. 3 (1998): 585–608. https://doi.org/10.2307/2500713.

Polishchuk, Leonid, Alexander Rubin, and Igor Shagalov. "Managing Collective Action: Government-Sponsored Community Initiatives in Russia." *Europe-Asia Studies* 73, no. 6 (July 3, 2021): 1176–209. https://doi.org/10.1080/09668136.2021.1935466.

Pop-Eleches, Grigore, and Joshua A. Tucker. *Communism's Shadow: Historical Legacies and Contemporary Political Attitudes.* Princeton Studies in Political Behavior. Princeton, NJ: Princeton University Press, 2017.

Powell, W. W., and Paul J. DiMaggio, eds. *The New Institutionalism in Organizational Analysis.* Chicago; London: University of Chicago Press, 1991.

Prasad, Monica, Mariana Borges Martins da Silva, and Andre Nickow. "Approaches to Corruption: A Synthesis of the Scholarship." *Studies in Comparative International Development* 54, no. 1 (March 2019): 96–132. https://doi.org/10.1007/s12116-018-9275-0.

Read, Benjamin Lelan. *Roots of the State: Neighborhood Organization and Social Networks in Beijing and Taipei.* Contemporary Issues in Asia and the Pacific. Stanford, CA: Stanford University Press, 2012.

Reddaway, Peter. *The Dissidents: A Memoir of Working with the Resistance in Russia, 1960–1990.* Washington, DC: Brookings Institution Press, 2020. https://search.ebscohost.com/login.aspx?direct=true&scope=site&db=nlebk&db=nlabk&AN=2087815.

Reisinger, William M., and Bryon J. Moraski. "Russia's Governors under Presidential Control, 2005–2012: A Survival Analysis of Gubernatorial Tenures." Chicago, IL, 2013. http://ir.uiowa.edu/polisci_pubs/102.

Remington, Thomas F. *Presidential Decrees in Russia: A Comparative Perspective.* 1st ed. New York: Cambridge University Press, 2014. https://doi.org/10.1017/CBO9781139629355.

Reno, William. *Corruption and State Politics in Sierra Leone.* African Studies Series 83. Cambridge; New York: Cambridge University Press, 1995.

Renzsch, Wolfgang. "German Federalism in Historical Perspective: Federalism as a Substitute for a National State." *Publius: The Journal of Federalism* 19 (Fall 1989): 17–33.

Reuter, Ora John. "Regional Patrons and Hegemonic Party Electoral Performance in Russia." *Post-Soviet Affairs* 29, no. 2 (2013): 101–35. https://doi.org/10.1080/1060586X.2013.780410.

Rimlinger, Gaston V. *Welfare Policy and Industrialization in Europe, America, and Russia.* New York: Wiley, 1971.

Robertson, Graeme. *The Politics of Protest in Hybrid Regimes: Managing Dissent in Post-Communist Russia.* Cambridge: Cambridge University Press, 2010.

Rochlitz, Michael, Anton Kazun, and Andrei Yakovlev. "Property Rights in Russia after 2009: From Business Capture to Centralized Corruption?" *Post-Soviet Affairs* 36, no. 5–6 (June 27, 2020): 434–50. https://doi.org/10.1080/1060586X.2020.1786777.

Rock, David. *Authoritarian Argentina: The Nationalist Movement, Its History and Its Impact.* Berkeley: University of California Press, 1993.

Rosenfeld, Bryn. "Reevaluating the Middle-Class Protest Paradigm: A Case-Control Study of Democratic Protest Coalitions in Russia." *American Political Science Review* 111, no. 04 (November 2017): 637–52. https://doi.org/10.1017/S000305541700034X.

Rosenfeld, Bryn. "State Dependency and the Limits of Middle Class Support for Democracy." *Comparative Political Studies* 54, no. 3–4 (July 6, 2020): 411–44. https://doi.org/10.1177/0010414020938085.

Rosenfeld, Bryn. "Survey Research in Russia: In the Shadow of War." *Post-Soviet Affairs* 39, no. 1–2 (December 5, 2022): 38–48. http://www.tandfonline.com/doi/abs/10.1080/1060586X.2022.2151767.

Ross, Michael L. "What Have We Learned about the Resource Curse?" *Annual Review of Political Science* 18, no. 1 (2015): 239–59. https://doi.org/10.1146/annurev-polisci-052213-040359.

Routledge, Clay, and Jamie Arndt. "Self-Sacrifice as Self-Defence: Mortality Salience Increases Efforts to Affirm a Symbolic Immortal Self at the Expense of the Physical Self." *European Journal of Social Psychology* 38, no. 3 (April 2008): 531–41. https://doi.org/10.1002/ejsp.442.

Rowland, Daniel B. *God, Tsar, and People: The Political Culture of Early Modern Russia*. NIU Series in Slavic, East European, and Eurasian Studies. Ithaca, NY: Cornell University Press, 2020.

Sadurski, Wojciech, Michael Sevel, and Kevin Walton, eds. *Legitimacy: The State and Beyond*. 1st ed. Oxford; New York: Oxford University Press, 2019.

Sakwa, Richard. "Putin's Leadership: Character and Consequences." *Europe-Asia Studies* 60, no. 6 (August 2008): 879–97. https://doi.org/10.1080/09668130802161132.

Salmenniemi, Suvi. "Struggling for Citizenship: Civic Participation and the State in Russia." *Demokratizatsiya* 18, no. 4 (2010): 309–28.

Sarkissian, Ani, and Ş. İlgü Özler. "Democratization and the Politicization of Religious Civil Society in Turkey." *Democratization* 20, no. 6 (October 2013): 1014–35. https://doi.org/10.1080/13510347.2012.669895.

Scott, James C. *The Art of Not Being Governed: An Anarchist History of Upland Southeast Asia*. Yale Agrarian Studies Series. New Haven, CT: Yale University Press, 2009.

Scott, James C. "Corruption, Machine Politics, and Political Change." *American Political Science Review* 63, no. 4 (December 1969): 1142–58. https://doi.org/10.2307/1955076.

Scott, James C. *Domination and the Arts of Resistance: Hidden Transcripts*. New Haven, CT; London: Yale University Press, 1990.

Seton-Watson, Hugh. *Nations and States: An Enquiry into the Origins of Nations and the Politics of Nationalism*. Boulder, CO: Westview Press, 1977.

Sharafutdinova, Gulnaz. "Gestalt Switch in Russian Federalism: The Decline in Regional Power under Putin." *Comparative Politics* 45, no. 3 (April 2013): 357–76.

Sharafutdinova, Gulnaz. *The Red Mirror: Putin's Leadership and Russia's Insecure Identity*. New York: Oxford University Press, 2020.

Sharafutdinova, Gulnaz. "Was There a 'Simple Soviet' Person? Debating the Politics and Sociology of 'Homo Sovieticus.'" *Slavic Review* 78, no. 1 (2019): 173–95. https://doi.org/10.1017/slr.2019.13.

Sharafutdinova, Gulnaz, and Rostislav Turovsky. "The Politics of Federal Transfers in Putin's Russia: Regional Competition, Lobbying, and Federal Priorities." *Post-Soviet Affairs* 33, no. 2 (2017): 161–75. https://doi.org/10.1080/1060586X.2016.1163826.

Shearer, David R. *Policing Stalin's Socialism: Repression and Social Order in the Soviet Union, 1924–1953*. The Yale-Hoover Series on Stalin, Stalinism, and the Cold War. New Haven, CT; Stanford, CA: Yale University Press; Hoover Institution, Stanford University, 2009.

Shefter, Martin. *Political Parties and the State: The American Historical Experience*. Princeton Studies in American Politics. Princeton, NJ: Princeton University Press, 1994.

Shen-Bayh, Fiona. "Strategies of Repression: Judicial and Extrajudicial Methods of Autocratic Survival." *World Politics* 70, no. 3 (July 2018): 321–57. https://doi.org/10.1017/S0043887118000047.

Shields Kollmann, Nancy. "Muscovite Political Culture." In *A Companion to Russian History*, edited by Abbott Gleason, 89–104. Blackwell Companions to World History. Chichester, UK; Malden, MA: Wiley-Blackwell, 2009.

Shkel, Stanislav. "Bastions of Tradition: The Ethnic Factor and Political Machines in Russian Regions." *Russian Politics* 4, no. 1 (February 27, 2019): 76–111. https://doi.org/10.1163/2451-8921-00401004.

Shkel, Stanislav. "Why Political Machines Fail: Evidence from Bashkortostan." *Demokratizatsiya* 29, no. 1 (2021): 31–62.

Shleifer, Andrei, and Daniel Treisman. "A Normal Country: Russia after Communism." *Journal of Economic Perspectives* 19, no. 1 (2005): 151–74.

Sidorkin, Oleg, and Dmitriy Vorobyev. "Extra Votes to Signal Loyalty: Regional Political Cycles and National Elections in Russia." *Public Choice* 185, no. 1–2 (October 2020): 183–213. https://doi.org/10.1007/s11127-019-00747-8.

Simpser, Alberto. *Why Governments and Parties Manipulate Elections: Theory, Practice, and Implications*. Political Economy of Institutions and Decisions. Cambridge; New York: Cambridge University Press, 2013.

Sipher, John. "Vladimir Putin Isn't as Russian as He Seems." *Foreign Policy*, December 6, 2017. https://foreignpolicy.com/2017/12/06/vladimir-putin-isnt-as-russian-as-he-seems/.

Skocpol, Theda. *States and Social Revolutions: A Comparative Analysis of France, Russia, and China*. Cambridge: Cambridge University Press, 1979.

Skowronek, Stephen. *Building a New American State: The Expansion of National Administrative Capacities, 1877–1920*. Cambridge; New York: Cambridge University Press, 1982.

Slater, Dan. "Iron Cage in an Iron Fist: Authoritarian Institutions and the Personalization of Power in Malaysia." *Comparative Politics* 36, no. 1 (2003): 81–101.

Slater, Dan. "Revolutions, Crackdowns, and Quiescence: Communal Elites and Democratic Mobilization in Southeast Asia." *American Journal of Sociology* 115, no. 1 (2009): 203–54.

Slater, Dan, and Hillel David Soifer. "The Indigenous Inheritance: Critical Antecedents and State Building in Latin America and Southeast Asia." *Social Science History* 44, no. 2 (2020): 251–74. https://doi.org/10.1017/ssh.2020.2.

Smith-Morris, Carolyn. *Indigenous Communalism: Belonging, Healthy Communities, and Decolonizing the Collective*. New Brunswick, NJ: Rutgers University Press, 2020.

Smyth, Regina. "The Putin Factor: Personalism, Protest, and Regime Stability in Russia: Personalism and Regime Stability in Russia." *Politics and Policy* 42, no. 4 (August 2014): 567–92. https://doi.org/10.1111/polp.12080.

Snegovaya, Maria. "Guns to Butter: Sociotropic Concerns and Foreign Policy Preferences in Russia." *Post-Soviet Affairs* 36, no. 3 (May 3, 2020): 268–79. https://doi.org/10.1080/1060586X.2020.1750912.

Snyder, Richard. "Scaling Down: The Subnational Comparative Method." *Studies in Comparative International Development* 36, no. 1 (2001): 93–110. https://doi.org/10.1007/BF02687586.

Soifer, Hillel David. *State Building in Latin America*. New York: Cambridge University Press, 2016.

Soifer, Hillel, and Matthias vom Hau. "Unpacking the Strength of the State: The Utility of State Infrastructural Power." *Studies in Comparative International Development* 43, no. 3–4 (December 1, 2008): 219–30. https://doi.org/10.1007/s12116-008-9030-z.

Solaz, Hector, Catherine E. De Vries, and Roosmarijn A. de Geus. "In-Group Loyalty and the Punishment of Corruption." *Comparative Political Studies* 52, no. 6 (May 2019): 896–926. https://doi.org/10.1177/0010414018797951.

Solomon, Sheldon, Jeff Greenberg, and Tom Pyszczynski. "The Cultural Animal: Twenty Years of Terror Management Theory and Research." In *Handbook of Experimental Existential Psychology*, edited by Jeff Greenberg, Sander Leon Koole, and Thomas A. Pyszczynski, 13–34. New York: Guilford Press, 2004.

Sperling, Valerie. "Putin's Macho Personality Cult." *Communist and Post-Communist Studies* 49, no. 1 (March 1, 2016): 13–23. https://doi.org/10.1016/j.postcomstud.2015.12.001.

Spruyt, Hendrik. *The Sovereign State and Its Competitors: An Analysis of Systems Change*. Princeton Studies in International History and Politics. Princeton, NJ: Princeton University Press, 1994.

Starodubtsev, Andrey. *Federalism and Regional Policy in Contemporary Russia*. Studies in Contemporary Russia. Abingdon, Oxon; New York: Routledge, 2018.
Stearns, Peter N., ed. "Pugachev, Emelyan Ivanovich (1742–1775)." In *Encyclopedia of European Social History*, 6:289. Biographies/Contributors. Detroit, MI: Charles Scribner's Sons, 2001.
Steinmetz, George. *The Devil's Handwriting: Precoloniality and the German Colonial State in Qingdao, Samoa, and Southwest Africa*. Chicago: University of Chicago Press, 2007.
Stellmacher, Jost, and Thomas Petzel. "Authoritarianism as a Group Phenomenon." *Political Psychology* 26, no. 2 (April 2005): 245–74. https://doi.org/10.1111/j.1467-9221.2005.00417.x.
Stepan, Alfred C. *The State and Society: Peru in Comparative Perspective*. Princeton, NJ: Princeton University Pres, 1978. https://doi.org/10.1515/9781400868926.
Stepan, Alfred. "State Power and the Strength of Civil Society in the Southern Cone of Latin America." In *Bringing the State Back In*, edited by Peter B. Evans, Dietrich Rueschemeyer, and Theda Skocpol, 1st ed., 317–44. Cambridge: Cambridge University Press, 1985. https://doi.org/10.1017/CBO9780511628283.014.
Stephenson, Svetlana. "The Kazan Leviathan: Russian Street Gangs as Agents of Social Order." *Sociological Review* 59, no. 2 (May 2011): 324–47. https://doi.org/10.1111/j.1467-954X.2011.02007.x.
Stokes, Susan C. *Brokers, Voters, and Clientelism: The Puzzle of Distributive Politics*. Cambridge Studies in Comparative Politics. New York: Cambridge University Press, 2013.
Stosny, Steven. *Soar Above: How to Use the Most Profound Part of Your Brain under Any Kind of Stress*. Deerfield Beach, FL: Health Communications, 2016.
Tackett, Nicolas. *The Destruction of the Medieval Chinese Aristocracy*. Harvard-Yenching Institute Monograph Series 93. Cambridge, MA: Harvard University Asia Center, 2014.
"Tatarstan." *Britannica Academic*. Accessed January 22, 2020. https://academic.eb.com/levels/collegiate/article/Tatarstan/71379.
Taylor, Brian D. *State Building in Putin's Russia: Policing and Coercion after Communism*. Cambridge; New York: Cambridge University Press, 2011.
Tilly, Charles. *Coercion, Capital, and European States, AD 990–1992*. Rev. paperback ed. Studies in Social Discontinuity. Cambridge, MA: Blackwell, 1992.
Tilly, Charles. "States and Nationalism in Europe 1492–1992." *Theory and Society* 23, no. 1 (1994): 131–46.
Tilly, C. "Trust and Rule." *Theory and Society* 33, no. 1 (February 2004): 1–30. https://doi.org/10.1023/B:RYSO.0000021427.13188.26.
Tkacheva, Tatiana, and Grigorii V. Golosov. "United Russia's Primaries and the Strength of Political Machines in the Regions of Russia: Evidence from the 2016 Duma Elections." *Europe-Asia Studies* 71, no. 5 (May 30, 2019): 824–39. https://doi.org/10.1080/09668136.2019.1613515.
Tocqueville, Alexis de. *Democracy in America: And Two Essays on America*. Penguin Classics. London: Penguin, 2003.
Treisman, Daniel, ed. *The New Autocracy: Information, Politics, and Policy in Putin's Russia*. Washington, DC: Brookings Institution Press, 2018.
Treisman, Daniel. "Presidential Popularity in a Hybrid Regime: Russia under Yeltsin and Putin." *American Journal of Political Science* 55, no. 3 (July 2011): 590–609. https://doi.org/10.1111/j.1540-5907.2010.00500.x.
Treisman, Daniel. "Putin's Popularity since 2010: Why Did Support for the Kremlin Plunge, Then Stabilize?" *Post-Soviet Affairs* 30, no. 5 (2014): 370–88. https://doi.org/10.1080/1060586X.2014.904541.
Trudolyubov, Maxim. "Drop the Corruption, Keep the Authoritarianism." *New York Times*, February 17, 2020, sec. Opinion. https://www.nytimes.com/2020/02/17/opinion/international-world/putin-russia-government.html.
Tsygankov, Andrei P. *The Strong State in Russia: Development and Crisis*. Oxford; New York: Oxford University Press, 2014.

Ure, John. *The Cossacks*. London: Constable, 1999.
Vaughan, Mary K. *Cultural Politics in Revolution: Teachers, Peasants, and Schools in Mexico, 1930–1940*. Tucson: University of Arizona Press, 1997.
Verkhovsky, Aleksandr, and Galina Kozhevnikova. "The Phantom of Manezhnaya Square: Radical Nationalism and Efforts to Counteract It in 2010." SOVA Center for Information and Analysis, 2011. http://www.sova-center.ru/en/xenophobia/reports-analyses/2011/05/d21561.
Vigilant, Lee Garth, and John B. Williamson. "Symbolic Immortality and Social Theory: The Relevance of an Underutilized Concept." In *Handbook of Death and Dying*, edited by Clifton D. Bryant and Chung Yuan, 173–84. Thousand Oaks, CA: SAGE Publications, 2003. https://doi.org/10.4135/9781412914291.
Viola, Lynne, ed. *Contending with Stalinism: Soviet Power and Popular Resistance in the 1930s*. Ithaca, NY: Cornell University Press, 2002.
Viola, Lynne. *Peasant Rebels under Stalin: Collectivization and the Culture of Peasant Resistance*. New York: Oxford University Press, 1996. https://public.ebookcentral.proquest.com/choice/publicfullrecord.aspx?p=4701715.
von Soest, Christian, and Julia Grauvogel. "Identity, Procedures and Performance: How Authoritarian Regimes Legitimize Their Rule." *Contemporary Politics* 23, no. 3 (2017): 287–305. https://doi.org/10.1080/13569775.2017.1304319.
Vu, Tuong. "Studying the State through State Formation." *World Politics* 62, no. 1 (2010): 148–75.
Wang, Yuhua. "China's State Development in Comparative Historical Perspective." *Newsletter of the Organized Section in Comparative Politics of the American Political Science Association* 29, no. 2 (2019): 50–57.
Wang, Yuhua. "The Political Legacy of Violence during China's Cultural Revolution." *British Journal of Political Science* 51, no. 2 (December 12, 2019): 463–87. https://doi.org/10.1017/S0007123419000255.
Way, Lucan. *Pluralism by Default: Weak Autocrats and the Rise of Competitive Politics*. Baltimore: John Hopkins University Press, 2015.
Weber, Max. *Economy and Society: An Outline of Interpretive Sociology*. Edited by Guenther Roth and Claus Wittich. 2 vols. Berkeley: University of California Press, 2013.
Weber, Max. *The Methodology of the Social Sciences*. Edited by Edward Albert Shils and Henry A. Finch. Glencoe, IL: Free Press, 1949.
Wengle, Susanne, and Christine Evans. "Symbolic State-Building in Contemporary Russia." *Post-Soviet Affairs* 34, no. 6 (November 2, 2018): 384–411. https://doi.org/10.1080/1060586X.2018.1507409.
Wengle, Susanne, and Michael Rasell. "The Monetisation of l'goty: Changing Patterns of Welfare Politics and Provision in Russia." *Europe-Asia Studies* 60, no. 5 (2008): 739–56.
White, Stephen. *Political Culture and Soviet Politics*. London: Macmillan, 1979.
White, Stephen, and Ian McAllistar. "Putin and His Supporters." *Europe-Asia Studies* 55, no. 3 (May 1, 2003): 383–99. https://doi.org/10.1080/0966813032000069304.
Wierzbicka, Anna. *Semantics, Culture, and Cognition: Universal Human Concepts in Culture-Specific Configurations*. New York: Oxford University Press, 1992.
Willerton, John P. *Patronage and Politics in the USSR*. Soviet and East European Studies 82. Cambridge; New York: Cambridge University Press, 1992.
Williams, Kipling D. "Ostracism." *Annual Review of Psychology* 58, no. 1 (January 2007): 425–52. https://doi.org/10.1146/annurev.psych.58.110405.085641.
Wintrobe, Ronald. *The Political Economy of Dictatorship*. Cambridge; New York: Cambridge University Press, 1998.
Yemelianova, Galina M. "Islam and Power." In *Islam in Post-Soviet Russia: Public and Private Faces*, edited by Hilary Pilkington and Galina M. Yemelianova, 61–116. London; New York: RoutledgeCurzon, 2003.
Yudina, Natalia. "In the Absence of the Familiar Article. The State against the Incitement of Hatred and the Political Participation of Nationalists in Russia in 2019." SOVA Center for

Information and Analysis, 2020. http://www.sova-center.ru/en/xenophobia/reports-analyses/2020/03/d42196.

Yudina, Natalia, and Vera Alperovich. "Summer 2011: A New Batch of Neo-Nazi Convicts and Dreams of a Second Manezh." SOVA Center for Information and Analysis, 2011. http://www.sova-center.ru/en/xenophobia/reports-analyses/2011/11/d22976.

Yurchak, Alexei. *Everything Was Forever, until It Was No More: The Last Soviet Generation.* In-Formation Series. Princeton, NJ: Princeton University Press, 2006.

Zavadskaya, Margarita. "On the Harmfulness of Russian Polls." *Riddle Russia* (blog), May 4, 2022. https://ridl.io/on-the-harmfulness-of-russian-polls/.

Байдакова, Анна. "'Реально 'Единую Россию' поддержали 15% избирателей'. Интервью физика Сергея Шпилькина." *Новая газета*, September 20, 2016. https://www.novayagazeta.ru/articles/2016/09/20/69897-realno-edinuyu-rossiyu-podderzhali-15-izbirateley.

Белановский, Сергей, and Михаил Дмитриев. "Политический кризис в России и возможные механизмы его развития." Москва: Центр стратегических разработок, 2011.

Белановский, Сергей, Михаил Дмитриев, Светлана Мисихина, and Татьяна Омельчук. "Движущие силы и перспективы политической трансформации России." Москва: Фонд "Центр стратегических разработок" в сотрудничестве с Российской академией народного хозяйства и государственной службы при Президенте Российской Федерации, November 7, 2011. http://www.svop.ru/public/docs_2011_11_7_1344238631.pdf.

Бобров, В. В., and А. А. Мить. "Кемеровская область." In *Всемирная История. Большая Российская энциклопедия*, 2003. https://w.histrf.ru/articles/kemerovskaya-oblast.

Бузин, А. Ю. *Административные избирательные технологии: московская практика.* Москва: Панорама, 2006.

Волков, Денис. "Почему россияне боятся активизма и благотворительности." *Левада-Центр*, September 14, 2020. https://www.levada.ru/2020/09/14/pochemu-rossiyane-boyatsya-aktivizma-i-blagovoritelnosti/.

Волков, Ю. Г., ed. *Казачество как этносоциальный феномен современной России (по результатам социологического исследования казачества Дона).* Ростов-на-Дону: Антей, 2011.

Восленский, М. С. *Номенклатура: господствующий класс Советского Союза.* Издание второе, исправленное и дополненное. London: Overseas Publications Interchange, 1990.

Галямина, Ю. Е. "Мы-они: Как в дискурсе Владимира Путина разных лет конструируется идентичность." *Политическая наука*, no. 3 (2016): 152–67.

Гончарова, О. А., ed. *Горный Алтай: история социального развития второй половины XX века.* Горно-Алтайск: РИО ГАГУ, 2010.

Группа Белановского. "Новый спектр политических настроений в российском обществе в 2020 году." 2020. http://sbelan.ru/Research-Presentations/NOVYJ-SPEKTR-POLITIChESKIH-NASTROENIJ-V-ROSSIJSKOM-OBShhESTVE-V-2020-g.pdf.

Гудков, Л. Д. *Абортивная модернизация.* Москва: РОССПЭН, 2011.

Гудков, Лев. "Доверие политикам и президентское голосование." *Пресс-выпуск Левада-Центра* (blog), September 3, 2020. https://www.levada.ru/2020/09/03/doverie-politikam-i-prezidentskoe-golosovanie/.

Гудков, Лев. "Механизмы кризисной консолидации." *Контрапункт*, no. 5 (September 2016): 1–14.

Гудков, Лев. "Политическое участие и отношения с государством в России." *Левада-Центр*, March 16, 2021. https://www.levada.ru/2021/03/16/politicheskoe-uchastie-v-otnosheniya-s-gosudarstvom-v-rossii/.

Гудков, Лев. "'Советский человек' сквозь все режимы: 30 лет исследовательского проекта." In *Демонтаж коммунизма: тридцать лет спустя*, edited by Кирилл Рогов. Москва: Новое литературное обозрение, 2021. Р. 268–97.

Гудков, Лев. "Характер и структура массовой тревожности в России." *Левада-Центр*, April 21, 2021. https://www.levada.ru/2021/04/21/harakter-i-struktura-massovoj-trevozhnosti-v-rossii/.

Гудков, Лев. "Человек в неморальном пространстве: к социологии морали в посттоталитарном обществе." *Вестник общественного мнения* 116, no. 3–4 (2013): 118–79.

Гудков, Л. Д., Б. В. Дубин, and Н. А. Зоркая. *Постсоветский человек и гражданское общество*. Москва: Московская школа политических исследований, 2008.

Гудков, Лев, and Евгений Сеньшин. "'На первом месте—армия, на втором—президент, на третьем — ФСБ'." *Znak.com*, March 26, 2021. https://www.znak.com/2021-03-26/doverie_naseleniya_k_prezidentu_snizhaetsya_no_k_massovym_protestam_eto_ne_privodit_pochemu.

Данилин, А.Г. *Бурханизм: Из истории национально-освободительного движения в Горном Алтае*. Горно-Алтайск: Ак-Чечек, 1993.

Дробижева, Л. М., Г. Ф. Габдрахманова, И. М. Кузнецов, Г. И. Макарова, Р. Н. Мусина, Н. М. Мухарямов, С. В. Рыжова, Л. В. Сагитова, Е. А. Ходжаева, and Е. Ю. Щеголькова. *Консолидирующие идентичности и модернизационный ресурс в Татарстане*. Москва.: Институт социологии РАН, 2012.

Камалов, Э., И. Сергеева, В. Костенко, and М. Завадская. "Большой исход: портрет новых мигрантов из России. Отчет по результатам опроса в марте 2022 проекта OutRush." 2022. https://outrush.io/report_march_2022.

Киреев, Александр. "Что может искоренить фальсификации на выборах в России." *Александр Киреев* (blog), September 30, 2016. http://kireev.livejournal.com/1309515.html.

Козеренко, Екатерина. "О недостижимости и прерванных интервью." *Левада-Центр*, November 15, 2022. https://www.levada.ru/2022/11/15/o-nedostizhimosti-i-prervannyh-intervyu/.

Козлова, Наталья. *Советские люди: сцены из истории*. Москва: Европа, 2005.

Лаборатория публичной социологии. "Далекая близкая война: Как россияне воспринимают военные действия в Украине (февраль 2022–июнь 2022)." 2022. http://publicsociologylab.com/war_report.

Лаборатория публичной социологии. "Смириться с неизбежностью: Как россияне оправдывают военное вторжение в Украину? (осень–зима 2022)." 2023. http://publicsociologylab.com/report2.

Левада, Ю. А, ed. *Простой советский человек: опыт социального портрета на рубеже 90-х*. Москва: Издательство "Мировой океан", 1993.

Левада-Центр. "Гордость и идентичность." October 19, 2020. https://www.levada.ru/2020/10/19/gordost-i-identichnost/.

Левада-Центр. "Основные источники информации и популярные журналисты." April 20, 2023. https://www.levada.ru/2023/04/20/osnovnye-istochniki-informatsii-i-populyarnye-zhurnalisty/.

Левада-Центр. "Ответственность и влияние." October 31, 2018. https://www.levada.ru/2018/10/31/otvetstvennost-i-vliyanie-2/.

Левада-Центр. "Права человека." November 20, 2019. https://www.levada.ru/2019/11/20/prava-cheloveka/.

Левада-Центр. "Чувство ответственности и возможности влиять на ситуацию." January 13, 2023. https://www.levada.ru/2023/01/13/chuvstvo-otvetstvennosti-i-vozmozhnosti-vliyat-na-situatsiyu/.

Левинсон, Алексей. "Внуки против бабушек." *Ведомости*, June 11, 2020. https://www.vedomosti.ru/opinion/columns/2020/06/11/832422-vnuki-protiv-babushek.

Лопатин, Леонид Николаевич. *История рабочего движения Кузбасса (1989–1991 гг.)*. Кемерово: Пласт, 1995.

Магун, В. С., and Ася В. Магун. "Идентификация граждан со своей страной: российские данные в контексте международных сравнений." In *Национально-гражданские идентичности и толерантность. Опыт России и Украины в период трансформации*, edited by Л. М. Дробижева and Е. И. Головаха, 202–40. Киев: Институт социологии НАН Украины, Институт социологии РАН, 2007.

Матвеев, М. Н. *Власть и общество в системе местного самоуправления России в 1993-2003 гг.* Самара: Издательство "Самарский университет," 2006.

Мукаева, Л. Н. "История административно-территориального устройства Горного Алтая в прошлом и настоящем." In *Административно-территориальное деление Горного Алтая. Сборник архивных документов,* edited by Р. К. Сагыдыева, Л. Н. Мукаева, and М. А. Яковлева, 8–25. Кемерово, 2016.

Николаев, В. В. *Этнодемографическое развитие коренного населения предгорий Горного Алтая: XIX-начало XXI века.* Новосибирск: Издательство Института археологии и этнографии СО РАН, 2012.

Орешкин, Дмитрий. "Гибридные выборы. Предварительный отчет 'Народного избиркома.'" *Новая газета,* September 20, 2016. https://novayagazeta.ru/articles/2016/09/21/69914-gibridnye-vybory.

Орешкин, Дмитрий. "Зазеркалье избирательной кампании." *New Times,* October 26, 2016. https://newtimes.ru/articles/detail/116599/.

"Политзаключённые и политические репрессии в России в 2021 году." *Правозащитный центр "Мемориал",* March 15, 2022. https://memohrc.org/ru/reports/politzaklyuchyonnye-i-politicheskie-repressii-v-rossii-v-2021-godu.

Понарин, Э. Д., and М. О. Комин. "Дилемма русского национализма: 'Имперский' и этнический национализм в постсоветской России." *Полития,* no. 4 (83) (2016): 82–93.

"Россия полностью и необратимо втянулась в войну." *openDemocracy,* February 24, 2023. https://www.opendemocracy.net/ru/pochemu-rossiyane-podderzhivayut-voinu/.

Русанов, В. В. *Национальный суверенитет и процессы суверенизации Горного Алтая (в первой половине XX века).* Барнаул: АлтГУ, 2010.

Сагитова, Л. В., and Н. М. Мухарямов. *Республика Татарстан: политика идентичности и ее акторы: монография.* Казань: Институт истории имени Ш. Марджани Академии наук Республики Татарстан. Отдел этнологических исследований, 2018.

Самаев, Г. П. *Горный Алтай в XVII— середине XIX в.: Проблемы политической истории и присоединения к России.* Горно-Алтайск: Горно-Алтайское отделение Алтайского книжного издательства, 1991.

Стецовский, Ю. И. *История советских репрессий.* Общественный фонд "Гласность". Москва: Издательство "Знак-СП," 1997.

Тадина, Н. А. "Два взгляда на бурханизм у алтай-кижи." *Журнал социологии и социальной антропологии* 16, no. 4 (2013): 159–66.

Тюхтенева, Светлана Петровна. "Личность и общество у алтайцев: От родовой принадлежности до общеалтайской идентичности." *Oriental Studies* 8, no. 4 (2015): 72–81.

Чемчиева, А. П. *Алтайские субэтносы в поисках идентичности.* Новосибирск: Издательство Института археологии и этнографии СО РАН, 2012.

Шаров-Делоне, Сергей. "Развилка 1400 г. и самодержавный выбор." *Свободная школа Сопротивления,* February 19, 2013. https://www.youtube.com/watch?v=jDpaA7_wTmA&list=WL&index=6.

Шерстова, Людмила. "Бурханизм и проблема новых идентичностей народов Горного Алтая." *Народы и религии Евразии* no. 6 (2013): 243–50.

Шерстова, Людмила. *Бурханизм: истоки этноса и религии.* Томск: Томский государственный университет, 2010.

Шпилькин, Сергей. "История кемеровской аномалии и немного конспирологии." *Podmoskovnik, Livejournal* (blog), October 14, 2016. http://podmoskovnik.livejournal.com/176737.html.

Эппле, Николай. *Неудобное прошлое: Память о государственных преступлениях в России и других странах.* Москва: Новое литературное обозрение, 2020.

Якупов, Валиулла. *Ислам в Татарстане в 1990-е годы.* Казань: Иман, 2005.

List of Cited Primary Sources

Broken Ties. A Film by Andrey Loshak, 2022. https://www.youtube.com/watch?v=5qmQs2LbnaE.

Melkonyants, Grigory. "Очередная 'бомба' с незаконным штабом при администрации." *Facebook* (blog), August 5, 2016. https://www.facebook.com/grigory.melkonyants/posts/1048035861900384.

Nemtsova, Anna. "Russia's Fatalism Has Fatal Consequences against COVID-19." *Daily Beast*, April 20, 2020. https://www.thedailybeast.com/up-against-covid-19-russias-old-fatalism-has-fatal-consequences.

Авалиани, Т. Г. "Наглость правит бал." *Патриот*, November 28, 2003. N 49.

Аграрное молодежное объединение Республики Татарстан. http://amo-rt.tatarstan.ru/, access date June 28, 2019.

Администрация города Кемерово. Постановление от 16 сентября 2016 года N 2382 "Об утверждении муниципальной программы 'Развитие общественных инициатив в городе Кемерово' на 2017—2019 годы." http://docs.cntd.ru/document/441678836, access date March 29, 2017.

Администрация Кемеровской области, Департамент образования и науки. *Основные виды социальной поддержки студентам, учащимся и сотрудникам учреждений образования Кемеровской области*. Кемерово, 2007.

Акимова, Валентина. "Проезд останется бесплатным." *Медицинская газета*, February 11, 2005. N 11. P. 1.

АНО "Информационно-ресурсный центр добровольчества Республики Татарстан." https://dobrovolets.tatarstan.ru/index.htm, access date June 9, 2024.

Антонов, Кирилл. "Депутатскую группу 'Татарстан—новый век' возглавил Артур Абдульзянов." *Коммерсантъ (Волга-Урал)*, September 25, 2019. https://www.kommersant.ru/doc/4103712, access date January 30, 2020.

"Архангельск: кандидат от 'Стоп Шиес' обжаловал недопуск к выборам." *Север.Реалии*, August 19, 2020. https://www.severreal.org/a/30791720.html.

Бальзанова, В. З. "Хороших дел немало." *Земляки*, August 12, 2005. N 33.

"Барометр общественных нужд." *Земляки*, August 8, 2003.

Белоусова, Татьяна. "Вписаны в Золотую летопись города." *Земляки*, June 15, 2007. N 24.

Брежнева, Нина. "На добровольных началах." *Кемерово*, July 6, 2007. N 27.

Будяковская, И. "Были 'ничейные', стали—наши!" *Земляки*, March 30, 2007. N 13.

Васильева, О. "Сажаем картошку и выращиваем кроликов." *Комсомольская правда*, April 15, 2009. N 55. P. 4.

"Ветеранские гостиные." *Ветеран*, April 2, 2013. N 13.

Всероссийская общественная организация ветеранов (пенсионеров) войны и труда. "Об организации." https://veteranorg.ru/about, access date June 9, 2024.

"В Кемеровской области появилось региональное отделение 'Российской партии пенсионеров.'" *Кузнецкий край*, August 17, 2006.

"В поле зрения—800 тысяч судеб." *Земляки*, October 14, 2005. N 42.

"В районах города." *Кемерово*, March 30, 2007, N 13.

ВЦИОМ (Всероссийский центр изучения общественного мнения). "Информационный бюллетень мониторинга." *Мониторинг общественного мнения*, no. 1 (1993).

ВЦИОМ (Всероссийский центр изучения общественного мнения). "Мониторинг перемен: основные тенденции." *Мониторинг общественного мнения* 44, no. 6 (1999).

"Выборы: уроки для проигравших." В круге света. *Эхо Москвы*, September 20, 2016. http://echo.msk.ru/programs/sorokina/1841260-echo/.

Галимова, Наталья. "В Кремле обсудили получение 70% голосов за своего кандидата на выборах." *РБК*, December 26, 2016. http://www.rbc.ru/politics/26/12/2016/58600eff9a794781b168ae26.

Гармоненко, Дарья. "Структуры Ходорковского помогут штабам Навального." *Независимая газета*, March 11, 2021. http://www.ng.ru/politics/2021-03-11/1_8100_politics1.html.

"Главное внимание первичкам." *Ветеран*, October 6, 2009. N 37.
"Главное не лениться." *С тобой*, April 12, 2009. N 28. Р. 2.
"Главы штабов Навального побеждают на муниципальных выборах в Томске и Новосибирске." *Коммерсантъ*, September 14, 2020. https://www.kommersant.ru/doc/4491782.
"Год юбилея." *Кемерово*, January 22, 2010. N 4.
Голованова, Алла. *О времени, о людях, о Тулееве*. Кемерово: Кемеровский полиграфкомбинат, 1999.
"'Голос': бюджетников Тамбова принуждают агитировать за Путина." *Радио Свобода*, January 26, 2018. https://www.svoboda.org/a/28998726.html.
"Голос старшего поколения." *Ветеран*, January 26, 2010. N 4.
Горкунов. "Пенсионный проездной." *Российская газета*, April 11, 2007. N 75. Р. 11.
"Город: анализ, успехи, проблемы, перспективы." *Кемерово*, June 7, 2002. N 23.
Государственное бюджетное учреждение Республиканский центр молодежных формирований по охране общественного порядка "Форпост". "Наша история." https://rcforpost.tatarstan.ru/nasha-istoriya.htm, access date June 9, 2024.
Государственное бюджетное учреждение Республиканский центр молодежных формирований по охране общественного порядка "Форпост". "Об организации." http://rcforpost.tatarstan.ru/rus/o_nas.htm, access date June 9, 2024.
"Губернатор дал поручение мобилизовать бюджетников на выборы." *Калуга 24*, March 5, 2018. https://kaluga24.tv/news/017915.
Гулик, Ольга. "Вместо блока 'Служу Кузбассу'—общественное движение." *Континент Сибирь*, February 16, 2007. https://tayga.info/92951, access date January 30, 2020.
Движение "Голос." "Голос—за честные выборы. История 'Голоса.'" *Голос—за честные выборы*. Accessed June 24, 2021. https://www.golosinfo.org/about#history.
Движение "Голос." "'Голос' обнаружил незаконный штаб 'по организации выборов' в Краснознаменске." *Голос—за честные выборы*, July 26, 2016. http://www.golosinfo.org/ru/articles/103221.
Движение "Голос." "Уговоры и шантаж: Как кандидаты агитируют на выборах 9 сентября." *Голос—за честные выборы*, September 3, 2018. https://www.golosinfo.org/articles/142237.
Джанполадова, Наталья. "Всеобщая мобилизация: как власти заманивают людей на выборы." *Радио Свобода*, March 9, 2018. https://www.svoboda.org/a/29087032.html.
"Дмитрий Гудков запустил 'политический Uber' в Петербурге." *РБК*. January 30, 2018. https://www.rbc.ru/politics/30/01/2018/5a708fe99a794755b1ea2ad7.
Драбкин, Леонид, and ОВД-Инфо. "Как теперь протестовать и защищать себя, оставаясь в России." *Как теперь / проект ОВД-Инфо*, October 25, 2022. https://www.youtube.com/watch?v=30j6EHL3Uho.
Ермакова, Нелли. "Вместе в добрый путь!" *Земляки*, June 9, 2006. N 23.
Ермакова, Нелли. "Когда дело ладится." *Земляки*, February 7, 2003. N 6 [639].
Ермакова, Нелли. "О чем скажут 'незабудки'." *Земляки*, January 12, 2007. N 2.
Ермакова, Нелли. "Преграды на пути первопроходцев." *Земляки*, November 3, 2006. N 44.
Затари, Амалия. "'Во-первых, они не воюют'. Кто и зачем в России собирает помощь для российских военных в Украине." *BBC News Русская служба*, April 8, 2022. https://www.bbc.com/russian/features-61000576.
Зинчук, Валентина. "Что знаете о льготах?" *Кемерово*, June 8, 2007. N 23.
Иванов, Сергей. "Аман Тулеев: 'Наберу больше голосов—Кузбассу будет легче жить.'" *Кузнецкий край*, March 10, 2000.
"... и много радости." *Кемерово*, September 14, 2007. N 37.
Ильина, Надежда. "Дойти до каждого." *Кемерово*, December 12, 2008. N 50.
Итоги Всероссийской переписи населения 2010 года. Приложение 7. Национальный состав населения по субъектам Российской Федерации. https://www.gks.ru/free_doc/new_site/perepis2010/croc/Documents/Materials/tab7.xls, access date February 12, 2020.

Итоги работы с населением за 2015 г. http://www.kemerovo.ru/administration/rabota_s_naseleniem_.html, access date April 22, 2016.

Итоги работы с населением за 2016 г. http://www.kemerovo.ru/administration/rabota_s_naseleniem_.html, access date March 29, 2017.

Канкия, Давид. "Как медики во время эпидемии коронавируса будут за поправки в Конституцию агитировать." *Голос—за честные выборы*, March 20, 2020. https://www.golosinfo.org/articles/144169.

Кикиой, Татьяна. "Решаем вместе." *Кемерово*, May 15, 2009. N 20.

"К кемеровчанам—с отчетом." *Кемерово*, December 17, 2010. N 51.

Команда Юлии Галяминой. "Проекты." Accessed June 24, 2021. http://galiamina.ru/projects.

Корня, Анастасия, and Петр Козлов. "Партия власти агитирует за себя с помощью неполитических мероприятий." *Ведомости*, August 11, 2016. http://www.vedomosti.ru/politics/articles/2016/08/12/652704-partiya-vlasti-agitiruet-sebya-pomoschyu-nepoliticheskih-meropriyatii.

Королева, Наталия, and Анна Хрусталева. "Интервью с дочерью легендарного конструктора Сергея Королева." *Российское историческое общество*, April 12, 2018. https://historyrussia.org/polemika/intervyu-s-istorikami/intervyu-s-docheryu-legendarnogo-konstruktora-sergeya-koroleva.html.

"Коротко." *Кемерово*, August 24, 2007. N 34.

"Коротко." *Кемерово*, February 8, 2008. N 6.

"Кремль определил явку на голосовании по поправкам к Конституции." *Радио Свобода*, June 8, 2020. https://www.svoboda.org/a/30658724.html.

Кузбасское соглашение между Федерацией профсоюзных организаций Кузбасса, Коллегией Администрации Кемеровской области и работодателями Кемеровской области на 2010-2012 годы. Document obtained from the Kemerovo regional library. Catalog number 66.72 K89 4/540726.

"Лидер 'Стоп-Шиес' Олег Мандрыкин собрался в Госдуму от партии 'Яблоко.'" *Znak.com*, May 7, 2021. https://www.znak.com/2021-05-07/lider_stop_shies_oleg_mandrykin_sobralsya_v_gosdumu_ot_partii_yabloka.

Логинова, Екатерина. "Шахтерский край города Кемерово." *Кемерово*, July 29, 2005. N 31.

Лукьянова, Инна. "Аман во спасение." *Профиль*, July 5, 1999. http://www.profile.ru/arkhiv/item/40853-items_3631.

Лукьянова, Ирина. "'Коллеги, регистрируемся, скриншот в личку!'. Учителей в Москве заставляют голосовать—почему они молчат?" *Новая газета*, June 15, 2020. https://novayagazeta.ru/articles/2020/06/13/85826-kollegi-registriruemsya-skrinshot-v-lichku.

Мерзликин, Павел. "'Голосование—это должностная обязанность.' По всей России бюджетников и работников предприятий сгоняют на голосование за поправки в Конституцию—несмотря на коронавирус. Вот как это устроено." *Meduza*, June 24, 2020. https://meduza.io/feature/2020/06/24/golosovanie-eto-dolzhnostnaya-obyazannost.

Микельсон, Татьяна. "Знать каждого—по паспорту." *Земляки*, November 9, 2007. N 45 (897).

Милютина, Наталья. "Ни дня без строчки." *Земляки*, March 28, 2008. N 13.

Милютина, Наталья. "Предназначение защищать." *Земляки*, December 14, 2007. N 50.

Министерство внутренних дел по республике Татарстан. "'Форпост' подвел итоги работы и наметил планы на будущий год." December 4, 2018. https://16.xn--b1aew.xn--p1ai/news/item/15152763/.

Министерство по делам молодежи Республики Татарстан. "Модель системы психологической помощи населению в Республике Татарстан." http://minmol.tatarstan.ru/rus/model-sistemi-psihologicheskoy-pomoshchi-naseleniy.htm, access date June 9, 2024.

Министерство по делам молодежи, спорту и туризму Республики Татарстан, Республиканский центр молодежных, инновационных и профилактических программ. *Деятельность учреждений по месту жительства: Информационный бюллетень за 2007 г.*, edited by М. З. Галеева, А. Г. Синеглазова, Э. И. Читалина, А. Ю. Галимова, and И. В. Герасимова. Казань: РЦМИПП, 2008.

Министерство по делам молодежи и спорту Республики Татарстан. *Материалы к коллегии "Итоги 2002 года и задачи Министерства по делам молодежи и спорту Республики Татарстан на 2003 год".* Edited by М. М. Бариев. Казань: РЦИМ, 2003.

Министерство по делам молодежи, спорту и туризму Республики Татарстан. *Материалы коллегии "Итоги работы Министерства по делам молодежи, спорту и туризму Республики Татарстан за 2005 год и задачи на 2006 год."* Edited by М. М. Бариев. Казань: РУМЦ, 2006.

Министерство по делам молодежи, спорту и туризму Республики Татарстан. *Материалы коллегии "Итоги работы Министерства по делам молодежи, спорту и туризму Республики Татарстан за 2008 год".* Edited by М. М. Бариев. Казань: РЦМИПП, 2009.

"Мухаметшин: Движение 'ТНВ' стало мощной опорой социально-экономической и духовной стабильности в РТ." *Татар-Информ*, June 28, 2019. https://www.tatar-inform.ru/news/society/28-06-2019/muhametshin-dvizhenie-tnv-stalo-moschnoy-oporoy-sotsialno-ekonomicheskoy-i-duhovnoy-stabilnosti-v-rt-5181328, access date January 30, 2020.

Мухаметшина, Елена. "Три четверти россиян говорят о необходимости сильной руки в руководстве страны." *Ведомости*, February 25, 2020. https://www.vedomosti.ru/society/articles/2020/02/24/823697-rossiyan-neobhodimosti.

"'Мы чужое не берем, а свое назад вернем'. Z-агитация в школах и детсадах." *Север.Реалии*, April 4, 2022. https://www.severreal.org/a/agitaziya-v-shkolah-i-detsadah/31781931.html.

Неворотова, Нина Павловна. "И с бедой и с радостью идут к нам ..." *Земляки*, September 26, 2003. N 43.

Неворотова, Нина Павловна, and Нелли Ермакова. "Милосердие нацелено в завтра." *Земляки*, December 29, 2006. N 52.

Неворотова, Н.П., М.М. Кушникова, and В.В. Тогулев. *Отдать свой опыт людям ... Из истории ветеранского движения Кузбасса.* Кемерово: Кузбассвузиздат, 2013.

"Ни дня без дела." *Кемерово*, December 17, 2010. N 51.

"Нина Павловна Неворотова." *Ветеран*, October 15, 2013. N 39.

Об итогах деятельности центров по работе с населением в 2013 г. (printed brochure at a community center; copied during fieldwork).

Общественная палата Кемеровской области. "Союз женщин Кузбасса." https://opko42.ru/soyuz-zhenshchin-kuzbassa/, access date June 9, 2024.

"Основа успеха—в первичных организациях!" *Ветеран*, October 21, 2003. N 40.

"'Ощущение, что школьников уже давно готовят к войне'. В школах Оренбурга проводят 'патриотические уроки'." *Radio Free Europe / Radio Liberty*, March 8, 2022. https://www.idelreal.org/a/31740500.html.

Полыгаева, Дарья. "'Соцработники часто настраивают пенсионеров голосовать за партию власти': Член УИК в Ново-Переделкино о ходе голосования." *Телеканал Дождь*, September 10, 2017. https://tvrain.ru/teleshow/here_and_now/sotsrabotniki_chasto_nastraivajut_pensionerov_golosovat-444406/.

Правительство Республики Татарстан. "Молодежные общественные объединения Республики Татарстан." http://prav.tatarstan.ru/rus/molodejj.htm, access date June 25, 2019.

Пресс-служба администрации города. "Пункты стали центрами." *Кемерово*, December 29, 2006. N 52.

Пресс-служба администрации города. "Центры есть, работа будет." *Кемерово*, August 12, 2005. N 33.

Пресс-служба Горсовета народных депутатов. "'Молодая гвардия' укрепляет тылы." *Кемерово*, February 16, 2007. N 7.
"Равных нет в рукопашном бою." *Кузбасс*, June 1, 2005. N 95.
Рассказова, Ирина. "Бой политического значения." *Кемерово*, October, 26, 2007. N 43.
"Республиканский центр молодежных (студенческих) формирований по охране общественного порядка 'Форпост.'" http://minmol.tatarstan.ru/rus/podvedy.htm?department_id=89916, access date February 3, 2020.
Республиканское общественное движение "Татарстан—Новый век"—"Татарстан—Яңа гасыр". "История." https://www.tnvrod.ru/about/history, access date June 9, 2024.
Росстат. *Демографический ежегодник России. 2012: Статистический сборник.* Москва: Росстат, 2012.
Росстат. *Регионы России. Социально-экономические показатели. 2012: Статистический сборник.* Москва: Росстат, 2012.
Росстат. *Регионы России. Социально-экономические показатели. 2013: Статистический сборник.* Москва: Росстат, 2013.
Росстат. *Регионы России. Социально-экономические показатели. 2014: Статистический сборник.* Москва: Росстат, 2014.
Росстат. *Регионы России. Социально-экономические показатели. 2015: Статистический сборник.* Москва: Росстат, 2015.
Росстат. *Российский статистические ежегодник. 2007: Статистический сборник.* Москва: Росстат, 2007.
Росстат. *Российский статистические ежегодник. 2008: Статистический сборник.* Москва: Росстат, 2008.
Росстат. *Российский статистические ежегодник. 2012: Статистический сборник.* Москва: Росстат, 2012.
Росстат. *Российский статистические ежегодник. 2014: Статистический сборник.* Москва: Росстат, 2014.
Росстат. *Российский статистические ежегодник. 2016: Статистический сборник.* Москва: Росстат, 2016.
Савин, Глеб. "'Жёлтая' инициатива: в Республике Алтай работников образования принуждают к выходу из профсоюза." *Солидарность*, November 23, 2011. https://www.solidarnost.org/thems/profsoyuznaya-zhizn/profsoyuznaya-zhizn_8462.html, access date February 28, 2020.
Сатановский, Сергей. "О чем говорили на форуме муниципальных депутатов в Clubhouse." *DW.COM*, March 21, 2021. https://www.dw.com/ru/o-chem-govorili-na-forume-municipalnyh-deputatov-v-clubhouse/a-56946079.
Сафиуллин, Л. К., Р. Р. Мухамадеева, and М. М. Тухватова. *Применение избирательных технологий в условиях города и сельской местности. Методические рекомендации для кандидатов в депутаты в органы местного самоуправления. Долгосрочная целевая программа "Сельская молодежь Республики Татарстан на 2011–2015 годы".* Казань: РЦМИПП, 2011.
Сваровский, И. В. "Заслужили всей жизнью." *Земляки*, October 3, 2008. N 40.
"Слово активистов." *Кемерово*, April 4, 2008. N 14.
Сорокин, Александр. "Коммунисты не станут угождать властям." *Край*, March 12, 2004.
Союз пенсионеров России. Общероссийская общественная организация. Кемеровская область. http://www.rospensioner.ru/region/122, access date March 15, 2017.
Старожилов, Антон. "Кузбасс прильнул к 'Медведю.'" *Эксперт*, November 29, 1999. N 45(208).
Старцев, П. А. "Ступенька в завтра." *Земляки*, October 10, 2008. N 41.
"ТОС—самая близкая власть." *Кемерово*, January 26, 2007. N 4.
Тотыш, Наталья. "С пользой и интересом." *Кемерово*, December 22, 2006. N 51.
Тулеев, Аман. *Оставаться самим собой. Кемерово*: Кемеровское книжное издательство, 1999.

"У нас пока нет сладких пилюль, чтобы давать вместе с горькими." *Новая газета. Понедельник*, June 8, 1998.

"Участники политического клуба студентов РТ встретились с депутатом Госсовета Татарстана." *Татар-Информ*, March 28, 2006. https://www.tatar-inform.ru/news/society/28-03-2006/uchastniki-politicheskogo-kluba-studentov-rt-vstretilis-s-deputatom-gossoveta-tatarstana-5619809.

Федорова, Галина Федоровна, and Нелли Ермакова. "Инициативы, продиктованные жизнью." *Земляки*, October 13, 2006. N 41.

Фефелова, Елена. "Город делится опытом." *Кемерово*, June 26, 2009. N 26.

Фефелова, Елена. "Готовимся к переписи." *Кемерово*, July 3, 2009. N 27.

Фохт, Елизавета, Сергей Горяшко, and Петр Козлов. "Независимые кандидаты назвали успехом выборы в Москве." *BBC News Русская служба*, September 11, 2017. https://www.bbc.com/russian/features-41222506.

Хамраев, Виктор, Ирина Нагорных, Наталья Корченкова, and Софья Самохина. "Валдайский клуб убедили в безальтернативности Владимира Путина." *Коммерсантъ*, October 23, 2014. N 193. https://www.kommersant.ru/doc/2595799.

"Центр работы—первички." *Ветеран*, March 27, 2007. N 12.

Черемнов, Сергей, and Григорий Шалакин. *Аман Тулеев—человек, политик, губернатор: оценки, признания, откровения*. Кемерово: Центр-Полиграф, 2004.

"Число новых сельских клубов в Татарстане к концу года вырастет до 285." *Татар-Информ*, October 15, 2018. https://www.tatar-inform.ru/news/2018/10/15/630072/.

Чурпита, В. М. "Бывших шахтеров не бывает." *Земляки*, July 25, 2008. N 30.

Шатская, Таисия. *Доверие*. Кемерово: Кузбассвузиздат, 2008.

Шилова, Мария. "Хорошее настроение делаем сами." *Кемерово*, December 12, 2008. N 50.

Шипачев, К. В., Р. М. Дерябина, and В. А. Шабанов. *Меры социальной поддержки жителей Кемеровской области: Сборник информационных материалов*. Кемерово: Кузбассвузиздат, 2008.

Штаб Навального в Санкт-Петербурге. "Муниципальные выборы 2019." September 27, 2018. https://shtab.navalny.com/hq/sankt-peterburg/595/.

Index

For the benefit of digital users, indexed terms that span two pages (e.g., 52–53) may, on occasion, appear on only one of those pages.

Tables and figures are indicated by an italic *t* and *f* following the page number.

active resistance. *See* resistance
activism, compliant, 137, 149, 154, 164–67, 174, 176–78
Ahmed, Abiy, 7–8
Alexander II, 151–52
Altai Republic
  autonomy and, 59–60
  China and, 59
  clan networks in, 72–74, 105–7
  ethnicity and, 53–54, 59–61, 72–74, 105
  Gazprom and, 60–61
  group loyalties and, 72, 105
  identity and, 59–61, 72
  interview list for, 223
  labor unions in, 96
  legitimate authority and, 72, 75–77
  loan money in, 73
  nonstate community leaders and, 75–77
  outsider state in, 72–77
  pluralist political environment in, 105–7
  political machines and, 105–12
  post-Soviet Russia and, 60–61
  presidential election of 2012 and, 49–50
  public organizations and, 72–74, 94, 96, 101
  regional history of, 59–61
  reproduction of boundary between civic and political and, 110–12
  Russian Old Believers in, 59–60
  safety net in nonstate communities and, 72–75
  settlement of, 59–60
  as small and predominantly rural, 51
  social norms and, 72–75
  socioeconomic profiles of, 50–54
  Soviet Union and, 60
  state-formation in, 59–61
  surrounding region of, 51
  tribal transition of, 59–61
  Tsarist Russia and, 59

utility maximization as driver of clientelism in, 107–10
analysis. *See* fieldwork data collection and analysis; interview list; quantitative analysis; Russian authoritarianism; social roots of authoritarianism
antistatist societies. *See* statist and antistatist societies
authoritarianism. *See* division-based authoritarianism; Russian authoritarianism; social roots of authoritarianism; statist and antistatist societies; unity and division; unity-based authoritarianism
authoritarian legitimacy, 21–22
authority, group. *See* group authority
authority, legitimate. *See* legitimate authority
autonomy
  Altai Republic and, 59–60
  Cossacks and, 62–63
  group authority and, 30–31
  psychological need for, 22, 134–35, 145
  public organizations and, 94–96
  Rostov region and, 62–63, 94–96
  statist and antistatist societies and, 22, 24, 30–31
  Tatarstan Republic and, 55–57

bargaining, 107–10
belonging, 22–23, 28–29, 72, 115, 141, 143, 145
blurred boundary between civil and political, 113–15, 166–67
building unity, 112–16
buying loyalty, 105–12

case selection, 46–50, 48*f*, 49*t*
Catherine II, 55, 149, 151
centralized public organizations. *See* public organizations

China
  Altai Republic and, 59
  aristocratic elites in, 25–26
  authoritarian regime in, 2, 4, 6–7, 17, 36
  formation of state in, 25–26
  group identity and, 17
  Huang Chao Rebellion in, 25–26
  local lineages in, 179–80
  political competition and, 25–26
  popular support for regime in, 4
  Russian authoritarianism's parallels to, 11
  as statist, 6–7
  team logic and, 26–28
  unity-based authoritarianism in, 8, 17
  unity cultivated within, 2
civil society, 32–36, 101–3
"collective institutions," 101–3, 113
community centers, 79–86, 116, 121–22
compliant activism, 137, 149, 154, 164–67, 174, 176–78
control of public space and discourse, 121–24
Cossacks, 62–63, 74–76, 105
Crimea invasion, 140–41, 142, 164, 170–71, 175

data sources and variables, 189–98, 190t, 193t, 194t, 196t, *See also* fieldwork data collection and analysis; interview list; quantitative analysis
Decembrist revolt (1825), 151
decentralized public organizations, 94–101
democracy as balance point, 6–9, 15–16
democratic institutions, 3, 5, 8, 137
developmental state, 69–71
distorted idea of representation, 115–16
division and unity. *See* unity and division
division-based authoritarianism, 4–5, 6, 8, 11, 15, 17, 40, 42, 64

economic inequality, 68–69, 162–63
economic modernization, 69–71, 145–46
election of 2012. *See* presidential election of 2012
electoral resilience, 46–47, 64
elements of democracy, 7–10, 15
Elena's residential council, 78–79
empirical approach of current volume, 11–13, 12t
Ethiopia, ethnic tensions in, 6–8
ethnicity
  Altai Republic and, 53–54, 59–61, 72–74, 105
  overview of, 8, 50, 53–54, 65
  Rostov region and, 61–63, 74, 106
  Tatarstan Republic and, 53–57
  See also identity
expansion of Veterans' Councils, 130–34

false consciousness, 20–21
fieldwork data collection and analysis
  developing the argument, 202–4
  interviews, 200, 201t
  local library research, 199–200
  overview of, 199
  See also data sources and variables; interview list; quantitative analysis
Forpost movement, 90–91, 102, 122
"Freedom in the World" report, 2

Galiamina, Yulia, 172, 173
Gazprom, 60–61
Golden Horde, 54–55, 147–48
GONGOs (government-organized nongovernmental organizations), 35, 92–93
Gramsci, Antonio, 20–21
grassroots politics
  civil society and, 32–36
  GONGOs and, 35
  infrastructural state power and, 32–36
  maintenance of, 32, 38
  overview of, 5, 6, 11
  recruitment of local activists and, 33–35
  social roots of authoritarianism and, 5, 6, 11
  statist and antistatist societies and, 31–40
group authority
  agency and compliance contradiction and, 20–21
  authoritarian legitimacy and, 21–22
  autonomy and, 30–31
  belonging and, 22–23
  corruption and, 30
  definition of, 20
  examples of, 20
  false consciousness and, 20–21
  legitimate authority and, 20–23
  monopolization of, 26
  political environment and, 26–28, 27f
  resistance and, 28–29
  scholarship on, 20–21
  sets of interests and, 21–23
  social norms and, 20
  statist and antistatist societies and, 17–18, 19–31, 27f, 33
  team logic and, 26–28
  third face of power and, 19–23
  voluntary compliance with, 20–22, 23
  women and traditional roles and, 20–21
  See also legitimate authority
group loyalties, 30, 72, 105–6, 111, 113, 117, 175
Gudkov, Dmitry, 172

INDEX 255

Haggard, Stephan, 182
hijacking a social movement by the state, 125–34
Huang Chao Rebellion (875-884), 25–26

identity
   Altai Republic and, 59–61, 72
   civic identity, 1, 5, 8
   collective identity, 4, 18, 26, 139, 140, 159
   group identity, 4, 13, 17, 19, 106
   inclusivity and, 140–41
   Kemerovo region and, 57
   Putin and, 139, 140–42
   Rostov region and, 61–62, 72, 106
   Russian authoritarianism and, 4, 139, 143, 145–46, 150–51, 154, 159
   social roots of authoritarianism and, 3–5
   statist and antistatist societies and, 5–7, 18–19, 26, 32, 141–42
   Tatarstan Republic and, 57, 70–71
   unity and division and, 8, 11
   See also ethnicity
imperial Russia. *See* Tsarist Russia
inequality, 68–69, 162–63
informality as driven by the state, 38–40
infrastructural state power, 17–18, 32–36, 34*f*, 47
intelligentsia, 150–52, 156–57, 158
interview list
   for Altai Republic, 223
   for Kemerovo region, 223
   for Rostov region, 224
   for Tatarstan Republic, 224
Iran
   authoritarian regime in, 2, 6–7, 24–25, 180–81
   Islamic Revolution in, 6–7, 180
   state and religion relationship in, 6–7, 24–25, 180–81
   unity cultivated within, 2
Ivan III, 147–48
Ivan the Terrible, 25–26, 54–55

Kaufman, Robert, 182
Kemerovo region
   activists as driving force in mobilization and, 118–19
   activities of centers and councils in, 82–86
   Aman Tuleyev's takeover of Veterans' Councils in, 128–30
   blurred boundary between civil and political in, 113–15
   collective institutions in, 101–3, 113
   community centers and, 79–86, 116, 121–22
   compliant activism and, 154
   control of public space and discourse and, 121–24
   distorted idea of representation and, 115–16
   economic inequality in, 68–69
   Elena's residential council and, 78–79
   expansion of Veterans' Councils and, 130–34
   functions of public organizations in, 117–25
   grassroot politics in, 64, 78
   hijacking of a social movement by the state in, 125–34
   identity and, 57
   infrastructure of public organizations and, 79–82
   interview list for, 223
   leadership of Veterans' Councils in, 132
   management of existing and potential discontent and, 119–21
   media complex in, 133
   mining industry in, 52–53, 57, 58
   mobilization and co-optation and, 117–19
   number of councils and activists in, 82*f*
   political machines and, 105–12, 125–34
   post-Soviet Russia in, 126–28
   presidential election of 2012 and, 49–50
   pride and loyalty in, 71–72
   public organizations and, 66–69, 77–94
   regional branches of Pensioners' Union and, 133–34
   residential councils and, 78–86, 82*f*
   short history of Veterans' Councils in, 126–28
   social policy in, 66–68
   social statism makes social movements vulnerable and, 134
   socioeconomic profiles of, 50–54
   Soviet Union and, 58, 126–28
   stability of electoral performance and, 124–25
   standardization of councils in, 81–82
   state as collective leader in, 71–72
   state as protector in, 66–68
   state-formation in, 57–59
   structure of Veterans' Councils in, 130–33
   surrounding region of, 51
   team logic and, 66–72
   Trans-Siberian railroad and, 57
   Tsarist Russia and, 57
   Tuleyev as caring patriarch in, 66–68
   urbanization of, 51
   Veterans' Councils in, 118–19, 122, 125–34
   workers movement in, 58
   World War II and, 58
   See also newspaper publications (residential committees and community centers); newspaper publications (Veterans' Organizations); Veterans' Councils

Khodorkovsky, Mikhail, 163, 168–69, 172, 173
Kisliuk, Mikhail, 128–29, 133
Kurultai of the Altai, 60–61

labor unions, 94, 96, 100, 125, 128–29
legitimate authority
   Altai Republic and, 72, 75–77
   authoritarian legitimacy and, 21
   definition of, 21
   group authority and, 20–23
   nonstate community leaders and, 75–77
   performance legitimacy and, 142–43
   public organizations and, 75–77
   Rostov region and, 72, 75–77
   statist and antistatist societies and, 24, 32
   See also group authority
Levada, Yurii, 157–58
Levchenko, Sergei, 171–72
Levitsky, Steven, 9–10
local library research, 199–200
Lukes, Steven, 20–21

Maduro, Nicolás, 1–2
management of existing and potential discontent, 119–21
Medvedev, Dmitry
   castling of, 43–44, 169
   investigation into properties and, 172
   presidential election of 2012 of, 43–44, 43*f*, 50*f*, 124
   as Putin's alter ego, 43–44
   region selection and, 46, 49
   youth organizations and, 99
Meeting Place Cannot Be Changed, The (film), 155
methodological approach to regional research, 46–50
Mexico, authoritarian regime in, 5, 29, 36
Migdal, Joel, 6
Aleksei Mikhailovich, 151
minimal interference, state strategy of, 97–101
mining industry, 52–53, 57, 58, 130–31
Minnikhanov, Rustam, 72
mobilization and co-optation, 117–19
model specification, 185, 186*t*, 187*t*

nationalism, 140–42
Navalny, Alexey, 169–70, 172, 173
nested analysis, 46–50
Nevorotova, Nina, 130–34
newspaper publications (residential committees and community centers), 209–14
newspaper publications (Veterans' Organizations)
   across Russia, 215–18
   Keremerovo region, 218–22
   organizational development and activities, 216–18, 220
   overview of, 215
   political positions, 215–16, 218–19
NGOs (nongovernmental organizations), 35, 40–41, 92–93, 94–96, 97, 100–2, 167–68, 170–72. *See also* GONGOs
Nicholas II, 152
nonstate community leaders, 75–77
nonstate groups, 24, 29–30, 31–32, 33–36, 72, 75–77, 103, 145–46, 180

Open Russia (NGO), 172, 173
Orthodox Church, 148
outsider state, 72–77, 101–3. *See also* public organizations; team logic; unity and division

passive resistance. *See* resistance
performance legitimacy, 142–43
personalism, 139
Peter III, 151
Pipes, Richard, 143, 145, 158
pluralist political environment, 105–7
political and the civic. *See* political machines
political competition, 2–3, 5, 6–7, 25–29, 27*f*, 31–32, 35, 37, 182–83
political machines
   Achilles' heel of state-led unity and, 134–35
   activists as driving force in mobilization and, 118–19
   Altai Republic and, 105–12
   Aman Tuleyev's takeover of Veterans' Councils and, 128–30
   in antistatist societies, 105–12
   blurred boundary between civil and political and, 113–15
   building unity and, 112–16
   buying loyalty and, 105–12
   challenge of stable electoral performance and, 110
   control of public space and discourse and, 121–24
   distorted idea of representation and, 115–16
   expansion of Veterans' Councils and, 130–34
   functions of, 117–25
   hijacking a social movement by the state and, 125–34
   history of Veterans' Councils and, 126–28

Kemerovo region and, 105–12, 125–34
management of existing and potential discontent and, 119–21
mobilization and co-optation and, 117–19
overview of, 104–5, 135–36
pluralist political environment and, 105–7
political functions of public organizations and, 117–25
regional political machines, 45
reproduction of boundary between civic and political and, 110–12
Rostov region and, 105, 106–12
social movement vulnerability and, 134
stability of electoral performance and, 124–25
statist and antistatist societies and, 105–16
in statist societies, 112–16
structure of, 105
Tatarstan Republic and, 105–12, 117–25
team logic and, 104, 112, 115–16
utility maximization as driver of clientelist forms of, 107–10, 117, 124
Veterans' Councils and, 125–34
post-Soviet Russia
active resistance and, 168–72, 173–74
Altai Republic and, 60–61
blending of civic and political functions and, 166–67
civic initiatives and, 170
community organizations and, 165
compliance and, 172–77
compliant activism and, 164–67
Cossacks and, 63
Kemerovo region and, 126–28
Open Russia and, 173
passive resistance and, 167–68, 176
public opinion polls and, 160–61, 170–71
regional leadership and, 69
repression and, 172–77
resistance and, 166–67, 172–77
Rostov region and, 63
Russian authoritarianism and, 159–77
search for a just state in, 159–77
social roots of Putin's support in, 164–67
Tartars and, 55
Tatarstan Republic and, 56–57
Ukraine and, 172–77, 181
Veterans' Councils and, 126–28
presidential election of 2012
Altai Republic and, 49–50
election of 2008 contrasted with, 46–47
electoral resilience and, 46–47
Kemerovo region and, 49–50

protests following, 44
puzzle of, 11–12, 43–44
regional political machines and, 45
results of, 44
Rostov region and, 49–50
Tatarstan Republic and, 49–50
variation in performance of regional political machines and, 46
pride and loyalty, 71–72
propaganda, 3, 4–5, 118, 126, 140, 153, 157, 170–71, 177
publications. *See* newspaper publications (residential committees and community centers); newspaper publications (Veterans' Organizations)
public discourse and space, 121–24
public opinion polls, 1, 90, 157–58, 160–61, 170–71, 174, 176–77
public organizations
activities of centers and councils, 82–86
Altai Republic and, 72–74, 94, 96, 101
autonomy and, 94–96
centralized public organizations, 77–94
civil society and, 101–3
"collective institutions" and, 101–3
community centers and residential councils and, 78–86
decentralized public organizations, 94–101
developmental state and, 69–71
economic inequality and, 68–69
Elena's Residential Council, 78–79
infrastructure and activities of youth organizations and, 88–91
infrastructure of residential councils and community centers and, 79–82
Kemerovo region and, 66–69, 77–94
legitimate authority and, 75–77
nonstate community leaders and, 75–77
origins of Tatarstan's youth organizations and, 86–88
outsider state and, 72–77, 101–3
overview of, 65, 103
political functions of, 36–38, 117–25
pride and loyalty and, 71–72
residential councils and, 78–79
Rostov region and, 72–77, 94–101
safety net in nonstate communities and, 72–75
social norms and, 72–75
state as protector and, 66–68
state leadership beyond the formal state and, 92–94
state strategy of minimal interference and, 97–101

public organizations (*cont.*)
  statist and antistatist societies and, 32–36
  Tatarstan Republic and, 69–72, 86–94
  team logic and, 66–72, 101–3
  youth organizations and, 86–94
public space and discourse, 121–24
Pugachev, Yemelyan, 150
Putin, Vladimir
  active resistance and, 168–72
  approval rating of, 43–44, 43*f*, 169, 170–71
  blending of civic and political functions and, 166–67
  castling of Medvedev and, 169
  civic initiatives and, 170
  community organizations and, 165
  compliance and, 172–77
  Crimea invasion under, 164
  identified with Russia, 139
  identity and, 139, 140–42
  macho image of, 139
  Medvedev as alter ego of, 43–44
  nationalism and, 140–42
  Navalny and, 169–70
  oligarch crackdown of, 163
  passive resistance and, 167–68
  performance legitimacy and, 142–43
  personalism and, 139
  political culture and, 143–47
  presidential election of 2012 of, 43–44
  psychology of leadership and, 139
  public image of, 138, 163–64
  public opinion polls and, 43–44, 43*f*, 169, 170–71
  regime overview of, 138–43
  repression and, 172–77
  resistance and, 166–67, 172–77
  Russian authoritarianism and, 138–43
  search for a just state and, 143–47, 146*f*
  social contract and, 142–43
  social roots of support for, 164–67
  statism and, 138–43
  team logic and, 163–67
  Ukraine and, 164, 172–77
  Yeltsin and, 138, 161–64
  See also presidential election of 2012

quantitative analysis
  cases excluded because of missing data, 198
  data sources and variables, 189–98, 190*t*, 193*t*, 194*t*, 196*t*
  influential observations, 198
  interpretation of population rather than sample model, 185–86
  Model 2 diagnostics, 198
  model specification, 185, 186*t*, 187*t*
  multicollinearity, 198
  notes on regression analysis, 189–98
  overview of, 185
  regression results, 186–89
  residuals, 198
  value change for the Moscow case, 189–98

Razin, Stepan, 150
regional inequality, 68–69, 162–63
regional research
  budgetniki and, 45
  case selection and, 46–50, 48*f*, 49*t*
  federal transfers and, 53*f*
  histories of state-formation and, 54–64
  impact of stress on performance and, 47–50
  methodological approach to, 46–50
  nested analysis and, 46–50
  overview of, 42–43, 64
  population share and, 51*f*
  puzzle of the 2012 presidential election and, 11–12, 43–44, 49
  regional governors and, 45
  regional political machines and, 45
  reliability and, 49–50
  school network and, 47
  socioeconomic profiles of regions and, 50–54, 51*f*, 52*f*, 53*f*
  state-formation and, 54–64
  state infrastructure and, 47
  titular and nontitular regions and, 49
  unity and division and, 42, 64
  variation by region and, 46–50
  See also Altai Republic; data sources and variables; fieldwork data collection and analysis; interview list; Kemerovo region; quantitative analysis; Rostov region; Tatarstan Republic
representation, distorted idea of, 115–16
repression, 8, 29, 30–31, 32, 38, 172–77
reproduction of boundary between civic and political, 110–12
Republic of Altai. *See* Altai Republic
Republic of Tatarstan. *See* Tatarstan Republic
residential councils, 36–37, 65, 78–86, 82*f*, 116, 117–18, 119–20, 125, 130–31, 166–67
resistance
  active resistance, 137, 156–57, 168–72, 173–74
  group authority and, 28–29
  passive resistance, 137, 154, 157–59, 167–68, 176

Russian authoritarianism and, 150–52, 172–77
social roots of authoritarianism and, 5, 7–9
Soviet Union and, 156–59
statist and antistatist societies and, 20–21, 24–26, 28–29, 30–31, 33, 38
Roizman, Evgenii, 171–72
Rostov region
  Armenian diaspora and, 62
  autonomy and, 62–63, 94–96
  bargaining in, 107–10
  challenge of stable electoral performance and, 110
  competition between groups in, 106
  conflict resolution and, 74–75
  Cossacks in, 62–63, 74–75, 105
  defensiveness about state budget in, 100
  ethnicity and, 61–63, 74, 106
  falsification of electoral results in, 111–12
  Greeks in, 74
  group loyalties and, 105
  identity and, 61–62, 72, 106
  industry in, 52–53
  interview list for, 224
  labor unions in, 96
  legitimate authority and, 72, 75–77
  NGOs in, 95–96, 100
  nonstate community leaders and, 75–77
  outsider state and, 72–77
  pluralist political environment in, 105
  political machines and, 105, 106–12
  post-Soviet Russia and, 63
  presidential election of 2012 and, 49–50
  public organizations and, 72–77, 94–101
  reproduction of boundary between civic and political and, 110–12
  Russian Civil War and, 62–63
  safety net in nonstate communities and, 72–75
  social norms and, 72–75
  socioeconomic profile of, 50–54
  Soviet Union and, 62–63
  state-formation in, 61–64
  state strategy of minimal interference and, 97–101
  surrounding region of, 51
  utility maximization as driver of clientelism in, 107–10
  youth programs in, 99
Russia. *See* Altai Republic; Kemerovo region; post-Soviet Russia; Putin, Vladimir; Rostov region; Russian authoritarianism; Soviet Union; Tatarstan Republic; Tsarist Russia

Russian authoritarianism
  active resistance and, 137, 156–57, 168–72, 173–74
  caricature as wanting benevolent tsar of, 11
  causes of, 145, 164–67
  China as parallel to, 11
  civic initiatives and, 170
  compliance and, 172–77
  compliant activism and, 137, 149, 154, 164–67, 174, 176–78
  Cossacks and, 150–51
  Crimea annexation and, 175
  definition of, 2
  distinctness of, 42
  foundations of, 52–56
  Golden Horde and, 52–54
  hesitating supporters of Ukraine invasion and, 176
  homo soveticus and, 158
  identity and, 4, 139, 143, 145–46, 150–51, 154, 159
  intelligentsia and, 150–52, 157
  nationalism and, 140–42
  Orthodox Church and, 148
  overview of, 1–2, 137, 177–78
  passive resistance and, 137, 154, 157–59, 167–68, 176
  peasant uprisings and, 150–51
  performance legitimacy and, 142–43
  personalism and, 139
  political competition and, 25–26
  political culture and, 143–47
  post-Soviet Russia and, 159–77
  psychology of leadership and, 139
  public opinion polls and, 160–61, 170–71
  Putin's regime and, 138–43
  repression and, 38, 172–77
  research site for, 10–11, 13
  resistance and, 150–52, 172–77
  returning nature of, 10–11, 137
  search for a just state and, 143–47, 146f, 149, 151, 152–77
  social contract and, 142–43
  social roots of authoritarianism and, 10–11, 13, 179–84
  social roots of Putin's support and, 164–67
  Soviet Union and, 152–59
  state-formation and, 25–26
  statism and, 138–43
  statist and antistatist societies and, 138–43
  symbolic role of tsar and, 148–49
  team logic and, 163–67
  Tsarist Russia and, 150–52

Russian authoritarianism (cont.)
  Ukraine invasion and, 137, 172–77
  unity and division and, 2, 4, 10–11, 17, 137
  Yeltsin vs. Putin and, 161–64
Russian Old Believers, 59–60

safety net in nonstate communities, 72–75
Scott, James, 20–21
search for a just state in post-Soviet Russia, 143–47, 146f, 149, 151, 152–77
Shaimiev, Mintimer, 56–57, 69, 114
Sharafutdinova, Gulnaz, 158
Shirshina, Galina, 171–72
Skocpol, Theda, 24
social contract, 26–28, 138, 142–43, 154–55, 156
social movement vulnerability, 125–34
social norms, 6, 18–20, 22, 23, 29, 35, 41, 72–75
social roots of authoritarianism
  aims and contributions of current volume on, 4, 13–15, 179–84
  autocracy-democracy-autocracy cycle and, 7–10
  challenges of studying, 10
  coercion's role in, 3, 14
  conceptual challenge of theorizing, 13–14
  continuum of democracy and autocracy and, 9–10, 9f
  democracy as balance point and, 6–9
  democracy support and, 15–16
  elements of democracy and, 7–10
  empirical approach of current volume on, 11–13, 12t
  grassroots politics and, 5, 6, 11
  identity and, 3–5
  motivation for current volume on, 11–12
  opposite logics and, 4–5
  overview of, 1–3
  prior scholarship on, 9, 14–15
  propaganda and, 4–5
  puzzle of the 2012 presidential election and, 11–12
  regional selection and, 12
  resistance and, 5, 7–9
  return of authoritarianism and, 1
  Russian authoritarianism and, 10–11, 13, 179–84
  statist and antistatist societies and, 5–7, 7f, 179–84
  structure of current volume on, 14–15
  subnational comparison and, 11–13
  team logic and, 5
  unity and division as, 3–5
  unity-based authoritarianism and, 8–9, 14
  See also Altai Republic; data sources and variables; fieldwork data collection and analysis; interview list; Kemerovo region; quantitative analysis; Rostov region; Tatarstan Republic
Soviet Union
  active resistance in, 156–57
  Altai Republic and, 60
  Communist party taking up attitude of tsar in, 152–53
  compliant activism and, 154–56
  diversity policies of, 8
  as example of statist authoritarian regime, 36
  GONGOs in, 35
  Great Purge in, 38
  intelligentsia in, 157
  Kemerovo region and, 58, 126–28
  passive resistance in, 157–59
  resistance in, 156–59
  resistance movement in, 28–29
  Rostov region and, 62–63
  as rupture with past, 152–53
  Russian authoritarianism and, 152–59
  search for a just state in, 152–59
  simple person analysis and, 158
  Stalinism and, 38, 62–63, 139, 155
  Tatarstan Republic and, 55–56, 86–87
  team logic and, 26–28
  Veterans' Councils and, 126–28
  See also post-Soviet Russia
Stalin, Joseph, 38, 62–63, 139, 155
state-formation
  Altai Republic and, 59–61
  histories of, 54–64
  Kemerovo region and, 57–59
  political competitiveness during, 25–29
  regional research and, 54–64
  Rostov region and, 61–64
  Russian authoritarianism and, 25–26
  statist and antistatist societies and, 25–29
  Tatarstan Republic and, 54–57
state strategy of minimal interference, 97–101
statist and antistatist societies
  around the world, 179–81
  autonomy and, 22, 24, 30–31
  civil society and, 32–36
  competitiveness during state-formation and, 25–29
  as continuum, 24–26, 30–31
  corruption and, 30
  definition of, 6, 17, 18–19, 24
  determining societies as, 30–31

explanatory power of distinguishing,
    6–7, 17–18, 24–26, 29–30, 33, 35–38,
    40, 181–84
GONGOs and, 35
grassroots politics in, 31–40
group authority and, 17–18, 19–31, 27f, 33
identity and, 5–7, 18–19, 26, 32, 141–42
informality as driven by the state and, 38–40
infrastructural state power and, 17–18, 32–
    36, 34f
legitimate authority and, 24, 32
nonstate groups and, 29–30, 31–32, 33–36
overview of, 5–7, 17–19, 40–41
pluralism and, 29–30
political competition and, 25–29, 27f, 31–
    32, 35, 37
political machines and, 105–16
public organizations and, 32–38
recruitment of local activists and, 33–35
regime change and, 31
repression and, 38
resistance and, 20–21, 24–26, 28–29, 30–
    31, 33, 38
Russian authoritarianism and, 138–43
scale of, 17–18
social institutions and, 23
social norms and, 18–20, 22, 23, 29, 35, 41
social roots of authoritarianism and, 5–7,
    7f, 179–84
state-formation and, 25–26
team logic and, 26–28, 35
third face of power and, 19–23
types of authoritarianism and, 6, 7f, 17–18
unity and division and, 5, 17–18, 19,
    31, 40–41
Sudan, division-based authoritarianism in, 17
Syria, Alawite minority obtaining resources
    in, 7–8

Tatarstan Republic
    activists as driving force in mobilization
        and, 118–19
    attempts to Latininize Tartar language in, 70
    autonomy of, 55–57
    blurred boundary between civil and political
        and, 113–15
    collective institutions in, 101–3, 113
    compliant activism and, 154
    control of public space and discourse
        and, 121–24
    developmental state and, 69–71
    distorted idea of representation and, 115–16
    economic modernization of, 69–71

ethnicity and, 53–57
Forpost movement in, 90–91, 122
Golden Horde and, 54–55
GONGOs in, 92
grassroot politics in, 64
identity and, 57, 70–71
industry in, 52–53
infrastructure and activities of youth
    organizations in, 88–91
institutionalization of, 55–56
international status of, 70
interview list for, 224
Kazan Khanate as precursor to, 54–55
management of existing and potential
    discontent and, 119–21
mobilization and co-optation and, 117–19
nationalist movement in, 56
origins of youth organizations in, 86–88
political machines and, 105–12, 117–25
post-Soviet Russia and, 56–57
presidential election of 2012 and, 49–50
pride and loyalty and, 71–72
public organizations and, 69–72, 86–94
"Selet" in, 91
Shaimiev's leadership in, 69–71
socioeconomic profiles of regions and, 50–54
Soviet Union and, 55–56, 86–87
stability of electoral performance
    and, 124–25
state as collective leader in, 71–72
state-formation in, 54–57
state leadership beyond the formal state
    and, 92–94
student council election in, 116
"Student Spring" in, 93
surrounding region of, 51
Tartar-Russian relations in, 55–57
Tatarstan—The New Age movement in, 114
team logic and, 66–72
Tsarist Russia and, 55
youth organizations in, 86–94, 89f, 101,
    119, 121–22
team logic
    definition of, 26–28
    group authority and, 26–28
    Kemerovo region and, 66–72
    political machines and, 104, 112, 115–16
    public organizations and, 66–72, 101–3
    Putin and, 163–67
    Russian authoritarianism and, 163–67
    social roots of authoritarianism and, 5
    Soviet Union and, 26–28
    statist and antistatist societies and, 26–28, 35

team logic (*cont.*)
   Tatarstan Republic and, 66–72
   See also outsider state; public organizations; unity and division
third face of power, 19–23
Trans-Siberian railroad, 57–58
Tsarist Russia
   Altai Republic and, 59
   Cossacks and, 150–51
   Decembrist revolt in, 151
   intelligentsia and, 150–52
   Kemerovo region and, 57
   peasant uprisings and, 150–51
   resistance and compliance in, 150–52
   Russian authoritarianism and, 150–52
   symbolic role of tsar in, 148–49
   Tatarstan Republic and, 55
   Tsygankov, Andrei, 144n.33
Tuleyev, Aman
   appointment of, 58–59, 79–80, 128
   as caring patriarch, 66–68
   early political career of, 128–29
   pacification history of, 58–59
   political affiliation of, 128
   regional branches takeover by, 133–34
   Veterans' Councils takeover by, 128–30
Turkey, authoritarian regime, 4, 29, 70

Ukraine
   civic identity in, 5
   democratic institutions and, 3, 5, 8
   invasion of, 1, 38, 136, 137, 140, 142, 164, 172–77
   Orange Revolution in, 99
   post-Soviet Russia and, 172–77, 181
   public opinion of, 1
   Putin and, 164, 172–77
   repression and, 38
   resistance by Russians to, 1
   Russian authoritarianism and, 137, 172–77
United Russia, the Young Guard, 121–22
unity and division
   continuum of democracy and autocracy and, 9
   definition of, 13–14
   democratization and, 8
   division-based authoritarianism, 4–5, 6, 8, 11, 15, 17, 40, 42, 64
   identity and, 8, 11
   regional research and, 42, 64
   Russian authoritarianism and, 2, 4, 10–11, 17, 137
   as social roots of authoritarianism, 3–5
   statist and antistatist societies and, 5, 17–18, 19, 31, 40–41
   unity-based authoritarianism, 4–5, 6–9, 11, 13, 14
   See also team logic
unity-based authoritarianism, 4–5, 6–9, 11, 13, 14
Urlashov, Evgenii, 171–72
utility maximization as driver of clientelist forms, 107–10, 117, 124

Venezuela, authoritarian regime in, 1–2, 4, 17
Veterans' Councils'
   Aman Tuleyev's takeover of, 128–30
   expansion of, 130–34
   history of, 126–28
   leadership of, 132
   political machines and, 125–34
   post-Soviet Russia and, 126–28
   Soviet Union and, 126–28
   structure of, 130–33
   See also newspaper publications (Veterans' Organizations)
Vietnam, regime legitimacy in, 180

Way, Lucan, 9–10

Yeltsin, Boris, 56, 58, 138, 161–64
youth organizations
   infrastructure and activities of, 88–91
   origins of, 86–88
   public organizations and, 86–94
   Tatarstan Republic and, 86–94, 89f, 101, 119, 121–22

Zemliakli (newspaper), 133